GOOD MAINE FOOD

"Damn her!" Cap Huff said. "She swears to God she don't know how to cook, and I'm beginning to believe her. It's a disgrace to the town of Arundel and the whole damned province of Maine, if you ask me! Can't cook! Gosh! I never expected to live to see the day that a Maine woman couldn't cook!"

Mary never looked at him, nor at me, but she spoke in a husky voice. "Maine woman? I? You take me for a filthy Bostonnais?"

Cap's jaw dropped. He put a hand on each knee, squatting, open-mouthed, to stare at her the more strickenly. "Filthy who?"

"Mind your own business!" I told him. "There's plenty of women in Maine that can't cook, either, not any more than a chipmunk can, though they call it cooking. Why don't you cook your own breakfast?"

"Well, mebbe I better," Cap said, straightening up. "Us filthy Bostonnais have got to have our food."

"What can we have?" I asked.

"Why," said Cap, in some surprise, "there ain't anything left in the world but pork, is there? Pork and wine wouldn't be bad for breakfast, Stevie: a little pork and a lot of wine."

—KENNETH ROBERTS, *Arundel*

GOOD
MAINE FOOD

By MARJORIE MOSSER

With an Introduction and Notes by
KENNETH ROBERTS

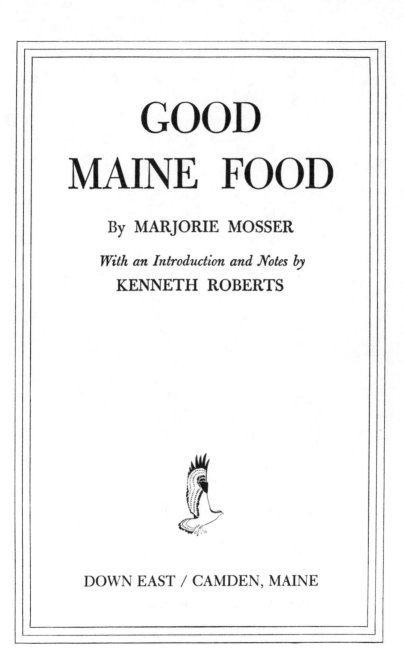

DOWN EAST / CAMDEN, MAINE

Down East Books / Camden, Maine

To

D. N. M.

WINGATE CRAM TO KENNETH ROBERTS CONCERNING ART, COOT AND COOKERY

Those that build a nobler pumpkin or berry pie, or cook a better bean, or know when to stop a lobster's boiling, seem to do it from pure unadulterated instinct—or is it art? Somebody once, as a stunt, measured the poundals in Paderewski's finger strokes, but they never got a Pianola that would pick it up.

My own wife excels all people in the cooking of the overrated grouse and the noble woodcock. Her recipe is simple. She has the oven just right and takes them out when they are just right.

The Anglo-Saxon of today neglects his cooking too much, anyway. Beans, mincemeat, even mushroom soup comes in cans, and even the good cooks take them thus, doll them up and let them go.

No one can ever replace the late Harold Sewall of Bath, whose chicken curries drew people from the Orient; whose bouillabaisse was famous in Marseilles. And his coot stew!

Those who parboil coot surely deserved parboiling in turn. Parboiling, forsooth! No, no! Skin 'em—that's important, and put 'em in cold water with a little vinegar over night, says the French woman; cold water and lemon juice, says my cook. The Filipino boy says lime with your cold water.

Here and there on the St. John River are women who can create pea soup sauriette—summer savory to you—that makes the pea soup of the Château in Quebec (good as it is) taste like mere gruel.

Or creton—a word I can't find in a French dictionary. The belle femme takes the lean pork bits she gets from the trying lard, blends it with the kidney and liver (and perhaps other things) from the inner of the critter, and makes it into a paste that excels pâté de foie gras. It is like true love; it cannot be bought but has to be given. I asked the last old French lady that made it for me how she did it. She said that as she only had a few English words and it took her four hours to make it, she was afraid she couldn't explain.

CONTENTS

FOREWORD

KENNETH ROBERTS was at work on *Trending into Maine* when I became his secretary. One of the chapters in that book dealt with the dishes which he, as a boy on a Maine farm, fondly remembered —such dishes as fish chowder, baked beans, corned beef hash, fish balls, finnan haddie, coot stew, tomato ketchup, chocolate custards.

A few months after that chapter was written it was published in the *Saturday Evening Post;* and for weeks after its publication I opened and helped answer letters from homesick, helpful or indignant residents and ex-residents of Maine.

They wanted to know why Mr. Roberts hadn't mentioned lemon pie. They were profoundly pained because he had said nothing about salt fish dinner. Where, they wanted to know, was the recipe for blueberry pie? For what reason, they demanded, did he put six tablespoonfuls of salt in his ketchup recipe, and why didn't he stick to writing novels instead of encroaching on a woman's province— the kitchen?

Ladies who had licked their first frosting spoon in the shadow of Mount Katahdin, on the fir-clad points of Boothbay, along the snakelike windings of the upper Kennebec, in salt-box houses on the edges of Kittery meadows, on the hill slopes looking out across the emerald islands of Casco Bay, took pen in hand to tell Mr. Roberts about Aunt Emma's marvelous recipe for oxtail soup; Grandma Perkins' stimulating cucumber relish; Cousin Jane Weaver's miraculous cracked pitcher for pancake batter; Cousin Mary's succulent red flannel hash; Dr. Emmons' wife's manner of preparing Indian pudding; Captain Stone's recipe for fried pies; Great-aunt Carrie's hermits.

"Keep those letters separate," he told me. "We'd better have some of that red flannel hash. I haven't had any since I was eleven years

viii

old. Get my grandmother's cookbook and see whether she made it
the same way."

Some of them annoyed him. "Sugar in ketchup!" he protested.
"That woman's family weren't seafarers or farmers. They were city
folks! Their tastes were ruined by tea parties! Sweet pickles! Bah!
Sugar in ketchup! Sugar in beans! Bananas and cherries on a salad!
Nuts! That's not the sort of good Maine food I used to know!"

Answering these letters, copying them and checking them in
Grandma's cookbook led to other things—led to consultation with
far-off aunts and cousins over recipes used by Grandma's cook
Katie, Aunt Lutie's cook Susy, Aunt Fanny's Maggie, Cousin Isabel's
Addie.

Our file of cooking letters grew. There were letters from educators,
male and female; from Africa; from the Dutch East Indies; from
England, New Zealand, Mexico and almost every state in the Union,
all dealing with Maine foods.

Cookbooks written in ink that had faded to the color of pallid
coffee were exhumed from attics; from behind spice tins in kitchens
that hadn't altered, except for the stove, in half a century.

Sea captains' wives lodged information concerning dishes discovered by them in far-off ports and brought back to Maine to provide
exotic company for baked beans and hash. Residents of Maine whose
forebears had come from Sweden to settle in Aroostook County, from
Finland to work the granite quarries near Tenants Harbor, from
Greece and Syria to conduct small businesses in Biddeford and Portland, from Yorkshire and the Midlands to work in the woolen mills
of Sanford and Saco, obliged us with recipes that had, they said,
been eagerly adopted by neighbors who were suspicious of all other
foreign dishes.

French Canadians have moved down into Maine in great numbers;
and French-Canadian concoctions that must have been well and
favorably known to the Jesuit Fathers have seemingly become common property in many sections of the state, so that they are now
Maine foods—and those addicted to them protest sharply when they
aren't included among Maine's culinary triumphs.

Out of all those letters, those tattered family recipe books, those
blankbooks bulging with personal notes from long-dead ladies ex-

plaining unusual methods of handling lobster stew, potato soup, corn muffins and other delicacies, came this book, which is a fairly comprehensive compilation of recipes that have long been approved by the rugged and straightforward people of a peculiarly rugged state.

—MARJORIE MOSSER

INTRODUCTION

By Kenneth Roberts

———————◆————————

I LIKE good food; and ever since I've known anything at all about such things, I've known that the best foods are the simplest. *Good Maine Food* ignores cookery that is namby-pamby, twiddly, cloying, fussy, messy and immature, and emphasizes foods that appeal to men and women whose tastes are sound and sturdy.

I suspect that the true nature of cookbooks which purport to give recipes for the making of desirable foods is revealed by their attitude toward pickles, salads and appetizers.

I doubt the worth of those that advocate the sugaring of pickles, ketchup, piccalillies and relishes; for good cooks in early New England shunned sweetened ketchups and pickles as they would have shunned vitriol in tea.

I question those that tolerate salads made of sliced pineapple and Maraschino cherries, of grapefruit fragments, of bananas sprinkled with chopped nuts, of little dabs of whipped cream tastefully arranged on pears and dates. Such mixtures aren't salads at all. They're desserts.

I have had reason to think, in recent years, that as cooking in America has become more elegant, it has arrived at the point known to veteran State-of-Mainers as "a pretty pass."

Not so many years ago, beneath the street level of a widely known Boston hotel, there was a grillroom that served food unsurpassed by any in the world. Its salads were flawless; its meats the best to be obtained, and cooked exactly right; its cocktails as good as could be mixed by the most accomplished of hosts; its wines perfection.

Its paneled walls somehow absorbed the prattle of its highly civilized patrons, and reflected it back in soft and soothing murmurs. Muted strains of music filtered from a muscians' balcony that bore, across its front, the pregnant German motto, *Wer nicht liebt Wein, Weib und Gesang, Der bleibt ein Narr sein Lebelang.*

In that restaurant I had my first glimpse of Richard Harding Davis, resplendent in a perfectly fitting dinner jacket—the dinner jacket of the war-correspondent hero of a romantic novel. I was close to him: so close that my fascinated gaze could follow every movement of his fork: so close that I could hear the awful severity of his voice when he bade his waiter summon the manager—and when that bearded dignitary arrived, I heard Mr. Davis request the privilege of being conducted to the kitchen so that he might express to the proper cook his keen personal appreciation of the ineffable excellence of the fillet of sole and chiffonade salad with which he had been served, as well as of the irreproachable consistency of the camembert cheese.

Not long after that I went away from Boston. When I came back, I took some friends, for old times' sake, to that paneled grillroom. The oaken walls were there no longer. In their place were sheets of black glass, from which the voices of undiscriminating patrons echoed with painful clarity. The musicians' balcony was gone, and in one corner of the room was a platform above which hung a microphone. From time to time a young lady mounted the platform and, in a voice that bubbled and slowly surged, like a minor eruption of cold molasses, sang drearily of love as envisioned by a New York song writer.

My companions let me order; so, again for old times' sake, I ordered fillet of sole and chiffonade salad; a dry, an extremely dry, white wine, and camembert cheese.

The fillets, when they came, were coffin-shaped slabs hewn from a giant fish; then breaded and brutally fried.

The chiffonade salad was made from lettuce heads split asunder by a South End hatchet man, and garnished with a dressing made from oil that might have come from a crankcase.

The wine was heavy and sickeningly sweet; the camembert cheese firm and resilient as sculptors' clay.

Such a change, it seems to me, is an American tragedy.

Restaurants that serve good American food have never been overplentiful. It was my good fortune to travel in various parts of America with the late George Horace Lorimer, a wise man who knew good food. Occasionally, in a restaurant, I'd be tempted to order a steak or a portion of fish. Lorimer would look at me coldly and say, "Better play safe with ham and eggs. Even a rotten cook can make *something* out of ham and eggs."

Lorimer's advice, I regret to say, was usually right. Good American food is hard to find; and the increase in cookbooks that extol the heavy, fussy, sickish and messy, leads me to suspect that good American food will become increasingly difficult to find in homes and restaurants. It shouldn't, of course, be so.

In the city of Munich, in the shadow of the Frauenkirche, in pre-Hitlerian days, was a smoky cellar restaurant, known as the Nürnberger Glöck'l, that was crowded from noon until midnight. Its plates and drinking cups were pewter, and its specialty was sausages no bigger than a man's little finger. The sausages were accompanied, as a matter of course, by sauerkraut, mashed potatoes and beer; but the sausages were what the patrons sought.

Travelers from England, from America, from the Scandinavian countries—surgeons, diplomats, newspapermen, artists—came to that smoky restaurant, lured by the reputation of those little sausages, or brought back to Munich by fond recollections of their savor.

They have lingered in my own memory for many a long year; and I never went to Munich, in the old days, without making an immediate pilgrimage to that small, dark restaurant in the shadow of the Frauenkirche and devouring sausages until my belt creaked.

Nowhere in Maine is there a restaurant half so popular as was that dingy little Nürnberger Glöck'l. Nowhere in Maine is there a restaurant where a traveler can obtain such pleasant nourishment; and this, it seems to me, is another American tragedy; for in Auburn, Maine, there is a packing house that makes sausages—little sausages—that I believe to be without a peer.

I'm as sure as I am of anything that those little Auburn sausages are more delicious and made of vastly better materials than the little Munich sausages whose reputation had spread all over the world. My acquaintance with them is long-standing, and I've refreshed my memories of them a dozen times a year ever since. Each time they tasted even better than I expected them to taste.

Penley's little link sausages[1] is the name, made by the E. W. Penley Company of Auburn, Maine; and this encomium has been neither

---

[1] Penley makes many sausages, but the "little link" are best.

solicited nor paid for. If it had been even solicited, I wouldn't have used it—probably because I followed Mr. Samuel G. Blythe in Washington as correspondent for the *Saturday Evening Post*, and had been instructed by Mr. Blythe that anybody who asked to have himself included in the *Post* page called "Who's Who and Why" should be instantly barred from consideration.

The sole reason for this enthusiastic mention of Penley's sausages is my belief that they are the best in the world; and when a state is able to produce a sausage that is the best in the world, there certainly ought to be, in that state, at least one restaurant that specializes in cooking them as they should be cooked and serving them as they should be served. There ought to be; but so far as I know, there isn't.

I wish that somewhere near my home there was a restaurant that specialized in baked beans, brown bread, tomato ketchup and chocolate custards, all cooked the way good Maine cooks used to cook them; but if there is one I never heard of it.

I wish, somewhere in Maine, I could find a restaurant that served nothing—nothing at all—but properly cooked salt fish and pork scraps: that dish so feelingly described on page 42 by Dr. Samuel Capen, Chancellor of the University of Buffalo. If I knew of one, I'd go to it as Harvard students were wont to go to Owen Wister's mythical Bird in Hand; but such restaurants, unfortunately, are as nonexistent as the ambrosial establishment of *Philosophy 4*.

I wish I knew little places that specialized in—that knew how to make, that is to say, and stuck exclusively to—the right sort of fish chowder, or the right sort of clam stew, or the right sort of corned beef and cabbage, or the right sort of blueberry pie. Are there such places? There are not!

What a godsend it would be to know dependable and unpretentious small places capable of giving hungry travelers just one toothsome dish and little else—tinker mackerel or broiled scrod, for example, cooked in the good Maine way that makes them the peer of any fish that ever swam in fresh or salt water. Or corned beef hash, moist inside and crusty brown outside, and juicy with homemade ketchup. Or thick split pea soup, a lettuce salad touched lightly with garlic, and lemon pie topped with meringue as soothing to the palate as though scooped from a creamy white thunderhead hovering on the verge of sweet solidity.

Such places, of course, don't exist and perhaps never will, because of the widespread and wholly erroneous notion that a light meal, no matter how perfectly cooked, is an indication of inhospitality and penny pinching, and that a large meal, wretchedly cooked, is generous and therefore preferable.

It's all a great pity, and I wish something could be done about it; but I suppose nothing *can* be done unless somebody invents a method by which the traveling public can acquire good taste without conscious effort and by some form of mass impregnation.

When my niece started to work on *Good Maine Food,* I turned over to her all my letters and all my family cookbooks, and had no hesitation in calling on my friends to give her whatever help they could. I'm glad I did; for to my way of thinking it has turned out to be the best cookbook ever assembled—one that I hope will long remind the cooks of Maine, as well as those of other states, that old recipes, like old friends, are usually most dependable.

Kenneth Roberts

COOKING TABLE

THE FOLLOWING cooking table is a basic table for those who wish their meats and vegetables cooked in such a way that flavor is unharmed, tenderness brought out, digestibility preserved.

The finest piece of tenderloin becomes tougher and tougher with each added minute of overcooking; the freshest asparagus grows soggy if cooked too long; the youngest and tenderest green corn is ruined by an extra five minutes in the boiler; the freshest of fish isn't worth eating if dried by overbaking.

Cooking, however, is an art; not only are the rules impossible to follow rigidly; they must be read with the brain as well as with the eye. The proper cooking time for venison is four minutes. This presupposes that the venison is cut from a tender young doe; that it is cooked in a sizzling hot oven or over coals. If cut from a fourteen-point buck, victor over many bitter enemies and bitterer winters, hero of innumerable exhausting love affairs—or if cooked in a dull oven or over a smoky fire of green wood—then all rules must be thrown overboard.

Similarly, young green corn, just picked from the stalk, cooks perfectly in seven minutes. But old corn, picked on a Tuesday, shipped a thousand miles on Wednesday and Thursday, exposed for sale on a Friday, purchased on Saturday by a cook who thinks that each ear of green corn is just another piece of green corn, can't be cooked at all in ten minutes. What's more, the unfortunate truth is that no amount of cooking can make it worth eating.

Headwork, therefore, must be applied to all cooking times here given. When cooking vegetables, add ½ teaspoon salt and ½ teaspoon sugar to water in which they're cooked.

VEGETABLES, BOILED

	Minutes		Minutes
Asparagus	15	Corn, green	7
Beans, string	20	Eggplant	15
Beans, lima	25	Onions	30
Beet greens	10	Parsnips	30
Beets	40	Peas	15
Broccoli	25	Potatoes	30
Brussels sprouts	15	Spinach	10
Cabbage	15	Squash, summer	15
Carrots	20	Squash, winter	25
Cauliflower	20	Tomatoes	15
Celery	15	Turnips	35

VEGETABLES, BAKED

	Minutes
Peppers	30
Potatoes	40
Beans	8 to 10 hrs.

POULTRY AND GAME

	Broiled	Roasted
Chicken (broiler)	20 min.	30 min. per pound
Duck, Wild		
small	12 min.	14 min.
medium	14 min.	16 min.
large	16 min.	18 min.
Duck, Tame		12–15 min. per pound
Goose		20 min. per pound
Turkey, 10-pound		3 hrs.
Squab	15 min.	45 min.
Venison	4 min.	
Partridge	12 min.	16 min.
Woodcock	8 min.	15 min.
Pheasant	20 min.	30 min.

MEATS, BROILED

		Minutes
Beefsteak		
1 inch thick		6
1½ inches thick		8
Lamb chops		
double		10
single		7
Pork chops		20

MEATS, BAKED

		Minutes
Beef, roast	per pound	8
Lamb	per pound	15
Mutton	per pound	12
Pork	per pound	30
Veal	per pound	20
Ham	per pound	20

EQUIVALENTS

Dash or pinch	1/16 teaspoon
Size of an egg	¼ cup
1 saltspoon	¼ teaspoon
3 teaspoons	1 tablespoon
4 tablespoons	¼ cup
16 tablespoons	1 cup
½ cup	1 gill
2 cups	1 pint
2 pints	1 quart
4 quarts	1 gallon
8 quarts	1 peck
4 pecks	1 bushel
16 ounces	1 pound
1 wineglass	¼ cup
1 teacup	½ cup

WEIGHTS AND MEASURES

1 pound eggs	. . . . .	10
1 pound flour	. . . . .	1 quart
1 pound butter	. . . .	2 cups
1 pound liquid	. . . .	2 cups
1 pound sugar	. . . .	2 cups
1 pound chopped meat	. .	2 cups
1 ounce salt	. . . . .	2 tablespoons
1 ounce liquid	. . . .	2 tablespoons
1 ounce butter	. . .	egg-size or rounding tablespoon
1 ounce flour	. . . .	2 tablespoons
12 ounces brown sugar	. .	1 pint
1 ounce chocolate	. . .	1 square

OVEN TEMPERATURES

Very slow oven	. . . . . .	250° F.
Slow oven	. . . . . .	300° F.
Moderately slow oven	. . . .	325° F.
Moderate oven	. . . . .	350° F.
Moderately hot oven	. . . .	375° F.
Hot oven	. . . . .	400° F.
Very hot oven	. . . .	450°–500° F.

MAINE MEALS: ONE WINTER MONTH

MOST Maine homes were run on a rotating diet, and in some parts of the state they will forever be so run. Economy was at the bottom of this diet, and, like all useful things, it was highly satisfactory. Leftovers were utilized; on certain days the top of the stove was left free for the week's wash; on Saturdays, when the fire burned all day for baking, the opportunity was always seized to bake beans.

Thursday was boiled-dinner day; Friday fish day; Saturday bean day; Sunday fish-cake day (when Friday's leftovers were used) and Monday hash day (when Thursday's leftovers were used). Housewives didn't have to rack their brains over such menus, and menfolk never tired of them.

FIRST WEEK

Sunday   Lunch: Onion Soup (1) p. 31; Salad, p. 190

            Dinner: Chicken Paprika, p. 103; Peas, Corn Bread; Salad; Snow Pudding, p. 318

Monday   Lunch: Broiled Lamb Chops, p. 137; Salad

            Dinner: Spaghetti, p. 238; Fiddleheads, p. 156; Salad; Indian Pudding, p. 331

Tuesday   Lunch: Rocky Pasture Pea Soup, p. 35; Salad

            Dinner: Lamb Stew, p. 138; Dumplings, p. 117; Salad; Banana Graham Pie, p. 296

Wednesday   Lunch: Sardine Rarebit, p. 62; Salad

            Dinner: Calf's Liver, p. 130, and Bacon; Asparagus Mold, p. 158, Mashed Potatoes, p. 177; Salad; Vanilla Ice Cream with Chocolate Sauce (1), p. 338

Thursday   Lunch: Cheese Omelet, p. 229; Salad

            Dinner: Baked Ham (2), p. 145, Corn Fritters, p. 167, Mashed Potatoes, p. 177; Salad; Spanish Cream, p. 315

Friday   Lunch: Rocky Pasture Fish Chowder, p. 26; Salad

            Dinner: Hot Ham Mousse, p. 148, Mashed Potatoes, p. 177; Salad; Lemon Pie, p. 302

Saturday   Lunch: Minestrone, p. 244; Salad

            Dinner: Baked Beans, p. 160, Brown Bread, p. 272, sliced thin and served cold, buttered; Salad; Chocolate Custards, p. 313, Vanilla Wafers, p. 374

SECOND WEEK

Sunday   Lunch: Pizza Alla Napolitana, p. 188; Salad

            Dinner: Roast Lamb, p. 137, Mint Sauce, p. 210,
                     Mashed Potatoes, p. 177, Boiled Winter
                     Squash, p. 183; Salad; Lemon Cream
                     Sherbet, p. 321

Monday   Lunch: Minced Lamb, p. 135; Salad

            Dinner: Spanish Sole, p. 65, Boiled Potatoes, p. 176,
                     Broccoli, p. 163; Salad; Sour Cream
                     Gingerbread, p. 273

Tuesday   Lunch: Clam Chowder, p. 24; Salad

            Dinner: Chicken Pie (1), p. 107, Boiled Beets,
                     p. 163; Salad; Prune Whip, p. 319

Wednesday   Lunch: Creamed Dried Beef (1), p. 130; Salad

            Dinner: Spaghetti, p. 238; Frozen Asparagus; Salad;
                     Apple Dumplings, p. 326

Thursday   Lunch: Black Bean Soup, p. 22; Salad

            Dinner: Baked Haddock Fillets, p. 53, Cucumbers
                     with Sour Cream, p. 169, Mashed Po-
                     tatoes, p. 177; Salad; Coffee Bavarian
                     Cream, p. 314

Friday   Lunch: Italian Rice, p. 243; Salad

            Dinner: Barbecued Oysters, p. 78, Mashed Potatoes,
                     p. 177, French Peas, p. 176; Salad; Choco-
                     late Soufflé, p. 320

Saturday   Lunch: Pepperpot, p. 35; Salad

            Dinner: Roast Turkey (2), p. 111, Mashed Potatoes,
                     p. 177, Boiled Onions, p. 173; Salad;
                     Walnut Mocha Cake, p. 360

THIRD WEEK

Sunday   Lunch: Spanish Turkey, p. 111; Salad

            Dinner: Roast Beef (1), p. 126, Mashed Potatoes, p. 177, Broccoli, p. 163; Salad; Cottage Pudding (Cottage Cake, p. 353, served warm with Cottage Pudding Sauce, p. 340)

Monday   Lunch: Cold Roast Beef; Salad

            Dinner: Codfish Puff, p. 47, Boiled Spinach, p. 182; Salad; Griddlecakes, p. 285

Tuesday   Lunch: Kedgeree, p. 56; Salad

            Dinner: Baked Spareribs and Sauerkraut, p. 151, Mashed Potatoes, p. 177; Salad; Orange Sherbet, p. 322

Wednesday   Lunch: Rocky Pasture Pea Soup, p. 35; Salad

            Dinner: Tuna Casserole, p. 66, French Beans, p. 162; Salad; Rice Pudding, p. 330

Thursday   Lunch: Curried Eggs (1), p. 230; Salad

            Dinner: Corned Beef, p. 115, Boiled Cabbage, p. 164, Boiled Potatoes, p. 176; Salad; Devil's Float, p. 331

Friday   Lunch: Oyster Stew (1), p. 33; Salad

            Dinner: Corned Beef Hash, p. 117, Harvard Beets, p. 163; Salad; Chocolate Bread Pudding, p. 329

Saturday   Lunch: Finnan Haddie Newburg, p. 50; Salad

            Dinner: Baked Beans and Spareribs, p. 160, Brown Bread, p. 272, sliced thin and served cold, buttered; Salad; Sea Moss Blancmange, p. 316

FOURTH WEEK

Sunday   Lunch: Egg Timbales, p. 228, with Tomato Sauce,
                    p. 213; Salad

            Dinner: Baked Chicken (3), p. 100, Mashed Po-
                    tatoes, p. 177, Broccoli, p. 163; Salad;
                    Rice Pudding, p. 330

Monday   Lunch: Macaroni Haddie Casserole, p. 245; Salad

            Dinner: Lamb Stew, p. 138, Dumplings, p. 117;
                    Salad; Squash Pie, p. 308

Tuesday   Lunch: Vichysoisse, p. 39; Salad

            Dinner: Broiled Honeycomb Tripe, p. 134, Stewed
                    Tomatoes, p. 183, Mashed Potatoes, p.
                    177; Salad; Lemon Sherbet, p. 322

Wednesday   Lunch: Cheese Fondue (1), p. 233; Salad

            Dinner: Canadian Meat Cakes, Sharp Sauce, p. 127,
                    Mashed Potatoes, p. 177, Creamed On-
                    ions, p. 174; Indian Pudding, p. 331

Thursday   Lunch: Corn Chowder, p. 24; Salad

            Dinner: Fried Shad Roe, p. 63, Bacon, Mashed Po-
                    tatoes, p. 177; Salad; Vanilla Ice Cream,
                    Meringues, p. 366, and Chocolate Sauce
                    (2), p. 339

Friday   Lunch: Finnan Haddie Florentine, p. 49; Salad

            Dinner: Salt Fish Dinner, p. 42; Salad; Banana
                    Fritters, p. 288

Saturday   Lunch: Chipped Beef Omelet, p. 228; Salad

            Dinner: Baked Veal, p. 140, Potatoes and Cheese,
                    p. 177; Salad; Wine Jelly, p. 318

BEVERAGES AND APPETIZERS

MAXIMS FROM MAINE KITCHENS

To remove a glass stopper from a glass bottle, heat a poker red-hot and run it around the outside of the neck of the bottle.

❦

To unscrew a tight cap from a jar or bottle, turn bottle bottom-side up and rap cap sharply on a table top. It will then turn easily.

❦

Ammonia in the water in which silver is washed will keep it bright a long time.

❦

Nickel is best cleaned by rubbing with woolen cloth saturated with spirits of ammonia.

BEVERAGES

HOT BUTTERED RUM (1)

HOT BUTTERED RUM, Maine's earliest drink, was doubtless of inestimable benefit to hardy pioneers who needed internal warmth to protect them from the rigors of a Maine winter. It's a dangerous drink, however, for delicately nurtured moderns. It's not only heavy in the stomach and violent in its action, but the butter seals the fumes of the alcohol within the drinker. When other drinks are poured in on top of hot buttered rum, the effects are frequently both disastrous and lasting.

Mr. Roberts described the mass production of hot buttered rum in *Northwest Passage:*

"Cap placed his keg upon a table; slapped it affectionately. 'This here's the medicine for food-poisoning, like what you fellers prob'ly got from your insides not being built up strong and seasoned. It aint no ordinary rum, that's had all the good taken out of it by being strained and doctored and allowed to grow weak with age. This here's third-run rum, real powerful, more like food than drink. When you drink it, you can taste it. Rum's intended to take hold of you, and that's what this does. There aint no way of concealing what it is, the way you can with old, weak-kneed rum. Why, this rum, you could put onions in it, or the powerfulest dead fish, and couldn't taste a thing different about it! It's real honest rum!' His eye fell on my wash-bowl and pitcher in the corner. 'Here, gimme that pitcher! First we'll try it raw; then we'll butter it, and you can see what I mean.'

"Worrying the bung from the keg, he decanted some of the contents into the pitcher. The room, on the instant, was permeated with an odor like that of a damp and dirty cellar in which quantities of molasses have become sour, mouldy and pungent.

"Cap raised the pitcher to his lips. When he lowered it, his eyes were watery, and he gasped spasmodically, like a dying haddock.

"He handed it to the man beside him. 'Now you try it, but don't spill none of it on you. You're a nice-dressed little gentleman, and you don't want holes et in your clothes.' He turned to Hunk. 'Don't waste time unwrapping that butter and the rest of the stuff we got in Boston. This rum's more penetrating than what I figured on.' . . .

"He seized a bucket and went to work. In it he put two cups of maple sugar, added an inch of hot water and stirred until the sugar was dissolved. He poured in two quarts of rum, added a lump of butter the size of his fist, threw in a handful of powdered cinnamon; then filled the bucket to the brim with steaming hot water. So briskly did he stir the mixture that it splashed his shirt. And as we passed him our cups to be filled, he lectured us on the subject of hot buttered rum.

" 'This here,' he said, 'aint the proper way to make it. I put hot water in this here, but what you ought to have is hot cider. You take three or four drinks of this, made the right way, and you don't worry about what kind of food you're eating, or about anything else, either. You can't even remember what you et five minutes after you et it.

" 'And it aint a temporary drink, like most drinks. That's on account of the butter. No matter how much you drink of anything else, it'll wear off in a day or so; but you take enough hot buttered rum and it'll last you pretty near as long as a coonskin cap. Fellers up our way drink it when they're going out after catamounts, on account of catamount-hunting being hard work and requiring considerable persistence. After a man's had two-three drinks of hot buttered rum, he don't shoot a catamount: all he's got to do is walk up to him and kiss him just once; then put him in his bag, all limp.'

"The rum in the drinks which Cap passed us had been miraculously changed. The mixture seemed mild and sweet—as harmless-tasting as a soothing syrup. Murmurs of pleasure arose from my friends as they sampled it; and the glances turned toward Cap were almost affectionate.

"At their gratified murmurs, Cap scooped up a cupful for himself and drained it; then stood with eyes upraised, meditating. 'Yes,' he admitted, 'that aint bad! A few of those and you could play with me like a kitten.' "

A single portion of hot buttered rum is made as follows:

Half fill an ordinary tumbler with boiling water; then throw out the water.

Into the hot tumbler put ½ inch of hot water, and in it dissolve 1 lump or 1 teaspoonful of sugar, either white or brown.

Add a pat of butter the size of an individual helping in a hotel. Pour in a jigger of rum—about ¾ inch.

Add ½ teaspoonful of powdered cinnamon, fill up the tumbler with hot water, stir vigorously and serve.

HOT BUTTERED RUM (2)

A more convenient method of making hot buttered rum was invented by Trader Vic, whose rum concoctions, dispensed in his Oakland, California, caravanserai, have made him world-famous. He called it Northwest Passage.

Make a batter by mixing together 5 pounds yellow sugar, 1 pound butter and 1 ounce vanilla. Put the batter in a mason jar. It will keep indefinitely. In a convenient box put a handful of stick-cinnamon, a handful of cloves and a handful of vanilla beans.

Into a fair-sized tumbler put 1 teaspoon of batter, and to it add a small piece of stick-cinnamon, 1 vanilla bean and 3 cloves. Pour in a good-sized jigger of rum that tastes like rum—preferably New England or Jamaica—and fill the tumbler with boiling water, using about three times as much water as rum. Stir and serve.

NEW YEAR'S PUNCH

1 pound loaf sugar	½ cup whisky
1 cup strong English break- fast tea	Juice of 3 large oranges Juice of 3 large lemons
Rind of ½ orange, pared thin	1 cup chopped pineapple
Rind of ½ lemon, pared thin	1 cup claret

Let these stand for 4 hours:
  then stir and add
	1 pint bottle Maraschino
	  cherries

½ cup old Medford rum	2 lumps ice as big as one's
½ cup brandy	fist

Put on ice for ½ hour; then, just before serving, add a quart of domestic champagne, extra dry or preferably brut.

OLD-FASHIONED

Moisten a lump of sugar with Angostura bitters, put it in the bottom of an old-fashioned whisky glass, add a little water and stir till the sugar dissolves (sugar won't dissolve in alcohol). Put two lumps of ice in the glass, add a generous jigger of bourbon or rye whisky (or rum), fill the glass with water, drop in a slice of orange peel, and serve.

RUM COCKTAIL

Dry martinis, in the balmy winter climate of the Bahamas and the West Indies, are apt to lose their savor, even when made with the best of gin and Noilly Prat vermouth.

Mr. Roberts and Mr. Ben Ames Williams experimented assiduously in the Bahamas with rum cocktail mixtures, using various sorts of rums—heavy, flavorful Jamaicas, lighter Barbados and Puerto Rican, and the even lighter Bacardis. They reported favorably on all of them; but in the end found themselves sticking to the light grade of Bacardi. The basic recipe for their rum cocktail, however, was the same, no matter what sort of rum was used.

1 tumbler sour fruit juice	1 teaspoon Angostura bitters
¼ tumblerful grenadine, Falernum or fruit syrup	1 grain saccharine
	2 tumblers light rum

Add 8 ice cubes, shake well in a cocktail shaker and decant immediately into a thermos jug. This same recipe makes an adequate daiquiri or bacardi.

RUMROUSAL

1 quart Jamaica rum	1½ cups liquid honey
3 quarts whole milk	½ pint bourbon

Serve either chilled or hot, as desired.

Those who wish it non-fattening can substitute 5 grains of saccharine for the honey. Powdered or evaporated milk can be used in place of whole milk.

FISH HOUSE PUNCH

(Official, by courtesy of Charlton Yarnall and J. Somers Smith, Governor, State in Schuylkill. "State in Schuylkill" is an exclusive Philadelphia society which was founded early in the eighteenth century. It built a clubhouse—the Fish House—at the falls of Schuylkill, where catfish, perch and rockfish abounded. There the members of State in Schuylkill met on every other Friday during the fishing season to fish, eat catfish and drink the punch that had originated with the members of the society. As many as 480 catfish were often devoured at a single sitting, but there is no record of the number of Fish House Punches consumed at the same time.)

2 quarts Jamaica rum	1 quart water
1 quart brandy	1 pound cut sugar
1 quart lemon juice	1 gill peach brandy
1 large lump ice	

Place sugar in the bottom of a large bowl with water, and let it slack down. Strain the lemon juice; then add it to the slacked sugar. Put into the bowl a lump of ice as large as can be got in. Mix the rum and brandy in a separate pitcher, then add to bowl. Add the peach brandy and stir by pouring the liquid over the ice with a dipper. Allow to brew for 4 or 5 hours before serving.

Serve in whisky glasses. The use of larger glasses is apt to be dangerous. The foregoing quantity should last a dozen people through a hot afternoon, if served in whisky glasses at the rate of once every 10 or 15 minutes.

CHRISTMAS PUNCH

1 quart Tom Collins Mixer	1½ pints dark rum
1 pint grape juice	1 quart ginger ale

Pour the Tom Collins Mixer, grape juice and rum into a large pitcher, stir; then pour over a block of ice in a punch bowl. Add the ginger ale and serve at once.

APPLE TODDY

Recipe from that ancient and honorable Philadelphia organization The Rabbit (by courtesy of Charlton Yarnall and J. Somers Smith).

12 apples (pippin variety)	1 quart boiling water
10 lumps sugar	2 quarts Jamaica rum
	1 quart brandy

Bake the apples whole in their skins and uncovered until cooked, but not soft enough to fall apart.

Put the sugar in a crock, add apples, boiling water, rum and brandy. Stand crock, covered with a plate, in front of the fire, but do not let it boil. The toddy should brew for 5 hours, and will continue to improve for 3 or 4 hours thereafter.

Serve in small glasses.

HARD PUNCH

1 pint cold green tea	½ pint Medford rum
Juice of 12 lemons, sweetened to taste	1 quart best bourbon whisky
3 quarts claret	½ pint French brandy
1 pint curaçao	1 pint Maraschino liqueur

For flavoring add a small bag of allspice and clove. Leave the mixture for 3 days; then add garnish of sliced orange, lemon, banana, fresh cherries, stoned, and strawberries. Serve over block of ice in large punch bowl and bruise mint on the ice.

RUM PUNCH (1)

1 quart tea	Juice of 6 lemons
2 cups sugar	Juice of 2 oranges
	1 bottle Jamaica or Medford rum

Add sugar and fruit juices to hot tea. Cool, add rum, let stand 24 hours: then serve over ice.

RUM PUNCH (2)

1 cup powdered sugar	1 bottle Jamaica rum
Rind of 1 lemon	½ cup curaçao
1 cup water	1 bottle champagne

Juice of 1 lemon

Put sugar and lemon rind into a bowl with the water, and when dissolved add remaining ingredients. Ice before serving.

HOT PUNCH

12 lumps sugar	½ cup old Jamaica rum
1 pint hot water	¼ cup brandy
Juice and rind of 2 lemons	¼ cup porter or stout

1 tablespoon arrack

Stir briskly while mixing ingredients. Continue till mixture foams.

CHERRY BOUNCE

12 pounds cherries	¼ teaspoon cinnamon
4 pounds sugar to each gallon	4 blades mace
of juice	1 quart brandy
¼ teaspoon allspice	1 quart rum

Strain the juice of the cherries through a coarse cloth, then boil it with the sugar and spices until all scum has disappeared. Cool; then add brandy and rum. Bottle.

CHRISTMAS EGGNOG

72 eggs	2 quarts applejack
8 quarts whole milk	4 quarts New England rum
10 quarts heavy cream	2 pounds powdered sugar

Separate yolks and whites of eggs. Beat yolks to a froth in punch bowl, and into them slowly pour the milk, cream and sugar, stirring hard. Add applejack and rum gradually, still stirring vigorously. Lastly stir in the beaten egg whites.

MANHATTAN

Put several cubes of ice in a small mixing pitcher. Over them pour two parts of rye whisky and one half that amount of Martini & Rossi Italian vermouth. Add a dash of Angostura bitters, stir briskly and strain into cocktail glasses. Experienced drinkers seldom bother to drop in a cherry.

DRY MARTINI

There are two ways of mixing a dry martini correctly—the easy way and the hard way.

EASY DRY MARTINI

3 parts gin   1 part Noilly Prat French
Thick piece of lemon rind   vermouth

In a small pitcher put several large pieces of ice. Over the ice pour the requisite amount of gin and one third that amount of the best French vermouth. With a spoon stir the ingredients briskly and steadily for about 3 minutes. Strain into cocktail glasses, and over each glass twist a piece of lemon rind so that the oil from the outer rind is sprayed onto the surface of the cocktail.

DIFFICULT (AND BEST) DRY MARTINI

Fill a large cocktail shaker with large pieces of ice. Pare the whole rind from two oranges and have them handy. On a table set out as many cocktail glasses as there are persons to be served.

Almost fill each glass with the best dry gin obtainable. Add to the gin in each glass enough Martini & Rossi Italian vermouth to give the gin a pale straw color—not more than ⅛ inch.

Pour the contents of all glasses into the shaker. Crumple the 2 orange peels into the shaker; then shake vigorously until outside of shaker is frosted with rime (not less than 5 minutes). Decant into glasses originally used. This will make slightly over two cocktails for each person served.

TOM (OR RUM) COLLINS

A "Collins" is a highball to which a dash of sweet and sour has been added. If ice, lemon juice, sugar syrup and a 2-ounce glass of gin are put in a highball glass and the glass filled with charged water, it's a Tom Collins. If rum is substituted for the gin, it's a Rum Collins.

CHAMPAGNE PUNCH (1)

2 quarts strong green tea	3 bottles brandy
Rinds of 12 lemons	1 bottle curaçao
3 cups powdered sugar	6 bottles champagne

Mix all except champagne in punch bowl and stir until sugar is dissolved. Put in 3 blocks of ice. Then pour in the champagne (brut or extra dry).

CHAMPAGNE PUNCH (2)

1 quart domestic brut champagne	4 ounces brandy
	8 dashes Angostura bitters
1 quart domestic dry white wine	4 grains saccharine dissolved in a little water

Put about 10 ice cubes in a large pitcher, then add the above ingredients. Stir slightly and serve in punch glasses.

CHAMPAGNE COCKTAIL

Into a pitcher pour 1 quart domestic champagne (brut), 2 ounces of brandy, 4 dashes Angostura bitters, 2 grains saccharine dissolved in 1 teaspoon of water. Stir slightly and decant into goblets containing ice cubes.

WASSAIL

England's outstanding Christmas drink, in the old days, was mixed in the wassail bowl. The English brought it to America; and in such New England towns as Kittery and Portsmouth, the wassail bowl was put to frequent use by the more substantial families.

Wassail was made thus:

Put a little grated nutmeg, 2 cloves, 1 teaspoon Jamaica ginger, a blade of mace, 1 teaspoon allspice and 2 teaspoons of cinnamon in a gill of water, and bring it twice to a boil. To it add 4 bottles of wine—claret, sauterne or burgundy—and heat over a moderate fire. In this dissolve 1 pound of sugar. While heating, beat separately the yolks and whites of 12 eggs. Fold the yolks into the stiffly beaten whites; then put them into a large punch bowl. Remove the wine from stove, pour it over the eggs, and beat the whole until light and frothy. While the liquid still foams, add 12 hot baked apples.

BURGUNDY CUP

| 1 lemon | 1 bottle charged water |
| Sugar to taste | 1 bottle burgundy |

Cut rind of lemon very thin and put in a bowl with the sugar. Let it stand until the sugar is dissolved, then add the charged water and remove the lemon peel. Add the burgundy.

EGGNOG

1 egg, well beaten	2 tablespoons sherry, whisky,
2 teaspoons sugar	rum or brandy
1 cup milk	Dash of nutmeg

Add sugar to egg, and gradually beat in milk and sherry. Serve in a tall glass and sprinkle nutmeg over top.

POSSET CUP

Put 1½ pounds of sugar into a quart of sherry. Strain into this the beaten whites and yolks of 24 eggs. Place on stove until scalding hot. Add 2 quarts of boiling milk into which a nutmeg has been grated, pouring milk into eggs and wine from as great a height as possible, and stirring constantly while pouring. Keep warm ½ hour before serving.

NEGUS

1 bottle port	1½ liqueur glasses brandy
1 quart boiling water	Nutmeg
1 lemon	Sugar

Warm the port. Rinse a pitcher with hot water, slice the lemon into it; then pour in the port and boiling water. Add the brandy and nutmeg, and sugar to taste.

MULLED ALE

1 quart ale	2 cloves
1 tablespoon sugar	1 gill rum
	Nutmeg

Heat the ale with the sugar and cloves. Warm a jug and pour ale into it; then add rum and some grated nutmeg.

SPRUCE BEER

In a large kettle put spruce tips, checkerberry leaves, dandelion root, yellow dock root, black cherry bark and spruce bark; cover with cold water and steep 6 hours over a slow fire. Drain and mix with 2 pails of cold water. Add 1½ pints of molasses to each pail of liquid. Dissolve 2 yeast cakes in lukewarm water and add to mixture. Strain through cheesecloth, put in jugs in a warm place until scum works off, then cork tightly.

FLIP

In a round-bellied pitcher mix ½ cup rum or brandy with 6 well-beaten eggs, 1 cup sugar and a grated nutmeg. In another receptacle heat 1½ quarts of ale till almost boiling. Pour the hot ale into the eggs: then pour back into the ale receptacle, and continue to pour back and forth till mixture is creamy smooth. Reheat by plunging a red-hot poker into the mixture. Serve at once.

COCKTAIL SWEETENER

For sweetening old-fashioneds, rum or champagne cocktails: attach a squirting-stopper to a pint bottle. Fill the bottle with warm water. Into it drop 50 grains of saccharine and shake till dissolved. Two or three squirts of the mixture will adequately sweeten one old-fashioned cocktail. Eight or ten squirts will sweeten a pitcher of champagne cocktails.

MINT JULEP

Put 3 sprigs of fresh mint, ½ tablespoon sugar and a little whisky in a tall glass. Set in refrigerator 15 minutes. Add some cracked ice and fill remainder of glass with whisky. Stir gently with a long-handled spoon until glasses are frosted. Decorate top with sprigs of mint.

WHISKY SOURS

Juice of 4 lemons   6 teaspoons sugar dissolved
Juice of 2 limes   in a little water
7 jiggers whisky

Put ingredients in cocktail shaker, add ice cubes and shake hard. Makes 8 cocktail glasses and a dividend all round. The sugar can be replaced with 2 grains of saccharine dissolved in 2 teaspoons of water.

WHISKY PUNCH

12 oranges   8 quarts water
6 lemons   2 bottles scotch or rye
4 pounds powdered sugar   12 egg whites

Squeeze oranges and lemons; grate rinds and add to juice. Add sugar and water and stir. Pour in whisky. Beat egg whites to a froth, stir them into the punch, pour all over cake of ice in punch bowl, and serve.

CIDER CUP

2 tablespoons sugar   1 liqueur glass curaçao
1 lemon   1 quart cider
1 liqueur glass brandy   1 bottle charged water

Put the sugar, lemon rind and juice into a jug. When the sugar is dissolved, pour over the brandy, curaçao and cider. Set in ice and when cool, add charged water. Remove lemon rind before serving.

MULLED CIDER

1 teaspoon cloves	3 sticks cinnamon
1 teaspoon allspice	2 quarts cider
	¾ cup brown sugar

Tie spices in a cheesecloth bag. Boil cider, sugar and spices 10 minutes. Remove spice bag and serve hot.

GRAPE JUICE

Cover Concord grapes with cold water (after removing the stems and washing thoroughly in a colander), then boil until tender. Press the juice through a wire sieve, add to it 1 cup of sugar for every 3 quarts of juice, and place over the fire just long enough to come to a boil. Do not let the grapes cook too long in the first place, or any more than boil up the last time, or the flavor will be impaired. Bottle hot.

HAYMAKERS' SWITCHEL[1]

1 cup brown sugar	½ cup molasses
½ teaspoon ginger	¾ cup vinegar
	2 quarts water

Mix all ingredients and chill with ice.

RASPBERRY SHRUB

Pick over and cover fruit with cider vinegar. Let stand overnight, then strain and to 1 pint of juice add 1 pint of sugar. Allow to boil freely at least 5 minutes. Bottle.

LEMONADE

Boil 3 pints of water and 1 pint of sugar 5 minutes; then add 1 pint of lemon juice. Chopped mint leaves improve the flavor.

---

[1]This mixture, if freely used during the haying season, is thought by Maine farmers to get hay into a barn in three quarters the time that would otherwise be consumed.

TEA

Pour boiling water into an earthen or china teapot to heat it; then pour out water. For each cup, put 1 to 2 teaspoons of tea leaves and 1 cup fresh boiling water into the pot. Let stand, covered, 3 minutes. Strain.

ICED TEA

Pour strong, hot tea over ice in glasses or pitcher. Garnish each glass with slice of lemon or orange.

HOT CHOCOLATE

2 squares chocolate	Dash of salt
4 cups rich milk	¼ cup sugar

Heat chocolate and 1 cup of milk together until the chocolate is melted; then add salt and sugar, and boil 3 minutes, stirring constantly. Scald the remaining 3 cups of milk in double boiler, add chocolate and beat until foamy.

HOT COCOA

Mix 2 tablespoons cocoa with 2 tablespoons sugar, and stir in enough boiling water to make it pour easily. Add this to 1 quart of scalded milk. Beat 2 minutes. Serve with whipped cream.

BOILED COFFEE

Use 2 level tablespoons of coffee to each cup of water. Put the coarsely ground coffee, a little cold water, the white of an egg and an eggshell into the pot; mix together and then add boiling water. Plug tissue paper into the spout, boil coffee 8 minutes; then reduce the heat and add ¼ cup cold water to settle the grounds.

CREAM CHEESE AND HORSERADISH SPREAD

1 3-ounce package cream cheese	1 teaspoon chopped chives
2 tablespoons horseradish	Dash of Worcestershire sauce

Put cream cheese in a bowl, and when soft work in the remaining ingredients. Spread on potato chips or crackers.

CRAB MEAT CANAPÉS

Pick over and shred 1 cup crab meat, and mix with enough mayonnaise to hold it together; then add a dash of Maggi's seasoning. Sauté 3-inch rounds of bread in butter until lightly browned. Peel and thinly slice a cucumber, and place a slice on each round of toast. Season lightly with salt and pepper, and spread on top of the cucumber a layer of crab-meat mixture. Place the canapés in a pan and broil until light brown. Garnish with sprigs of parsley and serve hot.

CREAM CHEESE AND ANCHOVY SPREAD

4 3-ounce packages cream cheese	¼ minced clove garlic
	⅓ cup anchovy sauce
2 tablespoons melted butter	Small can pimentos

Mash cream cheese, butter, garlic and anchovy sauce together with a fork until completely blended; then stir in finely chopped pimentos. Chill in refrigerator. Spread ¼ inch thick between thin slices of bread, and cut diagonally in quarters or in three strips.

ROQUEFORT CHEESE AND CAVIARE

Spread crisp crackers with thin layer of Roquefort cheese mashed into a spread with cream cheese. On the cheese spread red caviare.

SARDINES AND CRACKER CRUMBS

Roll sardines in cracker crumbs and set in the oven until brown. Squeeze lemon juice on them before serving.

SPECIAL SUNDAY FISH BALLS WITH CHILI SAUCE

Prepare small Special Sunday Fish Balls, p. 45, stick a toothpick in each, and pass with a side dish of Chili Sauce, p. 206.

DEVILED HAM

See Cold Ham Mousse, p. 148.

SOUPS

MAXIMS FROM MAINE KITCHENS

If food is too salty, stretch a clean cloth tightly over the container holding the food; sprinkle a tablespoonful of flour on the cloth, and let container simmer. In a few moments the flour will absorb the surplus salt.

✿

To clean silverware without rubbing, stand it overnight in sour milk. In the morning, heat milk to the boiling point.

✿

To remove too much salt from soup, add slices of raw potato, boil a few minutes and remove.

✿

Tinware is best cleaned with sifted wood ashes.

SOUPS

POT–AU–FEU

"POINT AUX TREMBLE, at this time, had assumed the appearance of a straggling village. . . . We enjoyed as much comfort as tight houses, warm fires, and our scantiness of clothing would admit. Provisions were in plenty, particularly beef, which, though small in bulk, was of an excellent flavor. . . . When these people slaughter their beasts for winter use, they cut up the meat into small pieces, such as a half pound, two pounds, etc. according to the number in the family. In the evening before bedtime, the females of the house prepare the dinner of the following day. It may be particularly described, as it was done in our view for a number of days together, and during the time was never varied. This was the manner: a piece of pork or beef, or a portion of each kind, together with a sufficiency of cabbage, potatoes, and turnips, seasoned with salt, and an adequate quantity of water, were put into a neat tin kettle with a close lid. The kettle was placed on the stove in the room where we all slept, and there it simmered till the time of rising, when it was taken to a small fire in the kitchen, where the stewing continued till near noon, when they dined. The contents were turned into a large basin. Each person had a plate; no knife was used, except one to cut the bread, but a five or six pronged fork answered the purposes of a spoon. The meat required no cutting, as it was reduced to a mucilage, or at least to shreds. . . . Our dinner followed in a few hours. The manner of our cookery excited astonishment in our hosts. As much beef was consumed at a single meal, as would have served this family for a week."

—JOHN JOSEPH HENRY, *Campaign Against Quebec*, entry for November 18, 1775. (*March to Quebec*, p. 361.)

POT–AU–FEU

4 pounds lean beef	5 allspice
6 quarts cold water	2 cups diced potatoes
2 cups diced turnips	Small piece of lemon rind
2 sliced onions	4 stalks chopped celery
2 cups diced carrots	3 tablespoons chopped
1 cup diced parsnips	parsley
2 whole cloves	2 teaspoons salt
1 bay leaf	¼ teaspoon black pepper
A pinch of sage	A pinch of baking soda

Cut the meat in pieces, put in cold water and heat slowly. As the scum becomes thick, remove it. After skimming well, add vegetables and seasonings and simmer, tightly covered, for 5 hours. The longer and slower it cooks, the better it is.

BOUILLON

4 pounds lean beef	4 peppercorns
2 pounds marrowbone	4 whole cloves
2 quarts cold water	1 onion, carrot and celery
1 tablespoon salt	stalk, chopped fine

Wipe and cut meat in 1-inch pieces. Soak half the meat in the water in a soup kettle ½ hour. Brown remainder of meat in hot frying pan with 2 tablespoons marrow from marrowbone; then add it with the bone to the kettle. Bring to a boil and skim. Cover and simmer 3 hours. Add seasonings and vegetables, cook 1 hour longer, strain and cool. When cold, remove fat. Makes about 1½ quarts.

WHITE STOCK

4-pound knuckle of veal	1 sliced onion
2½ quarts cold water	1 sliced celery stalk
1 tablespoon salt	½ teaspoon peppercorns
	1 bay leaf

Wipe meat, remove bone and cut in small pieces. Put meat, bone, water and seasonings in kettle. Heat to boiling point, and skim frequently. Reduce heat, cover, and simmer 4 hours. Strain. Makes about 1½ quarts.

BROWN STOCK

5-pound shin of beef	2 sprigs parsley
2 pounds marrowbone	1 tablespoon salt
3 quarts cold water	1 sliced carrot
½ teaspoon peppercorns	1 sliced celery stalk
Pinch of bay leaf, thyme	2 sliced onions
and marjoram	1 sliced tomato

Crack bone and extract marrow; cut lean beef in small cubes. Brown ½ of it in marrow, or in 2 tablespoons fat; add with remaining meat and bone to cold water, bring to boil and boil 10 minutes. Skim, cover and simmer 3 hours, removing scum as it forms; add vegetables and seasonings, and cook 1 hour longer. Strain stock; when cold, remove fat. Makes about 2 quarts.

CHICKEN STOCK OR BROTH

3-pound fowl	½ cup chopped celery
2 quarts cold water	½ bay leaf
1 sliced onion	Salt and pepper

Clean fowl; remove skin and fat, and cut in pieces. Put all the ingredients in a soup kettle, bring to a boil and skim. Cover and simmer 3 hours, or until meat is tender. Strain and clear; season to taste and serve hot, or chill for jellied soup. Makes 1½ quarts.

AROOSTOOK SOUP

6 small white onions	2½ cups diced potatoes
1 cup chopped celery	2 tablespoons butter
3 tablespoons butter	1½ tablespoons flour
1 quart milk	Salt, pepper, cayenne
Minced parsley	

Slice onions and sauté with celery in 3 tablespoons butter, stirring until yellow; then add to the milk and cook in the top of a double boiler for 45 minutes. Boil potatoes 10 minutes in salted water. Heat 2 tablespoons butter and mix with the flour, add the milk mixture and potatoes. Cook together until soft and thick. Season well and garnish with parsley. Serves 6–8.

HERB BOUQUET

An "herb bouquet" is made of sprigs of parsley, thyme, celery and bay leaves tied together. It is suspended for an hour in soup to add flavor and body.

CREAM OF ASPARAGUS SOUP

1 bunch cooked asparagus	2 tablespoons butter
1 slice onion	2 tablespoons flour
2 cups milk	Salt and pepper
1 cup heavy cream	

Cut off and reserve tips of cooked asparagus, and put remainder through a sieve. Put onion in milk and scald milk; remove onion; add strained asparagus. Combine butter and flour, add a little hot liquid and stir smooth; add to mixture with seasonings. Bring to a boil, then add asparagus tips and cream. Serves 6.

BARLEY SOUP

Cook 1 pound of lamb, covered with water, until nearly done; then add 1 cup pearl barley which has been soaked in salted water. As the barley becomes soft add 1 cup diced turnip and 1 cup diced potatoes, and simmer until vegetables are tender. Makes about 1½ quarts.

BORTSCH

1½ pounds lean beef	1 cup chopped carrots
2 quarts water	1 cup chopped raw beets
½ cup butter	1 tablespoon flour
2 chopped onions	1 cup chopped cabbage
2 slices diced bacon	4 diced potatoes
1 cup sieved tomatoes	Juice of ½ lemon
Sour cream	

Cook the meat in the water. Melt the butter in a large saucepan, and sauté bacon and onion in it till light brown. Add tomatoes, carrots, beets and flour, and cover with some of meat broth. When vegetables are almost soft, add them to kettle in which meat is cooking. Add cabbage and potatoes, and cook until potatoes are done. Add lemon juice. For each serving, put a slice of meat in the bottom of a soup bowl, fill with soup, and top with sour cream. Serves 8–10.

BEET SOUP

2-pound shoulder of lamb	½ minced onion
6 cups hot water	12 peppercorns
6 beets, sliced thin	1 teaspoon sugar

Salt and boil ingredients for 1½ hours. Remove lamb and use as separate course, or save for future dishes. Then add 2 tablespoons vinegar. Before serving add ¾ cup cream, either sour or sweet. Serves 6.

BAKED BEAN SOUP

2 cups cold baked beans	2 tablespoons butter
2 minced onions	2 tablespoons flour
1 quart cold water	1 tablespoon celery salt
2 cups canned tomatoes	1 cup cooked elbow macaroni

Simmer beans, onions and cold water ½ hour. Heat tomatoes, rub through a strainer and add to bean mixture. Mix butter and flour together and gradually add enough boiling water to make it thin; add to the soup. Add the salt, strain; then add macaroni and serve hot. Serves 8.

BLACK BEAN SOUP

1 pint black beans	¼ teaspoon pepper
2 quarts water	½ teaspoon mustard
1 ham bone	¼ teaspoon paprika
2 stalks chopped celery	1 clove garlic
2 tablespoons butter	2 tablespoons flour
1-inch cube salt pork	3 lemons: 2 squeezed, 1 sliced
½ teaspoon salt	
3 hard-boiled eggs	

Soak beans 12 hours overnight. Put in fresh water, add ham bone, celery and half the butter. Simmer 3 hours, adding more water as it diminishes with boiling. Rub through sieve, reheat and add salt, pepper, mustard, paprika and garlic. Cook butter and flour together until smooth and stir into soup. Cut eggs and lemon in thin slices. Put in tureen and strain soup over them.

CREAM OF CELERY SOUP

1 cup chopped celery stalks and leaves	1 tablespoon butter
1 pint chicken stock	1 quart scalded milk or light cream
2 tablespoons cornstarch	Salt and pepper

Boil celery in stock until soft, then press through sieve. Cream cornstarch and butter together and add to stock with scalded milk and seasonings. Serves 6–8.

CHEESE SOUP

Cheese Sauce (2), p. 207	1/4 cup minced green pepper
1/2 cup minced onion	1/4 cup butter
1/2 cup minced celery	1 cup chicken stock

Prepare Cheese Sauce (2), p. 207. Sauté onion, celery and green pepper in butter until soft, then add to the sauce with the chicken stock. Heat thoroughly. Serves 6.

CREAM OF CHICKEN, OR RABBIT, SOUP

2 tablespoons butter	3 cups chicken (rabbit) stock
1 tablespoon minced onion	1 cup diced cooked chicken or rabbit
2 tablespoons flour	2 tablespoons minced parsley
1/2 teaspoon curry powder	1 tablespoon celery salt
1 cup scalded milk	
1 cup cooked rice	

Sauté onion in butter 5 minutes; then stir in flour, curry powder, milk and stock. Add remaining ingredients and heat thoroughly. Serves 6.

CLAM BROTH

1 pint minced clams	1 teaspoon salt
Liquor from clams	1/8 teaspoon pepper
1 pint water	Blade of mace
Dash of cayenne	

Bring above ingredients to a boil and then strain through a cloth. Serve in cups and add large spoonful of thick cream to each cup. Serves 4.

CLAM BISQUE

1 quart shucked clams	2 tablespoons flour
1 slice onion	1 cup cracker crumbs
2 stalks celery	1 teaspoon salt
1 bay leaf	1/8 teaspoon pepper
2 tablespoons butter	1 quart scalded milk

1/2 cup light cream

Separate necks and bodies of clams. Simmer hard parts 1/2 hour with 2 cups water. Strain, reserving liquor. Cook liquor, onion, celery and bay leaf 3 minutes; then rub through a sieve. Mix butter, flour and crumbs; add liquor and soft parts of clams, and cook 6 minutes. Three minutes before serving add scalded milk and cream. Serves 6.

CLAM CHOWDER

1 quart shucked clams	3 slices salt pork
2 sliced onions	1 quart whole milk
6 cubed potatoes	2 tablespoons butter

Salt and pepper

Rinse clams in clam liquor and remove black portions. Chop clams fine in wooden mixing bowl. Cook onions and potatoes in just enough water to cover for 15 minutes; then add clams and cook another 15 minutes. Cut salt pork in 3/8 inch cubes, fry till brown and drain on brown wrapping paper. Add pork scraps and fat to clams and vegetables. Heat the milk and add it to the chowder. Add butter and season to taste. Serves 8.

CORN CHOWDER

1/3 cup diced salt pork	1 cup cooked corn, canned
1 sliced onion	or fresh
2 1/2 cups diced potatoes	1 cup hot milk
2 cups boiling water	1 cup light cream
Common crackers	Salt and pepper

Try out salt pork in large saucepan. Add onion and cook to a golden brown. Add potatoes, boiling water, corn and cook until potatoes are tender. To this add milk, cream and seasonings. Reheat and serve over a cracker placed in each dish. Serves 4.

CORN AND CHICKEN SOUP

1 cup cream-style canned corn	2 egg yolks
½ cup minced celery	2 cups hot milk
1 cup minced chicken	3 tablespoons butter
1 quart chicken stock	1 tablespoon celery salt
	Croutons

Heat the corn and force it through a coarse strainer; then add the strained corn, celery and chicken to the chicken stock. Bring to a boil, cover and simmer 15 minutes. Beat egg yolks slightly, gradually stir in hot milk; then add to soup. Cook 2 minutes, stirring constantly. Add butter and seasonings. Serve with croutons. Serves 8.

GREEN CORN AND TOMATO SOUP

8 pounds soup meat	2 chopped onions
12 ears sweet corn	2 diced carrots
2 quarts tomatoes, peeled and cut	Salt and pepper

Cover meat with cold water and simmer 2 hours, skimming as it boils. Cut corn from cobs and add cobs to boiling soup for 1 hour. Remove cobs and add corn and remaining ingredients. Cook until vegetables are tender. Dumplings may be dropped into the boiling soup by the spoonful if desired. Serves 8.

SALT CODFISH CHOWDER

½ pound salt codfish	3 cups boiled diced potatoes
1-inch cube salt pork	1 quart milk
1 tablespoon chopped onion	
8 soda crackers, softened in milk	

Flake codfish and soak it in lukewarm water until it is soft and the salt has been removed. Cut pork into small pieces and cook it until a light brown. Add onion, and when slightly browned add potatoes and cover with water. Boil until tender. Add milk and fish and reheat. Add crackers just before serving. Serves 4–6.

All fish chowder recipes are well adapted to making in bulk and freezing in small containers.

CORN BISQUE

1 cup cream-style canned corn	1½ tablespoons flour
1 pint milk	1 cup light cream
1 tablespoon butter	1 teaspoon salt

Chop cooked or canned corn and cook with milk in double boiler half an hour; then rub through strainer. Cook butter and flour together and add to corn-milk mixture. Just before serving add heated cream and salt. Serves 4.

CRAB STEW

6 hard-shell crabs	Salt and pepper
1 tablespoon butter	1 quart chicken stock
1 chopped onion	1 cup light cream
1 tablespoon flour	1 tablespoon minced parsley

Boil crabs. Remove meat from crabs, chop fine and sauté in butter with onion. When onion is brown add flour, seasonings and stock. Simmer 10 minutes, add cream and parsley, and serve. Serves 6.

ROCKY PASTURE FISH CHOWDER

4 sliced potatoes	1 pound diced haddock,
1 quart water	cod, striped bass, hali-
3 slices diced salt pork	but, or 1 can chicken
3 diced onions	haddie[1]
2 teaspoons curry powder	¼ teaspoon white sugar
Cracker crumbs	1 quart whole milk
Salt and pepper	1 cup heavy cream

Boil potatoes in the water; drain, mash and return to water in which they boiled. Fry pork, add onions and cook slowly in the fat until lightly browned; then add potatoes, curry powder, fish, sugar, milk and cream. Cook 30 minutes over slow heat. Thicken with cracker crumbs and season with salt and pepper. Serves 8.

Any one of the following may be substituted for the fish in the above recipe: 1 quart clams, the meat from 2 boiled lobsters, or 1 quart oysters.

This recipe can be quadrupled, placed in containers and frozen to good advantage, as it improves with age and freezing.

[1]Chicken haddie is lightly smoked haddock, canned in 14-ounce tins by W. H. Tidmarsh, Charlottetown, Canada, Connors Bros. Ltd., Black's Harbour, N.B., and other Canadian packing houses.

CREAM OF CRAB SOUP

3 tablespoons butter	1 teaspoon salt
1 minced onion	1/8 teaspoon pepper
3 stalks minced celery	2 cups chicken stock
3 chopped mushrooms	1 1/4 cups crab meat
1 1/2 tablespoons flour	3 cups milk

1 cup heavy cream

Melt butter, add onion, celery and mushrooms, and cook 5 minutes without browning. Blend flour and seasonings with the stock, and add with crab meat to the vegetables. Simmer 1/2 hour. Combine milk and cream, scald and add to soup. Let stand 5 minutes before serving. Serves 6–8.

FINNAN HADDIE CHOWDER

1 pound finnan haddie	2 sliced potatoes
2 ounces salt pork	1 quart milk
2 sliced onions	Salt and pepper
2 cups fish stock	1 cup heavy cream

Prepare Finnan Haddie (1), p. 49. Sauté onions in salt pork until soft, add stock and potatoes, and boil 25 minutes. Add flaked finnan haddie and milk and boil 10 minutes longer. Season with salt and pepper. Remove from heat, stir in cream and serve with a bowl of cracker crumbs as thickening. Serves 6.

FISH CHOWDER

3-pound haddock	8 common crackers
4 diced potatoes	1 pint milk
3 chopped onions	1 tablespoon butter
4 slices diced salt pork	Salt and pepper

1 pint light cream

Cook haddock in boiling water until done. Remove fish from water and add potatoes and onions to water. Cook until potatoes are soft. Fry salt pork until crisp. Add scraps and fat to chowder. Remove skin and bones from fish. Add fish to chowder. Split crackers, soak them in milk, and heat. When milk is hot, add to chowder. Before serving add butter, seasonings and cream.

LENTIL SOUP

2 cups lentils	½ cup olive oil
⅔ cup rice	2 onions

Salt and pepper

Pick over lentils and boil in 1½ quarts water 3 hours. Add uncooked rice and cook till rice is done, stirring often. Chop the onions fine and brown in oil. Add onions to lentils and boil 5 minutes. Season with salt and pepper. Serves 4–6.

LETTUCE SOUP

4 slices bacon	4 beef bouillon cubes dis-
2 heads lettuce	solved in 2 quarts water
2 chopped onions	2 cups cooked rice
2 thick slices bread	1 tablespoon celery salt

Try out bacon in a saucepan until crisp, then remove from fat. Chop lettuce and add it to the bacon fat with onions, bread, dissolved beef cubes and water. Simmer 1½ hours. Then add the cooked rice and serve. Serves 6.

LOBSTER BISQUE

2 medium lobsters, under-cooked	2 tablespoons flour
2 cups water	2 cups oyster crackers rolled to a dust
1 quart milk	1 teaspoon salt
6 tablespoons butter	Few grains cayenne

Remove meat from shell and large claws and pass through fine grinder. Break body and small claws, cover with water, bring slowly to boiling point and cook 20 minutes. Drain and add liquor to milk and scald. Melt butter; stir in flour and cracker crumbs; gradually stir in hot liquid and cook 5 minutes, stirring till smooth and thickened. Add seasonings and lobster meat, and heat thoroughly. Add remaining butter and serve. Serves 6.

LOBSTER STEW

Pick meat from a boiled lobster and chop it fine with crackers. Add chicken stock to moisten. For each pint of lobster mixture add a quart of rich milk. Season with butter, salt and pepper.

LIMA BEAN CHOWDER

1 slice pork shoulder	2 cups fresh lima beans
1 tablespoon butter	1 teaspoon salt
2 minced onions	½ teaspoon pepper
4 diced potatoes	2 cups water
3 diced carrots	1 tablespoon flour

Cut meat in small pieces and fry in butter until brown; then add onions. When light brown, add potatoes, carrots, beans, seasonings and water. Simmer until vegetables are tender. Thicken with flour and serve hot. Serves 6.

LIVER SOUP

½ pound calf's liver	2 teaspoons chopped parsley
2 cups water	1 tablespoon rice
1 medium-sized onion	1 egg
1 tomato	1 lemon
Salt and pepper	

Wash liver, slice into small pieces, and boil in water until tender. Cool, remove gristle and put through meat grinder. Add meat, sliced onion, tomato, parsley, rice and seasonings to the liver water and simmer until onion and rice are cooked. Before serving add the following egg sauce: Add the juice of 1 lemon to a well-beaten egg, and continue beating until well mixed. Gradually add to the soup. Serves 2.

MINESTRONE

(See p. 244)

Minestrone is an Italian soup whose ingredients are as diverse as they are satisfying and filling, and there is no such thing as a fixed recipe for it. It is different in every Italian province; and it even varies in each province, depending on the whims of the cook and the vegetables obtainable.

MULLIGATAWNY SOUP

1 chopped onion	½ cup butter
1 bunch celery, cut in 1-inch	½ cup flour
pieces	1 teaspoon curry powder
1 diced carrot	¼ teaspoon cloves
1 chopped green pepper	¼ minced clove garlic
1 cup diced uncooked	1 small can tomatoes
chicken	3 quarts White Stock, p. 19

3 cups boiled rice

Brown onion, celery, carrot, pepper and chicken in butter. Add flour, curry, cloves, garlic, tomatoes and white stock, and simmer 1 hour. Remove chicken, and rub vegetables through sieve. Add chicken to strained soup, season with celery salt and pepper, add rice and serve. Serves 6–8.

CREAM OF MUSHROOM SOUP (1)

¼ pound or 1 can mush-	1 quart consommé
rooms	Salt and pepper
3 tablespoons butter	1 pint light cream
2 tablespoons flour	1 tablespoon Worcester-
	shire sauce

Wash, peel and chop mushrooms; then sauté in butter 5 minutes. Stir in flour, consommé, salt and pepper. Bring to a boil and simmer 20 minutes. Add cream and cook 5 minutes. Before serving add Worcestershire sauce. Serves 8.

CREAM OF MUSHROOM SOUP (2)

½ pound mushrooms	1 pint light cream
¼ cup butter	1 teaspoon minced onion
1 pint chicken stock	Salt and pepper

2 tablespoons flour

Wash, peel and chop mushrooms; sauté in butter in stewpan 10 minutes. Heat stock, cream, onion, seasonings and flour in a double boiler; then add mushrooms. Serve hot. Serves 6–8.

MACARONI SOUP

2 quarts broth   ¼ pound macaroni

Prepare a good pot-au-feu or bouillon. Break macaroni into 2-inch pieces and boil 10 minutes in salted water. Then drain thoroughly and drop into boiling broth 15 minutes before serving. It may be served with Parmesan cheese, grated, if desired. Serves 6–8.

MADRILÈNE

2 cups chicken stock   1 diced carrot
2 cups beef stock   1 chopped onion
1 quart can tomatoes   1 tablespoon celery salt

Bring stocks and vegetables to a boil and simmer 1 hour. When partially cooked, add salt. Strain before serving. Serves 6.

OKRA SOUP

2 pounds beef without fat   Salt and pepper
      or bone   ¼ pound butter
1 chopped onion   4 quarts cold water
            2 cups chopped okra

Cut beef into small pieces, and season well with salt and pepper. Fry it in soup kettle with onion and butter until brown. Then add cold water and simmer 1 hour. Add okra and simmer 3 hours longer. Serves 6.

ONION SOUP (1)

10 medium-sized onions   1 teaspoon Worcestershire
¼ cup butter   sauce
1½ quarts beef bouillon   6 slices toast
            Grated cheese

Slice the onions thin and brown them in butter. Add bouillon, Worcestershire sauce, salt and pepper to taste, and simmer until onions are tender. Pour the soup in an earthenware tureen. Arrange slices of toast on top and sprinkle toast with grated cheese. Serves 6.

ONION SOUP (2)

1 onion for each person, sliced fine	2 tablespoons flour
	2 cans consommé
¼ cup butter	1 tablespoon celery salt

Sauté onion in butter till faintly brown. Add flour and gradually stir in consommé and salt. Simmer 1 hour. As liquid boils down, replace with water. Pour over slices of toast and sprinkle liberally with grated cheese.

CREAM OF ONION SOUP

6 chopped onions	1 egg yolk
2 tablespoons butter	1 tablespoon chopped
3 cups water	pimentos
1 tablespoon butter	1 tablespoon celery salt
1 tablespoon flour	¼ teaspoon pepper
2 cups scalded milk	Parmesan cheese

Sauté onions in 2 tablespoons butter until soft, then add water and simmer 20 minutes. Strain. Melt 1 tablespoon of butter, stir in flour and milk, and cook 5 minutes. Stir the sauce into onion broth, and when blended add well beaten egg yolk, pimentos and seasonings. Serve hot with Parmesan cheese (or any other hard cheese) grated over each serving. Serves 6.

OXTAIL SOUP

1 oxtail	3 whole cloves
1 chopped onion	1 tablespoon flour
2 chopped carrots	3 quarts consommé
1 bunch chopped celery	1 tablespoon celery salt
1 tablespoon chopped parsley	⅛ teaspoon black pepper
½ pound lean ham or beef	⅛ teaspoon cayenne
Grating of nutmeg	

Wash oxtail and cut in small pieces. Sauté oxtail and onion in butter 10 minutes. Then add carrots, celery, parsley and chopped ham or beef. When brown, add cloves, flour and consommé. Cover and simmer 4 hours. Add seasonings and strain. Serves 8.

OYSTER STEW (1)

3 pints milk
2 tablespoons flour
¼ cup oyster or common
     crackers rolled to a
     powder

Salt and pepper
1 quart oysters
2 tablespoons butter

Heat milk in double boiler. Add a little cold water to flour and cracker dust to mix smooth; then stir into milk and cook 6 minutes. Add seasonings and oysters and cook till they are puffed up. Add butter and serve at once. Serves 6–8.

OYSTER STEW (2)

1 quart oysters
1 quart milk

3 tablespoons butter
1 tablespoon celery salt

¼ teaspoon black pepper

Bring oysters to a boil in their liquor. Boil the milk and then add it to the oyster liquor. Add the butter, salt and pepper, and cook until the oysters are plump and the edges begin to curl. Serve immediately with oyster crackers. Serves 4–6.

OYSTER BISQUE

1 pint oysters
1½ tablespoons butter
1½ tablespoons flour
2 cups milk
1 cup light cream

1 teaspoon salt
¼ teaspoon pepper
2 egg yolks
2 tablespoons cold water
½ cup powdered oyster
     crackers

Bring oysters to the boiling point in their liquor. Drain, reserving the liquor. Chop and mash the oysters. Melt butter, add flour, then milk and cream, and cook until smooth. Add oysters with their liquor, salt and pepper. Beat egg yolks with water and stir into the bisque. Add powdered oyster crackers, simmer 2 minutes and serve. Serves 6.

OYSTER CHOWDER

2 slices diced fat bacon	¼ teaspoon pepper
2 chopped onions	1 pint milk
2 stalks minced celery	1 pint light cream
6 sliced potatoes	2 tablespoons butter
1 teaspoon salt	1 tablespoon flour
1 pint oysters	

Try out bacon, remove bacon from pan and add onions, celery, potatoes and seasonings. Cover with boiling water and cook till almost done. Add milk and cream, boil up and thicken with blended butter and flour. Add oysters and cook until edges curl. Serves 8.

PARSNIP SOUP

2 parsnips	1 teaspoon salt
2 tablespoons butter	¼ teaspoon pepper
1 quart milk	

Wash, pare and dice parsnips. Cook until tender with enough water to cover. Drain and mash parsnips, add butter, seasonings and milk, and simmer until hot. Serves 6.

PEA SOUP

2 cups dried peas	Ham bone or salt pork
1 quart boiling water	Salt and pepper
1 bunch chopped celery	1 quart milk
2 chopped onions	⅓ cup butter

Soak peas in cold water overnight; drain; then cover with boiling water, add celery, onions and bone or pork. Simmer until soft. When tender remove from stove and press through a sieve; add salt and pepper. Return soup to the fire, let it boil up once and add milk and butter, stirring well. Serve at once. Serves 8.

PUREE OF GREEN PEAS

1 quart young green peas	2 quarts milk
2 sliced onions	Salt and pepper

Cook the onions with the peas according to recipe for Boiled Green Peas, p. 176; then drain, rub through a sieve and add them to scalded milk. Do not boil after adding peas. Add seasonings.

ROCKY PASTURE PEA SOUP

3 cups split peas, or whole field peas	1 stalk chopped celery
2 pounds salt pork	1 can consommé or stock, or 4 chicken cubes dissolved in hot water
1 gallon water	
1 sliced onion	1 tablespoon celery salt
1 sliced carrot	1 teaspoon summer savory

Soak peas overnight in cold water to cover. Put salt pork in a kettle with the water, peas, onion, carrot and celery. Boil slowly for 1½ hours. Add consommé and simmer another 1½ hours. Add salt and savory, rub through a strainer and serve. Makes 3 quarts.

PEPPERPOT

¼ cup chopped celery	½ pound cooked honey-comb tripe, cut fine (p. 134)
½ cup chopped green peppers	
¼ cup chopped onion	1½ cups diced potatoes
4 tablespoons butter	½ teaspoon pepper
3 tablespoons flour	1 tablespoon celery salt
5 cups chicken stock	½ cup light cream

Cook vegetables in half the butter 15 minutes; then add flour and stir till well mixed. Add remaining ingredients, except cream. Cover and cook 1 hour. Before serving add cream and remaining butter. Serves 6.

ROCKY PASTURE POTATO SOUP

½ pound salt pork   4 cups water
5 potatoes   2 egg yolks
3 chopped onions   1 tablespoon flour
4 chicken bouillon cubes   1 cup scalded milk
                ¼ cup light cream

Cut pork in small pieces, try out in frying pan, remove pork scraps
and brown chopped onions in pork fat. Boil and mash the potatoes.
Dissolve bouillon cubes in the water, and add onions, pork fat and
mashed potato. Cook ½ hour, adding enough water to make up for
evaporation. Blend flour, egg yolks and scalded milk and add to
soup. Lastly add cream, salt and pepper to taste, and cook 10 minutes more. Serves 6–8.

POTATO SOUP

6 potatoes   1 cup grated American
2 slices bacon   cheese
1 chopped onion   1 teaspoon Worcestershire
2 tablespoons chopped parsley   sauce
1 tablespoon flour   1 tablespoon celery salt
1 quart scalded milk   ¼ teaspoon pepper

Boil potatoes and put through ricer. Cut bacon fine, cook in frying pan until crisp, then drain on brown paper. Sauté onion and
parsley in bacon fat; add flour, scalded milk, bacon, potatoes, cheese,
Worcestershire sauce and seasonings. Serves 6.

PURÉE OF POTATOES

2 tablespoons butter   1 quart scalded milk
2 teaspoons flour   1 teaspoon onion juice
2½ cups mashed potatoes   1 teaspoon salt

Rub butter and flour together and then add it to mashed potatoes.
Gradually stir in the scalded milk and add remaining ingredients.
Bring to a boil and serve garnished with minced parsley. Serves 6.

LEEK AND POTATO SOUP

1 bunch leeks	1 quart consommé
1 cup celery	3 cups diced potatoes
5 tablespoons butter	Salt and pepper

Cut leeks and celery in thin slices and cook in butter until soft. Add consommé and cook 40 minutes in double boiler. Parboil potatoes in boiling salted water 10 minutes, drain and add to soup. Cook until potatoes are soft, then season to taste. Serves 4–6.

RABBIT SOUP

2 young rabbits	1 bay leaf
2 quarts cold water	1 tablespoon butter
1 chopped onion	½ cup rice
Salt and pepper	

Skin and draw the rabbits and wash in warm water. Then cut the meat into small pieces and cover with the cold water. Add onion and bay leaf and simmer until meat is tender. Add rice and seasonings and simmer 1 hour longer. Serves 6.

SQUASH SOUP

1 quart whole milk	2 tablespoons butter
1 cup canned squash	Salt and pepper
2 tablespoons flour	Whipped cream

Heat milk, then stir in squash. Cream flour and butter, add to the milk and squash, and season to taste. Serve with whipped cream on top of each portion. Serves 6.

TOMATO AND RICE BROTH

Cook 1 can tomatoes, 1 minced onion, and 1 pint of water for ½ hour. Strain, return to fire and add ½ cup boiled rice and 1 cup water in which it was boiled. Season with salt, pepper and parsley. Make a white *roux* of 1 teaspoon sugar, 3 tablespoons butter, and 3 tablespoons flour; add to the soup. Put a pinch of soda in 1 cup hot milk and add to the soup. Boil and stir well. Serves 4–6.

TOMATO SOUP WITH DUMPLINGS

1 can tomatoes	3 tablespoons butter
1½ quarts water	¼ teaspoon salt
2 minced onions	⅛ teaspoon pepper

Boil the ingredients for 1½ hours and add more water if it becomes too thick. Make Dumplings, p. 117, and drop them into the soup 15 minutes before serving. Serves 4–6.

TURTLE SOUP

In West Indian waters all fish markets are plentifully supplied with green turtle, hawksbill turtle and loggerhead turtle. Four pounds of turtle meat are needed to make soup for 8 people. Green is best. Hawksbill and loggerhead are strong and must be soaked in lime juice overnight.

Scald the turtle meat ½ hour, replace with fresh water, add 1 sliced onion, 1 chopped celery stalk, 1 sliced sweet pepper, 1 tablespoon celery salt, and simmer 2 hours. Cut the soft portions of the meat back into the broth in small pieces, and before serving add 1 wineglass of sherry.

MOCK TURTLE SOUP

1 calf's head	½ cup butter
½ cup sliced onion	½ cup flour
½ cup diced carrots	2 cups beef extract
1 teaspoon cloves	1 cup condensed tomato soup
1 teaspoon pepper	¼ cup sherry
½ teaspoon allspice	Juice of 1 lemon
1 tablespoon celery salt	Grating of nutmeg

Soak calf's head in cold water for 1 hour. Bring a gallon of water to a boil and in it boil calf's head, onion, carrots and seasonings for 2 hours. Remove head and continue to boil soup till reduced to half. Remove from fire, strain through sieve and chill. Brown the flour with the butter, add beef extract and bring to boil. From calf's head cut 2 cups soft portions, and add to beef extract. Into this pour the head-stock, tomato soup, sherry and lemon juice and bring to a boil. Serve with small squares of toast. Serves 10–12.

TRIPE CHOWDER

Melt 3 tablespoons butter in a deep saucepan, add 4 tablespoons each of chopped celery, green peppers and onion. Cook 10 minutes, stir in 3 tablespoons flour and gradually add 1½ quarts chicken stock. Add ½ pound fresh honeycomb tripe, cut in fine strips, and 1 cup raw potato cubes. Cover and cook slowly 1 hour. Season with salt and pepper, and just before serving add ½ cup hot milk. Serves 6.

If pickled tripe is used instead of fresh, it must be boiled twice before adding to chowder (see p. 134).

VICHYSOISSE

1 tablespoon butter	2½ quarts hot water
3 sliced leeks	1 cup milk
1 sliced onion	1 tablespoon salt
2 ounces diced salt pork	1 teaspoon white pepper
2 bay leaves	½ cup light cream
8 sliced raw potatoes	1 tablespoon butter
2 tablespoons flour	

Melt butter and sauté leeks, onion, salt pork and bay leaves until soft and light brown. Add potatoes, hot water, milk and seasonings, and simmer, covered, for 1 hour. Strain through a sieve into another saucepan, cook 5 minutes, then add cream and butter blended with the flour. Stir and cook 1 minute longer. Serve with bread croutons. Serves 8–10.

VEGETABLE CHOWDER

⅓ pound bacon	4 diced potatoes
3 minced onions	2 tablespoons salt
2 diced carrots	¼ teaspoon pepper
1 diced turnip	2 tablespoons butter
2 tablespoons minced parsley	2 tablespoons flour
2 chopped green peppers	1 pint hot light cream

Try out bacon, remove bacon from pan and sauté onions in fat till a light brown. Add vegetables and seasonings. Cover with boiling water and simmer 1 hour, or until vegetables are tender. Add butter and flour, blended and moistened with a little milk. Cook 1 minute and then pour cream over all. Serves 8.

VEGETABLE SOUP

Put 1 quart of soup stock into a saucepan and add 1 diced onion, 1 diced carrot and 1 diced turnip. Let it simmer until vegetables are tender.

WINTER CHOWDER

½ cup diced salt pork	1 common cracker pounded
2 chopped onions	to a dust
2 diced potatoes	2 tablespoons flour
2 cups boiling water	2 cups canned tomatoes
2 cups canned corn	⅛ teaspoon soda
2 cups milk	1 tablespoon celery salt

Grating of nutmeg

Try out the salt pork and sauté the onion in the fat. Add potatoes and boiling water, and cook until tender. Add corn, milk and powdered cracker, and thicken with flour blended with cold water. Heat the tomatoes and add to chowder with soda and seasonings. Serves 6.

FISH AND SHELLFISH

MAXIMS FROM MAINE KITCHENS

If a fish sinks when placed in fresh water, it is fresh.

❧

To keep a baked fish hot and fresh, cover it with a greased paper. It will hold its heat and flavor for 15 minutes.

❧

To keep a dish on ice in a refrigerator, put a rubber ring, such as used on fruit jars, on the ice under it. Then it won't slip.

❧

To keep a silver dish hot in the oven without damaging the dish, set it on a double layer of blotting paper in a larger receptacle, and pour water around it.

❧

A refrigerator should be regularly washed with hot water in which two tablespoonfuls of soda or borax have been dissolved. The drain pipe will keep clean if a tablespoon of borax is put around it.

FISH AND SHELLFISH

SAMUEL P. CAPEN TO MR. ROBERTS
CONCERNING A SALT FISH DINNER

"As far as a layman can translate into the vulgar tongue the instructions of the experts, this is the way to make a salt fish dinner.

"About four hours before the meal is to be served tear a dry salt fish into pieces two or three inches long. Put it to soak for two or three hours in cold water. Boil it in the same water for half an hour. Then drain off the water. Boil potatoes, beets and carrots separately. Prepare a common egg sauce. Cut a quarter of a pound of salt pork into small dice and fry it brown.

"These are the ingredients. The assembling of them is important, however. Each person takes portions of fish and of the three vegetables, chops them up fine on his plate and mixes them together as hash is mixed. He then pours egg sauce over the mixture, and on top of that puts a few pork scraps and some of the juice produced by frying the pork. If the chopping and mixing have been well done, the flavor is different and far more heavenly than the taste of any of the component parts.

"My neighbor says that the only difference between her hash and your grandmother's is that she first sautés finely chopped onion until brown and mixes it into the hash before it is cooked; and that she thinks she cooks her hash somewhat longer, turning the outside in from time to time."

BOILED FISH
(Haddock, Halibut, Salmon, etc.)

Wash and clean fish, tie in piece of cheesecloth and plunge into warm Court Bouillon (see below), or water to which has been added 1 teaspoon salt and 1 tablespoon vinegar to every 2 quarts of water. Bring to boiling point and simmer 10 minutes to each pound, or till the flesh separates from the bones. Drain and serve with White Sauce, p. 214, Egg Sauce, p. 209, or Hollandaise Sauce, p. 209.

COURT BOUILLON

2 tablespoons butter	2 quarts water
½ cup chopped onions	1 cup vinegar
¼ cup chopped carrots	3 peppercorns
¼ cup chopped celery	3 whole cloves
1 teaspoon salt	

Sauté onions, carrots and celery in butter 5 minutes, add remaining ingredients and bring to boiling point.

FRIED FISH

Clean and wipe dry fillets of halibut, flounder, smelts, etc. Sprinkle with salt, dip first in flour, then in egg, then in crumbs. Fry in deep hot fat, 375 degrees. Serve with lemon halves, Lemon Butter Sauce, p. 205, or Bahama Fish-tenders, p. 280.

POACHED FISH

This method of preparing fish is used by cooks in the Bahamas when cooking fillets of yellowtails (about the size of a 1½-pound black bass). It works equally well with any delicate fish fillets, such as sole, haddock, striped bass, etc.

Poach fish 10 minutes in enough water to cover, or in Court Bouillon (see above).

While fish is cooking, prepare a sauce made of 2 tablespoons butter, 3 tablespoons light cream, 1 tablespoon vinegar, salt and pepper, and 1 cup of the boiling water in which the fish was cooked.

Remove fish from the pot, arrange on a platter, pour the sauce over it, garnish with parsley, and serve immediately.

BAKED STUFFED BASS
(Bluefish, Shad, Haddock or Whitefish)

Remove scales and wash thoroughly inside and out; wipe dry. Stuff with the following dressing: To 1 cup bread crumbs add 1 tablespoon melted butter, 1 tablespoon minced parsley, 1 teaspoon minced onion, ½ teaspoon salt, ⅛ teaspoon pepper. Sew and place on rack in dripping pan. Sprinkle with salt and pepper, brush over with melted butter, and dredge with flour. Cover bottom of pan with boiling water and dots of butter; bake 15 minutes to every pound of fish in a hot oven, 400 degrees. Baste every 10 minutes with the gravy in the pan. Serve with either White Sauce, p. 214, Lemon Butter, p. 205, or Egg Sauce, p. 209.

STRIPED BASS

Sauté 2 sliced onions in 1 tablespoon butter for 5 minutes. On them place 1 teaspoon salt, ½ teaspoon pepper, 6 fresh mushrooms, 12 raw oysters and ½ cup Tomato Sauce, p. 213. Over all lay a 1½-pound striped bass that has been cleaned and scaled. Cover pan and cook 5 minutes; then place pan in slow oven, 300 degrees, for ½ hour. Add 1 tablespoon butter and serve fish with sauce in which it was cooked.

BAKED BLUEFISH

Clean and scale a 3-pound bluefish, rub with salt, pepper and paprika, place in a buttered baking tin and pour over it equal parts of butter and lemon. Cover with greased paper and bake in a moderate oven, 350 degrees, for 30 minutes. Serve with Mustard Sauce, p. 211.

BUTTERFISH

In a saucer blend 1 teaspoon salt, ½ teaspoon pepper and 1 tablespoon olive oil. Wipe dry 6 prepared butterfish and dabble each one in the oil dressing. Broil 4 minutes on each side, and serve with lemon juice.

SALT CODFISH HASH

2 cups shredded salt codfish
3 tablespoons bacon fat
1 minced onion
1 minced clove garlic

3 cups diced cooked potatoes
½ cup water
⅛ teaspoon pepper

Soak fish a few hours in lukewarm water until soft. Drain. Melt the bacon fat in a frying pan and add the combined fish, onion, garlic and potatoes. Stir in the water and pepper. Cook over a slow fire, stirring occasionally, until browned underneath; fold, and turn like an omelet. Serve with liberal quantity of Tomato Sauce, p. 213. Serves 6.

SALT CODFISH WITH PORK SCRAPS

2 cups salt codfish
1 sliced onion
1 tablespoon butter

3 cold boiled potatoes
1½ cups stewed tomatoes
3 slices chopped salt pork

½ cup buttered bread crumbs

Soak codfish in cold water overnight. Drain and cut in small pieces. Sauté onion in butter a few minutes without browning it; then add to fish. Arrange alternate layers of fish, sliced potatoes, tomatoes and salt pork in a buttered baking dish, sprinkling with pepper. Cover with crumbs and bake in a moderate oven, 350 degrees, until crumbs are brown. Serves 6.

SPECIAL SUNDAY FISH BALLS

½ pound salt codfish
3 pounds potatoes

5 medium-sized eggs
2½ tablespoons butter

¼ teaspoon pepper

Place salt codfish in pan of cold water and soak overnight. Change water on following day, simmer fish until tender; then drain and flake. Boil and mash potatoes, and add chopped fish, butter, eggs and pepper, carefully blending everything together. Use a spoon or ice-cream scoop to form fish balls. Drop into hot deep fat, 385 degrees, and fry until light brown. Drain on brown paper. Serve with Tomato Sauce, p. 213, or Tomato Ketchup, p. 203. Serves 6.

SCALLOPED SALT CODFISH

2 cups shredded salt codfish	3 eggs, well beaten
2 cups boiled rice	Dash of pepper and paprika
1 cup milk	Pimento strips

3 tablespoons butter

Soak fish a few hours in lukewarm water until soft. Drain. Mix the fish and rice lightly with a fork and place in a buttered baking dish. Combine milk, eggs and seasonings and pour over fish mixture. Garnish with pimento strips and dot with butter. Bake in a moderate oven, 350 degrees, until well heated. Serves 6.

CODS' TONGUES AND CHEEKS

2 quarts water	1 bay leaf
5 chopped onions	1 cup vinegar
3 carrots	2 pounds cods' tongues and cheeks

Boil onions, carrots, bay leaf and vinegar in the water till vegetables are nearly cooked. Add cods' tongues and cheeks, boil up once and simmer 20 minutes. Drain vegetables and brown slightly in butter. Add a little of the liquor in which the tongues were cooked, thicken slightly with flour, season and pour over the tongues. Serves 6.

BACHAMELLE

"At King Dick's table that night, I had my first experience of bachamelle, which is salted codfish cooked in the Haitian manner —boned and stewed with potatoes, pimentos, oil, garlic, and butter, and the whole thickened with manioc flour, which is like oatmeal. Every Haitian, man, woman, and child, King Dick said, would eat bachamelle or some similar preparation of salt codfish for breakfast, dinner, and supper every day in the week, if given the chance. I thought at first he was exaggerating, but I know different now; and I never see or smell a salt codfish that all Haiti doesn't rise before me. . . ."

—Kenneth Roberts, *Lydia Bailey*

Tear dried salt codfish into strips and soak in cold water 3 hours. Boil in same water 1 hour. Cook 2 cups rolled oats and keep it moist.

To this add 2 diced boiled potatoes, a small can of pimentos cut in strips, a sliced avocado pear, a minced clove of garlic and the salt codfish. Mix well and serve with French Dressing, p. 190.

CODFISH PUFF

Wash and pare potatoes and cut in cubes, so there will be 1¼ cups. Add ½ cup flaked salt codfish. Cover with boiling water and cook until potatoes are soft. Mash the potatoes and codfish until smooth, and then add 1 teaspoon butter and a dash of pepper. Add 2 well-beaten eggs and beat until fluffy. Cover the bottom of a small frying pan with pork fat, put in the mixture and spread evenly. Cook slowly until a brown crust forms. Turn out on a hot platter and serve with Cheese Sauce, p. 207. This dish should be eaten without delay. Serves 4.

CREAMED CODFISH

1 cup salt codfish	1 cup light cream
1 tablespoon butter	⅛ teaspoon pepper
1 tablespoon flour	1 egg yolk, well beaten
1 hard-boiled egg, sliced	

Soak codfish in cold water several hours. Drain, cover with fresh cold water and simmer until fish is tender. Drain, and flake fish. Melt the butter and add flour, cream and pepper. Bring to the boiling point, stirring constantly. Add the codfish, and lastly the beaten egg yolk. Serve on buttered toast and garnish with slices of hard-boiled egg. Serves 4.

FISH CAKES

1 cup salt codfish	1 egg, well beaten
1 cup mashed potatoes	2 tablespoons light cream

Soak fish several hours in cold water. Drain, shred, add fresh water and heat to boiling point; repeat until fish tastes fresh. Mix codfish, mashed potatoes, egg and cream, and beat until fluffy. Form into small flat cakes, dip in beaten egg, then in bread crumbs, and sauté in melted butter until golden brown. Drain on brown paper. Serve with Tomato Sauce, p. 213, or Tomato Ketchup, p. 203. Serves 4.

DOGFISH

Small dogfish, scorned and flung away in America, are called
palombo *in Italy, and devoured avidly. I have eaten them many
times, both in Italy and in Maine, and found them delicious. The
meat is white and resembles halibut; and it has only one large bone
to be removed. Use small fish, 18 or 20 inches long. Skin, cut in 1½-
inch segments; fry or stew.*—K.R.

BAKED EELS

Clean and skin eels[1] and cut in 3-inch pieces without splitting open.
Twist out intestines with a knife, fork or piece of wood. Lay pieces
of fat salt pork in a baking pan and add the pieces of eel. Bake in a
moderate oven, 350 degrees, until done.

EEL JELLY

6 large eels	½ teaspoon allspice
1 quart water	¼ teaspoon cloves
1 pint vinegar	4 bay leaves
2 sliced onions	2 tablespoons gelatin dis-
1 teaspoon salt	solved in
½ teaspoon pepper	¼ cup cold water

Clean and skin eels,[1] and cut in 3-inch pieces. Do not split open.
Clean sections by twisting out intestines with a knife, fork or stick;
then wash. Add water, vinegar, onions and seasonings to eel sections
and boil until meat comes away from bone. Remove meat, put in
mold or earthenware dish. Strain liquor in which eels were boiled.
Bring it to a boil again, and add the gelatin which has been dissolved
in the cold water. Boil 15 minutes, pour over eel meat and chill in
refrigerator.

Hornpout may be substituted for eels.

---

[1]The best way to skin an eel is to leave the head on, slit the skin back
of the gills with an old safety-razor blade, nail the eel's head to a board,
get a tight hold on the skin with two pairs of pliers, and peel off the skin
as a person peels off a glove. Eel properly prepared is one of the juiciest and
most delicate of fish.

MATELOTE OF EELS

Skin 2 large or several small eels. Don't open belly. Cut in segments, twisting out intestines with fork or stick. Wash well. Put in saucepan with 1 cup stock, 1 cup red wine, clove garlic, whole pepper, sliced onion, bay leaf, thyme, cloves, parsley, and celery salt. Simmer gently till done.

Remove fish, strain liquor, add 2 ounces brandy. Melt 2 tablespoons butter in a saucepan, stir in 1 tablespoon flour, and gradually add sauce. Bring to a boil. Put bread croutons in a dish, arrange fish in center and pour sauce over all. Serves 6.

FINNAN HADDIE

To Flake Finnan Haddie:

(1) Cover finnan haddie with cold water, place over low heat and boil 10 minutes. Drain off water. Remove the skin and bones, and flake fish.

(2) Cover finnan haddie with milk and soak 1 hour. Bring it slowly to a boil, and simmer 25 minutes. Drain off milk. Remove the skin and bones, and flake fish.

FINNAN HADDIE DELMONICO

1 pound finnan haddie	1 cup diced boiled potatoes
1½ cups Cheese Sauce, p. 207	Grated Parmesan cheese

Prepare Finnan Haddie (1). Add flaked fish and potatoes to the cheese sauce. Cook 5 minutes, season with pepper, pour into a buttered casserole, sprinkle with cheese and dot with butter. Bake in a moderate oven, 350 degrees, until light brown. Serves 5–6.

FINNAN HADDIE FLORENTINE

Prepare Finnan Haddie (1) or (2). Make a Medium Cream Sauce, p. 215, add flaked finnan haddie to it, and cook 3 minutes. Season with salt and pepper. Place boiled spinach in the bottom of individual buttered casseroles, cover with creamed finnan haddie and sprinkle with grated Parmesan cheese. Bake in a moderate oven, 350 degrees, until the cheese is a light brown.

BAKED FINNAN HADDIE

Plunge fish into boiling water for 5 minutes; then remove skin. Place in baking pan, pour over 1 cup rich milk, dot with butter and bake in moderate oven, 350 degrees, 30 minutes.

BROILED FINNAN HADDIE

Soak finnan haddie in cold water for ¾ hour; drain, then cover with boiling water for 5 minutes. Drain, wipe dry, rub with olive oil. Broil till brown on both sides. Serve with Maître d'Hôtel Butter, p. 205.

FINNAN HADDIE NEWBURG

1 pound finnan haddie	3 tablespoons sherry
Medium Cream Sauce, p. 215	½ cup light cream
Dash of nutmeg	3 egg yolks, beaten

Prepare Finnan Haddie (1) or (2). Add flaked fish to cream sauce with the nutmeg. Bring to a boil, add sherry, and cream mixed with the beaten egg yolks. Do not cook after adding eggs. Serves 6.

FRIED FROGS' LEGS

Wash legs in cold water, skin and drain. Season with salt, pepper and lemon juice. Dip in beaten egg, then crumbs. Place in frying basket and fry 4 minutes in deep fat, 375 degrees. Drain and serve with Tartare Sauce, p. 213. 1 pair frogs' legs serves 1 person.

FROGS' LEGS NEWBURG

2 dozen frogs' legs	2 tablespoons butter
1 cup chopped mushrooms	1 cup chicken broth
1 tablespoon chives	1 tablespoon flour
1 minced clove garlic	¼ cup white wine
1 tablespoon minced parsley	3 egg yolks, beaten
½ cup light cream	

Clean and steam frogs' legs until tender. Sauté frogs' legs, mushrooms, chives, garlic and parsley in butter. Add chicken broth and flour mixed with white wine. Add cream to beaten egg yolks, then stir it into frogs' legs. Season with salt and pepper. Serves 6–8.

FISH HASH

2 cups flaked fish	1 tablespoon butter
2 cups diced boiled potatoes	1 egg, beaten
1 tablespoon minced onion	½ teaspoon salt

⅛ teaspoon pepper

Combine ingredients and fry in salt-pork fat until brown. Fold and turn like an omelet. Serve with Tomato Sauce, p. 213. Serves 6.

FISH OMELET

2 pounds fresh or canned mackerel, halibut, bass, swordfish or haddock	1 tablespoon celery salt
	¼ teaspoon pepper
	1 cup grated cheese
Milk	1 tablespoon butter
6 cold cooked potatoes	¼ cup cold water

Place fish in a baking dish, cover with milk and bake uncovered till done. Break flesh into small pieces. Mash the potatoes and add fish, seasonings and grated cheese. Melt butter in a large frying pan, add mixture and water. Cover, and cook over low heat 20 minutes, turning occasionally. Uncover, pat it flat and, when well browned underneath, fold and turn out like an omelet. Serve with Cheese Sauce, p. 207. Serves 6.

FISH PUFFS

2 cups canned or fresh cooked fish	1 tablespoon minced green pepper
1 tablespoon tarragon vinegar	1 teaspoon minced onion
2 tablespoons chopped celery	2 tablespoons butter
2 tablespoons chopped parsley	1 tablespoon celery salt
	3 eggs, separated

½ cup soft bread crumbs

Flake and mince fish after removing all bones. Marinate in vinegar. Sauté celery, parsley, green pepper and onion in butter until tender. Add to fish with salt, well-beaten egg yolks and bread crumbs. Mix thoroughly and fold in stiffly beaten egg whites. Place in greased custard cups. Bake for about 40 minutes in a 300-degree oven, or until puffed and golden brown. Serves 6.

FISH SCALLOP

2 cups milk	2 tablespoons sherry
½ cup flour	Yolks of 2 hard-boiled eggs
¼ cup melted butter	1½ cups flaked cooked
Salt and pepper	haddock
1 tablespoon chopped parsley	

Scald milk in top of double boiler and add flour mixed with melted butter. Season with salt and pepper and add parsley, sherry, yolks of eggs, mashed fine, and fish. Simmer 10 minutes in double boiler. Put in baking dish, sprinkle with bread crumbs and dot with butter. Bake in a hot oven until crumbs are brown. Serve with Tomato Sauce, p. 213. Serves 6.

FISH SOUFFLÉ

3 tablespoons butter	3 eggs, separated
3 tablespoons flour	¼ cup chopped parsley
½ teaspoon salt	1½ cups cooked, flaked fish
Dash of pepper	(haddock, tuna, sal-
1 cup milk	mon, etc.)

Melt butter, add flour and seasonings, and gradually stir in milk. When smooth and thick, add 1 egg yolk at a time, mixing well after each addition. Bring to a boil; then remove from heat and add parsley and fish. Fold in stiffly beaten egg whites. Pour into buttered casserole, set in a pan of hot water and bake in a moderate oven, 350 degrees, until firm. Serve with Tomato Sauce, p. 213. Serves 6.

HADDOCK SMOTHER

Cut haddock in pieces as for frying. Wash thoroughly but do not wipe or drain. Lay the pieces in stew kettle, cover with pieces of butter, and dredge with pepper, salt and flour. Cover closely and cook 1 hour or more, according to the thickness of the fish. Use plenty of butter but do not add any water, as the fish cooks in its own juice. Take up carefully on a platter and pour over it all liquor left in the kettle. Codfish, flounder, sea bass or cunners may also be prepared the same way. Serve with Lemon Butter Sauce, p. 205, or Tomato Sauce, p. 213.

BAKED HADDOCK

Clean and scale a 3-pound haddock. Place on a piece of heavily waxed paper in a shallow baking pan. Pour over it 1 cup olive oil mixed with the juice of 2 lemons, 1 cup of water and a minced clove of garlic. Bake in a moderate oven, 350 degrees, 45 minutes. Serves 6–8.

BAKED HADDOCK FILLETS

1 pound haddock fillets	1 tablespoon celery salt
1 cup Tomato Sauce, p. 213	½ teaspoon pepper
1 cup bread crumbs	1 teaspoon mustard
1 chopped onion	⅛ teaspoon paprika
1 teaspoon salt	Juice of 1 lemon

Heat tomato sauce in saucepan, remove from stove, and add bread crumbs, chopped onion and seasonings. Place half the haddock fillets in well-buttered baking pan and spread with the sauce. Add the second layer of fillets, dot with butter and season lightly with salt and pepper. Bake in a hot oven, 400 degrees, 15 minutes. Serves 4.

BAKED HALIBUT FILLETS

Put a slice of halibut in a dripping pan and cover with dots of butter, salt, pepper and cracker crumbs. Lay on top of this another slice of halibut and repeat with butter, salt, pepper and cracker crumbs. Bake in a moderate oven, 350 degrees, for 1 hour, basting frequently with the drippings. Serve with generous amount of Lemon Butter Sauce, p. 205.

This dish may also be made from fillets of flounder or slices of salmon.

FRANK FORRESTER'S HALIBUT

A halibut should be rubbed with salt and lemon before it is put in the water; have ready a large kettle half full of cold water, and to every 6 quarts of water put 1 pound of salt. Put in the fish, and set over a moderate fire. An 8-pound halibut should simmer 20 minutes; ¾ hour altogether in the water. When it begins to crack slightly, lift it up with a drainer, and cover with a napkin.

STUFFED HALIBUT FILLETS

2 halibut fillets
French Dressing, p. 190
2 cups bread crumbs

½ cup melted butter
½ teaspoon onion juice
1 minced pimento

Cover fillets with French dressing for 2 hours. Put one fillet in buttered baking dish, cover it with stuffing made of remaining ingredients; place second fillet over stuffing, and brush with melted butter. Bake, uncovered, in a moderate oven, 350 degrees, 40 minutes, basting frequently with melted butter. Serves 4–6.

HALIBUT LOAF

2 cups light cream
2½ cups bread crumbs
2 tablespoons butter
2 teaspoons minced onion

½ teaspoon celery salt
⅛ teaspoon pepper
2 cups ground raw halibut
4 egg whites

Heat cream in double boiler, stir in bread crumbs and cook several minutes; then add butter, onion, seasonings and halibut. Bring to a boil and cool. Fold in stiffly beaten egg whites. Pour into a buttered loaf pan, set in pan of hot water and bake in a moderate oven, 350 degrees, about 45 minutes, or until firm. Serve with Tomato Sauce, p. 213, or Egg Sauce, p. 209. Serves 8.

HALIBUT WITH TOMATO SAUCE

4 slices halibut, 1 inch thick
Melted butter
1 small can tomatoes
1 cup chopped celery
1 minced green pepper

1 minced clove garlic
½ pound grated American
    cheese
1 tablespoon butter
1 tablespoon celery salt

½ teaspoon pepper

Sauté halibut lightly in butter, then transfer to baking dish. Boil tomatoes, celery, pepper and garlic until soft. Sprinkle halibut with most of the grated cheese, dot with butter, add seasonings and cover with tomato mixture. Bake in a moderately hot oven, 375 degrees, 20 minutes. Sprinkle with remaining cheese, return to oven 2 minutes more, and serve. Serves 6.

HALIBUT AU GRATIN

Cheese Sauce (2), p. 207   ½ cup dry bread crumbs
2 cups cooked flaked halibut   ¼ cup grated cheese
                    ¼ cup butter

Heat the flaked halibut in the cheese sauce, then pour into a buttered baking dish. Sprinkle with crumbs mixed with grated cheese, and dot with butter. Bake in a hot oven, 400 degrees, until crumbs are brown. Serves 4.

FILLET OF MARINATED HERRING

12 herring (24 fillets)   6 medium-sized onions
1 quart sour cream   3 sour apples
1 cup vinegar   2 bay leaves
2 tablespoons olive oil   2 black peppercorns
                    ½ lemon, sliced

The best herring are the fat ones caught off Maine and Nova Scotia, usually sold as Nova Scotia herring. Best of the herring for marinating are the male fish, known as milters. Wash and soak 12 milters in cold water for 24 hours. Then cut out the milt sacs, chop them fine and mix them in a bowl with vinegar, sour cream and olive oil. Strain and add sliced onions, apples cut in thin strips, peppercorns, bay leaves and lemon. Cut head off herring, pull outer skin off, split the fish, cutting off all bones. Wash fillets, arrange in porcelain pot, pour dressing over them and keep in refrigerator. Let them soak 24 hours before serving.

HORNPOUT

6 hornpout   1 tablespoon flour
2 onions   1 can tomatoes
1 tablespoon olive oil   1 teaspoon salt
                ½ teaspoon chili powder

Clean and skin hornpout and cut in 2-inch lengths. Put in covered baking dish with tomatoes, onions and olive oil, and cook in slow oven, 300 degrees, ¾ hour. Add chili powder, flour and salt, stir lightly, so not to break fish, and cook another 15 minutes.

KEDGEREE (1)

1½ pounds cooked sole, salmon, tuna or rabbit, flaked; or shrimps, clams or scallops
5 tablespoons butter
4 tablespoons flour
3 cups scalded milk
2 teaspoons curry powder

1½ tablespoons French mustard
2 tablespoons Worcestershire sauce
¼ cup sherry
Salt, pepper, pinch of nutmeg and cayenne
3 egg yolks

¼ cup sherry

Prepare fish. Melt butter in a saucepan, stir in flour, and gradually add milk until mixture thickens; then add curry powder mixed with mustard, Worcestershire sauce, sherry and seasonings. When the mixture bubbles, remove from stove and stir in egg yolks beaten with sherry. Add fish, cover, heat through and serve on boiled rice or buttered toast.

KEDGEREE (2)

2 cups cooked rice
2 cups cooked flaked fish
4 chopped hard-boiled eggs

1 tablespoon butter
½ cup light cream
1 teaspoon salt

⅛ teaspoon pepper

Mix all the ingredients together in a double boiler and heat until hot.

MACKEREL GOULASH

2 tablespoons butter
3 minced onions
6 teaspoons Hungarian rose paprika, *not* Spanish

1 can flaked mackerel
6 chopped tomatoes
4 chopped green peppers
Slice of salt pork

Sauté onion in butter until brown. Remove pan from fire and stir in Hungarian rose paprika and mackerel. Return to fire and toss fish with a fork. When heated, add tomatoes and green peppers. Lay a small slice of salt pork on top, cover pan, and simmer until fish is tender.

BROILED MACKEREL

Split and clean a 2-pound mackerel. Sprinkle with salt and pepper and rub with melted butter. Place on greased broiler, skin side down. Broil 10 minutes, then turn and broil skin side until skin is crisp. Serve with Lemon Butter, p. 205.

BROILED TINKER MACKEREL

Split tinkers and bone for broiling, season with salt and pepper and dip in oil. Lay skin side down on broiler and cook not more than 4 minutes under moderate fire. It is only necessary to cook on flesh side. Remove to hot platter and serve with Lemon Butter Sauce, p. 205.

The less a tinker mackerel is cooked, the tenderer and juicier it is. Many Maine cooks consider 1½ minutes the proper length of time.

JELLIED TINKERS

2 tablespoons gelatin	1 quart boiling water
¼ cup cold water	Juice of 2 lemons
6 chicken bouillon cubes	1 teaspoon salt
4 tinker mackerel	

Soften gelatin in cold water. Dissolve bouillon cubes in boiling water, then stir the softened gelatin, lemon juice and salt into it. Pour ¼ inch of this liquid into each one of four oval individual casseroles.

Split tinker mackerel, broil the halves 1½ minutes under a hot flame; then place two tinker halves, skin side down, flat in each casserole. Pour the remaining chicken bouillon over the tinkers, and chill the casseroles in the refrigerator until the liquid is jellied. Serve in the casseroles without unmolding.

KENNEBEC SCRAPPLE

To 4 cups hot corn-meal mush add 2 cups flaked cooked salmon, cooked salt codfish or any leftover fish. Season highly with salt and pepper, and add 1 teaspoon onion juice. Pour into a mold which has been dipped in cold water. Chill; then slice and sauté in bacon fat. Serve with Tomato Sauce, p. 213, or ketchup.

SALMON AND SHAD

Discriminating cooks in northern Maine prepare shad and young salmon (grilse) in a manner highly esteemed by epicures.

A 3-pound shad or grilse is cleaned, scaled and wrapped in 5 yards of cheesecloth so that it forms a thick bundle.

Thus wrapped, the fish is placed in a washboiler half full of water into which 1 cup of vinegar has been poured. In this the fish is boiled 5 hours. It may be boiled longer, and cannot be boiled too long. Camp cooks sometimes put a fish on to boil in the morning and don't take it out till night. The vinegar in the water, coupled with the long cooking, dissolves small bones and so softens large ones that the entire fish may be eaten.

Another northern Maine method of cooking grilse is to put a long pan on the fire, fill it 1 inch deep with fat, and bring the fat to a boil. When it boils, the cleaned, scaled 3-pound grilse is slid into the boiling fat, left 1 minute and then removed. When the fat boils once more, the grilse is turned and again put in for 1 minute. It is then transferred to a baking pan and baked 25 minutes.

SALMON TIMBALES

2 cups flaked cooked salmon	2 eggs, well beaten
1 cup bread crumbs	1½ tablespoons chopped
2 tablespoons melted butter	onion
¼ cup milk	

Mix ingredients together and turn into buttered molds or custard cups. Set in a pan of hot water and bake in a moderate oven, 350 degrees, 20 to 30 minutes. Serve with Cheese Sauce, p. 207. Serves 6.

FRANK FORRESTER'S SALMON

The king of fishes is best plain boiled. His richness is sufficient, his flavor so excellent, that, so far from being improved, his natural qualities are destroyed and overpowered by anything of artificial condiment.

If you are ever so lucky as to catch a salmon, where incontinently you can proceed to cook him: in the wilderness, that is to say, within ten yards of the door of your shanty, with the fire burning and the pot boiling—good!

Stun him at once by a heavy blow on the head; crimp him by a succession of cuts on each side, through the muscle, quite down to the backbone, with a very sharp knife, in slashes parallel to the gill cover. Then place him for 10 minutes in a cold spring, or under the jet of a waterfall. In the meantime keep your pot boiling—nay, screeching—with intense heat, filled with brine strong enough to bear an egg. Therein immerse him, having cut out the gills, opened the belly and washed the inside, and boil him at the rate of 7½ minutes to the pound; dish him and, serving him with no sauce save a tureenful of the water in which he has been boiled, proceed to eat him, with no other condiment than a little salt and the slightest squeeze of a lemon. I do not object to cucumber sliced very fine, with a dressing of oil, 3 tablespoons to 1 of vinegar, salt, and black pepper *quantum suff;* but I regard green peas or any other vegetable with this grand fish as a cockney abomination.

If the salmon be not fresh enough to crimp, scale him and proceed as follows. Clean and prepare as before. Put your fish in cold water, using 1 pound of salt to every 6 quarts of water; let it be well covered with water, and set it over a moderate fire; when it begins to simmer, set it on the side of the fire. If the fish weighs 4 pounds, let it simmer ½ hour—if 8 pounds, ¾ hour, and so on in proportion; dish it on a napkin, and serve with lobster sauce.

FRANK FORRESTER'S LOBSTER SAUCE FOR SALMON

Put 12 tablespoonfuls of melted butter into a stewpan; cut a middling-sized hen lobster into dice, make ¼ pound of lobster butter with the spawn, thus: take out the spawn and pound it well in a mortar, then add ¼ pound of fresh butter, mix them well together, then rub it through a sieve; when the melted butter is upon the point of boiling, add the lobster butter, stir the sauce over the fire until the butter is melted; season with a little essence of anchovy, the juice of ½ lemon, and ¼ teaspoonful of cayenne; pass it through a sieve into another stewpan, then add the flesh of the lobster. When hot, it is ready to serve where directed. This sauce must be quite red; if not red in the lobster, use live spawn.

SALMON CUTLETS

2 cups cooked salmon	1 teaspoon lemon juice
1 cup heavy cream	1 egg, separated
1 tablespoon butter	1 teaspoon salt
1 slice white bread	Pinch of paprika

Mince salmon. Put cream, butter, crumbled bread and lemon juice in a saucepan, bring to a boil, then add beaten egg yolk. Pour this mixture over minced salmon, fold in stiffly beaten egg white, and chill for 2 hours. Add seasonings, shape into cutlets, dip in egg and bread crumbs. Place in a frying basket and fry in deep fat, 390 degrees, until light brown. Drain on brown paper. Serves 6.

SALMON MOUSSE

2 cups boiled salmon	2 eggs, separated
1½ tablespoons butter	1 tablespoon celery salt
½ tablespoon flour	¼ teaspoon pepper
¾ cup heavy cream	½ teaspoon onion juice

Put fish through a sieve. Melt butter, gradually stir in flour and cream, stirring till scalded. Add fish pulp, take from fire and add beaten egg yolks, seasonings and stiffly beaten egg whites. Turn into buttered mold. Set in pan of hot water and bake in a moderate oven, 350 degrees, 30 minutes. Serve with Medium Cream Sauce, p. 215, or Tomato Sauce, p. 213. Serves 6.

BAKED SALMON AND NOODLES

3 cups cooked noodles	1⅓ cups milk
2 cups flaked cooked salmon	1 egg
Buttered bread crumbs	

Put ⅓ of the noodles, seasoned with salt and pepper, in a buttered baking dish. Cover with half the salmon, dot with butter. Repeat with noodles, salmon, butter and noodles. Top with buttered bread crumbs and bake in a moderate oven, 350 degrees, until browned. Serves 4–6.

PLANKED GRILSE OR SALMON

A grilse is a young (3- to 5-pound) salmon. Scale a fresh grilse, split it down the back (removing the bone), lay it skin down on a hot buttered 1-inch-thick oak plank, put the plank in a hot oven and broil the grilse 12 minutes. No other manner of cooking can bring out to the full the succulence of a newly caught grilse. The same method of cooking is unrivaled for salmon steaks. Place 1-inch salmon steaks on a hot buttered plank, put under the broiler for 5 minutes, then set the oven at 450 degrees and bake 10 minutes longer.

FRESH SARDINES

Along the coast of Maine in spring, summer and autumn, sardines run in schools so enormous that the canning of them is one of the leading sources of revenue in Lubec and Eastport.

The canned sardine cannot compare for succulence with the fresh sardine, which costs next to nothing, and is as easy to cook as it is to prepare for cooking.

To cook fresh sardines, cut off their heads, slit them wide open down the stomach, and pin them to a pine board, using two pins to each sardine. Stand the board in the open air for an hour.

Put ⅓ cup of olive oil or a 2-inch cube of fat salt pork in a hot frying pan, and cover the bottom of the pan with sardines. Cook 1 minute on each side. Serve with liberal amount of Lemon Butter Sauce, p. 205.

CREAMED SARDINES

Drain oil from 1 small can˙ sardines, remove backbones from fish, then wash. Melt ¼ cup butter, add ¼ cup soft stale bread crumbs and 1 cup light cream. When thoroughly heated add 2 hard-boiled eggs finely chopped, and the sardines, salt, pepper and paprika to taste. Serve on toast. Serves 4.

SARDINE RAREBIT

2 tablespoons butter	⅛ teaspoon pepper
2 tablespoons flour	1 cup milk
1 teaspoon dry mustard	2 cups grated cheese
½ teaspoon salt	1 can sardines

1 teaspoon Worcestershire sauce

Melt butter in a double boiler, add flour and seasonings, and stir until blended. Gradually add the milk, stirring constantly until mixture thickens. Add cheese, and wnen it melts remove from fire and add sardines and Worcestershire sauce. Serve on toast. Serves 4.

SARDINES BORDELAISE

1 cauliflower divided into flowerets	½ cup olive oil
4 stalks celery, destringed and cubed	1 can mushrooms
2 green peppers, seeded and cut in strips	1 small bottle stuffed olives, sliced
1 cucumber, seeded and sliced	1 pint Tomato Ketchup, p. 203
	¼ cup wine vinegar
	3 cans sardines

Put cauliflower, celery, peppers, cucumber and olive oil in a deep saucepan and cook until vegetables are soft. Add mushrooms, olives, ketchup and vinegar and bring to a boil. Add sardines (oil included) and remove from stove. Chill thoroughly before serving. Serves 6–8.

PARBOILED SHAD ROE

Cook shad roe 20 minutes in boiling water to cover, with 1 tablespoon salt and 1 tablespoon lemon juice. Drain, cover with cold water and let stand 5 minutes. Drain again and prepare as desired.

BAKED SHAD ROE

Put Parboiled Roe (see above) in a buttered baking dish, cover with Tomato Sauce (1), p. 213, and bake in a hot oven, 400 degrees, for 20 minutes, basting every 5 minutes with the sauce in the dish. Serve with more tomato sauce.

BROILED SHAD ROE

Brush Parboiled Roe (see p. 62) with melted butter, seasoned with salt, pepper and a little lemon juice. Place in a shallow buttered pan and broil until a golden brown. Turn and broil other side. Baste frequently with melted butter. Serve with lemon.

FRIED SHAD ROE

Sprinkle Parboiled Roe (see p. 62) with salt and pepper. Dip in cracker dust, egg, and again in cracker dust. Fry in deep fat at 390 degrees, or sauté in butter until pale brown. Serve with lemon.

SHAD ROE CASSEROLE

Sprinkle 2 shad roes with salt, roll in flour, and sauté 5 minutes in butter. Turn and sauté another 5 minutes.

Place in buttered baking dish, surround with 2 cups cold diced boiled potatoes, and over them sprinkle 6 mushrooms, 1 green pepper, and 3 scallions, all finely chopped and mixed with 1 teaspoon salt and ¼ cup white wine. Cover, and bake in a hot oven, 400 degrees, 20 minutes. Serve with lemon.

PLANKED SHAD

Clean and split a 3- to 5-pound shad. Place skin side down on hot buttered oak plank. Sprinkle with salt and pepper, and brush with oil or melted butter. Bake in hot oven 20 minutes, basting frequently with butter. Garnish with parsley and serve at once. (See also Salmon and Shad, p. 58.) Serves 6.

BAKED SCROD

2-pound scrod	1 pint milk
2 tablespoons butter	¾ cup grated cheese
5 tablespoons flour	½ teaspoon salt

Put the scrod in a shallow baking pan. Make a sauce by melting the butter, adding flour, milk, cheese and salt. When smooth and well blended, pour over the scrod. Bake in a slow oven, 300 degrees, 45 minutes. Serves 4.

BROILED SCROD[2]

Split a young codfish down the back and remove backbone. Brush with melted butter and sprinkle with salt and pepper. Place on greased broiler and broil 1 minute over hot fire. Turn, brush again with butter, salt, and broil 1 minute. Turn, brush again with butter, and broil 5 minutes a little farther from fire. Turn for the last time, brush again with butter, and broil 3 minutes. Serve with Maître d'Hôtel Butter, p. 205.

BROILED SMELTS

Clean smelts; dip in olive oil, paprika and bread crumbs. Broil quickly until golden brown. Remove to hot platter and cover with melted butter.

FRIED SMELTS

Clean smelts, sprinkle with salt, pepper and lemon juice, cover and let stand 15 minutes. Then roll them in flour, dip in egg and roll in flour. Sauté in melted butter, or fry in deep fat, 370 degrees, until they are done and brown. Serve with Tartare Sauce, p. 213.

SAUTÉED SWORDFISH

Wipe slices of fish and sprinkle with salt and pepper. Melt a generous amount of butter in a hot frying pan, add fish and cook until brown on one side; then turn and brown the other side. Cook until it is done. Swordfish, being a fatless fish, dries up quickly if overcooked or if insufficient butter is used. Serve with Lemon Butter Sauce, p. 205.

---

[2]The true scrod is a small codfish, weighing between 1 and 2 pounds. When it is split wide open and the head, tail and bones removed, it becomes a scrod. It is a strictly New England dish, and is so designated in the Century Dictionary and Cyclopedia—"Scrod: a young codfish, especially one that is split and fried or boiled. [New Eng.]" State-of-Maine and Boston gourmets, confronted with such fish delicacies as pompano, Great Lakes whitefish or broiled scrod, are as apt to take the scrod as the whitefish or pompano.

Owing to the handicaps under which many modern fish markets labor, they are frequently unable to produce small codfish. Hence the fiction has grown up in fishmongering circles that a scrod is a fillet of any sort of fish, and that any fish may be "scrodded." Fish markets sell unsuspecting housewives "scrodded" pollack, and hotels serve revolting chunks of 20-pound cod and haddock as "scrod," which is a gross insult and a piece of barefaced misrepresentation.

BROILED SWORDFISH

Place 2-inch slices of swordfish in buttered baking pan. Season with salt and pepper and dot generously with butter. Broil until it begins to get brown; then turn and cook other side. Serve with Lemon Butter Sauce, p. 205.

FILLETS OF SOLE

8 flounder fillets	2 cups cold water
1 sliced onion	Salt and pepper
Sprig of parsley	2 tablespoons lemon juice
3 peppercorns	2 tablespoons white wine

Simmer fillets, onion, parsley and peppercorns in cold water 15 minutes. Place fillets in buttered pan, sprinkle with seasonings, lemon juice and wine. Cover and bake in a slow oven, 300 degrees, 10 minutes. Remove fish to hot platter and serve with Egg Sauce, p. 209. Serves 6.

SPANISH SOLE

1½-pound lemon sole or deep-sea flounder	1 tablespoon minced parsley
3 chopped onions	¼ cup melted butter
½ pound sliced mushrooms	½ cup white wine

Season fish with salt, pepper and lemon juice. Place in baking dish with onions, mushrooms and parsley. Pour butter and white wine over it and cover with bread crumbs. Bake in a moderate oven, 350 degrees, 25 minutes. Serves 4.

BAKED BROOK TROUT

Wipe, wrap each trout in a strip of bacon, place in baking pan, and bake in a moderate oven, 350 degrees, 20 minutes without turning.

SAUTÉED BROOK TROUT

Wipe, sprinkle inside with salt, and roll in corn meal. Sauté in butter until brown. Remove fish to a hot platter. Add ¼ cup butter, ½ teaspoon salt and juice of 1 lemon to the drippings in the pan. Permit it to brown, then pour it over the fish.

FRANK FORRESTER'S TROUT

This is the method of the woods, and in the woods I learned it; but having learned, I practice it at home, considering the trout one of the most delicious *morceaux,* when thus cooked, in the world. It must be cooked, however, in the open air, by a wood fire kindled on the ground or by a charcoal fire in a small Boston furnace.

Clean and scale your fish; open, clean and wash him internally; take for a 1-pound fish 2 small skewers of red-cedar wood; upon each thread a piece of fat salt pork ½ inch square; with these fasten the belly of the fish asunder, annex him by the tail to a twig of pliant wood, which suffer to bend over the fire so as to bring the fish opposite the blaze, place a large biscuit or a slice of thin dry toast under the drip of the gravy, cook quickly—for a 2-pound fish, 10 minutes will suffice—dish with the biscuit under him, and eat with salt and lemon juice.

I conceive, myself, that any piquante or rich sauce overpowers the flavor of the fish, and should therefore be eschewed.

PICKLED BROOK TROUT

1 quart water	1 sprig parsley
1 cup vinegar	1 bay leaf
1 small sliced onion	3 teaspoons salt
½ cup sliced carrots	6 whole peppercorns
1 stalk chopped celery	1 fresh trout for each person

Simmer all ingredients except trout in saucepan for 30 minutes; then strain, bring to a boil, add fish, and simmer slowly 8 minutes. Remove fish, chill and serve with lemon juice.

TUNA CASSEROLE

4 cold boiled potatoes	1 can drained peas
¼ cup melted butter	2 small cans tuna fish
Cheese Sauce (1), p. 207	

Cube the potatoes and put in a buttered baking dish with butter, peas and fish. Pour cheese sauce over the mixture and top with buttered bread crumbs. Bake in a moderate oven, 350 degrees, 45 minutes. Serves 4–6.

CREAMED TUNA FISH

2 cups White Sauce, p. 214 | ¼ cup minced onion
2 eggs | 2 tablespoons chopped
1 cup flaked canned tuna | pimento
    fish[3] | ½ cup bread crumbs
1 tablespoon lemon juice | 1 tablespoon butter

Remove white sauce from fire and stir in beaten eggs. Mix tuna fish with lemon juice, onion and pimento, and add to white sauce. Turn into buttered baking dish and top with bread crumbs which have been sautéed in butter. Bake in a moderate oven, 350 degrees, 15 minutes. Serves 4.

TUNA BOON ISLAND

Sprinkle slices of tuna with salt, dip in flour and sauté in small amount of oil. Brown 4 minced cloves of garlic in olive oil separately, add minced parsley, 2¼ pounds sliced tomatoes, salt and pepper, and cook 10 minutes. Pour sauce over tuna slices, add canned peas, and finish cooking in a moderate oven, 350 degrees.

TERRAPIN

Yolks of 2 hard-boiled eggs | Salt and red pepper
½ cup butter | 1 can terrapin
1 cup light cream | ¼ cup Madeira wine or
½ teaspoon India soi | sherry
Dash of allspice |

Sieve the egg yolks; then mash the butter into them. Scald the cream in a double boiler and gradually stir in mixed eggs and butter. Add the seasonings. If not thick enough, stir in a little flour mixed with water. Add terrapin, heat thoroughly; then add wine and serve.

---

[3]Before using canned tuna, place it in a colander and pour boiling water over it to remove oil.

CLAM AND CHICKEN PIE

12 little button onions	½ cup chopped celery
2 tablespoons butter	1 teaspoon salt
1 cup diced cooked chicken	¼ teaspoon pepper
1 pint chopped clams from which black necks have been removed	Pinch of cayenne pepper
	¼ cup dry sherry
	1 teaspoon flour
2 diced hard-boiled eggs	½ cup milk
1 cup diced cooked potatoes	Plain Pastry, p. 294

Sauté onions in butter until soft. Add chicken, clams, eggs, potatoes, celery, seasonings and sherry and simmer 5 minutes. Mix milk and flour to a paste, add to above mixture and simmer another 5 minutes. Pour into a baking dish, cover with thin pastry, and pierce pastry to allow steam to escape. Bake in a hot oven, 400 degrees, 15 minutes; then reduce heat to moderate, 350 degrees, and cook 15 minutes longer. Serves 8.

CLAM PIE

1 pint shucked clams	1 egg, beaten
¼ cup clam liquor	1 cup milk
½ cup cracker crumbs	1 teaspoon salt
1 tablespoon melted butter	⅛ teaspoon pepper
Plain Pastry, p. 294	

Drain clam liquor into a separate container, wash clams and chop fine. Mix all ingredients together, pour into a deep pie shell, cover with an upper crust and bake in a moderate oven, 350 degrees, 1 hour. Serves 6.

CLAM FRITTERS

2 cups shucked clams	½ cup milk
2 cups sifted flour	½ cup clam liquor
2 teaspoons baking powder	¼ teaspoon salt
2 eggs, beaten	⅛ teaspoon pepper

Drain clams and chop fine. Combine flour, baking powder, eggs, milk and clam liquor, and stir till smooth. Add the clams and seasonings. Drop from a spoon into deep hot fat, 375 degrees, and fry 2 minutes, or until golden brown. Serves 6.

KETTLE CLAMBAKE

Assemble 8 people around an outdoor fireplace. Put a layer of washed seaweed in the bottom of a large kettle, and on the seaweed put 8 live lobsters. Cover with a layer of seaweed, and on it place a layer of green corn in the husks. Add another layer of seaweed, top with clams, and add another layer of seaweed. Place a cover on the kettle, and put kettle over fire. The steaming time will vary, according to your fire, but 1½ hours will usually elapse before clams are shucked. Supply each participant with melted butter into which to dip clams. When the clams have been consumed, the corn will be ready to eat. Serve with butter and salt. The lobsters will then be done, and should also be served with melted butter. The conventional accompaniment is a large pot of boiled coffee.

DEVILED CLAMS

1 pint chopped clams	¼ cup chopped celery
½ cup clam liquor	¼ cup butter
1 tablespoon chopped onion	2 diced hard-boiled eggs
1 tablespoon chopped green pepper	¾ cup cracker crumbs
	1 teaspoon salt
⅛ teaspoon pepper	

Cook clams in their liquor 5 minutes. Cool. Sauté onion, green pepper and celery in half the butter for 5 minutes. Add this to the clams, eggs, cracker crumbs and seasonings. Put into individual buttered ramekins, dot with remaining butter, and bake in a hot oven, 400 degrees, 20 minutes. Serves 6.

FRIED CLAMS

Heat lard or vegetable shortening to 350 degrees. Select the required amount of clams, using only small ones, as the large are rubbery. Roll the clams in corn flour, and remove the loose flour by shaking them in a sifter. Drop into the fat and fry 1½ minutes. Drain in a colander placed over a platter (to catch the drippings). Sprinkle clams lightly with salt and serve at once.

STEAMED CLAMS

Wash clams in several waters, scrubbing the shells to remove sand, or wash thoroughly, cover with cold water, sprinkle with corn meal, set in a dark place for several hours, then drain. Place in large kettle and add ½ cup boiling water to 1 peck of clams. Cover kettle and steam over a low heat until shells open. With each portion serve melted butter seasoned with lemon juice. salt and pepper.

BROILED SOFT–SHELL CRABS

Wash crabs, remove pointed apron on belly, and cut off spongy material beneath points at each end of shell. Brush each crab with melted butter, sprinkle with salt and broil 3 minutes on each side over (or under) a moderately hot flame. Serve with lemon juice.

SAUTÉED SOFT–SHELL CRABS

Wash and clean crabs as above. Dredge lightly with flour and salt, and sauté in butter, 2 minutes on each side. Add lemon juice to the butter in the frying pan and pour this over crabs.

FRIED SOFT–SHELL CRABS

Wash and clean crabs as for Broiled Soft-shell Crabs above. Dip them in flour which has been seasoned with salt and pepper, then in slightly beaten egg, then in crumbs. Fry in deep fat, 375 degrees, until a golden brown. Turn while frying. Drain on brown paper. Serve with Tartare Sauce, p. 213.

CRAB MEAT TIMBALES

Medium White Sauce, p. 214	2 eggs, separated
1½ cups flaked crab meat	1 cup whipped cream

Add crab meat to sauce and cook several minutes. Cool. Fold in the beaten egg yolks and whipped cream, then the stiffly beaten egg whites. Pour into buttered molds or custard cups. Place molds in shallow pan of hot water, and bake in a moderate oven, 350 degrees, 30 minutes, or until a knife inserted comes out clean. Serves 4.

CRAB MEAT MOUSSE

2 egg yolks	2 tablespoons melted butter
1 tablespoon celery salt	1 cup milk
1 teaspoon dry mustard	1 tablespoon gelatin
2 tablespoons lemon juice	¼ cup cold water
2 cups flaked crab meat	

Beat egg yolks slightly and add salt, mustard, lemon juice, butter and milk. Cook in a double boiler until thick, stirring constantly. Soften gelatin in cold water 5 minutes, then stir into the hot mixture. Add the crab meat and turn into molds. Chill until firm. Serves 6.

CRAB CROQUETTES

2 cups chopped crab meat	⅛ teaspoon pepper
1 teaspoon onion juice	1 teaspoon minced parsley
½ teaspoon salt	1 cup Thick White Sauce, p. 214

Mix ingredients in order given. Chill, mold into croquettes, roll in cracker crumbs, dip in a slightly beaten egg, and then roll in the crumbs again. Fry in deep hot fat, 390 degrees, until brown. Drain on brown paper. Serve with Tomato Sauce, p. 213. Serves 4.

CRAB AND RICE CROQUETTES

1 egg	2 tablespoons ketchup
1½ cups cooked rice	½ teaspoon curry powder
2 cups flaked crab meat	1 teaspoon salt
2 tablespoons melted butter	⅛ teaspoon pepper

Beat egg and add remaining ingredients in order given. Mix well. Cool and shape into croquettes. Roll in egg and bread crumbs, and fry in deep fat, 390 degrees. Drain on brown paper and serve with Tomato Sauce, p. 213. Serves 6.

FRIED OYSTER CRABS

Wash and drain crabs. Roll in flour and fry in a basket in deep fat, 390 degrees, for 2 minutes. Drain on brown paper. Garnish with slices of lemon and serve with Tartare Sauce, p. 213.

CRAB NEWBURG

Melt 2 tablespoons of butter, and add 1 tablespoon of flour. When this is bubbling add 1 cup of milk, a little paprika, a dash of mace or nutmeg, and then 2 cups crab meat in large pieces. When boiling add 3 tablespoons of sherry and ½ cup heavy cream mixed with 3 beaten yolks of eggs. Do not cook after adding eggs. Serves 6.

CRAB MEAT AU GRATIN

3 cups flaked crab meat	1½ cups Cheese Sauce, p. 207
3 eggs, unbeaten	3 tablespoons melted butter
1½ cups soft bread crumbs	1 teaspoon salt

Combine ingredients, mix well and turn into a casserole or ramekins. Bake in a moderately slow oven, 325 degrees, 45 minutes. Serves 6.

NASSAU CRAWFISH[4]

3 crawfish	3 peeled and chopped tomatoes
¼ cup butter	½ cup white wine
1 minced clove garlic	1 cup consommé
2 teaspoons flour	½ cup light cream
1 teaspoon salt	½ cup finely crushed oyster crackers
Dash of cayenne pepper	

Boil crawfish, remove meat from shell and chop in small pieces in chopping bowl. Melt butter in frying pan and stir in remaining ingredients. Add chopped crawfish to sauce, pour into a buttered baking dish, and bake in a hot oven, 400 degrees, 5 minutes. Serves 4.

WHITEBAIT

Maine waters, during the summer, are filled with enormous schools of various sorts of minnows, sand eels and other fish bait. Occasionally the ocean is covered with half-mile-long pink drifts of baby shrimp. All these small fry, which come under the head of white-

[4]Lobster may be substituted for crawfish, using 2 medium-sized lobsters in place of crawfish.

bait, are scorned by many Maine cooks, but eagerly welcomed by some of the best, who prepare them thus:

Wash a quart of minnows in cold milk, put them in a sieve, and sprinkle with corn-meal flour. Put minnows in a frying basket with three slices of finely chopped bacon, and fry 1½ minutes in deep fat, 370 degrees. Serve immediately with Tartare Sauce, p. 213, and cold, buttered brown bread sliced thin.

(Whitebait needs no cleaning other than washing, and is cooked and eaten with heads and innards unremoved.)

BROILED LIVE LOBSTER

Kill the lobster by inserting a sharp knife between the body and tail shells, cutting spinal cord. Cross large claws and hold firmly. Make a deep cut at the mouth and continue down through the entire length of the body and tail. The cutting may be simplified by using a heavy butcher knife, placing it in position along the lobster's stomach, then hitting it smartly with a hammer. Open lobster as flat as possible, crack large claws and brush exposed meat with melted butter. Season with salt and pepper. Place in broiler, shell side down, so juices and fat won't run from the shell. Broil 6 minutes if the fire is hot and the lobster small. If the fire is only moderate and the lobster larger, it may stand as much as 15 minutes' broiling. Broiled live lobsters should be juicy and tender. If overcooked, they become dry and tough. Cooks must use their discretion and make their own rules when broiling lobsters. The newfangled and unfortunately widespread habit of covering the exposed portions of a lobster with a shell of cracker crumbs is thought by all good Maine cooks to be even more of a crime than petit larceny. Serve with liberal amount of melted butter.

BOILED LOBSTERS

Plunge live lobsters into kettle of boiling, heavily salted water, head downward. Add a pinch of curry powder. Cover, and boil from 15 to 20 minutes, depending on the size of the lobster. Remove from water, rinse in cold water to stop cooking and serve whole with a side dish of melted butter. Many connoisseurs insist that lobsters are tenderer if cooked in salted water that is cold at the start. As the water heats, the lobster dies painlessly (a fact confirmed by scientists). In using the latter method, take out the lobsters after the water has boiled 15 minutes.

LOBSTER AU GRATIN

1 cup lobster meat	2 tablespoons butter
1 cup crab meat or haddock	1 tablespoon flour
1 cup light cream	Salt and pepper to taste
2 egg yolks	1 tablespoon sherry
1 tablespoon rice	

Mix ingredients together and pour into a buttered casserole. Sprinkle with ground bread crumbs and dot with butter. Bake in a hot oven, 400 degrees, 15 to 30 minutes. Serves 4.

LOBSTER NEWBURG

2 cups boiled lobster meat	2 egg yolks
2 tablespoons butter	1 cup light cream
½ cup sherry	¼ teaspoon salt
⅛ teaspoon cayenne	

Cut lobster meat in small pieces and sauté in butter 3 minutes; then add sherry and cook another 3 minutes. Beat egg yolks and add cream; stir into lobster and continue to stir until mixture thickens. Add seasonings. Do not overcook, as sauce will curdle. Serves 4.

LOBSTER THERMIDOR

Split cold boiled lobster lengthwise. Remove meat and cut in small pieces. Make cream sauce as follows: Melt 1 tablespoon of butter, add 1 tablespoon flour and ¾ cup light cream, stirring constantly until sauce reaches boiling point. Boil 2 minutes, then add 1 teaspoon English mustard, ¼ teaspoon salt and dash of cayenne. Add lobster meat and ½ cup chopped cooked mushrooms and mix well. Fill empty shells with mixture, building it up above shell level. Sprinkle with grated cheese and place on broiler to brown.

LOBSTER AND NOODLE RING

Noodle Ring, p. 245
2 chopped onions
2 minced cloves garlic
2 tablespoons butter
1 can condensed tomato soup
1 cup chicken bouillon
1½ teaspoons curry powder

½ cup sherry
Salt and pepper
½ pound sautéed mush-
rooms
2 tablespoons flour
¼ cup heavy cream
4 Boiled Lobsters, p. 73

1 cup grated American cheese

Sauté onions and garlic in butter till brown, then add soup, bouillon, curry powder, cheese, sherry and seasonings. Simmer 30 minutes. Blend flour and cream, and add with sautéed mushrooms to sauce. Cook for 5 minutes. Remove meat from lobsters, cut in small pieces and add to sauce. Cook until lobster meat is heated, then pour into center of noodle ring and serve. Serves 8.

LOBSTER CROQUETTES

2 cups boiled lobster meat
1 cup Thick White Sauce,
p. 214

¼ teaspoon salt
¼ teaspoon dry mustard
2 eggs

Bread crumbs

Chop the lobster meat and add it to the white sauce with salt and mustard. Heat in a double boiler. Chill and shape into croquettes. Dip into beaten eggs and then into bread crumbs. Fry in deep hot fat, 390 degrees, and drain on brown paper. Serve with Mushroom Sauce, p. 210, or Tomato Sauce, p. 213.

LOBSTER RAREBIT

2 cups boiled lobster meat,
chopped fine
1 cup light cream
1 can condensed tomato soup

2 cups boiled rice
2 tablespoons each chopped
onion, celery and
green pepper

2-inch cube cheese, sliced thin

Mix the ingredients together, heat and serve on toast. Serves 6.

CREAMED BAKED LOBSTER

Squeeze ¼ cup lemon juice over 1 cup cooked flaked lobster meat, then add it to 1 cup Thick Cream Sauce, p. 215. Stir in 1 slightly beaten egg and 2 tablespoons sherry. Turn into baking dish, sprinkle with bread crumbs, season with salt and pepper and dot with butter. Bake in a hot oven, 450 degrees, until crumbs are brown. Serves 4.

TO PREPARE MUSSELS

Scrub and rinse mussels. Open by steaming, as for Steamed Clams, p. 70, or with a knife. Remove and discard hairy beard. For creamed or fried mussels use corresponding recipes for oysters.

BAKED MAINE MUSSELS

Scrub and wash 60 dark blue Maine mussels and steam, as for Steamed Clams, p. 70. Remove from shells, trim off bearded portions with scissors and place in a buttered baking dish. Season with salt, pepper and 1 teaspoon minced onion. Cover with thin slices of bacon and sprinkle with Parmesan cheese. Bake in a moderate oven, 350 degrees, 15 minutes.

PICNIC MUSSELS

Mussels often provide the chief dish at Maine picnics. A kettle is placed over a brisk fire. When hot, a piece of butter the size of an egg is tossed in with a minced clove of garlic, a cup of water and as many mussels as required. The kettle is covered. When the mussel shells open, they are cooked and can be eaten.

FRIED OYSTERS

Drain, wash and wipe oysters dry between towels. Mix 1 cup fine bread crumbs with ⅛ teaspoon salt and a little white pepper. Dip each oyster into the crumbs, then into a beaten egg, then into the crumbs. Fry in deep hot fat, 375 degrees, until brown. Drain on brown paper.

SCALLOPED OYSTERS

1 pint oysters	⅓ cup melted butter
½ cup oyster liquor	½ cup light cream
1½ cups cracker crumbs	Worcestershire sauce
1 teaspoon salt	Dash of mace
¼ teaspoon pepper	Roquefort cheese

Pick over oysters to remove any bits of shell; drain and reserve liquor. Combine cracker crumbs, salt, pepper and melted butter, stirring with a fork until mixed. Put a layer of crumbs in a greased baking dish and cover with half the oysters and oyster liquor. Add half the cream, and a few drops of Worcestershire. Add another layer of crumbs, oysters and liquor, cream and Worcestershire. Top with crumbs and mace, and dot generously with Roquefort cheese. Bake in a moderate oven, 350 degrees, 30 minutes. Serves 4–6.

BAKED OYSTERS AND MACARONI

1½ cups boiled macaroni	½ cup grated cheese
1 pint oysters	¼ cup butter
Salt and pepper	½ cup buttered bread crumbs

Put a layer of macaroni in bottom of buttered baking dish, cover with oysters, sprinkle with salt and pepper, some grated cheese, and dot with butter; repeat and cover with buttered crumbs. Bake in a hot oven, 450 degrees, 20 minutes. Serve with Tomato Sauce, p. 213. Serves 4–6.

CREAMED OYSTERS

1 cup diced celery	½ cup cracker crumbs
3 tablespoons butter	Salt and paprika
½ cup oyster liquor	½ cup light cream
1 pint oysters	

Simmer celery in butter 15 minutes; then add oyster liquor, crumbs, seasonings to taste and cream. Bring to a boil and add drained oysters. Cook until edges curl. Serve on toast or in patty shells. Serves 6.

CURRIED OYSTERS

1 quart oysters	3 tablespoons flour
½ cup butter	Pinch of salt
2 cups oyster liquor and whole milk	Pinch of pepper
	½ teaspoon curry powder

Sauté oysters in half the butter until edges curl. Remove from fire. Drain, keeping liquor, and add whole milk to make 2 cups. Melt remaining butter in saucepan, and stir in flour and seasonings. Add oyster liquor and milk gradually, and cook over low flame until thick, stirring constantly. Add oysters, bring to a boil and serve with boiled rice. Serves 8–10.

OYSTER PIE

2 cups White Sauce, p. 214	1 teaspoon lemon juice
½ teaspoon celery salt	1 dozen oysters
Plain Pastry, p. 294	

Add celery salt, onion juice and oysters to white sauce. Turn into pie plate lined with pastry, sprinkle with salt and pepper, cover with pastry and bake in hot oven, 400 degrees, 20 minutes.

OYSTERS COOKED IN SHELL

Wash oysters and rinse in cold water. Place in a baking pan with the deep shell down. Bake in a hot oven till the shells open. Season with a little butter, salt and pepper and serve immediately on the half shells.

BARBECUED OYSTERS

Clean oysters and dip in grated cheese, then in olive oil mixed with 1 minced clove of garlic. Roll in fine cracker crumbs seasoned with salt and pepper. Place in baking dish and bake in a hot oven, 400 degrees, 12 minutes. Serve on buttered toast with Lemon Butter Sauce, p. 205.

SAUTÉED OYSTERS

Drain oysters, season with salt and pepper and roll in fine cracker crumbs. Sauté in butter in hot frying pan till brown on both sides. Serve on buttered toast with Lemon Butter Sauce, p. 205.

BROILED OYSTERS

Clean and dry the oysters on a towel. Dip in slightly beaten egg, then in finely rolled cracker crumbs seasoned with salt and pepper. Place on greased broiler till brown on both sides. Serve with Lemon Butter Sauce, p. 205.

PANNED OYSTERS

Drain, wash and wipe the oysters dry. Melt 2 tablespoons butter in shallow dripping pan, add oysters and bake in hot oven, 400 degrees, until plump. Moisten slices of buttered toast with hot oyster liquor, place oysters on toast and serve.

SCALLOPED OYSTERS AND SCALLOPS

½ cup melted butter	⅛ teaspoon pepper
2 cups bread crumbs	¾ cup light cream
1 quart oysters	¼ cup oyster liquor
1 teaspoon salt	1 pint scallops, sliced or quartered

Mix melted butter and bread crumbs together and put a thin layer in the bottom of a buttered baking dish. Cover with oysters and seasonings; add some cream and oyster liquor. Add a layer of scallops, seasonings and crumbs; then a layer of oysters and liquids. Top with scallops and bread crumbs, and bake in a hot oven, 450 degrees, 30 minutes. Serves 8.

SCALLOPS EN BROCHETTE

1½ pints scallops	Dash of pepper
½ cup melted butter	12 slices bacon
1 tablespoon minced onion	12 mushrooms

Drain, pick over and dry scallops. Dip in mixture of melted butter, onion and pepper. Place scallops, bacon and mushrooms alternately on skewers, beginning and ending with scallops. Broil under high heat 5 minutes, or until the bacon is crisp. Turn frequently. Serve on strips of hot buttered toast and sprinkle with chopped parsley. Serves 6.

FRIED SCALLOPS

Wash and clean 1 pint scallops, drain and dry thoroughly. Dip scallops in beaten egg, then in rolled cracker crumbs seasoned with salt and pepper. Fry in deep fat, 385 degrees, 2 minutes and serve either with Tartare Sauce, p. 213, or with half a lemon to each portion. Before halving the lemons, warm them in hot water. Serves 4.

CREAMED SCALLOPS

¼ cup butter	1 cup heavy cream
1 small sliced onion	1 cup milk
¼ cup flour	1 sliced pimento
1 teaspoon salt	1 pint scallops
Dash of pepper	Buttered bread crumbs

Sauté onion in butter 5 minutes. Remove onion; add flour, salt and pepper. Gradually add cream and milk, stirring until mixture thickens. Add pimento. Put scallops in pan with enough water to cover, and cook 5 minutes. Strain and add to cream sauce. Fill ramekins with mixture, sprinkle with crumbs and bake until crumbs are brown. Serves 4.

SCALLOPS A LA CASINO

Wash and cut bay or tender small-size scallops into ½-inch pieces. Put a layer of scallops in a baking dish or scallop shells, sprinkle with salt and pepper and cover with strips of bacon. Bake in a hot oven, 400 degrees, 15 minutes. Serve with melted butter.

BOILED SHRIMP

Cook fresh shrimp 20 minutes in boiling salted water. Cool in water in which they were boiled. Drain, remove shells and cut out the black line (the intestinal tract).

CREAMED SHRIMP

Prepare Boiled Shrimp and heat in Medium Cream Sauce, p. 215.

SHRIMP FONDUE

2 cups buttered bread cubes
⅔ cup canned or boiled
   shrimp
Salt and pepper

2 cups grated American
   cheese
3 eggs
2 cups milk

Place bread cubes in a buttered casserole. Cover with a layer of shrimp and a layer of cheese. Sprinkle with seasonings. Repeat layers of shrimp, cheese and seasonings. Beat eggs and milk together, and pour over layers in casserole. Set casserole in pan of hot water and bake in a moderate oven, 350 degrees, 1 hour. Serves 8.

SHRIMP PIE

3 cups boiled shrimp
3 chopped onions
2 tablespoons butter
1 pint stewed tomatoes

2 tablespoons flour
6 boiled onions
2 hard-boiled eggs
1 small bottle stuffed olives

Plain Pastry, p. 294

Sauté chopped onions in butter until brown; then stir in tomatoes, flour and shrimp, and cook 3 minutes. Line a pie plate with pastry, put boiled onions around sides, pour in shrimp mixture, and slice eggs and olives on top. Cover with top crust and bake in a moderate oven, 350 degrees, 45 minutes. Serves 6.

SHRIMP NEWBURG

¼ cup minced onion
3 tablespoons butter
6 tablespoons flour
3 cups milk

1 teaspoon lemon juice
Salt and pepper
2 cups boiled shrimp
1 cup cooked green peas

3 tablespoons sherry

Sauté onion in butter until tender. Add flour and gradually stir in milk. Continue to cook and stir until thick and smooth. Remove from heat and add lemon juice, seasonings, shrimp and peas. Heat thoroughly and just before serving add sherry. Serves 6.

SHRIMP AND RICE

1 teaspoon grated onion
2 tablespoons butter
3/4 cup boiled rice
1/2 can condensed tomato
    soup

1 cup shrimp meat
1 teaspoon salt
1/3 cup milk
1 cup heavy cream

Put onion, butter, rice, soup, shrimp meat and salt in double boiler. Heat thoroughly and add milk. Just before serving pour in cream. Serves 3 or 4.

GAME AND POULTRY

MAXIMS FROM MAINE KITCHENS

Don't buy a goose unless he has plenty of pinfeathers. Pinfeathers are a sign of tenderness.

❦

If the skin of a chicken tears easily, it is tender.

❦

When the tail feathers may easily be pulled from a hung game bird, it is ready for cooking.

❦

Flour thrown on burning oil will extinguish it at once.

❦

A dish of charcoal placed in the pantry will keep food sweet and wholesome almost as well as ice. In warm weather change it every ten days.

❦

To remove rust from steel, moisten with kerosene and rub with sandpaper.

GAME AND POULTRY

SUGGESTIONS TO SPORTSMEN

In Maine, where a large proportion of males over seven years old knows how to handle a gun, the sporting books of Frank Forrester, famous at the time of the Civil War, are still read with respect and admiration.

When, at the age of twelve, I was allowed to have a side-snap 12-gauge shotgun and emphatically warned never to point it at any-one and never to climb over or through a fence without first un-loading it, I was presented with a copy of Frank Forrester's Field Sports, *and told to read it with care. I did so, and I never forgot it —particularly the chapter titled "Memoranda for Sportsmen." I think it belongs in this book for the benefit of all cooks and sports-men.—K.R.*

"It is well [says Forrester] that a Sportsman, without being any-thing of an epicure, should, like an old campaigner, know a little of the art of the cuisine; otherwise, in the country, even in this coun-try of abundance, he is very likely to fare badly, where, with a very little knowledge and a very little care, and having the precaution to carry with him a few simple condiments, he can live like a prince.

"In the first place, he should always carry his own black tea with him, if he would not be compelled to drink execrable rye-coffee. I commend him also to be his own liquor-bearer, as the spirits in country places are usually execrable, especially the rye whiskey of Pennsylvania and the West.

"If, however, he determine to take his chance in this matter, I advise him, in all cases, to eschew brandy, which is the most easily adulterated of all liquors, and, when adulterated, the worst.

"In New York and New Jersey, the cider-whiskey,[1] in country

---

[1]Applejack.

places, is decidedly the best thing to be got; it is too cheap to adulterate, and it is a wholesome liquor in itself—when very old, it is a very fine liquor—the taste, if disagreeable, as it is apt to be at first, is completely disguised by sugar and lemon-juice—and, whether hot or cold, it will be so found a very tolerable beverage.

"The best receipt I know for cold punch, and that which I always use, is, to one tumbler of crushed sugar, one and a-half of spirit, six of water, the peel of two lemons, and the juice of one.

"Or, if you use lemon syrup, which is far more convenient to carry, half a tumbler thereof to the above proportions.

"In cold weather, a very palatable hot drink may be made of common draft ale, or bottled porter, by simmering it slowly, with a few tablespoonsful of sugar, one of ginger, and a nutmeg grated to every quart of malt liquor, and two wine-glasses of spirit—gin is the best—to every quart.

"This will neutralize the acidity of the malt liquor, even if it is a little stale and even acid.

"To this end, and for all reasonable wants in the way of cookery, I say, carry with you a few pounds of black tea, a few bottles of lemon-syrup, one or two bottles of Harvey sauce, powdered ginger, a few nutmegs, some Cayenne pepper, some cloves; and, if you are wise, add thereunto a few pounds of rice, and the same of pearl-barley, and a flask or two of salad-oil.

"With these, if you can persuade your country hostess, instead of broiling the five-minutes-ago-slaughtered cock on which you are destined to dine, to skin it, quarter it, and stew it for at least three hours, with a bit of salt pork, an onion or two, ad libitum, and a few handfuls of rice or barley, which last should only be boiled one hour, you will feed like a prince, instead of breaking all your teeth, and dying afterward of indigestion.

"The same receipt for mutton, lamb, or veal, will be found invaluable to a campaigner—for meat in the country is, nine times out of ten, tough.

"As broiled cock is, however, the stand-by—and if you are travelling with your own horses, and arrive late at night, nine times out of ten, all that you can get, without waiting longer than is agreeable —it is an excellent plan to carry a pair of tender chickens with you from home, ready cleaned and prepared for cooking.

"These, when your cocks are killed at night, and ready for consignment to the gridiron, you prevail on your hostess to substitute, at the last moment; and carry hers forward, to serve the same purpose on the following day. This, with a little tact, you can generally manage, without offending the *amour propre* of the lady of the hostelry, though somewhat touchy they are wont to be, if they fancy the *droits* of the cuisine invaded or infringed.

"For breakfast, if you do not choose to wait to have a hot meal cooked (which, if you do, will lose you the better part of the day) have the remnants of your supper laid out, with bread, butter, and milk, before you go to bed; and the next morning beat up the yolk of a raw egg or two with your milk, add sugar and ginger to taste; but if you are wise, eschew the addition of the ardent, provided you aspire to a cool head and a steady hand.

"After the first day, it is your own fault if you do not fare well— or your gun's—which is the same thing; but observe: Instead of allowing them to attempt to roast or broil your game, by doing which they will infallibly spoil it, cause whatever you propose to use, Quail, Ruffed Grouse, Woodcock, Hare, Snipe (selecting those which are so hard hit as to be disfigured and unfit for keeping) to be cleaned, quartered, and placed in a large pot, with some pieces of fat pork, cut small, potatoes, an onion or two, a little chopped parsley, salt and black pepper to your taste. It will be a vast addition if you can get a red pepper-pod or two, which are generally to be found at every country tavern, and a mushroom or two, which you often find and pocket in your perambulation over upland pastures.

"The less water you put into the pot (provided there is enough to liquefy the mass, and prevent it from burning) and the slower you boil it, the better.

"When done, you will have a potage *à la Meg Merrilies,* which George IV. himself, or Apicius might envy you.

"Hawker says that if you skin and quarter any kind of Wildfowl, which are too fishy to eat, as Gulls, Coots, or Curlews, boil them four hours in a quart of water to each bird, with onions, and add to it, when on the point of serving, a spoonful or two of Harvey sauce, some lemon-juice, cayenne, and a gill of wine, you will have a very palatable mess.

"I never tried it, but it is well worth trying, especially on the seashore, where, in Bay Snipe, or Fowl-shooting, one is apt at times to fare hungrily enough.

"The little American Hare, *vulgo* Rabbit, would doubtless be delicious, either in this way, or stewed with rice and pork, as recommended for the fowl.

"At all events, nothing can be conceived better than a pie—not that abomination called a pot-pie, but a regularly baked pie, in a deep, earthen dish; if this cannot be had, a tin pan will serve the purpose—either of the Hare, nicely skinned and dissected, with some pieces of fat salt pork, a few hard eggs, a red pepper-pod or two, and mushrooms, if possible. I am supposing that you cannot obtain a rump-steak, for if you can, it should take the place of the pork. The mushrooms should be fried before being put into the dish, which should be well seasoned, and baked very slow. Either at home or abroad, it is an undeniable *plat,* and, after a hard day's shooting, it will act as a restorative worth all the ambergris and essences of all the cooks from the days of Lucullus to Ude."

WINGATE CRAM TO KENNETH ROBERTS ON WOOD-COCK, SHAD AND PORCUPINE LIVERS

"One Maine method of preparing woodcock and snipe was to roast them in clay, feathers and all. A blow from a hammer split the clay and the feathers came off with the clay.

"The Classical English method of preparing a woodcock for the kitchen was to hang it on a peg until the woodcock disappeared and then eat the peg.

"The late Dr. Nealley used a clay-pack method of cooking shad roe and bacon; but he made his clay from flour paste. The paste forms a shell as hard as a rock. The roe and bacon emerges with an anemic complexion but it 'eats damn well' as our grocer used to say. This method can be duplicated with rock salt, I'm told, but I've never seen it done.

"And, speaking of shad, you probably know that the farther north a thing can live the better its character. The best shad come from the St. John River in New Brunswick and I have a Filipino, Quesada, who bones them. By bones I mean he takes the bones out of the whole fish and not the fish away from the bones.

"Also, in New Brunswick and Nova Scotia they have smoked shad —findoned the way they do haddock.

"I had a friend in Nova Scotia who tried everything once (said to be the test of an English gentleman). He tried beavers' tails, moose's nose, muskrat, but as a result of experiment found nothing unusual except porcupine livers. They *are* good—more like duck livers than anything else."

PORCUPINE LIVER

Why the porcupine should be viewed with distaste or aversion, unless because of his malevolent appearance, is not easy to understand; for he feeds on the most delicate buds he can find, and pursues a semi-sedentary existence that is almost a guarantee of tenderness.

Perhaps because of his slow movements and his hearty meals, the porcupine has a relatively enormous liver, almost as large as a fat man's hand. Thousands of Maine gunners have eaten porcupine liver, and have unhesitatingly pronounced it one of the greatest delicacies.

To cook porcupine liver:

Soak the whole liver ½ hour in lightly salted water. Remove from water and cut in slices about ¾ inch thick. Drop slices into boiling water for 1 minute. Drain, cool and remove thin membrane from edge of each slice, and all gristle from interior. Wrap in strips of bacon and broil 5 minutes over coals, or fry 2 minutes in a blue-hot frying pan. Serve with lemon juice and boiled new potatoes.

WOODCOCK, SNIPE AND PHEASANT

Game birds, in Maine, are cooked in a score of ways. Some of the ways are products of necessity—of, for example, the long-standing custom, among Maine hunters, of carrying frying pans in the woods and cooking almost everything, from moose to trout and tea, in them. Others are handed down from ancestors who lived long ago in other lands.

Most State-of-Mainers, today, hold no truck with the manner of cooking snipe and woodcock followed for centuries by every great chef in France and England. Snipe and woodcock should, they maintained, never be drawn. The entrails or "trail" should be left in those birds and roasted with them: otherwise their true flavor is lost.

An old book by a French sportsman—*The Sportsman and His Dog,* by M. E. Blazé—touches on the woodcock:

"Woodcocks are found all over the world; in the ancient Continent as in the new; in Siberia as in Senegal. It is an excellent bird when plump, and always best during frost. They should never be drawn. By pounding woodcocks in a mortar a most delicious *purée* is made, and if on such *purée* you place the wings of partridges *piquées,* the happiest culinary result is obtained. The woodcock should not be eaten too fresh, otherwise its flavour will not be sufficiently developed: you will have meat without taste or delicacy: cooked as a *salmis,* its perfume mixes charmingly with that of truffles. Roasted with a breastplate of bacon, it should be watched over by the eye of a sportsman: a woodcock too much done is worthless; but a woodcock done to a turn, and placed on a toast black and unctuous from the trail, is a most delicate and delicious morsel, the most savory which a man can eat; and if he take the precaution to wash it down with some first-rate Burgundy, he may flatter himself that he has dined well."

Of the snipe, M. Blazé says:

"Snipes are everywhere to be found, as woodcocks. Their eating is delicate and delicious, and as regards their culinary preparation, we refer you to our receipt for the woodcock.

"From the cloisters of the Bernardins, who knew a thing or two, comes a recipe for a salmis of snipes.

"Take four snipes, roast them, but not too much: cut them up according to the rules of the art, then divide the wings, the legs, the breasts, and the backs, and arrange them on a dish. On the dish on which you dissect them, and which ought to be of silver, crush the livers and the entrails of the bird, on which squeeze the juice of four lemons and the rind, finely mixed, of one. On the members already prepared sprinkle a few pinches of salt and of allspice, two spoonsful of excellent mustard, and half a glass of first-rate sherry: then place the dish over a heater of spirits of wine, and stir it well, so that the whole be well impregnated with the seasoning, but let none unite. Take great care not to let it boil; but when it approaches that degree of heat, sprinkle it with some fine olive oil: diminish your heat, and continue to stir for several minutes. Then take off the dish, and serve it immediately, so that it may be eaten hot.

"Recollect, when you meet with this dish, to use your fork, as in case you touch it with your fingers you will devour them."

M. Blazé saves his greatest enthusiasm for the pheasant, and what he says of the pheasant applies equally to the partridge or ruffed grouse.

"This superb bird," writes M. Blazé, "when placed in your larder, should never be abandoned without reflection to the capricious arrangements of a cook, who will roast it two days too soon, or two too late, according to the number or quality of your guests. The pheasant should be roasted on the day it should be eaten: if your friends are there, so much the better for them.

"Some people hang them up by the legs, and when from the bird two or three drops of blood are seen to fall, then it is fit for those who do not like it somewhat high. Others hang them up by the tail, and when the pheasant falls they judge it worthy a place on their tables. Others, again, more difficult to please, believe that in order to eat a good pheasant he should be kept until he change his position without aid. These must permit me not to be of their opinion.

"If the pheasant be a splendid bird to shoot, if it be an ornament to your game-bag, it is nevertheless an equally superb decoration to your table in the second course.

"We are no longer in the time of the Emperor Heliogabalus, who, from ostentation or stupid prodigality, fed the lions of his menagerie with pheasants. When I kill one of these fine birds I eat it myself. A pheasant should not be eaten as other things are eaten; it requires a certain solemnity: neither is it without consideration that a subject of such importance should be treated: it should be delicately treated. Being, therefore, incapable to go into the depths of the subject, I shall borrow a page or two from a clever author on *The Physiology of Taste*.

" 'The pheasant is an enigma of which the name is only revealed to adepts; they alone know how to relish it in all its goodness. This bird, when it is eaten within the three days subsequent to its death, has nothing to distinguish it. It is neither so delicate as a spring chicken, nor has it so much flavour as a quail: but cooked at the proper time its flesh is tender, sublime; its high flavour combining that of poultry and of venison. The time so desirable to select is that when the bird commences decomposition: it is then the flavour develops itself, and is mixed with an oil which requires a little fermentation to exalt it, as the cup of coffee which is only obtained by torrefaction. This moment is made known to the uninitiated by a slight odour and by the change of colour in the breast of the bird; but the inspired derive it by instinct. A clever cook decides with the glance of an eye the moment when the bird should be taken from the spit, or allowed a few turns more.

" 'When the pheasant is perfectly fit, pluck it, not sooner; then lard it with great care, selecting the primest and freshest bacon. It is by no means an indifferent question, that of plucking a pheasant at the proper time. Experience has proved that those which are kept in their feathers are more perfumed and of better flavour than those which have been kept plucked, inasmuch as the air neutralises a portion of the flavour, or that the juice intended to nourish the plumage dries up and injures the flesh. Your bird being plucked, it should be stuffed in the following manner:— Take two woodcocks, and divide the flesh into one portion, the trail and liver into another. With the meat you make a stuffing, by hashing and mixing it with some beef marrow, a small quantity of scraped bacon, pepper, salt, and herbs; add truffles sufficient to fill up the remaining portion of the inside of the pheasant. Be careful to secure that stuffing so that none of it escape, which is difficult when the bird has been kept long. Nevertheless, there are several ways of obtaining this point, and, among others, that of placing a crust of bread over the orifice and attaching it with a thread. Prepare a slice of bread an inch thick, on which the bird rests in its length. Then take the trail and livers of the woodcocks, and mix them with truffles, an anchovy, some grated bacon, and a morsel of fresh butter: cover the bird with this paste, so that it shall be soaked through with the juice which melts while roasting. When the pheasant is done, serve it on the toast, surrounded with slices of orange, and be satisfied as to the event.'

"This delicious meat should in preference be washed down with some of the finest Burgundy, which I have fully decided after some experience. A pheasant thus cooked is food for angels. Already distinguished by its own flavour, it imbibes throughout the savoury and delicious odour which escapes from the woodcock and truffles. The toast, rich in itself, is impregnated in threefold combination by the juices which run through the bird when cooking; and thus, among all these good things, not an atom escapes its full appreciation: indeed such a dish is fit for the table of kings.

"Animals feed, man eats; but the man of mind alone knows how to eat."

COOT STEW

2 or 3 coot	3 tablespoons flour
Small piece salt pork	4 tablespoons water
Salt and pepper	2 cups diced boiled pota-
2 cups diced carrots	toes
1 turnip, cut in slices ¾ inch thick	Dumplings, p. 117

Skin birds, soak overnight in salted water to cover, cut into pieces for serving and wipe dry. Try out salt pork and place in the bottom of a kettle. Add meat, cover with cold water, season with salt and pepper and simmer 1½ hours; then add carrots, turnip and onions. When vegetables are tender, remove turnip *and do not replace it.* Remove the meat and vegetables from liquid and thicken it with mixture of flour and water. Replace meat and vegetables, add potatoes and dumplings, cover and cook 12 minutes before removing the lid.

ROAST COOT

Cut the wings from a coot and skin the body. Draw the bird, put carcass in a deep dish, and set dish in refrigerator. Do not put water in the dish. Unlike more highly esteemed waterfowl, a coot can be eaten the day it's shot, or at any later date. To cook, fasten strips of pork across breast and roast in a hot oven the same length of time that would be allotted to a mallard or black duck—16 minutes.

As dressing, take fluid from dish in which coot rested in refrigerator, and put it in a double boiler. To it add the drippings from the pan in which the coot was roasted, ¼ cup heavy cream and ¼ cup red wine. Stir and heat, but don't boil. Serve with Italian Rice, p. 243.

Thus prepared, coot is thought by many Maine gunners to be superior to any fresh-water duck, with the single exception of canvasback.

WILD DUCK

Heat oven as hot as possible. Put a peeled, quartered apple inside each duck and skewer 2 slices of thin salt pork over each breast. Roast mallards or black duck 16 minutes; medium-sized ducks, like pintails or bluebills, 14 minutes; teal, 11 minutes. The meat will look almost raw, but will taste better than if cooked longer. If cooked this way, duck can be eaten every night indefinitely. If cooked longer, they can't be endured after two or three eatings.

ROAST WILD GOOSE

The Canada goose is the only wild goose found in Maine. The goose and the gander cannot be told apart, and young birds and old birds look pretty much alike. Generally speaking, the plumage of an old bird is heavy and coarse, and the wing-spur at the "elbow" of his wing extremely large.

Few wild birds are more delicious than a young wild goose; and no sort of meat is tougher than the flesh of an old wild gander.

The only satisfactory way to cook an old wild goose is to remove all meat from its breast, cut it into strips, soak the strips overnight in cold water to which the juice of a lemon has been added; then place the strips in a bean pot, cover them with a quart of pea beans and a pound of salt pork, and bake 8 hours in a slow oven. This dish, in the south of France, would be called a *cassoulet*. An old goose, roasted, is too tough to eat at the end of 2 hours' roasting, and is apt to be tougher after 5 hours in the oven.

If the wild goose is young, let him hang from 2 to 5 days in a cool room; then pluck and singe him, remove pinfeathers and, before drawing, scrub with warm water and Ivory soap. This will give the goose grease a better chance to flow out during cooking. Then draw, put in a kettle with a sliced onion and a sliced potato, cover with cold water and parboil until the potato is done, changing the water twice during the process.

Stuff with Potato Stuffing, p. 253, and sew up the vent.

Put the bird in a roasting pan, breast down, and across his back pin strips of fat bacon or salt pork. Cover the pan with another pan to prevent drying, and roast until the tines of a fork will slip easily into the breast. This should be between 2 and 3 hours.

BEN AMES WILLIAMS' ROAST WILD GOOSE

In the morning bathe goose inside and out with lemon juice and place ¼ lemon in chest. Sprinkle with salt and pepper. Make a stuffing by putting dried bread through the meat grinder with 1 good-sized onion, goose liver and heart. Try out finely diced pieces of fat salt pork, enough so 2 tablespoons of golden-brown salt pork remain. Put this through grinder, add more bread, 1 teaspoon Bell's seasoning and a little salt. Add enough hot water to this mixture to make a firm paste, and stuff dressing firmly into the goose, filling all cavities. Skewer with toothpicks. Close neck tightly with toothpicks. Save the pork-fat drippings and, when they have solidified, rub over the goose. Let the goose stand until 2 hours before you wish to serve it, then place it in a covered roasting pan (without water) and roast in a very hot oven for ½ hour. Then pour 2 cups hot water over goose, replace cover, keeping holes in cover closed. Reduce heat to moderate and baste with drippings in pan frequently. A young goose will be roasted in 2 hours.

C. L. SIBLEY'S ROAST WILD GOOSE

Stuff a young wild goose with Potato Stuffing, p. 253, and sew up the vent. Place the bird in a roasting pan with a small amount of water. Cover and steam on the top of the stove for about 1 hour. Place strips of bacon on top of the bird and roast, uncovered, in a very hot oven until brown and tender. Baste every 15 minutes with the pan drippings. Partially bake apples in a baking dish, but finish cooking them in the roaster while the goose is browning.

BROILED FILLETS OF PARTRIDGE

Cut down along each side of the breastbone and remove breasts. Place in well-greased broiler and broil 8 minutes, turning frequently. Serve with Tarragon Sauce, p. 213.

BAKED FILLETS OF PARTRIDGE

Cut down along each side of the breastbone and remove breasts. Place a layer of bacon strips in bottom of baking pan, cover with partridge breasts and skewer another layer of bacon strips over the breasts. Bake in a hot oven, 400 degrees, 11 minutes. Remove top layer of bacon and broil 1 minute.

CANADIAN PARTRIDGE STEW

1 partridge	4 sliced onions
2 tablespoons butter	Salt and pepper
3 slices bacon	2 tablespoons chopped parsley
2 cups chopped cabbage	2 quarts water

Sauté partridge in butter until entire surface is seared. Wrap bacon around the bird and tie with a string. Put cabbage, onions, seasonings and parsley in pan used to sauté partridge, and place bird on top of vegetables. Add water, cover and simmer 2 hours. Stir occasionally. Serve on buttered toast. Serves 2.

ROAST PHEASANT

Singe, clean and wipe pheasant with a damp cloth. Rub inside with salt, stuff lightly with any desired stuffing, and truss. Rub with butter, sprinkle with salt and pepper, and roast, uncovered, 30 minutes in a moderately slow oven, 325 degrees. Baste frequently with a mixture of butter and hot water. Serve on buttered toast with a gravy made from the drippings in the pan. Serves 3 or 4.

POTTED PIGEONS

6 pigeons	1 sliced onion
3 slices bacon	1 quart boiling water
1 diced carrot	¼ cup butter
¼ cup flour	

Clean, stuff and truss pigeons. Place them upright in a stewpan on the slices of bacon, and add water, carrot and onion. Cover and simmer slowly 3 hours, adding boiling water when necessary. Make a sauce with butter, flour and 2 cups of stock remaining in pan. Place each bird on slice of toast and pour gravy over all. Serves 6.

BROILED QUAIL

Clean quails, split down back, brush with olive oil and sprinkle with salt and pepper. Place in well-greased broiler and broil 8 minutes. Serve on hot buttered toast, and garnish with parsley and sliced lemon. Allow 1 bird per person.

ROAST QUAIL

Pick, singe, clean, and wipe quail. Butter inside of each quail and sprinkle with salt and pepper. Rub outside lightly with butter; then truss and bind the body with a thin strip of bacon. Put 1 tablespoon butter in a roasting pan, set in the birds, and roast 20 minutes in a hot oven, 400 degrees, basting 3 times. Serve on buttered toast with a gravy made by adding 1 tablespoon of butter, 1 tablespoon of water and the juice of 1 lemon to the pan in which the quails were roasted. Cook 3 minutes and pour over the birds.

BROILED RABBIT

Clean a young rabbit and rub it inside and out with salt, pepper and flour. Lay it, back down, on a rack in an uncovered roasting pan. Dot with butter, but do not add water. Bake in a moderate oven, 350 degrees, 40 minutes, or until tender. Turn the rabbit over, baste with the drippings in the pan, and broil until brown. Thicken the drippings with flour and serve with the rabbit. Serves 2.

SAUTÉED RABBIT

2 rabbits, cut in pieces for serving	1 teaspoon salt
	½ cup butter
2 egg yolks, slightly beaten	½ cup boiling chicken
1 cup milk	stock
1 cup fine, dry bread crumbs	1 teaspoon minced onion
2 tablespoons Mushroom Ketchup, p. 203	

Combine egg yolks, milk, bread crumbs and salt. Dip pieces of rabbit into batter and sauté in hot butter in heavy frying pan 20 minutes. Add chicken stock, cover and cook in a slow oven, 300 degrees, 1 hour, or until tender. Make a gravy from the drippings and add onion and ketchup. Serves 4.

ROAST RABBIT

Hang a rabbit for 4 days after it has been killed. Dress it, wash in cold water, wipe with a clean cloth and squeeze lemon juice over all of it. Stuff with Moist Stuffing, p. 250, minus the onion. Lay the rabbit in a roasting pan, put strips of salt pork over it, and roast in a moderate oven, 350 or 375 degrees, for about 1½ hours, or until tender. Baste frequently. Serve with Bread Sauce, p. 204. Serves 2.

RABBIT STEW (1)

Cut rabbit in pieces for serving, cover with 1 pint of water and ¼ cup vinegar and let stand 3 hours. Drain, wipe, sprinkle with salt and pepper and roll in flour. Sauté in butter. Fasten a small piece of salt pork with a skewer to each piece of rabbit, add rabbit liver, salt and pepper, cover with water and simmer until tender. Remove liver, mash it and add to it ¼ cup port wine; add to rabbit mixture. Stir into the stock 4 tablespoons browned flour; cook 15 minutes longer, stirring constantly. Remove to serving dish and garnish with parsley. Serves 2 or 3.

RABBIT STEW (2)

Clean 3 rabbits and soak overnight in slightly salted water. The next morning place in a kettle, cover with cold water and simmer 1 hour, skimming often. Add 6 potatoes, 3 sliced onions, ¼ pound butter, salt and pepper, and simmer another hour. Add dumplings, if desired. Serves 6.

ROAST RACCOON

Clean all fat from coon, inside and out, and under all four legs. Cut off tail and feet at joints. Soak in salted water (½ cup salt in as much water as needed to cover coon) for 18 hours. Change salt water once. Stuff coon with potato or apple stuffing and sew up vent. Place in roaster with 1 cup water. Sprinkle lightly with salt and cover with 3 slices salt pork. Roast in a moderate oven, 350 degrees, until tender, about 1½ to 2 hours. When coon starts to brown, turn it. Baste frequently, or it will dry in cooking.

BURGOO

6 gray squirrels	1 can cream-style corn
1 chicken	1 can cooked yellow-eye
4 quarts water	beans
1 slice salt pork, ½ inch thick	1 tablespoon salt
1 sliced onion	1 quart whole milk
1 can tomatoes	1 handful flour

Skin gray squirrels and from forequarters remove small sac which has a bitter taste. Boil squirrels and chicken in water 1 hour and remove all bones. Add pork, onion, tomatoes, corn, beans and seasoning, and boil another hour. Just before serving add flour dissolved in milk.

This is an old hunter's dish, and is variable as the winds.

Maine hunters use rabbit, porcupine, muskrat,[2] woodchuck, big snapping turtles, venison, bear meat, as a base for burgoo. Some guides use skunk meat, which is said by those who have eaten it to be tender and delicious. In the spring, guides who have meat but no chicken for a burgoo will drift away from camp and later return with the carcasses of birds that look suspiciously like robins, blackbirds, yellowhammers, thrush or spruce partridges.

BROILED VENISON

Brush tender venison steaks or chops with olive oil, then sprinkle with salt and pepper. Put in broiler and sear 10 seconds on each side over hot fire. Brush again with olive oil and broil 2 minutes on each side. Serve with Maître d'Hôtel Butter, p. 205.

VENISON CUTLETS

Trim cutlets, rub well with salt and pepper and brush with melted butter. Place in broiler and broil 4 minutes, or sauté in butter. Serve with currant jelly.

---

[2]Rabbit and squirrel, in the dishes of Maine hunters and trappers, are frequently replaced by muskrat meat. Muskrats, which aren't rats at all, feed on roots, stems and leaves of water plants, on the eggs of birds, and on vegetables and fruits that grow near the waters they inhabit. Their flesh is sweet and tender, and by many is considered superior to rabbit. They have even been canned under the name of Marsh Rabbit. They should be cooked as rabbits or squirrels are cooked.

PAN–BROILED VENISON STEAK

Cut the steaks about ⅝ inch thick. Sprinkle 1 teaspoon salt into a blue-hot frying pan; then put in the steaks. Turn once, season with salt and pepper, and turn again. Cook, in all, not more than 1½ minutes. Overcooking only toughens them.

SIMMERED VENISON

6 pounds young venison	¼ pound butter
¼ pound salt pork	1 quart milk
1 quart water	

Cut pork in fine strips and insert in venison. Brown it well in the butter. Season with salt and add milk and water. Simmer, covered, 3 hours. Make a gravy of butter, flour and the stock from the kettle. After boiling 10 minutes add ½ cup sour cream and ½ cup red wine.

ROAST WOODCOCK

Pluck the bird's body, leaving the entrails in, and skin the head and neck. Tie the legs close to the body, insert the beak under a wing. In a dripping pan place as many slices of toast as there are birds. Place a woodcock on each slice of toast, and roast in a moderately hot oven, 375 degrees, for 17 minutes, basting frequently. Serve on the toast on which they were roasted. Allow 1 bird per person.

PAN–BROILED WOODCOCK

Skin the birds and lay off their breasts. Heat a frying pan blue-hot, pour in a teaspoon of salt or a tablespoon of olive oil, and broil the breasts 1 minute on each side. Allow 1 bird per person.

CAMPERS' WOODCOCK

Pluck birds without drawing. Wrap each one in a double thickness of the heaviest available paper, well buttered, oiled or greased. Bury beneath hot ashes for ½ hour. When removing paper, pour accumulated juices into a dish, season with lemon, salt and melted butter, and serve as sauce. Allow 1 bird per person.

BAKED CHICKEN (1)

3-pound chicken, cut in pieces for serving	3 tablespoons water
¾ cup sifted flour	1 cup bread crumbs
1 egg	3 tablespoons butter
	Salt and pepper

1 pint sour cream

Soak chicken overnight in cold salted water. In morning rinse, wipe dry and dredge with flour. Beat egg with a fork and add water. Dip chicken first in this mixture and then in bread crumbs. Put butter in frying pan, add chicken and brown on both sides. Place in roasting pan, sprinkle with salt and pepper. Bake in moderate oven, 350 degrees, for 30 minutes; then baste with some of the sour cream. Baste every 10 minutes until cream is gone. Bake 1½ hours in all, or until tender. Serves 4.

BAKED CHICKEN (2)

Cut 2 frying chickens in pieces, wash and dry. Sprinkle with salt and pepper and dip in flour. Sauté in butter in frying pan until golden brown. Place in self-roaster with an inch of water in the pan, cover and bake in a moderate oven, 350 degrees, 1½ hours. Use flour to thicken liquid in the pan for the gravy. Serves 8.

BAKED CHICKEN (3)

4-pound chicken, cut in pieces for serving	1 chopped clove garlic
1 teaspoon salt	1 tablespoon chopped parsley
⅛ teaspoon pepper	½ cup sherry or chicken stock
¼ cup butter	

Sprinkle chicken with salt and pepper; sauté in butter and garlic until browned. Place in roasting pan or baking dish, add parsley and sherry or chicken stock, cover and bake in a slow oven, 325 degrees, for 1½ hours, or until tender, basting frequently with juice in pan. Remove chicken and make a gravy by adding flour, cream and seasonings to drippings in pan. Serves 5–6.

BAKED CHICKEN PUDDING

2 young chickens, cut in pieces for serving	1 quart milk
	6 eggs, well beaten
Salt, pepper and mace	Flour to make thin batter
2 tablespoons butter	Pinch of salt

Season chicken with salt, pepper and a little mace. Put in a kettle, add butter, and cover with water. When half cooked remove them from kettle and cool. Make a batter of milk, eggs, flour and salt. Put a layer of chicken in the bottom of a baking dish, pour over it some of the batter; then another layer of chicken, and more batter, until the dish is full, having batter on top. Bake till a light brown. Break 1 egg into the gravy in which chickens were boiled, bring to a boil, and serve with the pudding. Serves 4–5.

BOILED CHICKEN

Clean and wash fowl. Place either whole or cut in pieces in a large kettle, and half cover with boiling water. Add salt after the first hour of cooking. Cook slowly, covered, until tender (2 to 3 hours). Serve with Boiled Wild Rice, p. 248, ½-inch slices of boiled bacon, and over all pour Egg Sauce, p. 209. The bacon may be boiled with the fowl or cooked separately.

PAN–FRIED CHICKEN

Cut young chicken in pieces for serving, season well with salt and pepper and dredge with flour. Sauté in chicken fat or butter in frying pan until brown and tender, turning occasionally.

ROAST CHICKEN

Dress and clean a roasting chicken. Rub it with salt inside and out, and stuff with desired stuffing. Truss the chicken and place it, breast side up, in a roasting pan. Sear, uncovered, in a very hot oven, 450 degrees, 20 minutes. Remove from oven and brush bird with Paste for Roast Chicken, p. 102. Reduce heat to moderate, 350 degrees. Baste every 20 minutes with a mixture of butter and hot water. Allow 15 to 20 minutes per pound for roasting. Remove paste crust before serving. Serve with Chicken Gravy, p. 102.

PASTE FOR ROAST CHICKEN OR TURKEY

3 egg yolks

1 minced clove garlic

1 teaspoon lemon juice

1 tablespoon onion juice

1 teaspoon dry mustard

½ teaspoon salt

¼ teaspoon pepper

Mix the above ingredients together, and add enough sifted flour to make a soft paste. This paste is most easily applied by painting it on with a 2-inch paintbrush.

CHICKEN GRAVY

To 4 tablespoons fat from roast chicken add 4 tablespoons flour and brown slightly, stirring constantly. Gradually add 1 cup chicken stock and 1 cup thin cream. Season with salt and pepper. Cook 5 minutes, then strain.

GIBLET GRAVY

Add finely chopped cooked giblets to Chicken Gravy.

JELLIED CHICKEN (1)

Cut up a fowl as for a fricassee and boil till tender. Remove chicken from kettle and chop meat into small pieces. Season broth in kettle with salt, pepper and summer savory. Dissolve 1 tablespoon gelatin in a little cold water and stir it into the broth. When it begins to thicken add the chicken and pour into a mold. Chill.

JELLIED CHICKEN (2)

1 package lemon Jello

1¾ cups boiling chicken stock

1 cup diced cooked chicken

1 chopped green pepper

1 cup chopped celery

3 tablespoons lemon juice

1 teaspoon salt

1½ cups chopped stuffed olives

1 teaspoon onion juice

Dash of cayenne

Dissolve Jello in boiling stock. Chill. Combine remaining ingredients, and when Jello is slightly thickened fold in chicken mixture. Turn into a mold and chill until firm.

CHICKEN PAPRIKA

4-pound chicken, cut in
    pieces for serving
Flour
1 tablespoon salt
1 teaspoon pepper

1½ tablespoons paprika
⅓ cup butter
2 chopped onions
2½ cups canned tomatoes
1 package noodles

Dip pieces of chicken in flour mixed with seasonings, and sauté in butter till brown. Remove chicken, and sauté onion in butter. Return chicken to frying pan with onion, pour tomatoes over it and simmer 1 hour, covered. Add the noodles, pressing them down into liquid and covering with chicken. Add water if necessary. Replace cover and simmer 1 hour longer. Serves 6.

BRUNSWICK STEW

5-pound fowl, cut in pieces
1 quart cold water
6 cubed potatoes
1 quart sweet corn
1 quart sliced tomatoes
    Salt and pepper

3 hard-boiled eggs
12 common crackers
2 tablespoons Worcester-
    shire sauce
½ cup butter

Stew fowl in water until tender enough to bone. Remove from kettle, skin, bone and dice. Put corn, tomatoes and potatoes into the kettle. When almost tender add the diced chicken and boil ½ hour. Chop 2 of the eggs fine and slice the other; add with the remaining ingredients to the stew. Serves 8.

CHICKEN CAKES

2 cups minced cooked chicken
    (or duck)
¼ cup minced onion
⅓ cup sautéed mushrooms
1½ cups bread crumbs

2 tablespoons butter
1 egg, slightly beaten
½ cup milk
½ teaspoon salt
¼ teaspoon pepper

Combine all ingredients, form into cakes and dust with flour. Melt 2 tablespoons butter in a hot frying pan and cook cakes until brown on both sides. Garnish with parsley. Serve with Tomato Sauce, p. 213. Serves 8.

CHICKEN CROQUETTES

½ cup bread crumbs   1 teaspoon melted butter
½ cup light cream   ¼ teaspoon salt
1 cup chopped cooked   ⅛ teaspoon pepper
    chicken   1 egg white, unbeaten

Soak the bread crumbs in the cream; then add to the chicken. Add butter, seasonings and unbeaten egg white. Form into balls, roll in fine cracker crumbs and fry in deep hot fat, 390 degrees. Drain on brown paper. Serve with Tomato Sauce, p. 213. Serves 4.

GUMBO

Have on hand a mason jar filled with crumbs made from crushing stale bread and toast slices with a rolling pin.

To make gumbo, melt 2 tablespoons butter in a stewpan. In the melted butter sauté 1 cup bread crumbs.

When the crumbs are browned, add 1 can chicken soup, 1 can tomatoes, 1 finely chopped clove of garlic, and any available odds and ends or any sort of canned goods—chicken, meat, fish, oysters, shrimp, crabmeat, singly or mixed. It may be served as is, or over rice.

A great deal of nonsense has been written in cookbooks about gumbo. Gumbo comes from the creole French word *gombo,* which merely means "a thick mixture."

CHICKEN GUMBO

Remove the bones from 1 medium-sized chicken and cut meat in small pieces; then brown chicken lightly in 2 tablespoons butter. Lift out chicken and stir in 2 tablespoons flour. Add 1 minced onion and brown lightly; then add a chopped tomato and cook 5 minutes. Add chicken, 2 finely chopped celery stalks, 2 quarts boiling water, 2 teaspoons celery salt and a dash of nutmeg, and simmer 1½ hours. Add 3 cups raw oysters and cook till they look plump; then add a wineglass of sherry, remove from stove and stir in 2 tablespoons filé powder.[3] Place a heaping tablespoonful of boiled rice in each soup plate, and serve the gumbo over the rice. Serves 8.

---

[3]Filé powder is an essential in Southern kitchens. It is made of powdered sassafras leaves, and is obtainable in all Southern grocery stores. It should be obtainable from any good Northern food store that carries a large stock of spices.

CHICKEN À LA KING

2 tablespoons butter	1 cup diced cooked chicken
1 tablespoon flour	½ cup sautéed mushrooms
1 cup hot chicken stock	2 tablespoons chopped
½ cup heavy cream	pimentos
Salt and pepper	1 egg yolk, slightly beaten

Melt butter, add flour and stir in chicken stock; then gradually add cream, stirring constantly. Season. Bring to a boil and cook 5 minutes. Add chicken, mushrooms and pimentos. Bring to boiling point again and add egg yolk. Also add ¼ cup sherry if desired. Serve on hot buttered toast or in patty shells. Serves 4.

CHICKEN LOAF

3 cups diced cooked chicken	¼ cup chopped pimento
2 cups fresh bread crumbs	3 cups milk
1 cup cooked rice	1 teaspoon salt
4 eggs, well beaten	

Mix ingredients in order given, pack in buttered loaf mold, set in pan of hot water and bake in moderately slow oven, 325 degrees, for 1 hour. Serve hot with Tomato Sauce, p. 213, or Mushroom Sauce, p. 210. Serves 8.

CHICKEN AND NOODLES

¼ cup butter	2 cups chopped cooked
2 tablespoons minced green	chicken
pepper	1 teaspoon salt
1 cup sliced mushrooms	⅛ teaspoon pepper
⅓ cup chopped pimento	2 egg yolks, beaten
1½ tablespoons flour	Cooked noodles
2 cups light cream	Grated Parmesan cheese

Simmer green pepper in butter until tender; then add mushrooms and pimento. Blend in flour, gradually add cream, and cook 10 minutes, stirring constantly. Add chicken and seasonings, and cook 3 minutes. Stir in egg yolks and remove from heat. Serve noodles on plates, top with chicken mixture, and serve with Tomato Sauce, p. 213, and grated cheese. Serves 6.

CHICKEN MOUSSE

2 cups minced cooked chicken	¼ teaspoon pepper
4 egg whites, unbeaten	Dash of nutmeg
½ teaspoon salt	1 tablespoon chopped parsley

½ cup heavy cream

Make a smooth paste of chicken and egg whites; then add seasonings, parsley, and gradually stir in cream. Pour into a buttered mold or custard cups. Cover with waxed paper to keep from burning. Set mold in pan of hot water and bake mousse in a moderate oven, 350 degrees, 30 minutes, or until firm. Unmold, and serve with Mushroom Sauce, p. 210, or Tomato Sauce, p. 213. Serves 4.

CHICKEN SOUFFLÉ

.3 tablespoons butter	1 cup chopped cooked chicken
3 tablespoons flour	
¼ teaspoon salt	3 eggs, separated
⅛ teaspoon pepper	1 tablespoon minced parsley
1 cup light cream	

Melt butter in double boiler, add flour and seasonings. Gradually stir in cream. Cook until sauce thickens. Add chicken, beaten egg yolks and parsley. Cook 1 minute longer. Remove from heat and cool slightly. Fold in stiffly beaten egg whites. Turn into buttered baking dish and bake 45 minutes in a moderate oven, 350 degrees. Serves 4.

CHICKEN AND OYSTER PIE

2 cups cooked rice	2 tablespoons butter
⅔ quart oysters	2 teaspoons celery salt
Liquor from oysters	1 cup Cheese Sauce, p. 207
2 cups chopped cooked chicken	½ cup sherry
	Plain Pastry, p. 294

Put layer of rice in buttered casserole; then a layer of chicken and oysters mixed; repeat layers. Over all pour oyster liquor, butter, cheese sauce and sherry. Cover with thinnest possible pastry, and bake in a hot oven, 400 degrees, 40 minutes. Serves 8.

BREAD–TOP CHICKEN PIE

3 carrots
1 minced onion
½ cup chicken broth
1 cup cooked green peas
2 cups diced cooked chicken

Salt and pepper
½ cup milk
1½ tablespoons flour
1 small can mushrooms
5 slices stale white bread

Swiss cheese, sliced

Cut carrots into strips and cook in boiling salted water 7 minutes. Pour off water, replace with enough to cover, add onion and boil 10 minutes. Add broth, peas, chicken and seasonings. Simmer 15 minutes. Add milk, flour, mushrooms and ⅓ their juice. Simmer several minutes and pour into baking dish. Cut bread in squares, toast one side, and place toasted sides down on top of pie. Cover untoasted sides with cheese and put pie in oven until cheese melts. Serves 6–8.

CHICKEN CREOLE

Sauté in a frying pan ¼ cup butter, ¼ cup chopped green pepper and 2 tablespoons minced onion until soft and yellow. Then add ¼ cup flour and 1 teaspoon salt. When absorbed add 2 cups stock and 1 cup tomato pulp or purée. When this boils add 2 teaspoons horseradish, 2 tablespoons lemon juice and 2 cups chopped cooked chicken. Heat thoroughly and serve on buttered toast. Serves 6.

CHICKEN PIE (1)

Cut a fowl in pieces for serving, place in a large kettle and half cover with boiling water. Add 2 slices onion and 1 teaspoon celery salt. Simmer slowly, adding small amounts of water as that in the kettle boils away. When tender, remove meat from the big bones. Mix 2 tablespoons flour and a little cold water, and add it to liquor in kettle; then stir in 2 tablespoons cream. If this fails to make 4 cups of gravy, add chicken broth to make 4 cups. Arrange meat and gravy in a casserole and bake until hot. Remove from oven and top with small, uncooked baking-powder biscuits, about ¼ inches thick. Return casserole to oven until biscuits are brown.

CHICKEN PIE (2)

Cut up chicken or fowl and boil it, seasoning broth to taste. Line
baking dish with rich pastry. Remove bones from chicken. Place
meat in dish, thicken broth to a gravy, adding butter generously.
Pour gravy over chicken until covered, as it dries out in baking. Put
thick pastry over all, pierce freely, and bake till top crust is done.

CHICKEN, TURKEY OR HAM TURNOVERS

3 tablespoons butter	Dash of nutmeg
3 tablespoons flour	2 teaspoons minced onion
1 cup milk or chicken broth	2 cups chopped cooked
½ teaspoon salt	chicken, turkey or ham
¼ teaspoon pepper	Plain Pastry, p. 294

Melt butter, stir in flour and gradually add milk or chicken broth.
Add seasonings, meat, and then cool. Roll pastry ⅛ inch thick, cut
with round, floured cooky cutter, allowing two pieces for each turn-
over. Place 1 tablespoon meat filling on one round; moisten edges
with cold water; cover with second round of pastry and press edges
together with a fork. Prick. Bake in hot oven, 450 degrees, about
20 minutes. Serves 6–8.

POACHED CHICKEN LIVERS IN SCRAMBLED EGGS

First prepare chicken livers:

3 teaspoons butter	½ cup chicken stock
2 teaspoons flour	¼ cup sherry
	8 chicken livers

Melt butter, gradually add flour and hot chicken stock, stirring constantly. Simmer a few minutes, then add sherry. Put the livers in
another saucepan, cover with chicken stock and poach them for 2
minutes. Remove the livers and chop fine; then add to the sauce.

Prepare Scrambled Eggs (2), p. 225, using 10 eggs. Heat 6 individual ramekins. Arrange the scrambled eggs around the sides of the
heated ramekins, leaving a hole in the center. Fill the holes with the
poached chicken livers and serve immediately.

CHICKEN AU GRATIN

½ cup sliced mushrooms
2 tablespoons butter
1½ cups Cheese Sauce, p. 207
2 cups diced cooked
  chicken

1½ cups diced cooked
  potatoes
1 tablespoon sherry
½ cup grated American
  cheese

Sauté mushrooms in butter 5 minutes, then add to the cheese sauce with chicken, potatoes and sherry. Pour into a shallow baking dish and bake in a hot oven, 400 degrees, 15 minutes. Serves 6.

CHICKEN CURRY[4]

2-pound chicken, cut in
  pieces for serving
3 tablespoons butter

2 sliced onions
1 tablespoon curry powder
1 teaspoon celery salt

1 tablespoon flour

Cover chicken with water, and simmer, covered, until tender. Sauté onions in butter until brown; then remove from pan. Put chicken in pan from which onions were removed, and fry them 4 minutes; then sprinkle with curry powder. Add chicken liquor to chicken and stew 5 minutes; then stir in flour, mixed until smooth with a little cold water. Stir until mixture thickens. Serve with hot boiled rice. Serves 4.

CHICKEN FRICASSEE

Cut up fowl and cook as for Boiled Chicken, p. 101. When tender, remove from water, sprinkle with salt and pepper, dredge with flour, and sauté in butter until browned. Serve with Chicken Gravy, p. 102.

CHICKEN IN SAUERKRAUT

Stuff chicken with mashed potato and cover with a paste of flour and water. Place 4 slices of bacon in casserole, then a layer of kraut, the chicken, and cover with kraut. Top with 4 slices of bacon, add water, and bake 3 hours.

---

[4]For another Chicken Curry recipe see p. 208.

CHICKEN GRIDDLECAKES

Prepare Griddlecakes, p. 285, and on each place 2 tablespoons of Chicken à la King, p. 105. Roll, and serve immediately.

ROAST DUCK

Dress, clean and truss duck. Sprinkle with salt, pepper and flour, and place on rack in roasting pan. Stuff with apples which have been pared, cored and cut in quarters. Roast in a moderate oven, 350 degrees, 20 minutes per pound. Baste every 15 minutes with hot orange juice. Remove apple before serving.

LEFTOVER DUCK

1 cup diced cooked duck	1 cup leftover gravy
2 chopped hard-boiled eggs	Salt and pepper
½ cup chopped olives	¼ cup red wine
1 tablespoon minced parsley	

Mix ingredients together in a double boiler and simmer until well heated. Serve on slices of buttered toast. Garnish with parsley. Serves 4.

ROAST GOOSE

Pluck, wash, scrub and draw a goose. Wash in cold water and dry. Stuff with apple, chestnut, potato or any desired stuffing. Truss, sprinkle with salt and pepper, and pin 5 strips of salt pork over breast. Place in roasting pan and roast, uncovered, in a moderate oven, 350 degrees, 20 to 25 minutes per pound. Baste every 15 minutes with fat in pan. Remove salt pork last half hour of cooking.

ROAST TURKEY (1)

Purchase a good young turkey weighing from 10 to 16 pounds and have the butcher draw and clean it. Wash it in cold water and dry it with a cloth. Make any desired stuffing, p. 250–53, such as Bread, Oyster, Potato or Chestnut. Stuff it lightly into the body cavity; then sew up with stout string. Also stuff the crop, and tie a string around the neck. Fasten legs and wings to body by skewers, and with strings from skewer to skewer across back. Stuffing should remain in bird overnight. When ready to roast, place bird breast side up on a rack in an uncovered roasting pan, without water. Roast in a 450-degree oven for about 20 minutes, or until brown all over. Make Paste for Roast Chicken or Turkey, p. 102. Remove turkey from the oven and brush half this paste onto the bird with a pastry brush. Turn the oven down to 325 degrees and put the turkey back into it for a few minutes; then paint it once more with the remainder of the paste. Do not add any water to the bottom of the pan, and do not put on a cover. Baste every 15 minutes with a mixture of hot water and butter. Allow 3½ hours for a 10-pound turkey; 15 minutes for each additional pound. Turn turkey on its back for last half hour. Remove the paste crust, string and skewers before serving. For gravy, boil liver, heart and gizzard until tender; chop fine and add to drippings in pan, which should be thickened with browned flour.

ROAST TURKEY (2)

Prepare turkey as for Roast Turkey (1). When ready to roast, place turkey breast side up on a rack in a roasting pan, add 1 cup of water and cover. Roast, the entire time, in a very slow oven, 250 degrees. Baste frequently with a mixture of hot water and butter. A 13-pound turkey will take 9 to 10 hours. The toughest turkey will become tender under this treatment, but the oven must never be allowed to go over 250 degrees.

SPANISH TURKEY

1 cup minced cooked turkey	Salt and pepper
¼ cup minced ham	2 cups hot boiled rice
1 cup mashed potatoes	1 minced clove garlic
½ cup turkey gravy	3 minced canned pimentos
¼ cup grated cheese	

Mix meats and potatoes with gravy and season to taste. Put into 6 buttered ramekins and cover with layer of rice into which garlic and pimentos have been stirred. Sprinkle with cheese and heat in a moderately hot oven, 375 degrees. Serves 6.

TURKEY SCRAPPLE

4 cups turkey meat   Giblet gravy
4 cups celery stuffing   1 teaspoon salt
Turkey bones   1 teaspoon poultry dressing
            1½ cups corn meal

Chop together in a chopping tray the meat and stuffing. Break up the turkey bones, cover with cold water, and boil slowly 45 minutes. Strain and pick all meat off bones. There should be about 12 cups of liquid. Add meat and stuffing, gravy, salt and poultry dressing. Put in a large kettle over a slow fire and gradually add corn meal, stirring constantly. When very thick put into well-buttered bread pans. This will keep 1 month. Slice as desired, and brown in frying pan in butter.

TURKEY BROILER

Sprinkle inside of turkey broiler with salt, and place breast side up in a floured pan. Make a paste of melted butter, flour, salt and pepper and spread over broiler. Roast in a hot oven until flour in pan gets brown; then add ½ cup water and reduce oven heat to moderate, 350 degrees. Baste the broiler frequently with drippings in pan. Cook about 1½ hours.

MEATS

MAXIMS FROM MAINE KITCHENS

Gravy will turn a rich brown if a tablespoonful of cream or condensed milk is added to it just before taking from stove.

✿

To clean ivory knife handles, rub them with cloth moistened with vinegar, turpentine or lemon and salt.

✿

Boiled meats improve if a little vinegar or sugar is added to the water.

✿

If the fat in a dripping pan catches fire, pour a little milk into it. The flame will instantly be put out.

MEATS

MRS. IVY GANDY TO MR. ROBERTS, ON CORNED BEEF HASH, INDIAN PUDDING, BAKED BEANS & FINNAN HADDIE

"Don't tell me that the water was thrown away in which your beans were parboiled! In my grandmother's house that water was used to soak the lamp burners in, to make them clean and bright, every Saturday morning. I did it! Then I filled the lamps with the kerosene oil, polished the lamp chimneys, and over each one placed a clean paper bag, and then the lamps were placed in a row on the mantelpiece in the kitchen.

" 'Slow oven' indeed; and who ever heard of a fast oven *down in Maine!* Brick oven was what we had. We built a fire of hard wood in the brick oven and let it burn until the beans were ready to be baked. Then the oven was brushed out, the beans were placed inside, with the brown bread, AND THE INDIAN PUDDING, and the whole baked all day Saturday and all Saturday night, and we had our beans for Sunday breakfast. Or, if we had them Saturday night for supper, we soaked them Thursday night and baked them all day Friday and Saturday. Like Long Island clam chowder, beans are better cooked a long time, if baked in a brick oven. There were no scorched beans, either, only brown ones on the top.

"But how, my dear Mr. Roberts, can we have corned beef hash unless we first have the real Maine corned beef? Didn't you know that nowhere in all the world do they know how to corn beef as it is done in Maine?

"All up and down the length of Long Island I have sought a meat market that has real corned beef, but all I can find is a tough length of reddened fibres, salty and bitter. My corned beef hash is made from meat that I corn myself by the old Maine recipe. After we have eaten corned beef and cabbage, sliced turnips and beets, carrots and boiled potatoes, until we are sated, I take a piece of the cold corned beef and chop it. I then take half as much cold boiled potato and chop that, then I mix the two, add pepper and salt, and moisten it all with milk. Iron kitchen utensils were used on my grandmother's farm, so I still use that metal. I take an iron pot with a tight top, with butter I grease it well, then place the hash in this pot, cover it tight and place it in my gas oven, set at 350 degrees. For half an hour I leave it there, while I mix up the johnny cake. Of course, we have johnny cake with corned beef hash, for what is corned beef hash without its complement? Condiments, of course, but we have piccalilli, made from green tomatoes, as well as that ketchup made from ripe tomatoes. Have you forgotten the cucumber pickles? Our chopping bowl was also used in concocting mincemeat, as well as all other things that had to be minced. Even the piccalilli was chopped in this same bowl.

"Finnan haddie is hard to get in the New York markets, and they never heard of scrod. My grandmother had seven sons, and one of them was a butcher, so we had a lot of meat. When I want to impress some person my husband brings home to eat with us, I cook an oxtail as my grandmother used to cook it."

CORNED BEEF

A New England boiled dinner, according to those Maine cooks whose reputations have gone farthest, is best made from corned beef made from the thick rib, or from a piece of flank next to the loin. These, they say, are more tender than regulation corned beef made from the throat and neck—the brisket.

They contend that corned beef made from the rump, thick rib or a piece of flank next to the loin can be perfectly cooked in 1½ or 2 hours, and is one of the best of the old New England dishes.

On the Maine coast, many families corn their own beef. They buy rump, flank or thick rib, rub the meat with coarse salt; then cover the meat with water. The water is salted with the same coarse salt until an egg or a potato will float in it. On top of the meat, to keep it submerged, is usually put a platter weighted with a doorstop. Many State-of-Mainers leave the meat in pickle only overnight. Others allow it to stay in pickle from a week to a month. Still others put fresh meat in heavily salted water, cook it until tender (usually about two hours), allow it to cool in the salted water, and serve it cold. The latter form of corned beef is called "corned in kettle."

Corned beef is best when served cold. Buy the fattest obtainable piece of corned beef, put it on the stove in cold water, and let it simmer until meat is tender. This will be somewhere between 1½ and 4 hours, depending on the meat. Save the broth in which the meat is cooked.

Let the meat stand in its liquor till cool; then take it from the liquor and lay in a deep bread tin with the meat fibers running the long way. Pull up layers of the meat with a fork, and into the interstices press pieces of fat from the outer edge. When the meat has been well larded, put a shingle on top of the meat, and weight it with a window weight or a flatiron. Chill thoroughly and serve cold on the following day, either as corned beef, or with hot vegetables as a boiled dinner.

BOILED DINNER

Two hours before the hour for serving dinner, boil the liquor in which the corned beef was cooked the day before.

In ½ hour add two carrots, scraped and cut in pieces. In 1 hour add 1 sliced turnip and 1 small cabbage cut in as many pieces as there are persons to be served. In 1½ hours add 8 peeled potatoes, halved, and a sliced summer squash.

At the end of 2 hours remove all vegetables, drain and arrange on a platter around the cold corned beef cooked the day before. To the vegetables add 2 cups of sliced pickled beets. Serve with tomato ketchup or vinegar.

CORNED BEEF CASSEROLE

4 sliced potatoes	¼ cup butter
¼ cup flour	Leftover sliced corned beef
Salt and pepper	1 cup milk

Place layer of sliced potatoes in bottom of buttered casserole. Sprinkle lightly with flour, salt and pepper, and dot with butter. Add a layer of corned beef. Repeat layers, ending with a layer of potatoes. Pour milk over all and bake in a moderate oven, 350 degrees, about 45 minutes. Serves 6.

CORNED BEEF HASH

Boil 6 medium-sized potatoes in their skins. Cool, peel and place in wooden chopping bowl with 1 onion and 4 cups of cooked corned beef from which all gristle has been removed. Chop extremely fine. Add pepper and salt. Melt ¼ cup butter in hot frying pan, and to it add ½ cup boiling water and the hash, stirring lightly until heated through. Cook over low flame until crust forms on bottom. Fold over like an omelet and serve with ketchup. Unless chopped very fine, hash is not hash at all, but merely food scraps. Serves 8.

INDIAN DINNER

1 pint yellow-eye beans	½ pound streaked salt pork
3 quarts hulled corn	2-pound chicken
3 pounds lightly corned (3 days) beef (thick rib)	6 potatoes
	1 small turnip

Pick over beans and soak all night. In morning bring twice to a boil, throwing away water each time; then simmer till soft, and mash to a pulp.

In a separate kettle put on corned beef and pork in cold water and bring to boil. Skim off scum. Boil 3 hours; then add chicken, sliced turnip and more water if necessary. Boil ½ hour more and add potatoes. Boil 30 minutes more.

Two hours before serving put on mashed beans and hulled corn in another kettle, and cover with water from cooking corned beef and chicken. Cook 2 hours, adding enough meat liquor from time to time to make mixture like a thick soup.

This dish is served in three containers: the pork and corned beef on one platter; the chicken, turnip and potatoes on another; and the beans and corn in a soup tureen. This mixture is better warmed over on the following day, and still better the third day.

DUMPLINGS

2 cups flour	½ teaspoon salt
4 teaspoons baking powder	1 cup milk

Sift flour, baking powder and salt; add milk and beat thoroughly. Drop by the spoonful on top of stews or in gravy, cover closely, and steam 10 minutes.

LOBSCOUSE[1]

4 cups bottom-round beef   ½ pound salt pork
1 quart raw potatoes   4 sliced onions
          4 cups cooked corned beef

Cut bottom round, potatoes and pork into small cubes, add onions and cover with water. Boil 1 hour; then add corned beef and simmer another ½ hour.

MULLIGAN

1 pound beef   2 diced carrots
1 pound lamb   1 diced parsnip
½ cup flour   2 stalks diced celery
1 tablespoon celery salt   2 chopped onions
½ teaspoon sage   6 diced potatoes
¼ teaspoon pepper   1 cup cooked elbow
¼ teaspoon paprika   macaroni
2 quarts water   2 tablespoons flour

Wash and dry meat; cut in pieces; roll in flour mixed with seasonings. Sear meat on both sides in butter in a frying pan. Put cold water, carrots, parsnip, celery and onions into a soup kettle, add meat and simmer 2½ hours. At end of 2 hours add potatoes and macaroni. Thicken soup with flour moistened with cold water. When possible, boil a soup bone with mulligan to add to its strength. Serves 6.

BEEF PIE

Put thin slices of cold roast beef on the bottom of a baking dish; dredge with a little flour, pepper and salt. Add a layer of minced onion; then another layer of beef, and seasonings and so on until the dish is filled. Add beef gravy if you have some; otherwise, add water enough to make a gravy. Boil and mash potatoes, add milk, butter and salt and spread 1 inch thick on top of the pie. Brush the top with egg and bake 20 minutes.

---

[1]Lobscouse was one of the most frequently used dishes in the galleys of Maine sailing ships.

IRISH STEW[2]

Put 4 pounds of round steak, cut in ¾-inch pieces, in a hot frying pan with a little butter. When brown, place in a stew kettle. Pour boiling water into frying pan; then over meat. Reduce heat so that stew will cook slowly. The longer and slower it is cooked, the better it will be. Let it boil 2 hours; then add 4 sliced onions, 4 diced carrots, 2 sliced potatoes, 1 can tomatoes, ½ teaspoon sage and 1 tablespoon celery salt. Cook ½ hour longer; 15 minutes before serving, add 1 cup cold water. This brings the fat to the top and it can be skimmed off, thus avoiding oily or greasy taste. Reheat and serve with Dumplings, p. 117. Serves 8.

BEEF STEW

Cut thick slice round beef in strips. Quickly brown on both sides in hot greased skillet, and remove. Add more grease to skillet, and slightly cook chopped onion, green pepper, can of tomatoes, ½ teaspoon sage, a pinch of baking soda, juice of ½ lemon and 1 tablespoon celery salt. When boiling, pour over the beef, which has been put in a pot; cover tightly and simmer 2 hours. The longer and slower it is cooked, the better it will be.

CHILI CON CARNE

2 pounds bottom-round steak	½ cup chopped onion
¼ cup chopped suet	3 cups boiling water
2 teaspoons salt	2 tablespoons chili powder
2 tablespoons olive oil	1 minced clove garlic

Cut meat in small cubes and add chopped suet and salt. Cook onion in olive oil, and when light brown add meat, stirring as it heats. When meat has browned, add boiling water, chili powder and garlic. Cover and simmer 2½ hours. Serve with kidney or yellow-eye beans. Serves 6.

---

[2]A letter to Mr. Roberts from Agnes Watkins on frozen Irish stew:
"Our Irish stew was made in a tremendous iron kettle in the beginning of the winter; then set out in the shed to freeze solid, chunks being hacked out as the occasion demanded, and the flavor of the whole improving the longer it stayed frozen."

YACHTSMAN'S MULLIGAN

Put 3 diced onions, 3 diced potatoes, 2 cloves garlic mashed with thumb, 1 handful beef cut in pieces, 6 slices dried beef, 6 slices diced bacon, 2 frankfurters cut in 1-inch pieces in a kettle. Add 1 cup sea water and fill ¾ full of fresh water. Simmer 1 hour; then add:

Two cans oxtail soup, 1 tablespoon Worcestershire sauce, 10 dashes Maggi sauce, ½ teaspoon peppercorns, small handful mixed spices, and 1 teaspoon each of paprika, curry powder and English mustard.

Simmer at least another hour. The longer and slower a stew is cooked, the better it will be.

This dish, served hot, with rum and water on the side, is said by Maine skippers to put hair on the chest and make childbirth easy.

POT ROAST

Rub a 3- to 6-pound boneless rump or chuck roast with salt, pepper and flour. In an iron pot heat enough fat to make 1 inch in the bottom of the pot. Brown the roast in the hot fat. Do not add any water. Cover the pot and simmer slowly 2 hours. Then add small peeled potatoes and onions. Simmer another hour, turning vegetables and beef so they brown evenly. Remove roast and vegetables to a platter and make a gravy by adding 3 tablespoons of flour and a little cold water to the drippings in the pot.

POT ROAST IN CASSEROLE

4 pounds beef	½ cup rum or sherry
3 tablespoons butter	2 tablespoons tomato paste
Salt and pepper	1 cup green olives

Season meat with salt and pepper and sauté in butter in frying pan until brown. Put in a kettle with rum or sherry. Cook ½ hour; then add tomato paste and simmer 3 hours. Add olives. Serves 8.

BEEF À LA MODE (1)

Mix 6 pounds round beef, ½ can tomatoes, 2 raw sliced onions, 6 whole cloves, 1 stick cinnamon, pepper and salt. Add ½ cup vinegar and 1 cup hot water and cook slowly for 4 hours. Strain gravy and thicken slightly. Pour over meat and serve.

BEEF À LA MODE (2)

1¼ pounds round steak
2 onions
1 teaspoon curry powder
1 teaspoon powdered ginger

1½ cups water
1 pint sour cream
1 tablespoon freshly grated
    horseradish

Salt and pepper

Cut steak in 1½-inch squares and simmer slowly with sliced onions, spices and water for ¾ hour. Add sour cream, horseradish and seasonings. Heat through, but do not let boil after adding sour cream, or it will curdle. Serves 4.

SLICED BEEF AND ONIONS

1½ pounds beef, cut in ½-
    inch slices
6 small onions
½ cup butter

1 cup water
½ cup vinegar
½ can tomatoes
Allspice, salt and pepper

Salt and pepper slices of beef, and sauté in butter with onions until brown. Put all in roasting pan with water, vinegar, tomatoes and allspice. Bake slowly 1½ hours. Serves 4.

SAUERBRATEN (1)

3-pound blade pot roast of beef
1 pint cider vinegar
1 pint water
3 bay leaves
¼ cup red wine

10 peppercorns
2 teaspoons salt
4 whole cloves
2 onions
8 gingersnaps

Place roast in a container. Heat the vinegar, water, bay leaves, peppercorns, salt and cloves. When hot, add sliced onions and pour over roast. If there is not enough brine to cover meat, add water to cover it. Place container in refrigerator for 3 days, turning meat daily. Remove meat from liquid, and brown in butter. Place the browned meat on a rack of a roasting pan, add 1 cup of the brine, cover the pan and simmer 3 hours over low heat. As brine cooks away, add more. Turn frequently. When done, remove to hot platter. Make a gravy by adding red wine and crumbled gingersnaps to broth. A little sugar may be added if desired. Serves 4–6.

SAUERBRATEN (2)

4 pounds rump roast	2 tablespoons ketchup
2 onions	3 bay leaves
½ cup vinegar	3 whole cloves
Juice of 1 lemon	2 teaspoons salt
1 cup water	¼ teaspoon pepper

6 gingersnaps

Sprinkle meat with flour, salt and pepper, and sear in a kettle. Add all ingredients except gingersnaps; then cover and simmer 2 hours. Add gingersnaps and cook ½ hour longer.

GOULASH

3 pounds lean beef (shinbone or shoulder)	6 tomatoes, cut up
2 tablespoons lard	6 coarsely chopped green peppers
3 chopped onions	1 piece pork, 2 by 4 inches
6 tablespoons Hungarian rose paprika, *not* Spanish	

Cut beef in 1½-inch cubes. Heat lard slowly, add onions and cook to a jelly. Remove pan and add paprika. Return to fire, add beef and brown lightly, tossing with wooden spoon. Add tomatoes, peppers and pork. Cover pan and simmer 2 hours, shaking occasionally. Do not use water or stock. Serves 6–8.

MEAT LOAF (1)

1½ pounds hamburg steak	¾ cup water
½ pound ground pork	2 hard-boiled eggs
1½ cups bread crumbs	3 slices bacon
1 chopped onion	1 tablespoon celery salt

1 teaspoon pepper

Soften bread crumbs in a little water and combine with hamburg, pork, onion and seasonings. Gradually add water and mix well. Put a layer of meat in a buttered loaf pan; then add slices of eggs. Cover with a layer of meat and top with bacon. Bake in a moderate oven, 350 degrees, 45 minutes. Serves 8.

MEAT LOAF (2)

2 pounds hamburg steak
1 pound ground veal
½ pound ground salt pork
6 soda crackers, rolled to
    crumbs

1 egg
1 pint milk
1 teaspoon salt
½ teaspoon pepper
1 chopped onion

Mix ingredients together, place in a greased loaf tin and bake in a moderate oven, 350 degrees, about 1 hour. Serve with Tomato Sauce, p. 213. Serves 8.

SMOTHERED BEEF

2 pounds round steak
½ cup flour
½ teaspoon salt
⅛ teaspoon pepper
3 tablespoons butter

2 tablespoons minced onion
½ cup boiling water
½ cup canned tomatoes
3 stalks chopped celery
1 chopped green pepper

Wipe meat with damp cloth, then roll in flour seasoned with salt and pepper. Sear meat in butter on both sides; then put in a casserole, adding any leftover flour. Sauté onion in butter until a light brown, add water and tomatoes, and bring to a boil. Sprinkle meat with celery and green pepper; then pour liquid mixture over all. Cover casserole and bake in a slow oven, 250 degrees, about 4 hours. Serves 6.

RED FLANNEL HASH

1½ cups chopped cooked
    corned beef
1½ cups chopped boiled po-
    tatoes
1½ cups chopped boiled
    beets

1 minced onion
¼ cup milk
1 teaspoon Worcestershire
    sauce
Salt and pepper
2 tablespoons butter

Mix together beef, potatoes, beets, onion, milk, Worcestershire sauce, and season to taste. Add mixture to butter in hot frying pan. Stir occasionally until thoroughly heated. Cook until hash is browned and crusty underneath. Fold over as for omelet and garnish with parsley. Serves 6.

MEAT HASH

Dredge meat with salt and pepper, and then put through meat chopper. Chop twice the amount of cold potatoes and mix with the meat. Put in frying pan with enough consommé or meat-cube consommé to moisten, and stir in a spoonful of butter. Heat slowly, stirring often. When warmed through, cover, and let it cook over very slow heat 20 minutes. Fold like an omelet and serve.

STUFFED MEAT LOAF

Mix together ½ pound each ground beef, pork and veal, 1 beaten egg, ½ cup milk, ½ teaspoon salt, ⅛ teaspoon pepper. Put half in buttered baking dish. Then add a stuffing made by combining 1½ cups toasted bread crumbs, ½ teaspoon salt, dash of pepper, 1 teaspoon minced onion, 1 tablespoon butter, ½ cup mushrooms and mushroom liquor to moisten. Top with remainder of meat. Bake in moderate oven, 350 degrees, 1½ hours and serve with Tomato Sauce, p. 213. Serves 6.

SWISS STEAK (1)

2 pounds lean steak, 2 inches thick	¼ cup chopped green pepper
Salt and pepper	2 cups stewed tomatoes
½ cup flour	Juice of ½ lemon
2 tablespoons butter	1 teaspoon mustard
3 thin slices onion	1 tablespoon horseradish

Season flour with salt and pepper and pound it into the steak. Brown meat in butter in heavy pan. Add onion, green pepper, lemon juice, mustard, horseradish and tomatoes. Cover and simmer 2 hours. Add water occasionally if needed. Serves 6.

SWISS STEAK (2)

Lay a tender round steak on meat board, sprinkle flour over it and pound it in vigorously. Cut in strips 1½ inches wide and arrange in a baking dish, lattice fashion, with bits of butter, pepper and salt, and small bits of onion. Garnish edge of dish with peeled potatoes. Put ½ cup water in dish, cover tightly and bake in moderate oven, 350 degrees, 1 hour.

PAN–BROILED STEAK

Heat 2 tablespoons bacon fat in a frying pan. Place a well-pounded 2-inch steak in the pan, sear it 30 seconds on one side, turn it over, using a spoon and not a fork, and sear the other side 30 seconds. Pour off the fat and add 2 tablespoons butter to the pan. Lower heat, cover the pan and cook 10 minutes. Just before serving (if desired), pour 1 ounce brandy over the steak and set it afire. Stir the liquid in the pan with a spoon, and pour over steak when served.

PAN–BROILED PICNIC STEAKS

Buy small tenderloin steaks cut ½ inch thick. Heat a frying pan blue-hot. In the frying pan sprinkle 1 tablespoon ordinary salt—nothing else. Put the small steaks in quickly and cook 30 seconds on each side. Serve immediately with lemon juice, or between slices of bread.

BAKED FLANK STEAK

Have a flank steak scored and place in roasting pan. Sprinkle sugar over surface and in cuts. Pour over it 1 tablespoon of lemon juice and enough water to make the gravy. Cover with sliced onions and sliced tomatoes. Dot with butter. Place small potatoes around steak, season with salt and pepper, dust with flour. Start in a moderately hot oven, 375 degrees; then reduce to 300 and cook 1 hour.

STUFFED FLANK STEAK

2 pounds flank steak, 1 inch thick	¼ teaspoon pepper
	1 tablespoon grated onion
1 cup bread crumbs	¼ cup chopped celery
½ cup stock	1 tablespoon chopped parsley
1 teaspoon salt	¼ cup suet

Treat steak, scoring and sugaring as above. Make a stuffing of crumbs, stock, seasonings, onion, celery and parsley. Wipe meat with damp cloth and spread stuffing over it. Roll meat with the grain; sew edges together and sprinkle with flour. Sauté meat in suet until well browned; then add almost enough hot water to cover. Cover kettle and simmer 2½ hours. Remove thread. Make gravy of drippings in the pan and serve over the steak.

SEAMAN'S STEAK

1½ pounds round steak	2 thinly sliced onions
6 sliced raw potatoes	Salt and pepper
1 cup beef bouillon	

Slice steak ½ inch thick and sear in butter; then put a layer of meat in a buttered baking dish. Sauté onions in butter and put on top of meat; then add a layer of potatoes; repeat. Season layers with salt and pepper. Pour bouillon over all and bake in a moderate oven, 350 degrees, 2 hours.

ROAST BEEF (1)

Good roast beef can be had only by buying the best cuts. The rib, loin and sirloin tip make the most desirable roasts. Remove meat from refrigerator and let it stand at room temperature for 1 hour before roasting. Wipe meat, rub with salt, pepper and flour. Put ½ cup water in the bottom of roasting pan and place beef in it, standing; not on its side. Sear in a very hot oven, 500 degrees, 20 minutes; then reduce heat to slow, 300 degrees, and continue roasting. Baste every 15 minutes for the first hour. Allow 16 minutes per pound for rare beef, 22 minutes per pound for medium, 30 minutes per pound for well-done roast.

ROAST BEEF (2)

Select and prepare beef as for Roast Beef (1); but place on a rack in an uncovered roasting pan without water. Put in oven preheated at 300 degrees, and roast at that temperature the entire time. Basting is not necessary. Allow same roasting times as for Roast Beef (1).

ROSEMARY ROAST BEEF

Order a standing rib roast and rub it with salt and pepper. Place on a rack in an uncovered roasting pan. Thatch the top well with rosemary. Sear in a very hot oven, 500 degrees, 15 to 20 minutes; then reduce heat to slow, 300 degrees, and roast 16 minutes per pound.

COLD MARINATED BEEF

3 tablespoons olive oil
Juice of 2 lemons
1 tablespoon chopped onion

½ tablespoon red pepper
1 teaspoon salt
½ teaspoon dry mustard

Stir ingredients vigorously. Slice cold rare roast beef, arrange on platter and pour dressing over it.

YORKSHIRE PUDDING

1 cup flour
1 cup milk

2 eggs
½ teaspoon salt

Gradually add milk to flour, and when smooth add eggs and salt. Beat well with an egg beater. Pour melted butter or beef drippings ½ inch thick over bottom of 2 bread pans. Pour half of mixture in each pan. Bake in a hot oven, 400 degrees, for 20 minutes, then reduce heat to moderate, 350 degrees, and bake 10 minutes longer. Cut in squares and serve with roast beef.

SHEPHERD'S PIE

Season 1 cup finely chopped cooked meat with butter, salt, pepper and 2 tablespoons chili sauce. Put in a baking dish and cover with 1 cup hot mashed potato. Brush potato with the yolk of an egg diluted with a little milk. Bake until light brown. Serves 2.

CANADIAN MEAT CAKES, SHARP SAUCE

1 pound finely chopped beef
    or venison
1 cup dried bread crumbs,
    rolled fine
1 teaspoon salt

¼ teaspoon pepper
½ cup milk
4 tablespoons flour
1 pint brown stock
½ cup tomato ketchup

1 cup sour cream

Mix chopped meat with bread crumbs, adding salt and pepper; then the milk. Make into 24 cakes and fry in butter until brown. Remove meat cakes from pan and stir flour into butter in which cakes were fried. When flour is smooth, add stock, ketchup and sour cream. Simmer the meat cakes in this sauce for ½ minute. Serves 4–6.

GERMAN MEAT BALLS

1½ pounds hamburg steak 2 slices of bread, crumbed
1 chopped onion 1 egg
Salt and pepper

Mix all ingredients together. Shape into balls and flatten thin. Fry in drippings until meat is well cooked. Serves 4–5.

MEAT BALLS

1 thinly sliced onion ½ pound fat pork
1 tablespoon butter 1 minced onion
3 tablespoons flour 1 tablespoon chopped
3 cups brown stock or water parsley
Salt and pepper 1 teaspoon pepper
1½ pounds bottom-round ½ teaspoon cloves
   beef ¾ cup soft bread crumbs
2 eggs, beaten

Make a gravy by sautéing sliced onion in butter and adding flour. When this is brown, stir in stock or water. Boil 5 minutes and then add seasonings. Put meats through food grinder and then add remaining ingredients. Form into balls and simmer 20 minutes in the gravy. Serves 8.

MINCED BEEF AND EGGPLANT

2 eggplants Salt and pepper
1 pound hamburg steak 1 chopped onion
½ cup butter 2 eggs, beaten
½ cup bread crumbs

Brown hamburg in 2 tablespoons of the butter. Add onion, salt and pepper. Soak eggplant in hot salted water 10 minutes; then drain, slice and fry with rest of butter. Place eggplant and meat in layers in a buttered baking dish. Pour the beaten eggs over the top, and on the eggs sprinkle bread crumbs. Bake in a moderate oven, 350 degrees, 50 minutes. Serves 8.

HAMBURG CAKES

2 pounds ground sirloin
1 raw egg
1 cup chicken broth
2 tablespoons chicken fat
½ teaspoon English mustard

1 tablespoon celery salt
1 teaspoon freshly ground
   black pepper
2 tablespoons Worcester-
   shire sauce

Mix ingredients in order given, form into cakes and pan-broil in hot skillet till brown on both sides. Serves 6.

CREAMED HAMBURG

½ pound hamburg
¼ cup butter
¼ cup flour
½ teaspoon salt
¼ teaspoon pepper

1 cup milk
1 cup brown stock
1 minced onion
Dash of Worcestershire
   sauce

Sauté hamburg in butter for 1 minute. Stir in flour, salt and pepper; gradually add milk and stock; then onion and Worcestershire sauce. Simmer briefly; serve on toast or waffles. Serves 4.

LOW MULL

As a base for low mull use either meat or fish, whichever is handiest. Cut meat into small cubes. Then put on the stove a large pot filled with water, as much as you're going to need, and let it come to a boil. Add sliced raw onion, chopped celery and sliced raw bacon. Fry more bacon; and when crisp remove from pan and transfer to mull pot. Add butter to fat in frying pan, fry some onions in it; then add the fried onions to mull pot. Also pour in 1 can of tomatoes, 1 can of condensed tomato soup, 1 sliced lemon. Put in several sliced cloves of garlic, and season with allspice, cloves, paprika, salt, pepper, pickled red pepper, tabasco sauce, Worcestershire and ketchup. Add a substantial supply of cubed potatoes, and 10 minutes later put in the meat or the fish. At the last, add butter or olive oil, sherry and chopped raw onions. Serve on rice, as you would curry. The whole process of preparation involves 3 or 4 hours over stove and cutting table; but the time is thought by Maine huntsmen to be well spent.

CREAMED DRIED BEEF (1)

½ pound dried beef   4 tablespoons flour
4 tablespoons butter   Dash of pepper
2 cups milk

Pour boiling water through the beef, cut it up a bit; then drain and
dry it. Sauté beef in butter until crisp. Remove beef and stir the
flour into the butter in the frying pan and cook until it is very brown,
almost burned. Add the pepper. Then pour in the milk and cook
until thick, stirring constantly. Add the crisp beef to the sauce and
serve at once. This browned sauce is regarded highly as a dressing
for fried tomatoes. Serves 6.

CREAMED DRIED BEEF (2)

½ pound chopped, smoked   1 cup milk
    dried beef   1 tablespoon butter
½ cup heavy cream   1 tablespoon flour
⅛ teaspoon pepper

Soak beef in boiling water 10 minutes. Drain. Melt butter in double
boiler, stir in flour; then gradually add cream and milk. Cook several minutes; then add beef and pepper. Cook 10 minutes and serve
on toast.

BROILED LIVER

Dip slices of calf's liver, ½ inch thick, in boiling water; remove
instantly. Remove gristle and peel outer skin from edges. Dry
thoroughly; brush with melted butter, sprinkle with salt and pepper, and place on greased wire broiler. Broil 5 minutes, turning frequently. Brush with butter and serve on hot platter. One pound
serves 4.

FRIED LIVER

Dip slices of calf's liver, ½ inch thick, in boiling water; remove instantly. Remove gristle and peel outer skin from edges. Dry thoroughly. Sauté in 3 tablespoons of butter 5 minutes, turning when
brown on one side. One pound serves 4.

BRAISED LIVER

1 pound calf's liver	1 bay leaf
Fat salt pork	2 whole cloves
2 cups stock or water	¼ cup diced carrot
6 peppercorns	¼ cup diced onion
¼ cup diced celery	

Wash and dry liver thoroughly. Remove gristle and edge skin. Lard with strips of salt pork. Place in a deep pan with any ends of pork used in larding. Add other ingredients, cover and bake 2 hours in slow oven, 300 degrees, uncovering the last 20 minutes. Remove liver from pan, strain liquor and make a gravy to serve around liver. Serves 4.

MOCK TERRAPIN

Cut three slices of bacon in halves and fry till crisp. Remove bacon and sauté 1 pound chopped calf's liver, with gristle and edge skin removed, and ¼ pound chopped mushrooms in the fat for 5 minutes, stirring constantly. Add 2 tablespoons flour, ¼ teaspoon dry mustard, 1 teaspoon salt and ¼ teaspoon pepper. When blended add 1 cup brown stock and stir until it boils; then simmer 20 minutes. Add 1 tablespoon lemon juice and 2 chopped hard-boiled eggs, bacon and 1 dozen stuffed olives, chopped fine. Serves 4.

LIVER CAKES

1 pound beef liver	1 teaspoon salt
1 medium-sized onion	⅛ teaspoon pepper
6 common crackers	2 tablespoons milk
1 tablespoon chopped parsley	2 eggs, slightly beaten

Remove gristle and edge skin from liver. Put liver, onion and crackers through meat grinder. Add other ingredients and mix thoroughly. Form into balls, and fry in 3 tablespoons melted butter until browned on both sides. Serves 4.

BRAISED OXTAIL JOINTS

(Mrs. Gandy enlightens Mr. Roberts on braised oxtail joints, vegetables and other tidbits.)

"To braise ox-tail joints, we first found a meat-man whose character and reputation were above reproach, and ordered from him two large ox-tails, weighing two to two and a half pounds each. He cut them cleanly at the joints, and before 7:30 the next morning we put the meat into a kettle of cold water and let it parboil for 15 minutes. Then we removed them from the kettle, threw away the water, and washed them in cold water; then put them in a colander and left them to drain.

"Then we broke out the old black iron kettle, the one with the air-tight cover, and in it tried out a quarter pound of fat salt pork cut up fine. When the pork scraps were about invisible we threw them away, and fried in the pork fat six large yellow onions, pared and sliced thin. When the onions were golden brown we left them, dredged the joints in white flour sifted with a little salt; then fried the joints until their complexion was like that of the onions. Finally we added to the onions and the joints, still in the old black iron kettle with the tight lid, not less than 8 cups of rich brown stock, heated, and let the whole simmer, simmer, simmer—and I mean SIMMER, not boil.

"While the simmering was going on there were lots of things to do. We assembled the makings of a noble salad. Greens. And so to set off the ox-tail dish, serve a salad of greens with dressing made from olive oil, some kind of vinegar, and whatever your taste likes.

"Well, an hour or so before dinner, we scraped and sliced some beautiful golden carrots, also a fine turnip, and parboiled them until tender but not really cooked. We then took off the lid of the iron kettle and if necessary added some of that brown stock to cover it all, and put the carrot and turnip slices in to give an added flavor to the whole.

"In the meantime we baked some large perfect Maine potatoes, one for each, and had them ready to serve with the joints. We also mixed a real New England johnny cake, and served it with the dinner. We made a big one, as we liked it cold the next day.

"For dessert, in winter, we had hot mince pie and a huge piece of strong cheese, with strong black coffee."

KIDNEY STEW

2 beef kidneys
2 tablespoons butter
1 cup consommé
1 cup tomato juice
¼ cup flour
1 tablespoon salt

¼ teaspoon pepper
1 cup sliced carrots
1 cup sliced onions
1 cup chopped celery
1 tablespoon Worcestershire
    sauce

Wash kidneys, remove skin and fat, split lengthwise and cut out core and hard membrane. Cut in small pieces and soak in cold salted water 1 hour. Drain. Sauté kidneys in butter in bottom of kettle until brown. Add consommé and tomato juice blended with flour, salt and pepper. Cover and simmer slowly 1 hour. Add vegetables and simmer another hour. Add Worcestershire sauce. Serves 4.

BOILED BEEF TONGUE

Wash tongue thoroughly. Place in kettle with boiling water to cover and add 1 tablespoon vinegar and 2 teaspoons salt. Bring to a boil, cover and simmer 2½ to 3 hours, or until tongue is tender. Cool slightly in liquid; then remove and peel off skin and fat. Cut in thin slices and serve hot or cold with Whipped Cream Horseradish Sauce, p. 210. Serves 8–10.

CASSEROLE OF TRIPE

2 pounds honeycomb tripe
2 tablespoons butter
2 minced onions
1 tablespoon minced green
    pepper

¼ teaspoon salt
⅛ teaspoon pepper
2 tablespoons flour
2 cups hot water
½ teaspoon Worcestershire
    sauce

Treat pickled honeycomb tripe with two boilings (as under Broiled Tripe). Cut in 2-inch strips. Sauté onion and green pepper in butter until soft. Add tripe and cook 5 minutes. Pour into a casserole and add salt and pepper, sprinkle with flour and add hot water. Cook in a slow oven, 300 degrees, 1½ hours. Add Worcestershire sauce before serving. Serves 8.

BROILED HONEYCOMB TRIPE

Cut tender fresh honeycomb tripe in pieces 6 by 4 inches. Always pick out what is known as "pocket" tripe. Season with salt and pepper, sprinkle with flour, dip in olive oil, and again sprinkle lavishly with bread crumbs. Broil slowly over charcoal and serve with Mustard Sauce (1), p. 211.

Fresh tripe has been supplanted in most markets by pickled tripe, and pickled tripe is difficult to broil satisfactorily. Pickled tripe should have two boilings of 15 to 20 minutes each in order to remove the sourness. One pound serves 4.

SPICED TRIPE

Cut fresh tripe into 4-inch squares. Put a layer of tripe in the bottom of an earthen jar, then sprinkle with cloves, allspice and whole pepper; repeat with a layer of tripe and spices until the jar is full. Cover and leave in a cool place several days. Cook and serve cold.

LAMB CURRY

1½ pounds shoulder of lamb, cut in 1-inch pieces	2 teaspoons curry powder
	1 teaspoon salt
2 tablespoons chopped onion	⅛ teaspoon pepper
1 tablespoon butter	1½ cups milk
1 cup diced raw potatoes	

Put lamb in hot frying pan and turn frequently until browned on both sides. Place in a buttered baking dish. Brown onions in butter, and add with curry, salt, pepper and milk to lamb. When well mixed, add potato. Cover and bake in a moderately hot oven, 375 degrees, ½ hour. Remove cover and bake 25 minutes longer.

CORNED LAMB

Sprinkle a piece of the shoulder or flank with salt and let stand overnight. In the morning put it in a kettle with 2 onions, 2 bay leaves, a little salt, 1 teaspoon of lemon juice, 1 teaspoon of cloves and 2 sticks of cinnamon, cover with cold water and simmer until well done. Discard all bones and gristle. Press in pan. This is good with scalloped potatoes.

CASSOULET (1)

Soak 2 pounds of beans overnight. Simmer 3 hours in plentiful amount of water with ¼ pound salt pork cut in cubes, 1 sliced carrot, 3 cloves garlic, celery salt, pepper, thyme and a bay leaf.

Cut a lightly roasted goose, or duck, into pieces and after browning them in fat combine them with the following:

1½ pounds lamb stew meat	1 pound smoked beef sau-
1½ pounds lean pork	sage (franks will do)
1 pound fresh pork sausage	1 pound onions

Blend all the above ingredients together, place in a pot, cover, and cook in a slow oven, 300 degrees, for 1½ hours. Do not allow the liquid to over-evaporate. At any sign of drying, add small amounts of boiling water. At the end of the cooking, the ingredients should just show through the liquid.

CASSOULET (2)

Soak a quart of white beans in a generous amount of water overnight; drain, place in a saucepan with 2 quarts water and boil 5 minutes; drain and place in a bean pot. Roast a 5- to 6-pound shoulder of lamb and a duck for 20 minutes; remove from oven, cut into medium-sized pieces and add to the beans with a 2-ounce piece of lean raw pork, 4 frankfurters, 1 quartered carrot, 1 onion and 3 whole cloves. Tie in a bunch 2 branches parsley, 1 branch chervil, 1 clove garlic, 1 bay leaf and a sprig thyme; add to the pot, season with 1 tablespoon celery salt and ½ teaspoon white pepper. Add 3 quarts of water, cover the pot and set in a slow oven for 8 hours. Remove the bunch of herbs, onion and carrots, cut the frankfurters and the pork into slices, and arrange on top of the pot. Sprinkle 1 teaspoon freshly chopped parsley over the meat. Serve from the pot.

MINCED LAMB

Heat 1 cup gravy and add to it 2 tablespoons heavy cream, ⅛ teaspoon mace, 1 minced onion, 1 tablespoon butter, 3 well-beaten eggs, salt and pepper. Stir well and add 2 cups finely chopped cooked lamb. Heat and serve on buttered toast, each helping topped with a poached egg. Serves 6.

MINCED LAMB AND EGGPLANT

1 eggplant	Salt and pepper
2 cups finely chopped cooked lamb	1 teaspoon chopped parsley
	Ripe tomatoes

Pare eggplant and cut in ¼-inch slices. Soak in salted water 30 minutes. Drain for 1 hour. Season lamb with salt and pepper, add parsley and mix well. Spread meat between slices of eggplant and sauté in butter. Arrange in shallow pan, cover top with slices of tomato, and bake in a moderate oven, 350 degrees, until tomatoes are done. Serves 8.

MINCED LAMB IN EGGPLANT

Peel an eggplant, and slice it the long way in slices ¼ inch thick. Salt each slice, pile the slices on top of each other, put a weighted dish on top of the pile to expel moisture, and let stand for an hour or more. Grind up 1 pound of lean raw lamb and into it stir 1 finely chopped clove garlic, 1 small can of mushrooms chopped fine, 1 teaspoon curry powder and 1 teaspoon celery salt. Divide the lamb mixture into as many parts as there are slices of eggplant. Place one part on a slice of eggplant and roll the eggplant around it. Around the rolled eggplant roll a slice of bacon, fastening the bacon with a skewer or toothpick. Put the rolls in a baking pan and bake in a hot oven, 400 degrees, 1 hour. Serve with Italian Rice, p. 243, and a liberal amount of Tomato Sauce, p. 213.

LAMB AND ARTICHOKES

2 pounds lamb	3 pints water
½ cup butter	8 artichokes
1 minced onion	3 eggs
Salt and pepper	Juice of 1 lemon

Cut lamb in small pieces and sauté in butter. Add onion, salt and pepper. When brown add water and boil ½ hour. Discard dried artichoke leaves. Cut tips from tender leaves, remove chokes, halve and add to meat. Boil 1 hour. Beat eggs, add lemon juice and 1 cup of meat broth. Heat—don't boil—till thick, stirring constantly. Pour over meat and serve at once. Serves 8.

BROILED LAMB CHOPS

Lamb chops are easier to spoil than any form of meat—usually by overcooking.

Rib chops have the best flavor. The length of cooking depends on whether they are single (1 inch thick) or double (2 inches thick).

Dip chops in lemon juice.

Place in broiler, close to heat, and sear 10 seconds on each side to hold in the juices.

Then, if chops are single, broil 2 minutes on one side; turn and broil 1½ minutes on the other side.

If chops are double, broil 4 minutes on one side after searing; turn and broil 3 minutes on the other side.

ROAST LAMB

5-pound leg of lamb	1 slivered clove garlic
Salt and pepper	Juice of 1 lemon
¼ cup butter	

Wash lamb and place in pan. Mix salt, pepper and slivers of garlic. Make holes in lamb with skewer, and into each hole put pinch of butter and seasoned slices of garlic. Sprinkle lamb with salt, pepper, lemon juice and remaining butter. Roast, uncovered, in a slow oven, 300 degrees, 2½ hours. Serves 8.

MINTED LAMB

1 boned leg of lamb	½ cup chopped mint leaves
2 tablespoons chopped celery	½ cup water
3 tablespoons minced onion	1 teaspoon salt
6 tablespoons butter	½ teaspoon pepper
2 cups bread crumbs	

Sauté celery and onion in butter, add mint and water, and simmer 5 minutes. Add seasonings and crumbs. Skewer lamb to form a pocket, sprinkle inside with salt and pepper, fill with stuffing, and sew opening. Roast in a very hot oven, 500 degrees, 15 minutes; then reduce heat to 250 degrees, and roast 2½ hours.

LAMB HASH

1 minced green pepper	½ cup chopped cooked
1 chopped onion	potatoes
1 tablespoon butter	3 chopped tomatoes
2 cups finely chopped cooked	1 cup stock
lamb	1 teaspoon salt

¼ teaspoon pepper

Sauté green pepper and onion in butter 5 minutes; then add remaining ingredients. Mix well, cover pan and bake in a moderate oven, 350 degrees, about 45 minutes. Serves 6.

LAMB STEW

Use either trimmed lamb chops, heavily cut, or shoulder cut by butcher into pieces, bone and all. Brown the meat in an iron pan, using chicken fat if possible. Put the meat in a kettle and add raw sliced onions, or small potatoes, carrots, green peas and sliced turnip. Season with salt and pepper, a little sage and a bay leaf. Add cold water to cover and cook slowly for about 3 hours. Follow directions for Irish stew. Pour onto a platter and serve with hot corn bread.

LAMB WITH PEAS AND TOMATO SAUCE

1 pound lamb	1 chopped onion
1 tablespoon butter	1 small can tomatoes

1 can peas

Cut lamb in small pieces and sauté in butter. When on verge of browning, add onion and cook well. Stir in tomatoes, allow the mixture to thicken, and then add peas. Serve with steamed rice. Serves 4.

BREADED LAMB CHOPS

Wipe and trim chops, sprinkle with salt and pepper, roll in flour; then dip in beaten egg and then in dry bread crumbs. Sauté in butter 4 minutes on each side.

BRAISED KIDNEYS

6 lamb kidneys	1 cup brown stock
3 tablespoons lemon juice	1 cup chopped sautéed
2 tablespoons butter	mushrooms
1 tablespoon flour	½ teaspoon salt
¼ teaspoon pepper	

Scald, skin and soak kidneys 30 minutes in cold water. Cut in small pieces and mix with lemon juice. Sauté kidneys in butter 5 minutes; then add flour, stock, mushrooms and seasonings. Cook 5 minutes. Serve on buttered toast.

RAGOUT OF KIDNEYS

6 lamb kidneys	¼ cup white wine
¼ cup butter	¼ cup sour cream
3 tablespoons flour	1 teaspoon salt
1 cup brown stock	¼ teaspoon pepper

Scald, skin and soak kidneys in cold water 30 minutes. Drain and slice thin. Stir flour into butter and brown slightly. Gradually add stock and cook 5 minutes, stirring until thickened. Add kidneys, wine, sour cream and seasonings. Cook 10 minutes.

BROILED LAMB KIDNEYS

Wash kidneys in cold water, remove the skin, and split in halves lengthwise. Brush each half with melted butter. Broil about 5 minutes on each side, or until brown. Place on buttered pieces of toast and serve with Maître d'Hôtel Butter, p. 205.

VEAL CUTLETS IN SOUR CREAM

Sprinkle veal cutlets with salt and pepper; then dip in flour. Sauté in butter until browned on both sides. Pour over meat enough sour cream almost to cover. Cover pan and let simmer 45 minutes. Add a few drops of Kitchen Bouquet. Serve gravy over meat.

BAKED VEAL CUTLET

Sauté 1 slice veal cutlet, 1 inch thick, in butter until brown; seasoning well. Place in buttered baking dish and cover with 1 can condensed mushroom soup. Bake in a moderate oven, 350 degrees, 40 minutes.

BAKED VEAL

Place a fat breast of veal in a baking pan with 1 quart of boiling
water. Cook ½ hour, pour off half the water and dredge with flour
and a little salt. Bake in a slow oven, 300 degrees, 1 hour, dredge
with flour and butter, and bake another ½ hour. Serve with a gravy
made by adding a little flour to the drippings.

VEAL DANDY

Season a pan with butter, salt, pepper and a little sage. Then place
in the pan strips of fat pork, then the veal. Add squares of thinly
cut dry bread, season again, use more strips of pork, and add
enough water to make 1 inch in the bottom of the pan. Bake in a
slow oven, 300 degrees, until tender. This veal will be rose color.

VEAL SAUTÉ

3 pounds veal shoulder	1 green pepper, cut in strips
½ cup salad oil	1 quart tomatoes
¼ pound sliced mushrooms	1½ tablespoons flour
1 minced clove garlic	1½ tablespoons cornstarch
¼ cup chopped celery	2 teaspoons salt
1 cup sliced and quartered onions	¼ teaspoon pepper

Cut veal in 1-inch cubes, season, place in roasting pan and pour
¼ cup salad oil over it. Bake in a moderate oven, 350 degrees, 1 hour.
Add 3 tablespoons water to free juices. Make a sauce by heating the
remaining oil in frying pan. Add mushrooms and garlic and sauté
5 minutes. Add celery and onions and sauté till tender. Add green
pepper and tomatoes. Blend flour and cornstarch with water to make
a paste, and add to sautéed vegetables with seasonings; cook 5
minutes. Add veal and juice to the sauce, bring to a boil and serve.
Serves 8.

VEAL CROQUETTES

2 cups chopped cooked veal	1 tablespoon chopped parsley
½ teaspoon salt	Yolk of 1 egg
⅛ teaspoon pepper	1 cup Thick White Sauce,
1 teaspoon chopped onion	p. 214

Mix ingredients, cool, shape into croquettes and crumb. Dip in beaten eggs and crumb again. Fry in deep hot fat, 390 degrees, until light brown. Drain on brown paper. Serve with Tomato Sauce, p. 213, or Mushroom Sauce, p. 210. Serves 6.

VEAL PIE

1 pound veal shoulder	1 celery stalk
¼ pound pork	Flour
1 bay leaf	2 eggs, well beaten
2 whole black peppercorns	2 tablespoons melted butter
1 teaspoon salt	3 tablespoons light cream
1 carrot	1 cup grated American cheese
1 onion	Plain Pastry, p. 294

Cut veal and pork into small pieces and put in a kettle. Add peppercorns, salt, carrot, onion and celery. Cover with water and simmer until tender. Remove meat, discard vegetables and thicken stock with 2 tablespoons flour to each cup of stock. Return meat to gravy, then pour all into partially baked pie shell and bake in hot oven until crust is done. Remove from oven and pour mixed eggs, butter, cream and cheese over the top. Return pie to slow oven, 300 degrees, and cook until top is browned. Serves 4.

VEAL STEW

1 pound veal shoulder	¼ cup chopped celery
2 tablespoons butter	2 chopped onions
2 cups hot water	½ teaspoon Worcestershire
½ cup each diced potatoes	sauce
and carrots	Salt and pepper
½ cup green peas	Grating of nutmeg
1 cup Tomato Sauce, p. 213	

Cut veal in 1-inch cubes, roll in flour and sauté in butter till brown. Add hot water and simmer 1 hour. Add vegetables, Worcestershire sauce and seasonings, and cook another 30 minutes. Stir in tomato sauce and bring to a boil. If desired, make Dumplings, p. 117, and drop by spoonful onto stew. Cover pan tightly and steam 10–15 minutes. Serves 4.

SWEETBREADS

Sweetbreads must first be parboiled. *To parboil:* first put sweetbreads under cold running water for 1 hour. Drain and put into boiling, salted water. Add 2 tablespoons lemon juice to each quart of water. Cook slowly 20 minutes. Drain, carefully pick out membranes, and place in cold water.

To broil, split in halves crosswise, and sprinkle with salt and pepper. Broil 10 minutes, turning to brown both sides. Serve with Lemon Butter, p. 205.

CREAMED SWEETBREADS AND MUSHROOMS

2 pairs Parboiled Sweetbreads (see above)	Dash of mace and nutmeg
1 can chopped pimentos	1 tablespoon flour
Juice of ½ lemon	2 tablespoons butter
1 cup light cream	2 egg yolks
1 cup veal stock	1 cup chopped sautéed
1 small onion	mushrooms

Cut sweetbreads into small pieces and add pimentos and lemon juice. Heat cream, stock, onion and spices in double boiler. When hot, stir in flour which has been mixed with the butter, and add beaten egg yolks. Stir until thick. Strain and add sweetbreads and mushrooms. Serve on buttered toast. Serves 6.

SWEETBREAD TIMBALES

½ pound sweetbreads	1¾ cups milk
4 eggs, beaten	1 teaspoon celery salt
½ teaspoon paprika	

Parboil sweetbreads (see above), chop fine and distribute evenly in 8 buttered custard cups. Combine remaining ingredients and pour over sweetbreads. Place cups in pan of hot water and bake in a moderate oven, 350 degrees, 25 minutes. Garnish with long slices of dill pickle.

BAKED CALF'S HEAD

Have butcher clean calf's head and remove eyes. Soak in cold water 1 hour to draw blood; then wash thoroughly. Place in a kettle of cold water and simmer until meat drops from bone. Cool, remove cheeks, tongue and brain, and chop fine. Moisten chopped meat with the liquor in which head was cooked. Add ½ teaspoon cloves, 1 teaspoon allspice, and ½ cup sherry. Pack in baking dish, scatter with bread crumbs and bake until crumbs brown. Serve with slices of lemon.

CREAMED CALF'S BRAINS

Parboil brains, remove all bits of skin and cool in bowl of cold water. Cut in small cubes and add to Thin White Sauce, p. 214. Stir until well heated; then add beaten yolk of 1 egg and 2 tablespoons sherry. Cook 1 minute longer. Serve on buttered toast.

BROILED VEAL KIDNEYS

Pare fat from kidneys, leaving about ½ inch. Split, and spread each half ¼ inch thick with prepared mustard. Broil 10 minutes or until thoroughly done. Serve with wild rice.

ROAST SUCKLING PIG

Wash a 10- to 12-pound suckling pig inside and out with water, and dry thoroughly. Fill inside with any desired stuffing. Sew up vent securely. Skewer forelegs forward and hind legs backward. Place a small block of wood in pig's mouth to keep it open. Place in roasting pan, brush with melted butter and sprinkle with salt and pepper. Put 1½ cups boiling water mixed with ¼ cup melted butter in bottom of pan. Cover and roast in a moderately hot oven, 375 degrees, about 4 hours, basting with the drippings every 15 minutes. Place pig on hot platter, garnish with fresh watercress, and remove piece of wood from mouth and replace with small red apple. Put cranberries in eye sockets.

GEORGE RECTOR'S SAUCE FOR ROAST PIG

Pour ½ cup tarragon vinegar into a saucepan, and add 2 mashed cloves of garlic, 1 tablespoon dry mustard, 1 bay leaf, 12 whole black peppercorns, 1 teaspoon paprika, ½ teaspoon salt and ½ teaspoon cayenne. Simmer down to half the quantity and strain. Heat 2 small cans condensed tomato soup and add strained spice mixture. Cook a few minutes, then add 1 tablespoon beef extract dissolved in ⅓ cup of boiling water, 1 teaspoon Worcestershire sauce, 3 tablespoons A-1 sauce, and 2 tablespoons butter. Serve hot.

ROAST PORK LOIN

Wipe meat with damp cloth, season well with salt and pepper. Dredge with flour and place in roasting pan in a hot oven, 500 degrees, for 15 minutes; then reduce heat to slow, 325 degrees, and cook 50 minutes to the pound. Add 1 cup hot water after the first hour, and baste frequently. Serve with brown gravy made from drippings in the pan, to which lemon juice has been liberally added.

PORK CHOPS (1)

Place thick loin chops in baking dish and season with salt and pepper. Cover with slices of tomato, chopped green pepper and chopped onion. Bake in a moderate oven, 350 degrees, until tender. Remove chops to hot platter, thicken sauce in baking dish, add juice of one lemon and pour around chops. Serve with rice.

PORK CHOPS (2)

2 pork chops	2 teaspoons paprika
1 pound sauerkraut	½ cup canned tomatoes

Sear chops in frying pan. Place remaining ingredients on them and cook slowly, covered, 30 minutes.

PORK CHOP CASSEROLE

Slice and parboil 4 potatoes. Brown 2 pork chops and 2 sliced onions in fat. Place chops in bottom of a casserole and arrange potatoes and onions in layers. Pour on milk to cover. Bake in a moderate oven, 350 degrees, 1 hour. Serves 2.

DICED PORK

4 sliced potatoes	2 tablespoons butter
1 teaspoon salt	2 cups hot milk
¼ teaspoon pepper	2 sliced tomatoes
¼ cup flour	¼ cup sifted, dried bread
½ pound diced cooked pork	crumbs
4 sliced onions	

Arrange half the potatoes in a greased casserole. Sprinkle with half the salt, pepper and flour. Dot with 1 tablespoon butter. Cover with half the cooked pork and half the onions. Repeat the layers of potatoes, seasonings, flour, butter, pork and onions. Pour hot milk over all the ingredients. Place sliced tomatoes on top and cover with crumbs. Dot with remaining butter. Bake in a moderate oven, 350 degrees, for 1½ hours.

PORK AND PARSNIP STEW

Cover a fresh pig's knuckle or lean pork with water, and when nearly done put in diced parsnips, diced potatoes, salt and pepper. When vegetables are tender, stir in enough flour to thicken. Serve hot.

BAKED HAM (1)

Place a boiled ham in a roasting pan. Make gashes across the surface of the ham and stick in whole cloves ½ inch apart. Make a paste of 1 cup brown sugar, 2 tablespoons flour, 1 teaspoon dry mustard, ¼ cup maple syrup and 3 tablespoons water. Pour this over the ham and bake, uncovered, in a hot oven, 400 degrees, 45 minutes.

BAKED HAM (2)

Place a 10-pound ham on the rack of a self-roasting pan, add water until it nearly reaches the rack. Cover pan and cook in a 350-degree oven 2 hours. Add more water if necessary.

Cool ham; then remove skin, stick in 1 teaspoon whole cloves, brush on cider vinegar and cover with 1 cup brown sugar or honey. Bake 2 hours in a 300-degree oven, basting every ½ hour with cider vinegar to which brown sugar has been added.

BAKED SLICED HAM (1)

Trim fat from a slice of ham, 1 inch thick, and place in baking pan. Put fat through meat chopper, mix with 6 tablespoons brown sugar, and sprinkle over ham. Stick with cloves. Put just enough water in the bottom of pan to keep from burning, and bake in a moderate oven, 350 degrees, 1 hour.

BAKED SLICED HAM (2)

Cut and trim a slice of ham, 1½ inches thick. Cover surface with light brown sugar and ¼ teaspoon dry mustard. Fill the baking dish with milk almost to cover the meat. Cover and bake in a moderate oven, 350 degrees, about 1½ hours.

BAKED SLICED HAM (3)

Slice of ham, 1½ inches thick	6 strips orange peel
1 tablespoon butter	1 cup water
1 chopped onion	½ cup orange juice
2 tablespoons raisins	1 tablespoon flour

Sear ham on both sides in butter. Add onion, raisins, orange peel and water. Cover and simmer 1½ hours. Make a paste of the flour and orange juice, pour over ham, and cook 5 minutes, stirring until liquid thickens. Serves 6.

HAM À LA KING

¼ cup butter	3 cups cooked diced ham
2 tablespoons chopped green pepper	2 diced hard-boiled eggs
2 tablespoons chopped onion	1 teaspoon dry mustard
½ cup sliced mushrooms	1 tablespoon chopped pimento
¼ cup flour	1 tablespoon chopped parsley
1 quart milk	

Melt butter and in it sauté green pepper, onion and mushrooms until onion is tender. Sprinkle with flour and stir in milk gradually. When thickened, add ham, eggs, dry mustard and pimento. Cook until thoroughly heated. Garnish with parsley and serve on rounds of buttered toast. Serves 8.

HAM AND VEAL LOAF

2½ pounds ground veal
½ pound ground smoked
    ham
1 cup cracker crumbs
1 cup milk
1 minced onion

4 tablespoons ketchup
4 tablespoons minced green
    pepper
1 teaspoon salt
¼ teaspoon pepper
1 cup mushrooms

1 egg

Mix ingredients, pour into a baking dish, cover with 2 slices of bacon, and bake in a moderate oven, 350 degrees, 1½ hours. Serve with Tomato Sauce, p. 213. Serves 8.

HAM LOAF WITH PICKLE

6 common crackers, pounded
    and rolled to fine crumbs
2 cups scalded milk
2 eggs, well beaten
1 pound finely chopped ham
1 pound finely chopped pork

½ teaspoon celery salt
½ teaspoon white pepper
¼ teaspoon sage
4 finely chopped dill pickles
3 finely chopped sweet
    peppers

1 cup sherry

Mix milk and cracker crumbs; then add ham, pork, eggs, salt, pepper and sage and stir thoroughly. Into a buttered bread pan pour the pickles, peppers and sherry. On top of this put the meat mixture. Bake in moderate oven, 350 degrees, 45 minutes. Chill, invert on platter and serve cold with hot Tomato Sauce, p. 213. Serves 8.

HAM CROQUETTES

5 tablespoons melted butter
2 heaping tablespoons corn-
    starch
½ teaspoon salt

Dash of pepper and celery
    salt
2 cups scalded milk
4 cups finely chopped ham

Add cornstarch and seasonings to butter; gradually add scalded milk and boil 2 minutes, stirring constantly. Add ham and let cool. Shape, roll in sifted bread crumbs, dip in beaten egg and roll in crumbs again. Fry in deep hot fat, 390 degrees. Serve with Tomato Sauce, p. 213. Serves 8.

HOT HAM MOUSSE

2 cups finely ground cooked   Few gratings nutmeg
      ham   1 cup heavy cream, or
2 eggs, separated   Thick Cream Sauce,
⅛ teaspoon pepper   p. 215
                    ¼ cup sherry

Press ham through a sieve; add egg yolks, seasonings, cream and
sherry, and lastly stiffly beaten egg whites. Pour into a buttered mold
or baking dish, and set in a pan containing hot water. Bake in a
moderately slow oven, 325 degrees, until mousse is firm (about 35
minutes). Unmold on a hot platter, garnish with watercress, and
serve with Hollandaise Sauce, p. 209, or Tomato Sauce, p. 213.
Serves 8.

COLD HAM MOUSSE

1 tablespoon gelatin   1 teaspoon celery salt
¼ cup cold water   2 teaspoons dry mustard
1 cup boiling water   2 cups finely ground cooked
2 beef bouillon cubes   ham
1 tablespoon Worcestershire   ¼ cup chopped olives
      sauce   ½ cup mayonnaise
                  1 minced onion

Soak the gelatin in cold water, then add to boiling water with meat
cubes, Worcestershire sauce, celery salt and mustard. Combine ham,
olives, mayonnaise and onion, then add hot gelatin mixture. Stir
well, pour into mold and chill in refrigerator. No cooking required.
Serve with Béchamel Sauce, p. 203, or Tomato Sauce, p. 213. Serves
8. Or use as deviled ham in sandwiches or on canapés.

HAM LOAF

2 pounds ground smoked ham   ½ cup condensed tomato soup
½ pound ground fresh pork   1 egg
1 cup bread crumbs   ⅛ teaspoon pepper

Mix ingredients together, form into a loaf and arrange in a pan.
Pour tomato soup over the loaf and sprinkle with ¾ cup bread
crumbs. Bake in a moderately hot oven, 375 degrees, 1 hour. Serve
with Cider Sauce, p. 208. Serves 8.

HAM WITH MAPLE SYRUP SAUCE

Place a slice of ham ¾ inch thick in a baking pan and cover with a sauce made by stirring together 2 tablespoons vinegar, 2 teaspoons dry mustard and ¾ cup maple syrup. Cover and bake in moderate oven, 350 degrees, 45 minutes.

BOILED HAM

Scrub ham with a stiff brush, place in a kettle with boiling water and let simmer 25 minutes per pound. Cool in water in which it was cooked, and remove the fatty rind.

FRANKFURTER SCRAMBLE

6 sliced frankfurters	6 eggs, beaten
¼ cup butter	½ teaspoon salt
3 cups cooked rice	¼ teaspoon pepper

Brown frankfurters in melted butter, then add remaining ingredients. Cook slowly, stirring constantly, until eggs are set. Serve with Tomato Sauce, p. 213. Serves 6.

FRIED SALT PORK

1 pound salt pork	¼ cup flour
Boiling water	2 tablespoons salt pork
½ cup corn meal	drippings
3 tablespoons lard	2 cups milk

Slice salt pork ¼ inch thick. Pour boiling water over slices and drain. Dip slices in corn meal and fry slowly in hot lard until golden brown. Make a gravy by adding flour and milk to salt pork drippings. Serves 6.

PORK SAUSAGES

Cut apart. Prick deeply and put in a cold, ungreased frying pan over low heat. Put a lid over three quarters of the pan. Cook slowly until one side is brown; then turn and brown the other. Partially covered, the steam keeps them moist. Remove and drain on brown paper. Serve with Tomato Sauce, p. 213, and mashed potatoes.

SAUSAGE

For 20 pounds of meat, mix together 2 parts lean, 1 part fat, 7 table-spoons salt, 3¼ tablespoons black pepper, 2½ teaspoons sage, ¼ teaspoon savory and ½ teaspoon sweet basil.

SAUSAGE MEAT

Nine pounds of fresh pork, using the trimmings, 1 cup salt, 2 table-spoons pepper, 2 tablespoons sage, and 1 teaspoon red pepper. Put meat through chopper and mix with seasoning. Pack close into cotton bags 3 inches wide and 12 inches long. Keep in cool place. To cook, turn back end of bag, cut in ½-inch slices and brown in frying pan. They will keep weeks in winter.

SAUSAGE ROLLS

1 pound Penley little link sausages	¼ teaspoon salt
	½ cup butter
¼ cup cornstarch	½ teaspoon lemon juice
¾ cup flour	1 teaspoon baking powder

Prick sausages with a fork and boil 5 minutes. Mix and sift flour, cornstarch and salt. Rub in butter and make a stiff paste with water and lemon juice. Roll out evenly; fold in three. Repeat process 3 times, each time sprinkling over it ⅓ of baking powder. On last rolling make it ⅛ inch thick, cut in 4-inch squares, wet edges, put cooked sausage in center, roll paste around it, pressing together at ends and top. Brush with egg and bake in hot oven, 450 degrees, until delicately brown. Serve with Tomato Sauce, p. 213.

SCRAPPLE (1)

Make a corn-meal mush, and to each cup of corn meal used add 2 cups of fresh pork, cut in small pieces. Cook pork with mush and season highly with salt, pepper, powdered herbs and sage. When thick, pour into buttered loaf pan and cover to prevent crust form-ing. When cold, slice ¼ inch thick and sauté in bacon fat or butter until browned on both sides. Serve with Tomato Sauce, p. 213.

SCRAPPLE (2)

Use pig's head and liver and all available lean scraps of pork. Boil until meat falls from bones; then remove meat from liquor, remove all bone and gristle, and chop fine. Put all back into the kettle in the liquor and season well with salt and pepper; let boil again. When boiling, thicken with corn meal, as you would when making ordinary corn-meal mush, by passing it slowly through the fingers to prevent lumping. Cook 1 hour, stirring constantly at first. When done pour into pans. After it is cold it can be sliced and fried brown. In cold weather scrapple will keep two months.

HEADCHEESE

Have butcher scrape and clean 1 hog's head, remove eyes and brain, scrape ears, scrub tongue, and rinse well. Cover with cold, salted water, add an onion and mixed herbs, and bring slowly to a boil. Simmer until meat is tender, 2 to 3 hours. Cool in stock. Place meat in a colander to drain, remove bones. Cut ears and tongue in thin slices. Season meat to taste with salt, pepper, sage, cloves and allspice. Add ½ cup vinegar, mix well and pack in molds. Cover with plate and place heavy weight on top. The headcheese will be ready to use in two or three days. Cut in thin slices and serve with Tomato Sauce, p. 213, or dip in egg and cracker crumbs and fry.

BAKED SPARERIBS AND SAUERKRAUT

Wipe spareribs, sprinkle with salt and pepper and place in a roasting pan. Add sauerkraut, cover pan and bake in a moderate oven, 350 degrees, 1½ hours. Serve with mashed potatoes.

BOILED PIGS' FEET

Wash, scrape and rinse pigs' feet; then put in a pan with ½ sliced onion, 1 bay leaf and ½ teaspoon salt. Cover with cold water and simmer 4 to 6 hours. Store in stock until used. Serve cold or hot with vinegar; sauerkraut and mashed potatoes on the side. One pig's foot serves one person.

JELLIED PIGS' FEET

2 pigs' feet, split in half	2 bay leaves
Salt and pepper	¾ teaspoon peppercorns
½ onion	8 whole allspice

Put pigs' feet in kettle and cover with water. Add remaining ingredients and simmer till meat begins to fall from bones, about 4 hours. Remove meat from broth and remove bones. Put meat in loaf pan and strain broth over it. Chill in refrigerator. Unmold, garnish with slices of lemon and use vinegar as a sauce. Serves 2.

PICKLED PIGS' FEET

Pour hot vinegar over Boiled Pigs' Feet, p. 151, and leave them in the liquid several days. Serve cold.

BROILED PIGS' FEET

Sprinkle Boiled Pigs' Feet, p. 151, with salt and pepper, place on a greased broiler and broil about 5 minutes on each side. Serve with vinegar, lemon juice or Maître d'Hôtel Butter, p. 205.

FRIED PIGS' FEET

Dip Boiled Pigs' Feet (see p. 151) into a batter of flour, salt and water. Fry in deep hot fat, 390 degrees, until brown. Serve with Maître d'Hôtel Butter, p. 205, or Mustard Sauce, p. 211.

VEGETABLES

MAXIMS FROM MAINE KITCHENS

Young turnips should be boiled with the skins on, and peeled after cooking.

❦

Never cover the following vegetables when cooking: Dandelion, spinach, green peas, cauliflower, cabbage, brussels sprouts.

❦

To bake potatoes quickly, put them first in boiling salted water for ten minutes; then take out and put in oven.

❦

Butter potatoes when putting them into the oven to bake. They will look more appetizing, and skins won't thicken.

❦

To remove odor from frying pan after frying onions, pour a little vinegar in the pan and let it heat.

❦

When boiling sweet corn, add a tablespoon of vinegar. This makes it whiter and tenderer.

VEGETABLES

<hr>

FIDDLEHEADS

MR. WINGATE CRAM, president of the Bangor & Aroostook Railroad, repeatedly insisted to Mr. Roberts that fiddlehead greens have long been one of the best-known foods in northern Maine, but are never found in any cookbook anywhere.

"The fiddlehead," wrote Mr. Cram in one of his letters, "is the soft budding stem of a kind of fern or brake that grows on the shores of streams, usually much below high-water mark. It is gathered in great quantities, particularly by the Indians on the Tobique. When I was a lad you had to pick it yourself or know someone that would share his. Now it is a common article of commerce in the spring at any of the stores in Aroostook. My barber tells me it is known as far south as Unity, Maine,—you may have it down your way, but I never heard of it south of Bangor.

"Strangely enough it has eluded the books (its edible quality, I mean). An encyclopedia of my father's (around 1875) says there is 'a highly edible' form of 'bracken.'

"You take the things when the frond is young and tender (and how!) and shaped like a fiddle-head, i.e., before it has unfurled, and it is covered with brown bitter pollen. When you wash the pollen off very very carefully and cook the fronds as you would broccoli, you have something that some serve as greens and others with bordelaise sauce, like asparagus. It is far above broccoli and closely approaches asparagus.

"I've been trying to find what it is. The University of Maine sends word that there are several varieties but that I mean *Osmunda cinnamomea*. This must come from their second-sight department.

"The only trouble is that fiddleheads retain their lusciousness for only a day or so after plucking, and the season is short. The good ladies of Aroostook 'put them down' (technical term for putting

FIDDLEHEADS

OSTRICH FERN

CROSS SECTION OF STEM

BRAKE FERN OR BRACKEN

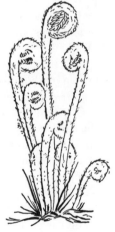

CINNAMON FERN

CROSS SECTION OF STEM

them up) in jars, vying with one another and exhibiting the bottled product at fairs."

☙

Stirred by Mr. Cram's letters, Mr. Roberts opened a fiddlehead correspondence with Professor F. H. Steinmetz of the University of Maine and Mr. Edward D. Johnson, Assistant State Horticulturist, in order to clear up the light fog in which the fiddlehead situation seemed to be shrouded. The results were as follows.

☙

Three types of fern, all known as fiddleheads because their tips, when young, are curled like the head of a violin, are picked and eaten in great quantities in Maine.

In Aroostook the liking for fiddleheads is so well developed that each May sees a heavy traffic in them. They are shipped to Faneuil Hall Market in Boston, sold in grocery stores in Aroostook County, preserved in mason jars and cans by countless Aroostook housewives and, just across the border, canned commercially. Canned fiddlehead greens, in 1939, sold in eastern Canada for $3.60 a case of 24 cans.[1]

The most popular of the fiddlehead ferns is the Ostrich Fern, known to botanists as *Pteretis nodulosa*. Gray's Manual calls it *Onoclea struthiopteris*.

Ostrich Ferns grow in clumps on low lands that are flooded in the early spring. As the waters go down, the ferns come up, and all Aroostook County goes out picking them. On each curled frond is a sort of brown scale, resembling loosely attached bits of brownish cellophane, which is easily removed by wiping or washing, or by soaking in water and then wiping. The inner side of the stem of the Ostrich Fern is deeply grooved, so that the curved tip, lying in the groove, is protected from the brown scale.

Aroostook residents usually break off and use the curled tip of the fern shoot and from ½ to 2 inches of the stalk below it.

Fiddleheads are eaten or preserved as soon as possible after picking—always within 2 days. For canning purposes they are cooked

---

[1] Canned fiddleheads may be obtained from Devon Community Cannery, South Devon, N.B.; Maritime Coöperative Egg & Poultry Exchange, St. John, N.B.; and Mrs. Gordon Boyd, R.R. No. 6, Fredericton, N.B.—K.R.

10 minutes in boiling, salted water; and when they are taken from the can they are simmered from 5 to 10 minutes in salted water.

Freshly picked fiddleheads of this variety have a delicate and pleasing flavor, like a faint blend of asparagus and mushrooms.

When cooked for the table, fiddleheads are boiled 20 minutes in lightly salted water. They are served on toast like asparagus, and over them is poured melted butter diluted with some of the water in which they were boiled.

Fiddlehead salad is made by chilling cooked fiddleheads, putting them in a bowl with large quantities of sliced onion, and covering them liberally with olive oil, lemon juice and salt.

Almost exactly like the Ostrich Fern or true fiddlehead, except that its stem is ungrooved on the inner side, is the Cinnamon Fern, known to botanists as *Osmunda cinnamomea*. The Cinnamon Ferns come up in clumps, just as do Ostrich Ferns, and their tips are curled in the same way. Instead of having a covering of brown scales, they are covered with a grayish-yellow wool. When the ferns are about 8 inches tall, this woolly covering splits and loosens from the fern stalks. At their most edible period, the yellowish fuzz may be removed from the stalks with comparative ease, but is almost inextricably fastened into the curled tips.

Cinnamon Ferns are prepared for cooking by soaking; then by rubbing with a cloth. They are cooked from ½ to ¾ of an hour in boiling water, and the water is salted just before the ferns are taken from the water. If the fuzz refuses to disentangle itself readily from the curled ends, the ends are thrown away and only the stalks eaten.

The third type of edible fern in Maine is the Brake Fern or Bracken. Botanists call it *Pteridium latiusculum*. Gray's Manual calls it *Pteris aquilina*.

Brake Ferns grow on higher land than either Ostrich or Cinnamon Ferns, and instead of coming up in clumps, like the other two, they come up in single green stalks, covered with a delicate silvery bloom which must be removed before cooking. They usually appear a week or two after the Cinnamon Fern. They are picked just before the three leaves at the tip begin to unfold, which means that they are picked when they are from 4 to 8 inches tall. They are prepared for cooking by removing the bent leafy ends and the tough bases. The gray bloom is then rubbed from the stalks, and the stalks broken into 2-inch lengths. These are cooked ½ hour in boiling salted water. They are served either hot with butter or cold in a salad.

ARTICHOKES

Cut off stem close to leaves, remove outside bottom leaves, trim artichoke, cut 1 inch from top of leaves, pry open leaves in middle and remove furry substance (the choke) between lower end of leaves and meaty base. Tie artichoke with a string to keep it in shape; then soak ½ hour in cold water. Drain, and cook 30 minutes in boiling salted water with a little lemon juice. Remove from water, place upside down to drain, take off string, and serve with melted butter, Hollandaise Sauce, p. 209, or Béarnaise Sauce, p. 204. The edible portions of an artichoke are the meaty leaf-bottoms, which are pulled off one by one, dipped in the sauce and scraped between the teeth until the marrow-like base is reached. This is the "heart" —the best part—of the artichoke.

BREADED ARTICHOKE BOTTOMS

Dry canned artichoke bottoms with a soft cloth. Beat together 1 egg and 2 tablespoons of milk; dip bottoms one by one into egg mixture; then into sifted bread crumbs. Fry in deep fat until amber color. Drain and serve with Tartare Sauce, p. 213.

ASPARAGUS MOLD

3 tablespoons butter	¼ teaspoon pepper
3 tablespoons flour	1 cup diced cooked chicken
2 cups milk	4 eggs, beaten
½ teaspoon salt	1 cup fresh or frozen
	asparagus tips

Melt butter in top of double boiler, add flour and gradually stir in milk. Add seasonings, chicken and beaten eggs. Parboil asparagus tips 5 minutes; then line a buttered mold with the tips. Pour in the chicken mixture. Set mold in a pan of hot water and bake in a moderately slow oven, 325 degrees, 30 to 40 minutes. Serve with Hollandaise Sauce, p. 209. Serves 6.

ASPARAGUS

Cut off lower parts of stalks, wash, and tie in bundles. Boil 10 to 20 minutes standing in kettle half filled with boiling salted water. Then the entire stalk will be edible. Length of boiling depends on whether asparagus has just come from the garden or was shipped several thousand miles a week ago. Drain, untie string and serve on toast that has been well moistened by dipping edges in water in which asparagus was cooked. Over all pour butter diluted half and half with asparagus water. Never try to cook asparagus in a pressure cooker. The taste and texture are ruined by so doing.

KENNEBUNKPORT BEANS

3- by 5-inch piece salt pork	1 cup grated American
1 pound beef, cubed	cheese or crumbled
1 chopped clove garlic	Roquefort cheese
1 can yellow-eye, kidney or	1 large can Italian tomatoes
any other sort of beans	1 tablespoon celery salt
½ cup chopped stuffed	1 teaspoon dry mustard
olives	1 tablespoon chili powder
1 small bottle pimentos	1 tablespoon soybean sauce

Sauté pork, beef and garlic for 5 minutes, then put in bean pot. Over them pour beans, olives, pimento, onion and cheese. Mix well. Heat tomatoes with salt, mustard, chili powder and soybean sauce, then pour into bean pot. Cover pot and cook in a slow oven, 250 degrees, for 2 hours. Serve with hot buttered toast.

BEANS BAKED IN BEAN HOLE

Put 4 quarts of dry beans in a 4-gallon iron pot, cover with water, hang over a fire and boil 5 minutes, stirring constantly. Remove from fire, add 3 pounds of pork, 1 cup molasses, pinch of mustard and handful of salt. Cover with closely fitting sheet-iron cover. In dry ground, preferably gravel, dig a hole 2 feet deep and 2 feet across and in it build a brisk hardwood fire. When the fire has burned to coals, take out a part of the coals with a shovel, place iron pot in the hole, and cover with the coals shoveled out. On top of the coals place the gravel originally taken from hole. Leave the pot in the hole all day.

BAKED BEANS

1 quart pea, yellow-eye, kidney, wax or any other sort of dried beans
1 pound salt pork

1 onion
3 tablespoons molasses
2 tablespoons celery salt
1 teaspoon dry mustard
1 teaspoon pepper

Soak beans in cold water overnight; then parboil them for ½ hour, or till skin cracks when blown upon. Put onion in pot, then part of beans, pork near top, more beans, molasses, salt, mustard and pepper. Cover with boiling water and bake all day (10 hours) in extremely slow oven.

At end of the first hour and every little while thereafter add boiling water to replace that which has boiled away. The most important trick in bean baking is to keep the water level constant by adding only a little boiling water, and often. If the water is allowed to boil far down, so that a lot must be poured in, the beans will be greasy. An hour before supper remove cover to let salt pork brown. Add no more water. Serves 8–10.

BEANS AND SPARERIBS

In place of the conventional pork in baked beans, State-of-Mainers frequently place 6 spareribs of pork in the bottom of the bean pot.

CANNED BAKED BEANS

3 cans oven-baked beans
1 tablespoon dry mustard
3 tablespoons molasses
⅛ cup brandy
1 teaspoon salt

Dash of pepper
1 grated onion
Grated rind of ½ lemon
1 or 2 cups boiling water
½ pound salt pork

Put beans in bean pot. Make a sauce of remaining ingredients except salt pork and pour sauce over beans. Boil beforehand salt pork, partly sliced down to rind. When beans are ready, lift pork carefully and set in top of beans, skin side up. Bake 1 to 2 hours in slow oven, 250 degrees, leaving top off bean pot. Enough water should be added to beans before baking so that they will remain thoroughly moist beneath the exposed top.

CORN–BREADED BEANS

Soak 1 cup of any sort of beans overnight. On the following morning boil them 1½ hours.

Brown ½ pound hamburger and ½ pound bagged sausage in a frying pan; then stir in ¼ cup flour and 1 tablespoon celery salt. Add the beans and spread in the bottom of a small cake tin. Over the top of the meat and beans sprinkle 1 tablespoon minced onion. To the Corn Cake mixture, p. 275, add 2 teaspoons Hungarian rose paprika; then pour it over the meat and beans, spread evenly and bake in a 400-degree oven 30 minutes.

Turn out on a plate, corn bread on the bottom, and serve with Tomato Sauce, p. 213.

BEANS AND COOT

Coot is also cooked with baked beans. In such a case salt pork is used. The breasts are removed from 6 coot; and when the beans are put to soak, the coot breasts are placed in a bowl and ¼ cup lemon juice or lime juice poured over them.

In the morning the coot breasts are put at the bottom of the bean pot, with the pork, and covered with beans.

WHITE BEANS
(French Canadian)

1 pint beans	1 chopped onion
1 quart water	2 chopped cloves garlic
1 cup chicken bouillon	½ pound salt pork
1 cup tomato purée, paste or soup	1 tablespoon salt
	1 teaspoon white pepper

Soak beans in cold water to cover overnight. Drain, add fresh water and parboil till soft. Put beans in casserole and cover with the quart of water and remaining ingredients. Cook in a slow oven, 250 degrees, 2 hours. These may be used as a basis for daily soups, mixing them with rice, macaroni and any leftovers in the refrigerator. Serves 8.

DRIED LIMA BEANS

2 cups dried lima beans
1 sliced onion
3 tablespoons butter

1 ½ teaspoons prepared mustard
Salt and pepper

1 can condensed tomato soup

Soak beans overnight in cold water to cover; then cook in the same water until soft. Drain, reserving liquor. Put beans in a buttered baking dish. Sauté onion in butter until brown, then add to the beans with the remaining ingredients. Cover halfway up the dish with bean liquor. Bake in a moderately slow oven, 325 degrees, 1 ½ hours. Serves 4.

BOILED LIMA BEANS

Shell beans and soak them in cold water 10 minutes. Cook, uncovered, in boiling salted water 1 hour, or until tender. Drain and season with salt, pepper and butter.

BOILED STRING BEANS

Break off both ends, removing strings from both sides. Wash in cold water and drain. Cut lengthwise in thin slices. Cook in boiling salted water, uncovered, 20 minutes, or until tender. Drain and season with salt and butter. Small pieces of ham, bacon or salt pork, cooked with the beans, improve their flavor. One pound serves 4.

FRENCH BEANS, À LA MAÎTRE D'HÔTEL

Prepare 1 pound Boiled String Beans. Drain thoroughly and reheat in ¼ cup melted butter, 1 teaspoon chopped parsley, 1 teaspoon lemon juice and ½ teaspoon salt. Shake pan over fire and cook 5 minutes. Serves 4.

STRING BEANS AU GRATIN

Prepare 1 pound Boiled String Beans. Sauté 1 teaspoon minced onion and 1 cup diced celery in ¼ cup butter until soft, then add to hot beans. Season with salt and sprinkle ¼ cup grated cheese over top. Serves 4.

BOILED BEETS

Cut off tops and soak beets several minutes in cold water. Wash well. Cook young beets, covered, in boiling salted water 30 to 50 minutes, older beets 1 to 2 hours. If the beet is wilted or tough, no amount of cooking will make it tender. Drain, plunge in cold water and rub off skins. Serve whole, sliced or diced, seasoned with salt, pepper and butter. One pound serves 4.

HARVARD BEETS

2 cups diced boiled beets	¼ cup vinegar
⅓ cup sugar	¼ cup water
1 tablespoon cornstarch	½ teaspoon salt
2 tablespoons melted butter	

Mix cornstarch and sugar, add the water, vinegar and salt, and bring to a boil, stirring until thick and smooth. Add beets, and cook over slow fire 15 minutes. When ready to serve, add butter and bring to a boil. Serves 4.

SHARP BEETS

12 small beets	¼ cup vinegar
¼ cup butter	¼ cup heavy cream
¼ cup flour	2 teaspoons salt
1 cup hot water	¼ teaspoon dry mustard

Scrub and boil beets till done. Peel and slice. Melt butter, stir in flour, add hot water and stir smooth. Add vinegar, cream and seasonings; pour over beets and serve. Serves 4.

BEET GREENS

Cook the same as Spinach, p. 182.

BROCCOLI

Remove tough stems and coarse leaves. If stems are large, split into pieces for serving. Cook, uncovered, in boiling salted water until tender (15 to 30 minutes). Drain, and season with butter, salt and pepper. Serve with plenty of Hollandaise Sauce, p. 209. One pound serves 4.

BRUSSELS SPROUTS

Remove wilted leaves and soak ½ hour in cold salted water. Drain and cook, uncovered, in boiling salted water until tender (15 to 20 minutes). Drain, and serve with melted butter or Hollandaise Sauce, p. 209.

CABBAGE

Remove outer leaves, cut in thin slices and quarter the slices. Cook, uncovered, in boiling salted water 10 minutes, or until tender. Do not overcook. Drain, season and serve as desired.

CREAMED CABBAGE

Reheat chopped boiled cabbage in cream.

STEWED RED CABBAGE

1 small head shredded **red** cabbage	1 cup cold gravy
	¼ teaspoon pepper
1 sliced onion	1 teaspoon salt
1 tablespoon butter	¼ cup vinegar

Brown onion slightly in butter and then add remaining ingredients. Cover and cook slowly 1 hour, or until cabbage is tender. Stir occasionally, and serve hot. Serves 6.

HOT SLAW

1 small head cabbage	1 tablespoon butter
½ cup vinegar	1 teaspoon dry mustard
1 egg yolk, beaten	1 teaspoon flour
½ cup heavy cream	

Chop cabbage fine. Cover with boiling water and a little salt, and let stand a few minutes. Heat vinegar, butter, mustard and flour in double boiler until mixture thickens, then add cream. Pour hot dressing over the cabbage. Serves 6.

COLE SLAW

Shred or chop cabbage and soak it in cold water 1 hour. Drain and dry it between towels and chill. Just before serving marinate it in French Dressing, p. 190, Boiled Dressing, p. 197, or heavy cream.

SAUERKRAUT

Shred cabbage, pack lightly in quart jars, add 1 teaspoon sugar and 1 teaspoon salt to each jar, and fill slowly with boiling water. Then add a little dill, seal tightly, and in six weeks the kraut will be ready to use.

When serving, rinse the kraut, put in a saucepan with cold water and cook until soft. Add a grated raw potato for thickening. Cut 4 slices of bacon in small pieces, fry, and add to kraut. Serve with pork chops, sausage, spareribs or a chicken dinner.

CANNED SAUERKRAUT

1 large can sauerkraut	½ teaspoon salt
1 medium-sized potato	Dash of pepper
4 tablespoons pork drippings	

Wash sauerkraut in cold water; then cover with fresh water and cook 2½ hours over a low flame. Grate in potato and cook ½ hour longer. Add seasonings and pork drippings. Serve with roast pork.

CARROTS

Cut off tops, wash and scrape. Cook whole or sliced, covered, in boiling salted water: 15 to 20 minutes for young carrots, 30 to 50 minutes for winter carrots. Drain, season and serve as desired. One pound serves 4.

CARROTS AND ONIONS

Cut raw carrots in small slices and sauté a little in butter; then add sliced onions and sauté until brown.

BAKED CARROTS

2 cups thinly sliced carrots	⅛ teaspoon pepper
½ teaspoon salt	2 tablespoons butter
1 cup light cream	

Wash, scrape and cut carrots. Arrange in baking dish, sprinkle with salt and pepper, dot with butter and add cream. Bake, covered, in moderate oven, 350 degrees, until carrots are tender. Serves 4.

BOILED CAULIFLOWER

Remove the leaves and stalk. Soak, head down, in cold salted water 20 minutes. Drain. Cook, head up, in boiling salted water 20 minutes, or until soft. Drain, serve whole, or separate into flowerets. Pour over either melted butter or Cream Sauce, p. 215.

CAULIFLOWER AU GRATIN

Separate a boiled cauliflower into flowerets and put a layer in the bottom of a buttered baking dish. Then add a layer of Medium White Sauce, p. 214, and grated cheese; alternate layers of cauliflower, sauce and cheese until cauliflower is used, having last layer sauce. Cover with buttered crumbs and bake.

CAULIFLOWER CASSEROLE

2 cans tomatoes	¼ cup flour
2 tablespoons sugar	4 cups sliced onions
4 teaspoons salt	⅓ cup butter
1 small head cauliflower	

Drain tomatoes, add sugar, salt and flour, place alternate layers of tomatoes and onions in buttered casserole. Dot with butter. Remove tough stem from cauliflower, leaving just enough to hold head together. Parboil head a few minutes, then drain and place on top of casserole, pressing it into tomatoes and onions and allowing just the top to protrude. Cover and bake in a moderate oven, 350 degrees, for about 1 hour. Serves 6.

CREAMED CELERY

Wash, scrape and cut in 1-inch pieces. Cover with boiling salted water and cook until the celery is soft. Drain, and to 1½ cups celery add 1 cup Medium White Sauce, p. 214. Mix well and serve hot.

CHESTNUTS

To Shell Chestnuts: Cut a slit in each nut, place in heavy frying pan and add ½ teaspoon of olive oil to each cup of nuts. Shake over fire about 10 minutes. When cool, remove shells and skins with sharp knife.

Creamed Chestnuts: Shell chestnuts and cook in boiling water till tender. Drain, and add an equal amount of cream sauce.

Chestnut Purée: Chestnuts are used in Italy as a substitute for mashed potatoes by shelling 2 cups of chestnuts, boiling them till soft, mashing them in a mortar or pressing through a sieve; then adding 2 cups milk, 2 tablespoons flour, ½ cup butter or margarine, 1 tablespoon celery salt and a few bits of chive or 1 thin slice of garlic mashed.

CORN ON THE COB

Remove the husks and silk. Cook, covered, in boiling water 7 minutes, or until tender. Place on platter covered with napkin and draw corners of napkin over corn. Serve with salt and butter. Every farmer and gardener knows that no corn on the cob is worth eating unless it is fresh out of the garden. Old corn is much better made into corn fritters, corn pudding or corn chowder.

CORN FRITTERS

2 cups grated raw corn	2 eggs, separated
Dash of salt	

Beat egg yolks and add to corn; then add salt and stiffly beaten whites. Melt a small amount of butter in a hot frying pan and drop batter into it by the spoonful. When the fritters bubble and are brown on the bottom, turn and brown on the other side. Serve with chicken or meat as a vegetable, or with maple syrup as a dessert. Serves 6.

CORN SOUFFLE

1 tablespoon butter	Dash of paprika
1 tablespoon flour	1 teaspoon salt
½ cup milk	2 cups fresh grated corn
2 eggs, separated	

Melt butter and stir in flour; gradually add milk. Cook about 5 minutes, stirring constantly. Add seasonings and corn, and remove from stove. Cool slightly, then add the well-beaten egg yolks and fold in stiffly beaten egg whites. Turn into a buttered dish, set in a pan of hot water and bake in a moderate oven, 350 degrees, 30 minutes. Serves 6.

CORN OYSTERS

1 pint grated corn	2 eggs, well beaten
¼ cup light cream	1 tablespoon butter
3 tablespoons flour	1 teaspoon salt
1 teaspoon baking powder	⅛ teaspoon pepper

Mix ingredients in order given. Drop by spoonfuls and fry in deep fat, 370 degrees, or cook on hot griddle in bacon fat. Drain on brown paper. Serves 6.

MAINE SUCCOTASH

Cut green corn from the cobs. Place cobs in enough water to cover them and boil 1 hour. Shell cranberry beans or young lima beans in equal quantity to the cut-off corn. Remove cobs from boiling water and add beans; boil 1 hour. Add corn and boil until it is tender. Drain off water. Add salt, pepper, butter and cream. True Maine succotash was never made from lima beans, as is usual today.

CORN AND SCRAMBLED EGGS

¼ pound diced bacon	¼ cup milk
1 can cream-style corn	1 teaspoon salt
4 eggs, well beaten	Dash of pepper

Fry bacon till brown. Drain off half the fat. Add corn and bring to a boil. Mix milk, eggs and seasonings and pour over corn and bacon. Cook slowly until eggs are thickened. Serves 3–4.

CORN PUDDING

2 cups grated fresh corn	⅛ teaspoon pepper
3 eggs, well beaten	2 cups light cream
1 teaspoon salt	2 tablespoons butter

Mix corn, eggs and seasonings. Pour into buttered baking dish, cover with cream, and dot with butter. Bake in a moderate oven, 350 degrees, 30 minutes. Serves 6.

BAKED CUCUMBERS

Cut cucumbers lengthwise and scoop out pulp, leaving the shells. Sauté a chopped onion and chopped head of celery until soft. To them add the cucumber pulp, and simmer 5 minutes. Fill cucumber shells, set them in a pan with water and bake in a moderate oven, 350 degrees, 6 minutes. Sprinkle thickly with grated American cheese and replace in oven another 5 minutes.

SAUTÉED CUCUMBERS

4 large cucumbers	4 tablespoons butter
4 tablespoons flour	3 tablespoons horseradish
Salt and pepper	½ cup melted butter

Peel cucumbers and cut in ½-inch slices. Chill in ice water, drain and dry. Dredge with flour, salt and pepper. Sauté in butter until light brown. Drain and serve with blended horseradish and melted butter. Serves 8.

CREAMED CUCUMBERS

Peel and slice 6 small cucumbers, and cover with salt for an hour. Sauté 1 minced onion in 2 tablespoons butter until brown. Dry the cucumbers by pressing in a towel, add to the onion and simmer 10 minutes. While they simmer, melt ⅛ pound crumbled American cheese in 1 cup of light cream with 1 teaspoon salt, ½ teaspoon pepper and 1 tablespoon soybean sauce. Add the cream to the cucumbers and serve at once.

CUCUMBERS WITH SOUR CREAM

2 large cucumbers	1 cup sour cream
1 tablespoon salt	¼ cup vinegar
	⅛ teaspoon pepper

Peel cucumbers, slice thin, sprinkle with salt, cover with cold water and leave in refrigerator 1 hour. Make a dressing of sour cream, vinegar and pepper. Squeeze liquor from cucumbers and cover with the dressing.

CUCUMBERS IN EVAPORATED MILK

Peel cucumbers, slice thin, sprinkle with salt, cover with cold water and chill in refrigerator 1 hour. Scald 1 can of evaporated milk, put in refrigerator until chilled, then whip until thick. Add 2 tablespoons of lemon juice, 1 tablespoon grated onion, and salt and pepper to taste. Drain cucumbers and press liquid from them with a cloth. Cover with the dressing. Serve with fish.

DANDELION GREENS

Wash leaves three times and soak overnight in cold water, with 1 tablespoon salt and juice of ½ lemon in it. Greens will otherwise be bitter. Simmer greens 1 hour in small amount of water with marrow from a ham bone. Drain and serve with lemon juice squeezed copiously over them. One pound serves 4.

SAUTÉED EGGPLANT

Pare, cut in ¼-inch slices and soak in salted water 30 minutes. Stack slices beneath a weighted plate, and let drain for 1 hour. Dry slices thoroughly, sprinkle with salt and pepper, and dredge with flour. Sauté slowly in butter until crisp and brown.

FRIED EGGPLANT

Pare eggplant, cut in ½-inch slices; then dip in egg which has been seasoned with salt and pepper, then in fine dry bread crumbs. Fry in deep fat, 370 degrees. Drain on brown paper.

EGGPLANT CASSEROLE

Soak eggplant in salted water 15 minutes. Pare, cut in small cubes and boil for 5 minutes in very little water. Drain, and put a layer of eggplant in a buttered casserole; then add a layer of finely chopped green peppers; ½ an onion, minced; bread crumbs mixed in melted butter. Repeat. Pour over the whole mixture ¾ cup light cream. Top with buttered bread crumbs. Bake 30 minutes in moderate oven, 350 degrees.

SPANISH EGGPLANT

1 eggplant	2 dozen chopped stuffed
1 chopped green pepper	olives
1 thinly sliced onion	1 cup parboiled diced
2 tablespoons butter	celery
1 teaspoon salt	2 cups canned tomatoes

Peel eggplant and cut in 1-inch cubes. Cook in boiling salted water until tender. Sauté green pepper and onion in butter until tender, then add olives and parboiled celery. Heat the tomatoes, add the drained eggplant and the pepper mixture, and salt. Pour into a buttered baking dish, cover with buttered bread crumbs and bake in a moderate oven, 350 degrees, until crumbs are brown. Serves 6.

STUFFED EGGPLANT

1 eggplant	1 teaspoon lemon juice
Salt and pepper	½ cup water
2 tablespoons butter	2 cups fine bread crumbs

Cut eggplant in quarters lengthwise. Remove pulp, leaving rind about ½ inch thick. Cover shells with cold water. Force pulp through food chopper. Add salt, pepper, butter, lemon juice and water, and cook 15 minutes, stirring constantly. Remove from stove and add 1 cup of bread crumbs. Drain the shells, sprinkle with salt and pepper, and fill them with mixture. Sprinkle with remaining crumbs. Bake in a moderate oven, 350 degrees, 20 minutes.

HOT LETTUCE

3 slices bacon	¼ cup light cream
½ teaspoon salt	½ cup claret vinegar[2]

Try out bacon, and when crisp add cream, salt and vinegar, stirring until very hot. When it bubbles, add outer leaves of 4 heads of lettuce and press into sauce, turning over and over until well wilted.

[2]Claret vinegar may be obtained from any Italian grocery in New England cities. An old established firm is Charles Torrielli, 171 Hanover St., Boston, Mass.—K.R.

LETTUCE WITH SOUR CREAM DRESSING

Wash lettuce, cut in small pieces, and marinate with this dressing: To 1 cup thick sour cream add 1 tablespoon lemon juice, 1 teaspoon salt and ¼ teaspoon pepper. Mix well.

KOHLRABI

Wash and peel kohlrabi. Slice or quarter, and cook, uncovered, in boiling water until tender. Drain thoroughly, season with butter, salt and pepper. Kohlrabi may be served with a cream or Hollandaise Sauce, p. 209.

BAKED MUSHROOMS

Wash, remove stems and peel caps. Place in a shallow dish with bits of butter and season with salt and pepper; add ½ cup light cream. Bake in a hot oven, 400 degrees, 10 to 15 minutes. Serve on toast.

CREAMED MUSHROOMS

2 cups mushrooms	1 tablespoon flour
½ cup boiling water	½ cup light cream
2 tablespoons butter	1 teaspoon salt
⅛ teaspoon pepper	

Prepare mushrooms and stew them in boiling water 6 minutes, or until tender. Melt butter and stir in flour; gradually add cream and seasonings. Add mushrooms, without draining, to the cream sauce. Serve hot on buttered toast. Serves 4.

BROILED MUSHROOMS

Wash, stem and peel mushrooms. Place them on broiler, cap side down. Broil 3 minutes, turn, and broil other side. Serve on buttered toast, sprinkle with salt, pepper, and dot with butter.

SAUTÉED MUSHROOMS

Wash and peel ½ pound mushrooms, and cut in pieces. Melt 2 tablespoons butter in a hot frying pan, add mushrooms and sauté 6 to 8 minutes. Turn frequently. Serve on toast.

STUFFED MUSHROOMS

12 large mushrooms
2 teaspoons chopped parsley
2 tablespoons butter
2 egg yolks, slightly beaten

1 tablespoon fine bread
  crumbs
1/4 teaspoon salt
Few gratings nutmeg

Wash mushrooms, remove stems and chop fine. Peel caps. Mix chopped stems with parsley and cook 10 minutes in melted butter. Stir in crumbs, salt and nutmeg. Remove from stove and add egg yolks. Fill mushroom caps. Place in shallow buttered pan and bake in a hot oven, 400 degrees, 15 minutes. Serves 3 or 4.

OKRA STEW

1 pound okra
1 pound lamb
2 tablespoons butter
2 chopped onions

1 cup lamb or beef broth
2 cups strained tomatoes
Juice of 1 lemon
1 teaspoon salt

1/4 teaspoon pepper

Cut meat into 1-inch cubes and sauté in butter with onions. Wash okra, cut off stems and slice crosswise. Add to meat with broth. Cook 5 minutes; then add strained tomatoes, lemon juice and seasonings. Simmer until thick and serve with rice. Serves 6.

BOILED ONIONS

Put onions in cold water and remove skins under water. Drain, put in saucepan and cover with boiling salted water; boil 5 minutes, drain, and cover again with boiling salted water. Cook 1/2 hour, or until soft, but not broken. Drain, add a small quantity of cream or white wine, butter, salt and pepper, and cook 5 minutes. One pound serves 4.

FRENCH–FRIED ONIONS

Wash and peel onions, cut in 1/4-inch slices, and separate into rings. Dip into milk, then into finely ground bread crumbs or flour. Fry in deep fat, 370 degrees, until lightly browned, drain on brown paper, and sprinkle with salt.

CREAMED ONIONS

Cover Boiled Onions with White Sauce, p. 214.

SAUTÉED ONIONS

6 medium-sized onions   2 tablespoons butter

Wash, peel and cut onions in thin slices. Sauté in butter until brown, stirring frequently. Season with salt and pepper. Serves 6.

ONIONS AND PEAS

Cook 8 small onions in boiling, salted water until tender; drain and place 4 of them in a buttered baking dish. Brown ¼ cup bread crumbs in 1 tablespoon of butter; add to onions. Add a layer of cooked or canned green peas, salt and pepper; then the remaining onions. Pour rich milk over all, cover with bread crumbs and bake 12 minutes.

ONIONS AU GRATIN

Cover the bottom of a buttered baking dish with medium-sized Boiled Onions; over the onions pour Cheese Sauce (2), p. 207. Heat in a moderate oven, 350 degrees, and serve.

STUFFED ONIONS

6 large onions   Cream to moisten
½ cup chopped ham   ½ teaspoon salt
½ cup soft bread crumbs   ⅛ teaspoon pepper

Peel onions and parboil 30 minutes in boiling salted water. Drain, and remove the centers. Chop the onion that was removed from centers and combine it with ham, crumbs, cream and seasonings. Fill the onion shells. Place in baking dish with small amount of water. Sprinkle with more crumbs and dot with butter. Cover. Bake in a moderate oven, 350 degrees, until tender, removing cover last 10 minutes. Serves 6.

BOILED PARSNIPS

Wash and scrape parsnips, dice or cut in strips, and cook in boiling salted water until soft. Drain, and season with salt, pepper and butter. Reheat. One pound serves 4.

CREAMED PARSNIPS

Add Boiled Parsnips to 1 cup of light cream, slightly thickened with flour, or reheat Boiled Parsnips in Cream Sauce, p. 215.

PARSNIP CAKES

2 cups cooked mashed parsnips	1 tablespoon flour
	1 teaspoon salt
1 tablespoon butter	2 egg yolks

Mix ingredients together well; then shape into flat cakes. Dip into powdered cracker crumbs and sauté in butter until brown.

SAUTÉED PARSNIPS

Wash and scrape parsnips, and cook in boiling salted water until soft. Cut in strips and sauté in melted butter until light brown. Season with salt and pepper.

SCALLOPED PARSNIPS

Dice Boiled Parsnips and put into a buttered baking dish in layers with cracker crumbs and grated cheese. The top layer should be crumbs, cheese and dots of butter. Lastly, pour over the top 1 cup of Medium White Sauce, p. 214, and bake in a moderate oven, 350 degrees, till brown.

PARSNIP STEW

Slice an equal quantity of potatoes, onions and parsnips. Cover with water and cook until vegetables are tender. Season with salt and pepper and add some milk. Fry 3 slices of salt pork and add to the stew. Simmer until ready to serve.

BOILED GREEN PEAS

Shell, cover with cold water, and let stand ½ hour. Remove peas which rise to top, and drain remaining peas. Cover and cook until tender in a small amount of boiling salted water. If there is any water left after cooking, drain it off. Season with butter, salt and pepper, and add 1 tablespoon sugar.

FRENCH PEAS

To 1 cup canned peas add 1 minced onion and cook until onion is done. Drain and add 1 tablespoon butter and 1 teaspoon celery salt.

STUFFED PEPPERS

6 green peppers	½ cup cream-style canned corn
1 cup bread crumbs	1 tablespoon chopped
½ cup chopped chicken	onion
1 tablespoon melted butter	Salt and pepper

Cut peppers in half, lengthwise, remove seeds, and parboil in boiling salted water 3 minutes. Combine crumbs, chicken, butter, corn, onion and seasonings. Stuff peppers with mixture and place in baking dish with water 1 inch deep. Bake in a hot oven, 400 degrees, about 30 minutes. Serves 6.

BOILED POTATOES

Select potatoes of uniform size, wash thoroughly, but never pare. Cover with boiling water seasoned with salt, and boil 20 to 30 minutes until tender. Drain, sprinkle thickly with salt, shake over stove until all moisture has evaporated from container and outside of potatoes; then serve at once.

RICED POTATOES

Peel hot boiled potatoes and force through a ricer or strainer. Add 2 tablespoons butter.

MASHED POTATOES

6 potatoes	3 tablespoons butter
⅓ cup of hot milk or light cream	1 teaspoon salt
	Dash of pepper

Boil potatoes, rub off skins, put through ricer and add remaining ingredients. Beat with a fork until creamy and light. Reheat. Serve piled lightly on hot dish. Dot with butter and sprinkle with paprika.

FRENCH–FRIED POTATOES

Pare and slice raw potatoes into long, even pieces. Let stand in cold water for 1 hour. Drain and dry between towels. Fry in deep fat, 390 degrees, until brown and thoroughly cooked. Drain on brown paper and salt before serving.

POTATOES AND CHEESE

1 quart diced potatoes	2 tablespoons cornstarch
1 grated onion	1 teaspoon salt
1 can slivered pimentos	½ teaspoon pepper
1 pint scalded milk	½ pound American cheese

Cook potatoes, onion and pimentos 5 minutes in boiling salted water. Then drain. Make a sauce of the milk, cornstarch, seasonings, and into it crumble the cheese. Cook till cheese is melted. Put potatoes in baking dish, cover with sauce and bake in moderate oven, 350 degrees, 45 minutes.

BAKED POTATOES[3]

Select medium-sized potatoes; scrub, rinse, dry and brush skins with butter or margarine. Place on baking rack and bake in a hot oven 40 minutes. Cut two gashes across the top to permit the steam to escape. Serve with butter.

To vary, mix horseradish and melted butter into the baked potato.

---

[3]In Mr. Roberts' copy of the first edition of this book appears a directive for the use of cooks: "Don't for ———— sake keep trying to bake potatoes. It can't be done—not so that the potatoes are one-tenth as good as properly boiled potatoes. Every Irishman knows that."

POTATO CROQUETTES

3 egg yolks	Dash of nutmeg
1 egg white	Salt and pepper
2 tablespoons heavy cream	1 teaspoon minced parsley
2 cups hot riced potatoes	2 tablespoons sherry

Beat egg yolks and white until light, then beat in cream and add to the potatoes. Beat in remaining ingredients. Shape into croquettes, roll in flour and fry in deep fat, 390 degrees, or until a small cube of bread dropped into the fat will brown in 1 minute. Drain on paper. Or shape into potato cakes, dredge with flour and sauté in butter in frying pan. Serves 6.

NORWEGIAN POTATOES

6 potatoes	Salt and pepper
3 tablespoons melted butter	1 can Norwegian sardines

Boil and mash potatoes. Mash sardines and combine with potato, butter and seasonings. Place in individual ramekins, dot with any high-flavored cheese and serve with Tomato Sauce, p. 213.

POTATO BALLS

2 cups mashed potatoes	½ teaspoon salt
1 cup stale bread crumbs	⅛ teaspoon pepper
1 tablespoon butter	⅛ teaspoon celery salt
1 egg, separated	

Sauté bread crumbs in butter and then add them to mashed potatoes. Stir in seasonings and yolk of egg. Fold in stiffly beaten egg white and beat until light. Form into balls and fry in deep hot fat, 375 degrees, until brown. Serves 6.

POTATO CAKES

Season 2 cups riced potatoes with salt, paprika and ¼ cup melted butter. Add enough flour to roll. Roll ½ inch thick and cut into circular cakes. Bake in hot oven, 400 degrees. Serve with butter.

STUFFED BAKED POTATOES

3 large potatoes	½ teaspoon salt
1 tablespoon butter	⅛ teaspoon pepper
1 tablespoon light cream	1 egg white, stiffly beaten

Bake potatoes, p. 177. Remove from oven, cut in halves lengthwise, and scoop out inside. Mash, adding butter, salt, pepper and cream. Fold in the stiffly beaten egg white. Refill potato shells and bake in a hot oven, 400 degrees, 8 to 10 minutes.

POTATOES AU GRATIN, OR DELMONICO

2 pounds potatoes, cut in ½-inch cubes	Salt and pepper
	Grated nutmeg
1 beaten egg	3 cups boiled milk
¼ pound grated American cheese	

Thoroughly mix ingredients in order given. Grease earthenware casseroles, rub with garlic and pour in mixture. Sprinkle with grated cheese, dot with butter and cook in a moderate oven for 40 to 45 minutes.

POTATO PANCAKES

3 cups grated raw potatoes	2 eggs, beaten
1 grated onion	1 teaspoon celery salt
½ teaspoon pepper	

Peel potatoes, cover with cold water and let stand 2 hours. Drain and grate them. Add grated onion, eggs and seasoning. Mix well. Drop by spoonfuls, spreading thin with spatula, into hot buttered frying pan. Turn once. Serve with sour cream.

LYONNAISE POTATOES

Sauté 1 tablespoon chopped onion in 1 tablespoon butter until light brown. Add 1 tablespoon vinegar, 2 cups diced, cold boiled potatoes, and season with salt and pepper. Stir gently with a fork till potatoes absorb the butter. Add 1 tablespoon chopped parsley. Cook until potatoes brown. Serves 4.

POTATO PUDDING

4 grated raw potatoes	1 cup milk
2 eggs	⅛ teaspoon pepper
½ cup melted butter	½ teaspoon salt
	½ cup flour

Mix ingredients together. Pour in shallow baking dish and bake 1½ hours in moderate oven, 350 degrees.

GERMAN–FRIED POTATOES

Pare and thinly slice potatoes; let stand in cold water ½ hour, drain and dry. Place in heavy frying pan with melted butter; sprinkle with salt and pepper. Cover pan and cook slowly until tender and brown, stirring occasionally.

HASHED BROWN POTATOES

2 cups cold boiled potatoes	1 tablespoon celery salt
⅓ cup fat	⅛ teaspoon pepper

Melt fat in frying pan, add finely chopped potatoes and seasonings. Fry for 3 minutes, stirring constantly. Brown on bottom, turn and fold like an omelet on serving dish. Serves 4.

SCALLOPED POTATOES

Pare and slice 4 potatoes, ¼ inch thick. Cover with cold water and boil 10 minutes. Drain, and put a layer of potatoes in the bottom of a buttered casserole. Sprinkle with salt and pepper and dot with butter. Repeat layers. Add enough milk so it appears through top layer. Bake in a moderate oven, 350 degrees, 1 hour, or until potatoes are soft. Serves 6.

BOILED SWEET POTATOES

Scrub. Cook in their jackets in boiling water to cover. Add 2 teaspoons salt to 1 quart water. Cook until soft, about 20 minutes.

SCALLOPED SWEET POTATOES AND APPLES

6 boiled sweet potatoes	1½ cups sliced apples
½ cup brown sugar	¼ cup butter
½ teaspoon salt	

Drain, peel and slice potatoes in ¼-inch pieces. Put a layer of sweet potatoes in buttered baking dish, then a layer of apples. Sprinkle with sugar and salt, and dot with butter. Repeat until the dish is filled with a top layer of apple. Bake in a moderate oven, 350 degrees, 50 minutes.

CANDIED SWEET POTATOES

Peel and slice 6 boiled sweet potatoes and put a layer in the bottom of a buttered baking dish. Sprinkle with brown sugar, add another layer of potatoes, another of brown sugar, and dot with butter. Bake in a hot oven, 400 degrees, till brown. Serves 6.

CREAMED SWEET POTATOES

Cut cold boiled sweet potatoes in small cubes. To 2 cups of potatoes add 3 tablespoons melted butter. Cook together 3 minutes, season with salt, pepper and a dash of paprika. Then sprinkle over mixture 2 tablespoons flour; add 1 cup thin cream and cook slowly for 20 minutes.

SPINACH MOLD

3 pounds spinach, or 2 boxes	2 tablespoons flour
frozen spinach	1½ cups hot milk
2 tablespoons butter	Pinch of salt
2 eggs, separated	

Prepare spinach as for boiled spinach, cook 15 minutes, drain, chop fine, or put through coarse sieve. Melt butter in saucepan, stir in flour and gradually add milk and salt. When smooth, pour over spinach and mix well. Beat and add egg yolks, then fold in stiffly beaten egg whites. Pour into buttered ring mold and set in a pan of hot water. Bake 45 minutes in a moderate oven, 350 degrees. Turn mold onto platter and pour Hollandaise Sauce, p. 209, in the center. Garnish with riced hard-boiled eggs. Serves 8.

BOILED SPINACH

Remove roots, tough stems and wilted leaves. Wash in warm water twice, then three times in cold water. Drain, place in a large kettle with ½ cup of water and cook, covered, 10 to 15 minutes. Drain, chop spinach, and season with salt, pepper and butter. Serve garnished with slices of hard-boiled eggs.

CREAMED SPINACH

2 cups chopped cooked spinach	¾ cup milk
3 tablespoons butter	½ teaspoon salt
2 tablespoons flour	⅛ teaspoon pepper
	⅛ teaspoon nutmeg

Melt butter in saucepan, add the flour and blend. Gradually add the milk, stirring constantly until mixture thickens. Then add the spinach and seasonings. Serves 4.

SPINACH TIMBALES

1½ cups cooked spinach, finely chopped	½ teaspoon onion juice
½ teaspoon salt	2 tablespoons melted butter
	2 eggs, well beaten
1 cup milk	

Combine all the ingredients. Turn into buttered timbale molds, set in pan of hot water, and bake in a moderate oven, 350 degrees, 30 minutes. Unmold and serve with tomato ketchup.

BOILED SUMMER SQUASH

Wash, slice and cook in a small amount of boiling salted water, covered, 15 to 20 minutes. Drain, mash and season with butter, salt and pepper.

SAUTÉED SUMMER SQUASH

Cut in thin slices and dip in flour seasoned well with salt and pepper. Sauté in butter until browned.

ACORN (OR DES MOINES) SQUASH

Acorn squash, when fully grown, have hard dark green shells. To cook, cut them in half lengthwise, remove seeds, put a dab of butter and a teaspoon of brown sugar, maple sugar or maple syrup in each half, and bake 1½ hours. Serve one half for each person.

When only half grown, the acorn squash is about the size of a tennis ball and has a pale green or pale yellow skin. If halved and cooked in the same way as their more mature relatives, they are the most succulent of all squashes, and the skin is tender and delicious.

BOILED WINTER SQUASH

Cut in pieces, remove seeds and stringy portion, and pare. Cover with boiling salted water and cook, covered, 30 minutes. Drain, mash and season with butter, salt and pepper.

BAKED WINTER SQUASH

Cut in large pieces and remove seeds and stringy portion. Place in shallow pan, spread with softened butter and sprinkle with salt and pepper. Bake about 1½ hours in a moderately slow oven, 325 degrees.

BAKED TOMATO AND EGG

Butter muffin pans and put 1 thick slice of tomato in each cup; season with salt and pepper. Break 1 egg on each tomato slice and again season with salt and pepper. Dot each egg with butter. Bake in moderate oven, 350 degrees, 15 minutes. Serve on toast.

STEWED TOMATOES

Drop tomatoes in boiling water 2 minutes, remove, and peel off skins. Cut in pieces and cook slowly 20 minutes, stirring occasionally. Season with salt, pepper and butter. A small amount of sautéed onion may be added if desired.

SCALLOPED TOMATOES

1 minced onion
1 chopped green pepper
¼ cup melted butter
Salt and pepper

1 cup bread or cracker
crumbs
2 cups tomatoes

Sauté onion and green pepper in half the butter. When yellow add remainder of butter and crumbs. Place a layer of tomatoes in a baking dish, sprinkle with salt and pepper, then add a layer of crumb mixture; repeat, having top layer crumbs. Bake in a hot oven, 400 degrees, until crumbs are brown. Serves 4.

TOMATO SAVORY

2 cups of ½-inch bread
cubes
½ cup melted butter
1 cup ½-inch pieces American cheese
2 cans tomato purée

½ cup hot water
1 teaspoon celery salt
1 teaspoon hickory smoked
salt
1 teaspoon dry mustard
1 minced clove garlic

Put cubes of bread in a baking dish, cover with butter and dot with cheese. Place tomato purée, water and seasonings in a saucepan and bring to a boil; then pour over bread. Cover dish and bake 30 minutes in a 375-degree oven.

BAKED STUFFED TOMATOES

Wash and remove stem ends from 6 medium-sized tomatoes. Scoop out pulp and sprinkle shell with salt. Invert and let stand ½ hour. Mix an equal amount of soft bread crumbs to the pulp and season with salt, pepper and 1 tablespoon chopped onion. Refill tomatoes with stuffing and place in a buttered baking dish. Sprinkle with buttered crumbs and bake in a moderately hot oven, 375 degrees, 20 minutes.

BROWNED TOMATOES

Wipe tomatoes and cut in halves. Lay cut side up in baking pan, sprinkle with salt and cover with finely chopped onions. Moisten soft bread crumbs with melted butter and put a layer over the tomatoes. Place the pan in hot oven until crumbs are browned.

SAUTÉED TOMATOES

Wash firm, ripe tomatoes and cut in ½-inch slices. Dip in fine crumbs seasoned with salt and pepper. Sauté in butter, turning to brown both sides.

TOMATOES AU GRATIN

Cover the bottom of a shallow casserole with bread or cracker crumbs; then add a layer of tomatoes, peeled and cut in ½-inch slices. Sprinkle with salt and pepper and add a layer of grated American cheese. Bake in a moderate oven, 350 degrees, about 20 minutes, or until tomatoes are soft and cheese has browned.

MEAT AND TOMATO SCALLOP

Put a layer of meat cut in small pieces in the bottom of a baking pan, then a layer of canned tomatoes and a layer of bread crumbs, sprinkle with salt, pepper and bits of butter, then another layer of meat, having the bread crumbs on top. Bake in a moderate oven, 350 degrees, 30 minutes.

BUTTERED TURNIPS

Pare and dice the turnips. Parboil and drain, then cover with boiling water and finish cooking. Drain, and season with salt, pepper and butter.

MASHED TURNIPS

Wash, pare and dice turnips. Cook in boiling salted water until tender. Drain, mash and season with butter, salt and pepper.

TURNIP PUFF

Mix together 2 cups hot mashed turnip and 2 cups hot mashed potato. Season with celery salt and pepper, and stir in 3 tablespoons butter, 2 tablespoons light cream, 1 well-beaten egg and 1 teaspoon dry mustard. Pour into a buttered casserole and bake in a hot oven, 400 degrees, 20 minutes. Serves 6.

CREAMED TURNIPS

Wash, pare and dice turnips. Cook in boiling salted water until tender. Drain, add 1 cup milk thickened slightly with flour, and 1 tablespoon butter. Season with salt and pepper.

BOILED ZUCCHINI

Wash and slice zucchini and boil in salted water, covered, until tender, about 15 minutes. Drain, pour on melted butter, or serve with Tomato Sauce, p. 213, or Hollandaise Sauce, p. 209.

SAUTÉED ZUCCHINI

Wash and cut zucchini in ¼-inch slices. Sauté in butter, stirring constantly. Season with salt and pepper.

SCALLOPED ZUCCHINI

Prepare Boiled Zucchini and place in bottom of a buttered casserole. Add a layer of grated cheese and 2 tablespoons minced onion. Pour on Medium White Sauce, p. 214, and cover with buttered bread crumbs. Bake in a moderately hot oven, 375 degrees, until the crumbs are brown, about 25 minutes. Serve with crisp bacon.

DOLMA

4 medium-sized tomatoes	2 minced onions
4 medium-sized green peppers	¼ cup chopped parsley
1 pound ground meat	2 teaspoons salt
	¼ teaspoon black pepper
1 cup rice	

Wash tomatoes and peppers, scoop out insides, and salt slightly. Keep tomato pulp to use later. To meat add onions, parsley, salt and rice which has been washed. Mix all together, adding a little water at a time until softened and mixture holds together. Fill tomatoes and peppers with it, and arrange alternately in a deep kettle close together. Strain pulp and juice of tomatoes over this and hold it down in the kettle with a plate. Cover kettle, place in moderate oven, 350 degrees, for ½ hour. Remove cover and leave in oven until mixture browns on top.

BEAN POT SMOTHER

2 pounds stew beef	¼ cup diced turnip
2 bouillon cubes	1 sliced onion
1½ cups diced potatoes	1 tablespoon celery salt
½ cup diced carrots	1 tablespoon dry mustard

Flour

Cut meat into pieces for stewing and place in bean pot. Dissolve bouillon cubes in hot water and add enough to pot to cover meat. Place cover on pot and cook in a slow oven about 3 hours, replacing hot water as it boils away. When meat is almost done, add remaining ingredients and cook till vegetables are tender. Add a little flour to thicken, and serve.

VEGETABLE CASSEROLE

½ cup diced potatoes	1½ cups chopped cooked
½ cup diced carrots	meat
½ cup diced celery	1 cup gravy
¼ cup chopped onions	½ teaspoon salt

¼ teaspoon pepper

Boil the vegetables in salted water for 10 minutes; then drain and combine with meat, gravy and seasonings. Pour into a buttered casserole and bake in a hot oven, 400 degrees, 30 minutes.

VEGETABLE TIMBALES

1½ cups cooked corn	1½ cups soft bread crumbs
1½ cups cooked peas	3 eggs, well beaten
1 cup drained canned	¼ cup melted butter
tomatoes	½ teaspoon salt
1 tablespoon minced onion	¼ teaspoon pepper

Mix together and turn into buttered molds. Set in pan of hot water and bake in a moderate oven, 350 degrees, 45 minutes, or until firm. Unmold and serve with Cheese Sauce, p. 207. Serves 6 to 8.

VEGETABLE SMOTHER

Fry 2 slices of salt pork in a frying pan, add sliced raw potatoes, carrots and turnip, almost cover with water. Simmer, covered, until vegetables are tender. A few minutes before serving place split baking-powder biscuits, slices of bread or dumplings on top. Water may need to be added while vegetables are simmering in order to have it juicy. Serve with dill pickles cut in strips.

PIZZA ALLA NAPOLITANA
(Naples Pie)

Butter a large pie plate and line with thin flaky pastry. Drain juice from 1 quart canned tomatoes, mash pulp, season with salt and pepper, and spread it evenly on pastry. Cut American cheese into strips ½ inch wide, 2 inches long and ¼ inch thick, and distribute strips on surface of tomato pulp. Between the strips of cheese place anchovy filets. Too many anchovies will tend to make the pizza too salty. Over all sprinkle orégano, dill or any other savory herb. Bake 20 minutes in a 400-degree oven. Serve either hot or cold, cut in pie-shaped segments.

SALADS

MAXIMS FROM MAINE KITCHENS

Wash green vegetables in warm water; rinse in cold.

❦

To keep cucumbers tender and digestible, slice cucumber, place slices on plate and sprinkle with sugar. Rinse and drain just before using.

❦

To peel tomatoes, drop in boiling water for 3 seconds. The skins then break and come off easily.

❦

To bake tomatoes or peppers more handily, put them in muffin tins, which hold them securely upright.

❦

The odor of garlic or onion may be removed from hands and mouth by eating celery tops and rubbing the hands with the tops.

❦

To clear cloudy or frozen olive oil, add 1 teaspoon of salt to each quart and in 24 hours it will be clear.

❦

To tenderize boiled meat or fowl, boil in water to which 2 spoonfuls of vinegar have been added.

SALADS

LETTUCE SALAD: FRENCH DRESSING

THERE IS only one staple, infallible and wholly satisfying green salad to the minds of Maine gourmets: the separated leaves of any non-iceberg lettuce, marinated with French dressing.

French dressing can be mixed and applied properly to a salad only in a large bowl, preferably earthenware. The only ingredients needed are any non-rancid olive, vegetable or mineral oil,[1] lemon juice, salt (preferably a vegetable salt, such as Vegesal), a slice of dry toast and a clove of garlic.

From the slice of toast break a piece 1 inch square. Cut the clove of garlic in half. Rub both sides of the piece of toast with the cut face of the garlic. Throw away the garlic, put the piece of toast in the bottom of the bowl, and on it put 1 teaspoon of salt. On the salt pour 2 tablespoons of oil, and into the oil pour 1½ tablespoons of lemon juice. Just before making the salad, stir this mixture with a wooden spoon.

Remove and throw away the garlic-rubbed toast.

Separate and wash the leaves of a head of Boston lettuce, roll them in a towel and squeeze out the water.

Put these leaves in the bowl with the dressing, and with a wooden fork and spoon turn the leaves over and over until their surfaces are covered with the dressing. This salad will serve 3 people.

For 4, 5 or 6 persons make the dressing of 4 tablespoons of oil, 2 overflowing tablespoons of lemon juice, and 1½ teaspoons of salt, and use 2 heads of lettuce, but do not use more toast and garlic.

---

[1] A great deal of claptrap has been written about the absolute necessity of using high-grade olive oil in salad dressings. Few epicures can tell the difference between a dressing made of garlic-flavored mineral oil and one made from olive oil. The mineral-oil dressing, moreover, can be eaten with impunity by dieters; and it does not, as rumored, destroy Vitamin A in the system.—K.R.

For 7, 8 or 9 persons, use 6 tablespoons oil, 3 tablespoons lemon juice, 2 teaspoons salt, and no more toast and garlic than was used for 3 persons.

For more persons, keep on increasing at the same rate.

For variation, sliced tomatoes, cucumbers, minced chives, etc., may be marinated with the lettuce leaves.[2]

ASPIC

4 pounds strung knuckle of veal

3 pounds veal bones, well broken

3 pounds strung knuckle of beef

3 calf's feet, boned and blanched

½ pound fresh pork rind, blanched and with fat removed

Add 8 quarts cold water to meat, boil and skim. Then add 1 ounce salt, and simmer gently 4 hours. Remove meat, skim off fat; and add ½ pound carrots, 6 ounces onions, 2 ounces leeks, a stalk of celery and a bundle of herbs. Simmer 2 hours longer; then strain and cool. Remove fat and then pour off into a stewpan so to prevent the deposit at bottom of kettle from mixing with the clear liquor. This should form a firm jelly. If not, add small amount of gelatin. Add to the stock 2 pounds of lean beef, minced and pounded together with the white of 1 egg and the juice of ½ lemon. Boil another ½ hour. Strain and flavor with any available wine.

GAME ASPIC

Prepare game aspic in the same way as aspic, substituting game, such as deer or rabbit (previously browned in oven), for the beef. When possible, add partridges too tough for broiling.

---

[2]The greatest boon yet discovered for salad addicts who have a kitchen garden is Slobolt lettuce. When the heads mature, their outer leaves can be removed, and the heads miraculously continue to renew themselves for weeks without turning bitter or going to seed. The best way to plant Slobolt is to drop a small pinch of seed at 15-inch intervals in two 15-foot rows. No thinning out is necessary. When the heads are half grown, plant additional pinches of seed halfway between each head. This method of planting will keep a family of five hearty lettuce eaters liberally supplied with lettuce for two months. In fertile soil, Slobolt heads grow to be 24 inches in diameter two months after seed is planted, and all leaves are equally tender.

QUICK CHICKEN OR FISH ASPIC

2 chicken bouillon cubes
2 tablespoons gelatin
¼ cup cold water
1 cup boiling water

1 cup dry white wine
½ cup diced cucumber
¼ cup diced celery
2 cups cooked diced
    chicken or flaked fish

Soak the bouillon cubes and gelatin in cold water until soft. Add the boiling water and stir till gelatin is dissolved. Then add the wine. Let cool, and when almost set, add cucumber, celery and diced chicken or flaked fish. Pour the aspic into a chilled mold. Chill, unmold on lettuce leaves and serve with mayonnaise. Serves 6.

TURKEY ASPIC

2 tablespoons gelatin
¼ cup white wine
½ cup hot white wine
1 cup canned tomatoes or
    tomato sauce
¼ teaspoon salt

½ cup chopped celery
1 cup chopped cooked
    turkey meat
2 tablespoons chopped
    green peppers
1 minced clove garlic

Soak gelatin in cold wine and dissolve in hot wine, then pour over tomatoes or sauce, add salt, and beat with rotary beater until smooth. Chill until mixture begins to thicken. Stir in celery, turkey meat, green pepper and garlic. Turn into a chilled mold. Place mold in refrigerator, and when firm, unmold on lettuce leaves and serve with mayonnaise. Serves 6.

AVOCADO MOLD SALAD

1 package lemon gelatin
1 cup boiling water
2 tablespoons lemon juice

1 teaspoon salt
1 cup mayonnaise
1 cup mashed avocado

Dissolve gelatin in boiling water, chill until partially set, then beat with an egg beater. Add lemon juice, salt and mayonnaise. Fold in avocado. Pour into a ring mold or individual molds and chill. Serve on lettuce leaves which have been marinated in French dressing. Serves 6.

AVOCADO
(Alligator Pear)

Cut an avocado in half, lengthwise, leaving rind on. Remove stone and fill hole with juice of half a lemon, a heaping teaspoon of finely-chopped onion or garlic, and a scant teaspoon of vegetable salt. Serve as salad without trimmings.

TOMATO ASPIC

2½ cups canned tomatoes	1½ tablespoons vinegar
1 chopped onion	1 teaspoon salt
1 chopped clove garlic	⅛ teaspoon pepper
8 whole cloves	1 tablespoon gelatin
¼ cup cold water	

Mix tomatoes, onion, garlic, cloves, vinegar and seasonings in a saucepan and simmer 20 minutes. Strain and reheat. Soak gelatin in cold water a few minutes, then add to hot tomato mixture and stir until gelatin dissolves. Dip molds in cold water and shake but do not wipe dry. Pour tomato mixture into molds and chill until firm. Unmold. Use as a soup or on a salad.

MOLDED CABBAGE SALAD

2 tablespoons gelatin	Juice of 1 lemon
¾ cup cold water	1 cup shredded cabbage
¼ cup vinegar	2 cups minced celery
2 cups boiling water	¼ cup chopped pimento
1 teaspoon salt	¼ teaspoon minced onion

Dissolve gelatin in cold water; then add vinegar, boiling water, salt and lemon juice. Cool until partly jellied. Add remaining ingredients, turn into molds and chill. Serve with mayonnaise. Serves 6.

LOBSTER SALAD

Combine 2 cups diced boiled lobster meat and 2 diced dill pickles. Salt well with celery salt; then either marinate in French dressing or mix with mayonnaise or cold Boiled Dressing (3), p. 197. Serve on lettuce and garnish with slices of tomato, alligator pear or anchovy filets.

CHICKEN SALAD

1 chicken	1 teaspoon mustard
5 hard-boiled eggs	2 tablespoons grated horse-
½ cup melted butter	radish
1 tablespoon salt	1 cup strong vinegar
1 teaspoon pepper	1 cup chopped celery

Boil chicken till tender, skin, pick from bones and chop fine. Mash eggs and add butter, salt, pepper, mustard, horseradish and vinegar. Mix celery with chicken and just before serving add the sauce.

CRAB MEAT SALAD

2 cups flaked crab meat	Salt and pepper
1 cup chopped celery	1 pimento
½ cup mayonnaise	1 avocado

Combine crab meat, celery and mayonnaise. Season to taste. Chill and place on lettuce leaves. Garnish with strips of pimento and avocado. Serves 6.

CUCUMBER CREAM SALAD

2 tablespoons gelatin	Juice of 1 lemon
2 tablespoons cold water	½ cup chopped cucumbers
1 cup heavy cream, whipped	Dash of salt and cayenne

Dissolve gelatin in cold water and then add to whipped cream. Stir in remaining ingredients. Fill molds and chill. Garnish with sweet red peppers and serve with Boiled Dressing, p. 197. Serves 4.

POTATO SALAD

4 cups diced cold boiled	¼ cup minced parsley
potatoes	1 minced onion
½ cup diced celery	2 sliced hard-boiled eggs
½ cup chopped dill pickles	2 cups Boiled Dressing (2),
½ cup diced cucumbers	p. 197

Mix all the ingredients together and serve on lettuce. Serves 10.

POTATO SALAD WITH SLICED PENLEY SAUSAGES

5 diced cold boiled potatoes
1 diced cucumber
1 tablespoon minced onion
1 diced tomato
1 pound Penley little link
    sausages

French dressing (8 table-
    spoons oil; 5 of lemon
    juice)
1 teaspoon prepared
    mustard
1 tablespoon celery salt

Combine potatoes, cucumber, tomato and onion. Cook sausages in boiling water, cool, slice and add to potato mixture. Moisten with French dressing combined with mustard and salt.

FRENCH POTATO SALAD

4 hot boiled potatoes
3 thinly sliced onions
2 teaspoons salt

¼ teaspoon white pepper
4 tablespoons lemon juice
6 tablespoons olive oil

Boil potatoes in their skins in salted water until soft; preferably new potatoes. In a bowl place salt, pepper and onion, then add lemon juice and oil slowly, beating constantly with a wooden spoon. When all is blended well, slice the hot potatoes thin, add to dressing and chill. Serves 4.

MACÉDOINE SALAD

1 cup diced cold cooked
    chicken
1 cup diced cooked carrots
1 cup diced cold boiled po-
    tatoes
1 cup chopped cooked string
    beans

1 cup cooked peas
Juice of 1 lemon
Vinegar
¾ cup olive oil
Salt and pepper
1 cup diced celery
1 cup diced apples

1 diced green pepper

Mix carrots, potatoes, beans and peas together. Put lemon juice in cup and then fill cup with vinegar. Beat well lemon juice, vinegar, olive oil and seasonings. Pour over vegetables and let stand overnight. Drain in morning and add remaining ingredients. Serve on lettuce with mayonnaise.

MARCH SALAD

¼ pound macaroni	1 chopped green pepper
½ cup chopped celery	1 medium-sized can tuna
2 tablespoons chopped onion	fish
2 cups chopped cabbage	½ cup mayonnaise

Remove oil from tuna by pouring boiling water over it. Cook macaroni until tender, drain and chill. Mix macaroni with chopped vegetables and flaked fish. Add salt and paprika to taste; then blend in mayonnaise. Garnish with strips of green pepper and pimento.

SALMON SALAD

Marinate an equal amount of flaked cooked salmon and diced cold boiled potatoes in French dressing or mayonnaise. Season with salt and pepper. If desired, add sliced cucumbers, slivered dill pickles or chopped celery. Serve on lettuce leaves and garnish with strips of pimento.

TUNA FISH SALAD

Put the tuna in a colander and pour boiling water over it to remove oil; then flake it and marinate it in French dressing. Drain, add an equal amount of diced celery, and ½ a green pepper shredded. Mix with mayonnaise and place on lettuce leaves. Garnish with sliced hard-boiled egg.

VEGETABLE SALAD

1 thinly sliced cucumber	1 minced green pepper
3 thinly sliced onions	3 diced tomatoes
1 bunch chopped radishes	

Mix ingredients together and just before serving marinate in French dressing.

HERRING SALAD

Mix together an equal amount of flaked cooked salt herring and diced cold boiled potatoes. Add 1 minced onion. Marinate in French dressing and chill. Serve on lettuce leaves.

BOILED DRESSING (1)

2 tablespoons flour
1 teaspoon salt
1½ teaspoons dry mustard
1 egg

⅓ cup vinegar
½ cup water
1 cup milk
2 teaspoons butter

Beat together dry ingredients and egg; add liquid and mix. Cook in double boiler till thick, stirring constantly. After removing from fire add butter.

BOILED DRESSING (2)

3 tablespoons butter
2 tablespoons flour
1 cup milk

3 eggs
¾ cup vinegar
¾ tablespoon salt

1 tablespoon dry mustard

Melt butter and gradually stir in flour and milk. Beat eggs and add to them the vinegar, salt and mustard; add to the first mixture and cook until creamy. Cool, and then bottle and place in refrigerator.

BOILED DRESSING (3)

Bring to a boil 2 cups water and ½ cup lemon juice; then add 4 tablespoons flour mixed with 4 tablespoons olive oil. Boil 5 minutes; add slowly beaten yolks of 4 eggs; beat until smooth. When cold, add 2 cups olive oil seasoned with 2 teaspoons salt, 1 teaspoon mustard and a dash of pepper. This will keep for months in a cool place.

CHIFFONADE DRESSING

5 tablespoons olive or mineral oil
3 tablespoons lemon juice
2 tablespoons chopped pimento
2 tablespoons minced parsley

1 tablespoon finely minced onion
2 finely chopped hard-boiled eggs
1 heaping teaspoon celery salt

½ teaspoon pepper

Mix ingredients, chill in a tightly closed jar. Shake the jar well before serving the dressing.

CREAM SALAD DRESSING (1)

1 tablespoon dry mustard	⅔ cup boiling vinegar
1 teaspoon salt	⅔ cup butter
3 eggs	1 pint heavy cream

Mix the mustard and salt with the slightly beaten eggs, and add to boiling vinegar. Cook in double boiler 5 minutes. Add butter and chill; then fold in stiffly beaten cream.

CREAM SALAD DRESSING (2)

Mix the yolks of 4 hard-boiled eggs with 1½ teaspoons salt, 2 teaspoons dry mustard, ⅛ teaspoon paprika. Gradually add 1 pint sour cream. When smooth and creamy add ½ cup vinegar. Lastly add the finely chopped whites of the eggs.

SALAD DRESSING

1 can condensed tomato soup	1 onion, quartered
¾ cup lemon juice	1 clove garlic
1 teaspoon salt	1 tablespoon dry mustard
½ teaspoon pepper	1 tablespoon Worcestershire
½ teaspoon paprika	sauce
1½ cups olive oil	

Shake all ingredients together in a quart jar.

MAYONNAISE

1 teaspoon mustard	2 tablespoons vinegar
½ teaspoon salt	2 tablespoons chilled lemon
Dash paprika	juice
2 egg yolks	1 pint chilled olive oil

Mix dry ingredients, add egg yolks, mix thoroughly, add vinegar, stirring constantly. Beat with egg beater while adding chilled olive oil drop by drop. When it begins to thicken, add lemon juice and oil alternately. Keep in a cool place. Whipped cream may be added as used.

REDUCER'S MAYONNAISE

1 cup mineral oil   ½ teaspoon mustard
1 egg yolk   Salt and pepper
            2 tablespoons lemon juice

Beat egg yolk, mustard, salt and pepper together. Add mineral oil drop by drop till mixture begins to thicken. Then add alternately mineral oil and lemon juice, and season to taste.

VARIATION OF REDUCER'S MAYONNAISE

To ½ cup of Reducer's Mayonnaise add 2 tablespoons chopped celery, 1 tablespoon chopped pimento, 1 tablespoon chopped green pepper, ½ chopped hard-boiled egg and minced onion or pickle if desired.

ROQUEFORT DRESSING

4 tablespoons olive or mineral   ¼ teaspoon paprika
        oil   ⅛ teaspoon pepper
3 tablespoons lemon juice   4 tablespoons mashed
1 teaspoon celery salt   Roquefort cheese
            Few drops onion juice

Mix ingredients together. Serve on lettuce.

DEAN SMITH'S SALAD DRESSING

Sydney Smith, canon of St. Paul's, wrote a celebrated salad dressing recipe in verse, which boils down to:

½ cup oil   2 teaspoons salt
¼ cup wine vinegar   1 teaspoon anchovy sauce
½ clove garlic, well mashed   Mashed yolks of 2 hard-
2 mashed potatoes   boiled eggs
1 teaspoon dry mustard

SAUCES, KETCHUPS AND PICKLES

MAXIMS FROM MAINE KITCHENS

Marbles in the bottom of a kettle will prevent ketchup, milk, sauces, etc., from burning.

❧

To keep olives from spoiling in an opened bottle, pour in a teaspoonful of olive oil.

❧

When bottling grape juice, ketchup or any liquid, boil the corks to soften them, and press them into the bottle while hot. When they cool, the bottle will be tightly sealed.

❧

To prevent dill pickles in an opened jar from becoming moldy, shake the jar each day.

SAUCES, KETCHUPS AND PICKLES

———————◆————————

"So FAR as I know, every ketchup on the market has a sweetish, artificial, shallow flavor that revolts the descendants of Maine's seafaring families.

"In most parts of early New England, tomatoes were called 'love-apples,' and were shunned as being poisonous; but that wasn't true among Maine's seafaring families. Sea captains brought tomato seeds from Spain and Cuba, their wives planted them, and the good cooks in the families experimented with variants of the ubiquitous and somewhat characterless tomato sauce of Spain and Cuba. The ketchups they evolved, in spite of the aversion to tomatoes throughout early America, were considered indispensable with hash, fish cakes and baked beans in Maine, even in the days of love-apples.

"Such was the passion for my grandmother's ketchup in my own family that we could never get enough of it. We were allowed to have it on beans, fish cakes and hash, since those dishes were acknowledged to be incomplete without them; but when we went so far as to demand it on bread, as we often did, we were peremptorily refused, and had to go down in the cellar and steal it—which we also often did. It had a savory, appetizing tang to it that seemed —and still seems—to me to be inimitable. I became almost a ketchup drunkard; for when I couldn't get it, I yearned for it. Because of that yearning, I begged the recipe from my grandmother when I went away from home; and since that day I have made many and many a batch of her ketchup with excellent results."

—KENNETH ROBERTS, *Trending into Maine*

GRANDMA'S TOMATO KETCHUP

1 gallon strained tomatoes[1]	2 tablespoons mustard
6 tablespoons salt	1 tablespoon cloves
1 teaspoon black pepper	¼ teaspoon red pepper
4 tablespoons allspice	1 pint sharp vinegar

One peck of ripe tomatoes, cooked and strained, makes 1 gallon. Mix all the ingredients together and simmer 4 hours, stirring frequently to prevent spices from sticking. Cool and bottle. Olive oil poured in neck of bottle will preserve this indefinitely.

MUSHROOM KETCHUP

Lay fresh mushrooms in a deep dish, strew salt over them, then a fresh layer of mushrooms. Let them stay in this brine 3 days; then mash them fine, and add to each quart 1 tablespoon vinegar, ½ spoon pepper and 1 teaspoon cloves. Pour all this in a stone jar and place the jar in a pot of boiling water. Let it boil 2 hours, then strain it without squeezing the mushrooms. Boil the juice 15 minutes and skim it well. Let it stand a few hours to settle. Bottle and pour olive oil on top to keep from fermenting. Keep in a cool place.

BÉCHAMEL SAUCE

1 slice onion	1 cup chicken stock
1 slice carrot	2 tablespoons flour
½ bay leaf	2 tablespoons butter
Sprig of parsley	½ cup light cream
6 peppercorns	½ teaspoon salt
¼ teaspoon pepper	

Cook onion, carrot, bay leaf, parsley and peppercorns in stock 20 minutes. Strain, and if necessary add enough water to make ½ cup. Melt butter, add flour, and gradually hot stock and cream. Cook 5 minutes, stirring constantly. Add seasonings. Serve on chicken timbales, croquettes, etc.

---

[1]This ketchup is more easily made if, for the strained tomatoes, 8 pint cans of tomato purée are substituted, or one hotel-size (gallon) can. If this substitution is made, the mixture need be simmered only one hour. One brand is Iona Purée, sold by A & P stores.

BARBECUE SAUCE (1)

2 tablespoons butter	½ cup tomato ketchup
2 tablespoons vinegar	1 cup stock
2 tablespoons Worcestershire	¼ cup chopped celery
sauce	¼ teaspoon salt
½ teaspoon dry mustard	¼ teaspoon pepper
1 teaspoon chopped onion	

Mix ingredients and heat to boiling point. Use to baste meats while roasting.

BARBECUE SAUCE (2)

1 minced onion	½ cup tomato ketchup
1 minced green pepper	¼ cup Worcestershire sauce
1½ cups tomato juice	⅓ cup butter
1 cup vinegar	1 teaspoon salt

Mix ingredients together and simmer 1 hour, stirring occasionally. Serve hot on steak.

SAUCE BÉARNAISE

4 egg yolks	1 tablespoon lemon juice or
¼ cup hot water or white	wine vinegar
wine	½ teaspoon salt
¼ cup olive oil	Dash of cayenne

Beat egg yolks until creamy; add water or wine and oil. Cook over hot water until it thickens. Remove from fire and add vinegar and seasonings. Mix well.

BREAD SAUCE

1 cup fine, stale bread crumbs	1 teaspoon salt
1 onion	¼ teaspoon paprika
3 whole cloves	1 pint milk
1½ tablespoons butter	

Cook crumbs, onion stuck with cloves, seasonings and milk in double boiler 1 hour. Remove onion and add butter. Beat until smooth. Serve on game or egg timbales.

LEMON BUTTER

½ cup butter   2 tablespoons lemon juice

Cream butter until soft and gradually stir in lemon juice. If butter is unsalted, add ½ teaspoon salt. Serve on fish.

LEMON BUTTER SAUCE

½ cup melted butter   ¼ cup lemon juice
2 teaspoons chopped parsley

Mix the above ingredients together and heat. Serve on fish, lobster, crabs, shrimp.

MAÎTRE D'HÔTEL BUTTER

2 tablespoons butter   ½ teaspoon salt
1 tablespoon chopped parsley   ¼ teaspoon pepper
1 tablespoon lemon juice

Cream butter until soft; add parsley, seasonings and lemon juice, beating until fluffy. Spread on broiled meat or fish.

BROWN SAUCE

2 tablespoons butter   1 cup brown stock
3 tablespoons flour   ½ teaspoon salt

Melt butter, stir in flour and cook until browned, stirring constantly. Gradually add stock, bring to boiling point, and boil 3 minutes. Add salt and pepper to taste.

CAPTAIN NASON'S CHILI SAUCE

30 ripe tomatoes   ½ cup sugar
2 hot peppers   2½ cups vinegar
4 large onions   2 tablespoons celery salt
2 teaspoons allspice

Scald and peel the tomatoes, remove the seeds from the peppers, peel onions. Chop onions and peppers fine. Chop tomatoes and combine ingredients. Cook for 2½ hours. If additional warmth is wanted, add more peppers.

CHILI SAUCE (1)

6 chopped tomatoes
2 chopped onions
1 chopped green pepper
⅔ cup vinegar
1 teaspoon cinnamon
1 teaspoon allspice
½ teaspoon cloves

Combine ingredients and cook slowly until thick.

CHILI SAUCE (2)

8 quarts ripe tomatoes, peeled and cut up
4 cups ground onions
4 cups ground sweet red peppers
6 tablespoons salt
6 tablespoons mustard seed
6 tablespoons celery seed
2 cups granulated sugar
1 quart vinegar
1 teaspoon cloves
1 teaspoon cinnamon
2 tablespoons pickling spices, tied in cheese-cloth bag
½ teaspoon dried hot pepper, tied in cheese-cloth bag
½ cup brown sugar

Combine ingredients in a kettle and simmer slowly, stirring frequently. Leave hot pepper bag in only until mixture suits taste. After 2½ hours, put through coarse sieve and remove spice bag. Simmer until desired thickness is reached. Pour into clean hot jars and seal.

CAPER SAUCE
(For crab meat, lobster, cold fish, etc.)

5 chicken bouillon cubes dissolved in
2 cups boiling water
2 tablespoons butter
2 tablespoons flour
2 tablespoons lemon juice
1 tablespoon heavy cream
2 tablespoons capers
2 tablespoons caper liquid
1 teaspoon celery salt
½ teaspoon pepper

Melt butter, add flour and gradually stir in boiling water in which chicken cubes have been dissolved. When smooth and slightly thickened stir in remaining ingredients.

CHEESE SAUCE (1)

3 tablespoons butter	¼ teaspoon pepper
3 tablespoons flour	¼ teaspoon paprika
½ teaspoon salt	1 cup milk

1 cup grated sharp cheese, or 1½ cups diced soft cheese

Melt butter, add flour and seasonings, and stir till blended. Gradually stir in milk; then add cheese and cook till melted.

CHEESE SAUCE (2)

4 tablespoons butter	1 teaspoon dry mustard
4 tablespoons flour	2 teaspoons Worcestershire
1 teaspoon celery salt	sauce
¼ teaspoon pepper	1½ cups grated sharp
2 cups milk	cheese

Melt butter, add flour, salt and pepper, and stir till blended. Pour in milk, stirring constantly. Add remaining ingredients and cook till cheese is melted.

CLAM SAUCE

¼ cup butter	1 teaspoon minced parsley
1 chopped onion	2½ cups canned tomatoes
1 minced clove garlic	1 quart chopped clams

Salt and pepper

Sauté onion and garlic in butter until brown, then add parsley and tomatoes. Simmer 45 minutes. Wash and steam clams; then add the juice to the sauce. Add the chopped clams. Season with salt and pepper. Serve on baked fish.

NAPLES CLAM SAUCE

In a saucepan put 2 cans minced Maine clams and their liquor, or 1 quart coarsely chopped clams, from which the head has been removed. Add 1 chopped clove garlic, 2 tablespoons butter, 2 teaspoons celery salt, 3 tablespoons chopped parsley and a dash of cayenne pepper. Heat. Serve on spaghetti. Serves 4. This is the sauce known in Naples as Vongole Sauce.

CIDER SAUCE

2 tablespoons minced onion
2 tablespoons minced celery
3 tablespoons butter
3 tablespoons flour

Salt and pepper
1 teaspoon prepared
   mustard
1 cup cider

Sauté onion and celery in butter 3 minutes, then stir in remaining ingredients. Simmer until the sauce thickens. Serve on Ham Loaf, p. 148, or Ham Croquettes, p. 147.

CREOLE SAUCE

¼ cup butter
3 tablespoons minced green
   pepper
3 tablespoons chopped onion
¼ cup flour

½ cup stewed and strained
   tomatoes
1 cup bouillon
1 teaspoon celery salt
⅛ teaspoon pepper

Sauté onion and pepper in butter 5 minutes; add flour and stir until browned; add tomatoes; then add bouillon and heat to boiling. Add seasonings and strain.

CURRY SAUCE

2 apples, thinly sliced
3 tablespoons butter
1 minced onion
¼ teaspoon ground cloves
½ cup thin cream

1 tablespoon curry powder
3 teaspoons lemon juice
4 chicken cubes dissolved in
2 cups rice water

Sauté apples and onion in butter. Mash, simmer and stir in cloves, curry powder and lemon juice. Gradually add chicken-rice water and cook until thickened. Add cream and simmer 20 minutes. The sauce may be strained or not, as desired. Serve on rice to which peeled boiled eggs, chicken, shrimp, lobsters, oysters or crab meat have been added.

CUCUMBER SAUCE (1)

Pare, seed and grate 2 cucumbers. Add juice of 2 lemons, 2 teaspoons celery salt, ½ teaspoon pepper, and blend. Serve on fish.

CUCUMBER SAUCE (2)

Slice 4 large cucumbers thinly and parboil in salted water for 10 minutes; then drain. Over the cucumbers pour 1 cup sour cream. Season plentifully with celery salt and pepper and simmer ½ hour; then add 1 teaspoon mustard, 2 tablespoons horseradish, and beat smooth. Serve on fish.

EGG SAUCE

2 tablespoons butter	Salt and pepper
2 tablespoons flour	½ cup sliced sautéed mush-
1 cup fish stock or water	rooms
2 egg yolks	1 teaspoon chopped parsley
2 tablespoons heavy cream	2 tablespoons white wine

Melt butter, then stir in flour and stock. Then add slightly beaten egg yolks, salt and pepper. When well blended remove from fire and add mushrooms, parsley and white wine.

HOLLANDAISE SAUCE (1)

¼ pound butter	Pinch of salt
3 egg yolks	Dash of cayenne
2 tablespoons lemon juice	

Cut butter into 3 pieces, and put 1 piece in double boiler with egg yolks, seasonings and lemon juice. Cook and stir constantly until butter melts. Add second piece of butter and stir until melted. Add third piece, and stir until that in turn melts. Remove from stove and serve at once. If sauce gets too thick, add a little chicken broth or warm water, and stir.

HOLLANDAISE SAUCE (2)

4 egg yolks	1 tablespoon lemon juice
½ cup melted butter	½ teaspoon salt
Few grains cayenne	

Beat egg yolks, gradually add the butter and seasonings. Cook in double boiler, stirring constantly until the sauce thickens. Remove from fire, stir in lemon juice and serve at once.

WHIPPED CREAM HORSERADISH SAUCE

1/4 cup grated horseradish   1/2 teaspoon salt
1 tablespoon cider vinegar   1/4 teaspoon paprika
          1 cup heavy cream

Mix horseradish, vinegar and seasonings. Just before serving, fold in stiffly beaten cream. Serve with cold meats.

MADRILÈNE SAUCE

2 tablespoons butter   1/2 cup red wine
2 tablespoons flour   Dash of salt and pepper
          1 cup madrilène or chicken stock

Melt butter and stir in flour. When well blended gradually add hot madrilène or stock, red wine and seasonings. Serve on steak.

MIGNONETTE SAUCE
(For raw oysters)

To 1 quart bottle of vinegar add 1 tablespoon coarsely ground peppercorns, 1 tablespoon celery salt, 1 tablespoon celery seed and 2 finely chopped onions.

MINT SAUCE

1/4 cup finely chopped mint   1 cup sugar
          1/2 cup vinegar

Wash and chop mint in chopping bowl. Mix sugar and vinegar and cook until it makes a syrup. Add mint. Serve on lamb.

MUSHROOM SAUCE

1/2 pound sliced mushrooms   3 tablespoons flour
1/4 cup butter   1 cup thin cream

Sauté mushrooms in butter, add flour slowly. Brown slightly; then add the cream and cook till thick. Serve on steak or chicken.

MUSTARD SAUCE (1)

1 tablespoon butter
1 tablespoon finely chopped
   onion

2 tablespoons sharp vinegar
2 teaspoons powdered Eng-
   lish mustard

1 cup brown gravy

Sauté the onion in butter. Add the vinegar and boil 2 minutes. Moisten the mustard, stir it into the brown gravy, and add gravy to vinegar and onion. Boil 5 minutes, strain through a sieve and serve hot. This is the sauce which the Parker House in Boston serves with broiled tripe.

MUSTARD SAUCE (2)

2 egg yolks
3 tablespoons melted butter
1 tablespoon vinegar

2 tablespoons dry mustard
1 teaspoon celery salt
1 teaspoon flour

½ cup water

Beat egg yolks well, add remaining ingredients, mixing well; then bring to a boil. If the sauce is too stiff, add more vinegar or water.

NEWBURG SAUCE

2 tablespoons butter
½ teaspoon salt
¼ teaspoon paprika

1 cup heavy cream
¼ cup sherry
4 egg yolks

Melt butter, add seasonings and cream. Cook until heated. Add egg yolks and sherry and stir until thickened. Heat 2 cups of lobster or crab meat in sauce.

OYSTER COCKTAIL SAUCE

½ cup tomato ketchup
1 teaspoon celery salt
Dash of pepper

2 teaspoons horseradish
¼ cup lemon juice
2 drops Tabasco sauce

Mix ingredients together and chill. Serve chilled with oysters on the half shell.

RAISIN SAUCE
(For ham)

1 cup raisins	¼ teaspoon salt
1 cup water	⅛ teaspoon pepper
4 whole cloves	1 tablespoon butter
¾ cup brown sugar	1 tablespoon vinegar
1 teaspoon cornstarch	1 teaspoon Worcestershire sauce

Cook raisins, water and cloves for 10 minutes. Then add the mixed sugar, cornstarch, salt and pepper. Stir until slightly thickened and then add remaining ingredients.

SAUSAGE GRAVY

2 tablespoons sausage fat	2 cups milk
2 tablespoons flour	½ teaspoon salt
⅛ teaspoon pepper	

Melt fat in a frying pan and stir in flour until smooth. Gradually add milk and seasonings. Stir slowly until gravy begins to simmer, then cook 6 minutes, until creamy and well blended.

SHRIMP SAUCE

1½ cups chopped cooked shrimp	1½ cups Medium White Sauce, p. 214
3 tablespoons lemon juice	2 hard-boiled eggs

Soak shrimp in lemon juice ½ hour and then add them to white sauce. Before serving add the finely chopped eggs. Serve on fish.

STEAK SAUCE

¾ cup butter	1 teaspoon dry mustard
1 tablespoon Worcestershire sauce	2 teaspoons lemon juice
	1 tablespoon tomato ketchup

Cook all the ingredients in a saucepan over low heat until the butter is melted and the sauce is smooth. Stir constantly. Serve on steak.

TARRAGON SAUCE

1 teaspoon lemon juice	1½ tablespoons butter
1 tablespoon tarragon vinegar	1 egg yolk
2 tablespoons hot water	⅛ teaspoon salt

Mix the lemon juice, vinegar and water together. Melt the butter in double boiler, add the egg yolk and beat until creamy. Add the salt and then the liquids. Stir constantly until it thickens.

TARTARE SAUCE

1 cup mayonnaise	1 teaspoon onion juice
1 tablespoon finely chopped cucumber pickles	1 tablespoon chopped capers
1 tablespoon chopped parsley	1 teaspoon celery salt

Combine ingredients, mix well and serve with fish.

TOMATO SAUCE (1)[2]

(For fish, meat loaves, rice, macaroni, omelets, hash, hams, gnocchi, etc.)

3 tablespoons butter	1 cup canned tomatoes
3 tablespoons flour	½ teaspoon allspice
	Salt and pepper

Brown butter, add flour, strained tomatoes and seasonings. Bring to boiling point.

TOMATO SAUCE (2)

(For fish, egg dishes or thinly sliced meats such as lamb, veal, pork or tripe)

Bring to a boil in a saucepan 1 cup canned tomatoes, 1 cup water, 2 whole cloves, 2 allspice berries, 2 peppercorns, 1 teaspoon chopped parsley and 1 teaspoon mixed herbs. Sauté 1 tablespoon chopped onion in 1 tablespoon butter, and stir in 1 heaping tablespoon cornstarch; then add to tomato mixture. Simmer 10 minutes. Season with ½ teaspoon salt, ¼ teaspoon pepper and juice of 1 lemon. Strain and serve.

---

[2]Additional Tomato Sauce recipes on pp. 214, 240–41.

ITALIAN TOMATO SAUCE

4 pork chops	2 cans tomato juice
2 tablespoons butter	2 cans tomato paste
1 chopped onion	1 cup fresh mushrooms
1 chopped green pepper	½ cup chopped celery

Salt and pepper

Brown chops in butter with onion and green pepper; then place in a kettle with tomato juice and paste. Season and simmer 3½ to 4 hours. A half hour before serving add mushrooms and celery. Remove bones and gristle from chops, cut to bits, replace in sauce and use on spaghetti, macaroni, noodles, gnocchi, etc.

VINAIGRETTE SAUCE

½ cup tarragon vinegar	1 teaspoon chopped capers
2 tablespoons olive oil	1 teaspoon chopped
8 chopped olives	pimentos
8 chopped sour midget pickles	¼ teaspoon paprika

1 teaspoon celery salt

Combine ingredients in order given; stir vigorously before serving on fish.

THIN WHITE SAUCE

1 tablespoon butter	1 cup milk
1 tablespoon flour	½ teaspoon salt

⅛ teaspoon pepper

Melt butter, add flour and blend. Gradually add milk, stirring constantly until mixture thickens. Add seasonings.

MEDIUM WHITE SAUCE

Follow recipe for Thin White Sauce, but use 2 tablespoons butter and 2 tablespoons flour.

THICK WHITE SAUCE

Follow recipe for Thin White Sauce, but use 4 tablespoons butter and 4 tablespoons flour.

CREAM SAUCE

Substitute cream for milk in any of the White Sauce recipes, p. 214.

PLAIN CUCUMBER PICKLES

Wash and wipe small pickling cucumbers and place in earthen jar. To every quart add 2 teaspoons of salt. Set for 3 hours, then turn off brine. Fill up jar with cider vinegar and add ½ cup allspice. Pour into jars and seal.

RIPE CUCUMBER PICKLES

Peel and seed 24 large cucumbers, too large for the table. Chop fine with 8 onions. Mix with 1 cup salt and let stand all night. Drain off liquid and add 1 heaping tablespoon mustard, 2 teaspoons black pepper and enough vinegar to mix well. Put up in stone jars without sealing.

CUCUMBER PICKLES

One peck small cucumbers, 1 gallon cider vinegar, 4 onions, 2 red peppers, ¼ pound salt, ¼ pound ground mustard, 1 ounce white ginger root, 2 ounces white mustard seed, 1 ounce stick cinnamon, 1 ounce whole cloves, ½ ounce peppercorns, 1 ounce horseradish. Mix in a stone crock. Stir from bottom daily for 3 weeks.

BREAD AND BUTTER PICKLES

30 5-inch cucumbers	1 cup water
12 small white onions	2 cups sugar
½ cup salt	1 tablespoon white mustard
Ice water	seed
1 quart vinegar	1 tablespoon turmeric
1 tablespoon celery seed	

Cut unpeeled cucumbers and peeled onions in thin slices. Sprinkle with salt, cover with chopped ice and ice water, and let stand 3 hours. Drain. Mix remaining ingredients and bring to a boil. Add cucumbers and onions and simmer 5 minutes. Pour into hot sterilized jars and seal at once.

PICKLE FOR 100 POUNDS OF HAM, ROAST, BACON, ETC.

3 pounds fine salt
3 pounds rock salt
1 pound brown sugar

1 quart molasses
1 ounce saltpeter
1 ounce soda

6 gallons water

Boil the salts, sugar, molasses, saltpeter and soda with about 3 gallons of water. Add the remaining water and when cold pour on meat.

CHOPPED PICKLES

1 peck green tomatoes
2 quarts onions
2 quarts peppers
3 cups salt

½ pound mustard seed
2 tablespoons allspice
2 tablespoons cloves
1 cup grated horseradish

3 quarts boiling vinegar

Chop tomatoes, onions and peppers fine, cover with salt and let stand overnight. Drain and add remaining ingredients.

SPICED BANANAS

¼ cup cider vinegar
1 cup water
½ cup sugar

Stick of cinnamon, broken
25 whole cloves
3 bananas

Boil vinegar, sugar, water, cinnamon and cloves until a thick syrup forms. Peel bananas, cut into thirds and drop in syrup. Cook slowly 3 minutes; then cool and serve with meat.

BEET RELISH

1 cup chopped, cold cooked
   beets
3 tablespoons horseradish

2 tablespoons lemon juice
1 tablespoon powdered
   sugar

2 teaspoons salt

Mix ingredients in order given.

PICKLED BEETS

Cook small beets in boiling salted water until tender; then drop in cold water, drain and peel off skins. Pack in jars and pour over boiling vinegar spiced with 1 teaspoon salt, 1 tablespoon white mustard seed, 1 teaspoon each cloves and allspice, and ½ cup sugar to 1 quart of vinegar.

PICKLED CABBAGE

2 cabbages	¼ cup celery seed
1 quart small onions	½ teaspoon cayenne
2 dozen red peppers	½ cup white mustard seed
1½ cups salt	½ ounce turmeric
1 gallon vinegar	Sliver of alum

Chop vegetables fine, cover with salt, mix well and let stand overnight. Drain. Bring remaining ingredients to a boil and pour over vegetables. Cover and let stand 1 week.

SHARP RELISH

6 carrots	1 cup salt
6 medium-sized onions	3 pints vinegar
12 sweet green peppers	2 tablespoons celery seed
6 pounds of cabbage	2 tablespoons mustard seed

Chop all the vegetables, stir in the salt and let stand 3 hours. Drain, add remaining ingredients and bottle cold.

WINTER RELISH

2 medium cabbages (4 pounds)	½ cup salt
8 carrots	1 teaspoon turmeric
4 green sweet peppers	1 teaspoon celery seed
4 red sweet peppers	1 teaspoon mustard seed
2 peeled onions	4 cups sugar
	5 cups vinegar

Grind vegetables, add salt and let stand 2 hours. Drain off juice. Mix spices and sugar together and add to vegetables. Add vinegar and bottle.

CHOWCHOW PICKLES

1 quart small onions	1 cauliflower, separated into
1 quart small cucumbers	flowerets
1 quart large cucumbers,	4 chopped red peppers
sliced	4 quarts water
1 quart small green tomatoes	3 cups salt

Make a brine of water and salt, pour over vegetables and leave for 24 hours; then cook until vegetables are soft. Drain, and while still hot cover with following dressing:

1 cup flour	1 ounce turmeric
6 tablespoons dry mustard	Vinegar

Moisten dry ingredients to paste with cold vinegar. Add vinegar to make 2 quarts. Boil until thick, stirring constantly.

SPICED CURRANTS

6 pounds currants	1 tablespoon cloves
4 pounds sugar	2 tablespoons cinnamon
	1 pint vinegar

Wash, drain and remove stems from currants. Put in a kettle, add remaining ingredients and simmer 1½ hours.

SPICED GOOSEBERRIES

5 pounds gooseberries	2 tablespoons cinnamon
8 cups sugar	1 tablespoon cloves
2 cups cider vinegar	1 tablespoon allspice

Pick over, wash and drain gooseberries. Put in kettle and add sugar, vinegar and spices. Bring slowly to boiling point and cook 2 hours, stirring frequently. Pour into jars and seal.

POTTED MACKEREL

One dozen mackerel, ½ cup salt, ½ ounce allspice, ½ ounce cloves. Cider vinegar to cover them. Roll the mackerel in the salt, pack closely in a stone jar, put the spices in a bag and lay on top. Cover with the vinegar and bake 6 hours in a moderate oven. These will keep for months.

CORN RELISH

1 dozen ears corn
1 cup chopped celery
2 chopped onions
2 chopped green peppers

1 cup chopped cabbage
2 tablespoons salt
1/4 teaspoon pepper
1 1/2 tablespoons dry mustard

2 cups vinegar

Cut corn from cob and mix with celery, onions, peppers and cabbage. Add remaining ingredients and cook slowly 1 hour, stirring occasionally. Pour into jars and seal.

PICKLED MAINE MUSSELS

3 or 4 quarts mussels
Sliced onion
Garlic buds
Mixed pickling spices
Salt

Freshly ground black
    pepper
Cider vinegar (or white
    wine vinegar)

Wash and scrub mussels carefully. Steam them open in large kettle with 1 cup water. Lift out mussels and shell, removing beard. Reserve the mussel broth. In a crock or glass jar arrange layers of shelled mussels, onion slices, garlic, spices, salt and pepper. Add strained mussel broth to 1/3 the depth of mussels, then pour on vinegar to cover. Let stand open, at least 3 days before using, stirring once or twice. Serve as a relish or appetizer.

OLIVE OIL PICKLES

50 2-inch cucumbers
1 cup salt
6 teaspoons white mustard
    seed

4 teaspoons white pepper
2 teaspoons celery seed
1 quart small white onions
1 cup olive oil

Vinegar

Slice cucumbers paper-thin, cover with salt and let stand 3 hours. Drain. Add the mustard seed, white pepper and celery seed to the olive oil. Slice the onions thin, add them to the oil, then pour over sliced cucumbers. Cover the mixture with vinegar and seal in sterilized jars.

MUSTARD PICKLES (1)

1 quart cucumbers	1 cup flour
1 bottle small onions	2 tablespoons mustard
1 quart vinegar	1 tablespoon salt
1 pint water	2 teaspoons turmeric

Chop cucumbers fine. Heat vinegar and water. Stir in dry ingredients moistened with a little of the water. Strain sauce, add cucumbers and onions, and bring to a boil. Pour into jars and seal.

MUSTARD PICKLES (2)

2 quarts cucumbers	1 ounce turmeric
1 quart small onions	2 ounces mustard
2 large cauliflowers	1 teaspoon pepper
1 cup salt	1 teaspoon vinegar
1 gallon water	3 tablespoons butter
2 quarts vinegar	½ cup flour

Cut vegetables fine, cover with salt and water, and let stand overnight. In the morning scald in the brine, drain and cool. Cream butter, flour, spices and teaspoon of vinegar together, add to vinegar and bring to a boil. Pour over vegetables. Pour into jars and seal.

PICKLED ONIONS

Peel small white onions and scald in salted water. Drain, put into a stone jar, and sprinkle with white mustard seed and pepper. Cover them with boiling vinegar. When cold, put in jars and seal. 1 tablespoon olive oil may be added to the top of the mixture.

PICKLED OYSTERS

1 quart oysters	1 teaspoon mace
1 quart oyster liquor	½ teaspoon cloves
1 teaspoon salt	½ teaspoon allspice
	1 cup hot vinegar

Wash and clean the oysters. Boil the liquor and skim. Add the oysters and seasonings and cook until oysters are plump. Add the hot vinegar and pour into jars. Seal.

PICKLED PEACHES

6 pounds peaches	3½ pounds brown sugar
1 pint vinegar	1 ounce stick cinnamon

1 teaspoon whole cloves

Rub the fuzz from peaches with a towel. Boil the sugar and vinegar; put the cinnamon and cloves in a bag and add to the vinegar. Put peaches into the syrup and cook until soft, using half the peaches at a time. Pack into hot sterilized jars, fill with syrup and seal.

BRANDIED PEACHES (1)

Select large white peaches and place them in a wire basket. Plunge the basket into boiling water for 2 minutes. Remove the skins from peaches when cool and drop them into cold water to keep them from losing color. Make a syrup of 1 pound of sugar and a little water to each pound of fruit. When it boils, drop peaches in, a few at a time. Cook until they look clear, lift them out carefully and put in glass jars. Fill jars with ½ syrup and ½ brandy. Seal.

BRANDIED PEACHES (2)

Dip peaches in boiling water and rub off skins. Pack a layer in bottom of a crock and fill space between peaches with sugar. Continue till crock is filled. Weight with a rock on a plate. On the following days replace shrinkage with more peaches and sugar. When shrinkage stops in 6 to 8 days put cover on crock and leave in a moderate temperature to ferment. Skim off scum. At the end of 6 weeks' fermentation the peaches will be brandied and can be sealed.

PEPPER RELISH

3 pounds red peppers	2 dozen small onions
3 pounds green peppers	1 tablespoon salt

3 pints vinegar

Clean peppers, remove core and seeds, and put separately through food chopper. Cover with boiling water and boil separately for 10 minutes. Drain, mix together, and add salt, chopped onions and vinegar. Boil 30 minutes, pour into jars and seal.

PICKLED PEPPERS

Wash, cut open, and remove seeds from red or green peppers. Cut into long, thin strips, scald and drop into cold water for 5 minutes. Drain and pack into jars. Make a pickle of 1 teaspoon each of salt, allspice, cloves and cinnamon to 1 quart of vinegar. Simmer 10 minutes, strain and pour over peppers. Seal jars.

TOMATO MUSTARD

1 peck ripe tomatoes	1 tablespoon cinnamon
6 red peppers	1 tablespoon ginger
2 onions	1 tablespoon cloves
2 tablespoons salt	2 tablespoons mustard

½ pint vinegar

Boil tomatoes, peppers and onions in water 1 hour; strain through a sieve. Add the other ingredients and boil 2 hours more.

TOMATO RELISH

2 quarts green tomatoes	2 seed cucumbers
2 quarts red tomatoes	3 green peppers
1 bunch celery	3 red peppers
3 large onions	½ cup salt
1 small cabbage	3 pints vinegar

1 teaspoon mustard

Chop all the vegetables and stir in the salt. Let stand overnight. Drain, add vinegar and mustard, and bring mixture to a boil. Cook slowly ½ hour. Pour into jars and seal.

EGGS AND CHEESE

MAXIMS FROM MAINE KITCHENS

To keep eggs from popping while frying, sprinkle a little flour in the fat before putting in the eggs.

❁

To boil cracked eggs, add a tablespoonful of salt to a quart of water, and no whites will run out.

❁

To keep eggs for long periods, place a few at a time in boiling water for ten seconds. They will then keep for months in an ice chest.

❁

To make scrambled eggs go further, add bread crumbs.

❁

Torn table or shelf oilcloth can be mended by sticking a piece of white adhesive tape under the tear on the wrong side of the oilcloth. The tape should be cut a little wider and a little longer than the tear.

EGGS AND CHEESE

CODDLED EGGS

PUT the eggs in warm water for a few minutes to remove chill. Then lower gently into container half full of boiling water. Leave on stove 5 seconds; then remove from fire, cover and let stand 5 minutes.

POACHED EGGS

Boil 1 quart water, 1 tablespoon vinegar and 1 tablespoon salt in frying pan. Break eggs, one by one, into a saucer and slide quickly into boiling water. Cook until the white is firm, spooning the boiling water over the tops of the eggs so that they will cook evenly. Remove with spatula to buttered pieces of toast. To keep the whites from spreading, place muffin rings on the bottom of the pan and drop one egg into each ring.

FRIED EGGS

Melt 1 tablespoon butter or bacon fat in frying pan; then slip in eggs and cook until white is firm. Spoon fat over eggs to cook tops evenly. Sprinkle with salt and pepper before serving.

DEVILED EGGS

Hard-boil eggs and cut them in halves. Remove yolks and mash, moistening with melted butter and lemon juice. Add a generous amount of dry mustard, celery salt, pepper, and 1 tablespoon anchovy paste. Refill whites with the mixture.

CREAMED EGGS

Boil eggs 10 minutes, then put them under cold water 1 minute, after which remove shells. Halve eggs and pour Medium Cream Sauce, p. 215, over them.

SCRAMBLED EGGS (1)

¾ cup light cream   Salt and pepper
6 eggs   2 tablespoons butter

Heat a frying pan, add cream and bring to a boil. Beat eggs in a bowl with a fork, add seasonings to taste and pour into bubbling cream. Stir at intervals and scrape from bottom and sides of pan. Cook until eggs are a creamy consistency. Remove from pan while still moist. Add butter and serve at once. Serves 4.

SCRAMBLED EGGS (2)

Into a bowl break 2 eggs per person. Add 2 tablespoons of milk for each egg, and season with salt and pepper. Beat with egg beater until foamy. In a frying pan heat 1 tablespoon of chicken, bacon or sausage fat, or butter, for every 2 eggs. The fat should be hot when eggs are poured in, but not bubbling or smoking. Lower heat as soon as eggs are added. When eggs begin to get firm on bottom, scoop with a large spoon from one side of pan to the other. Uncooked liquid will seep into cleared part of pan. Repeat scooping until the eggs run no more, but are still moist. They are then done. Serve with fried bacon, or with Pork Sausages, p. 149.

DOUBLE BOILER SCRAMBLED EGGS

6 eggs   1 teaspoon celery salt
½ cup milk or light cream   ¼ teaspoon pepper
            2 tablespoons butter

Beat eggs, salt and pepper until light and fluffy; gradually beat in milk. Melt butter in the top of a double boiler, set over boiling water. Add egg mixture and cook without removing the cover for 15 minutes. Stir, and continue to cook 10 or 15 minutes longer, or until firm. Serves 4.

DEVILED SCRAMBLED EGGS

2 tablespoons butter
4 eggs, well beaten
1 teaspoon dry English
   mustard

1 teaspoon minced onion
1 teaspoon minced parsley
¼ cup sour cream
1 teaspoon anchovy paste

Salt and pepper

Melt butter in frying pan. Mix remaining ingredients together and add to melted butter. Cook slowly, stirring constantly, until creamy. Serve at once. Serves 3 or 4.

SCRAMBLED EGGS WITH TOMATOES

1 large tomato
2 slices Spanish onion

2 tablespoons butter
Salt and pepper

4 eggs, beaten

Remove skin from tomato and mince fine. Melt butter, add tomato, onion and seasoning and sauté until onion is cooked, but not brown. Add eggs and stir constantly until set. Serve at once. Serves 2 or 3.

ROCKY PASTURE EGGS

For one serving break 2 eggs into a custard cup. Stir lightly and season with salt, pepper, celery salt and a dash of mustard. Place cup in a pan of hot water and simmer 15 minutes. Then chill to stop cooking.

SPANISH EGGS (1)

1 clove garlic
2 tablespoons butter
1 chopped tomato

6 eggs
1 teaspoon salt
¼ teaspoon pepper

Pinch of basil

Rub the inside of a frying pan with a clove of garlic; then add butter and tomato and cook 5 minutes. Add well-beaten eggs and seasonings to tomatoes. Cook slowly, stirring occasionally, until eggs are done. Serve on buttered toast. Serves 4.

SPANISH EGGS (2)

2 tablespoons butter
1 cup tomatoes
1 minced onion
1 teaspoon cornstarch

6 eggs
½ teaspoon salt
⅛ teaspoon pepper
1 teaspoon chopped parsley

½ teaspoon celery salt

Melt butter in hot frying pan, add tomatoes and onion and cook 5 minutes. Stir in cornstarch and cook 3 minutes. Then stir in slightly beaten eggs and remaining ingredients. Stir constantly until creamy. Serve on hot buttered toast. Serves 4.

SHIRRED EGGS

Put 1 tablespoon heavy cream, 1 teaspoon butter and 1 tablespoon tomato ketchup in a custard cup; break an egg into it, sprinkle with salt and pepper, place on baking sheet or in shallow pan, and bake in a moderate oven, 350 degrees, 15 minutes.

SHIRRED EGGS WITH SAUSAGES

Cut Penley's little link sausages into ½-inch pieces, cook lightly and drain off fat. Cover bottom of 8-inch baking dish with sausages, pour over 1 cup ketchup or Tomato Sauce, p. 213. Break 6 eggs in the ketchup and bake in a moderate oven, 350 degrees, 15 minutes.

SHIRRED EGGS IN MACARONI

1 tablespoon butter
1 tablespoon flour
1 cup milk
1 cup grated cheese

2 teaspoons salt
¼ teaspoon pepper
2 cups hot cooked macaroni
4 eggs

Melt butter, stir in flour and gradually add milk. Cook 5 minutes, stirring until smooth. Add cheese and seasonings, and cook until cheese is melted. Put macaroni in buttered baking dish and cover with cheese sauce. Make 4 depressions with a spoon in mixture and drop an egg in each hollow. Bake in a moderate oven, 350 degrees, 15 minutes. Serves 4.

MONHEGAN EGGS

1 cup light cream	1 teaspoon butter
1 tablespoon ketchup	1 teaspoon chopped onion
1 teaspoon celery salt	6 eggs
	6 slices toast

Scald cream, ketchup, salt, butter and onion; then drop eggs, one at a time, into hot mixture. Baste until whites are firm. Serve on toast.

EGGS IN BACON RINGS

Sauté strips of bacon until nearly done. Butter bottom of muffin tins and line them with bacon. Drop into each pan 1 egg, sprinkle with salt and pepper and bake in a moderate oven, 350 degrees, 15 minutes. Serve on rounds of buttered toast.

DUCK HUNTER'S BREAKFAST

Mix equal parts of cooked chopped meat and cracker crumbs, season with salt, pepper and butter or gravy. Moisten with milk; heat, and fill muffin pans about ¾ full. Break an egg on top of each. Bake in a moderate oven, 350 degrees, until eggs are cooked.

EGG TIMBALES

Beat 6 eggs until light; then add 1 cup of milk and a dash of salt. Put into buttered molds or custard cups, set in a pan of hot water and bake in a moderate oven, 350 degrees, until firm. Serve with Tomato Sauce, p. 213. Serves 6.

CHIPPED BEEF OMELET

Shred 1 cup of chipped beef and moisten with 1 cup Medium Cream Sauce, p. 215. Beat 6 eggs with ½ cup heavy cream, and season with 1 teaspoon salt and ½ teaspoon pepper. Grease the bottom and sides of a pan, pour in the eggs and place on the stove, shaking until they set. Cover with creamed beef, fold over and place on a hot platter. Surround with the remaining creamed beef, sprinkle with grated cheese and serve at once. Serves 4.

CHEESE OMELET

6 eggs   1 teaspoon salt
6 tablespoons water   ⅛ teaspoon pepper
½ cup grated cheese   1 teaspoon gin
                  2 tablespoons butter

Beat the eggs slightly and add water, cheese, seasonings and gin. The gin increases fluffiness. Melt butter in frying pan, pour in egg mixture and cook over low heat, shaking pan constantly. As it cooks, lift with spatula, letting uncooked mixture run underneath. Increase heat so it will brown quickly. Fold and slide out on hot platter. Grated cheese may be sprinkled over the omelet before it is served. Serve with Tomato Sauce, p. 213. Serves 4.

PUFFY OMELET

4 eggs, separated   ⅛ teaspoon pepper
½ teaspoon salt   ¼ cup milk
                  1 tablespoon butter

Beat egg yolks until thick and light; add seasonings and milk; fold into stiffly beaten egg whites. Turn into buttered, hot frying pan and cook over low heat until omelet puffs up and browns on bottom. Place in moderate oven, 350 degrees, for 10 minutes. Fold by slipping spatula under half of omelet and folding over. Slip on hot platter and pour Thin White Sauce, p. 214, around it. Serves 4.

FRENCH OMELET

4 eggs   ⅛ teaspoon pepper
½ teaspoon salt   ⅛ cup water
                  2 tablespoons butter

Beat eggs until whites and yolks are blended; add seasonings and water. Melt butter in hot frying pan, turn in mixture, and lower heat. As the egg solidifies, lift edges with spatula toward center, letting uncooked mixture run under the cooked portion. When bottom is browned, fold over and slip on hot platter. Serves 2.

SPANISH OMELET

Make a French Omelet, and before folding, place a liberal amount of Everyday Sauce, p. 240, on one half of the omelet; then fold the other half over on it. Pour more sauce around it on the serving platter.

GRAVIED EGGS

8 poached eggs   ½ cup grated cheese
½ cup fine bread crumbs   Celery salt and pepper
                    ½ cup leftover gravy

Put poached eggs in buttered baking dish which has been sprinkled with ¼ cup crumbs, ¼ cup cheese and salt and pepper. Pour gravy over eggs, add remaining crumbs and cheese. Bake in a moderate oven, 350 degrees, until cheese is melted.

CURRIED EGGS (1)

For each individual serving, boil 2 eggs 10 minutes and chill immediately, to leave the insides somewhat soft. Peel eggs, place on hot cooked rice and cover liberally with Curry Sauce, p. 208.

CURRIED EGGS (2)

Sauté 2 small sliced onions in 3 tablespoons butter. Remove onion and stir in 1 tablespoon curry powder, 1 teaspoon Worcestershire sauce and 6 well-beaten eggs. Stir and cook quickly. In another frying pan heat 1 pint rich tomato sauce and poach 2 eggs in it. Remove them to a hot platter, and poach 2 more. Continue until necessary number are poached. Serve on hot buttered toast, pour curry sauce around them, and sprinkle with grated Parmesan cheese.

COTTAGE CHEESE

Heat 1 gallon rich sour milk on back of stove till curd separates like a white jelly from the watery whey. Place doubled cheesecloth over an open dish, pour curds and whey into it, tie corners together to form a bag, and hang bag over sink to drain. After 2 hours' draining about 1 pint of curd will remain. Empty curd into bowl and chill. When chilled, mash into it ½ cup heavy cream, butter the size of an egg, and 1 tablespoon salt.

CREAM CHEESE

½ cup butter
2 quarts dry cottage cheese
1 tablespoon salt

1 teaspoon soda
1 pint heavy cream

Work the butter into the cottage cheese with the hands, then add soda. Place in large kettle, set kettle in a pan of hot water and put over low heat. Cook and stir until it becomes gummy and sticky. Add cream and salt, stirring well. Pour into a greased loaf pan and cover with oiled paper while hot.

CHEESE CASSEROLE

2 tablespoons butter
1 tablespoon flour
1 cup milk
1 teaspoon salt
½ teaspoon pepper
1 teaspoon dry mustard

1 cup grated American
  cheese
2 cups chopped celery
1 cup cooked macaroni
1 minced onion
½ cup buttered crumbs

Melt butter and into it stir flour and milk. Add salt, pepper and mustard. Bring to boil and add cheese. Stir briskly till cheese is melted. Parboil celery 10 minutes, drain and mix with macaroni. Stir in the onion; then pour all ingredients into buttered casserole with crumbs on top. Bake in a moderate oven, 350 degrees, 30 minutes. Serves 6.

CHEESE RING

6 eggs
3 cups milk
3 cups soft bread crumbs
2 tablespoons melted butter
2 cups grated American
  cheese

1 teaspoon salt
¼ teaspoon pepper
1 teaspoon dry mustard
1 teaspoon onion juice
1 teaspoon Worcestershire
  sauce

To slightly beaten eggs add milk and bread crumbs. Stir in butter, cheese and seasonings and pour into a buttered 8-inch ring mold. Place in pan of hot water and bake in a moderate oven, 350 degrees, 45 minutes. Serves 8.

WELSH RAREBIT

3 tablespoons butter
1 pound American cheese,
    the older and sharper
    the better
1 teaspoon cornstarch

1 teaspoon salt
½ teaspoon mustard
½ teaspoon paprika
1 cup beer or ale
2 eggs

Melt butter over low heat or in top of double boiler. Break cheese in small pieces on top of butter and sprinkle with cornstarch, salt, mustard and paprika. When cheese melts, add beer little by little, stirring briskly, always in one direction, until thoroughly blended. When mixture bubbles, add eggs, continuing to stir hard until consistency is creamy and all stringiness eliminated. Cover, let mixture simmer until it thickens; then stir briskly again and serve on toast or warmed saltines. The toast should be toasted on one side only. Unless eggs are stirred in vigorously, the rarebit will not blend and will have the leathery texture of molasses candy, similar to the rarebits served in restaurants. Once the stringiness is stirred out, the rarebit will remain creamy permanently. Serves 6.

FRIED CHEESE BALLS

1 cup grated mild cheese
½ cup bread crumbs
¼ teaspoon salt
1 tablespoon light cream

1 egg, beaten
½ teaspoon mustard
1 teaspoon Worcestershire
    sauce

Mix ingredients and form in balls. Dip in beaten egg, roll in cracker dust and fry in deep fat, 390 degrees. Drain on brown paper and serve hot.

CHEESE CURDS

1 cup rich milk
1 cup stale bread crumbs
1½ cups grated cheese
1 teaspoon salt

¼ teaspoon paprika
½ teaspoon dry mustard
½ teaspoon mushroom ketchup
2 eggs, slightly beaten

Cook milk, crumbs and cheese in double boiler until cheese is melted. Add seasonings and eggs and cook 1 minute, stirring constantly. Serve on hot toast with Tomato Sauce, p. 213. Serves 6.

CHEESE SOUFFLÉ

3 tablespoons butter	½ cup grated cheese
3 tablespoons flour	Salt and pepper
1 cup milk	4 eggs, separated
2 teaspoons minced chives	

Melt butter, stir in flour and gradually add milk. Stir constantly until thick; then add cheese and seasonings. Remove from fire and add well-beaten egg yolks. Fold in stiffly beaten egg whites and chives. Turn into buttered baking dish, set in pan of hot water and bake in a moderate oven, 350 degrees, 25 or 30 minutes. Serve with Tomato Sauce, p. 213. Serves 4.

CHEESE CROQUETTES

3 tablespoons butter	⅔ cup milk
¼ cup flour	1½ cups grated mild cheese
2 egg yolks	Salt and pepper

Melt butter, add flour and milk, and stir until thick. Add unbeaten egg yolks and mix well. Add grated cheese. As soon as cheese melts remove from fire, add seasonings and spread in a shallow pan to cool. Then cut in strips ½ inch thick and 3 inches long. Dip in crumbs, eggs, and crumbs again. Fry in deep fat, 390 degrees. Serve with Tomato Sauce, p. 213. Serves 6.

CHEESE TIMBALES

Make Cheese Sauce (1), p. 207, and add to it 2 well-beaten eggs. Mix well and pour into buttered molds or custard cups. Set in a pan of hot water and bake in a moderate oven, 350 degrees, for 20 minutes, or until firm. Unmold onto a platter and serve with Tomato Sauce, p. 213.

CHEESE FONDUE (1)

Beat together 1 cup scalded milk, 1 cup soft stale bread crumbs, 1 cup mild cheese cut in small pieces, 1 tablespoon butter, ½ teaspoon salt, 3 eggs. Pour into buttered baking dish and bake in a moderate oven, 350 degrees, 20 minutes. Serve with Tomato Sauce, p. 213. Serves 4.

CHEESE FONDUE (2)

6 slices white bread   3 eggs, beaten
½ pound grated American   2 cups milk
    cheese

Butter the bread and cut off crusts. Place bread in a shallow baking
dish and sprinkle with the cheese. Add the milk to the beaten eggs
and pour over all. Bake in a moderate oven, 350 degrees, about 30
minutes; then serve with Tomato Sauce, p. 213, and a green salad.
Serves 4.

WHITE GREEK CHEESE
(Seta)

*White Greek cheese, prior to World War II, came from Greece,
packed in layers in kegs with a strong solution of milk and brine,
which kept the cheese moist and tangy. When the war put an end to
Greek exports, Mexico and Colorado produced kegged Greek cheese
that compares favorably with the original Greek variety. It is a pure
white cheese, salty, mildly sharp, and with a texture between that of
Swiss and cottage cheese. It is unrivaled for light snacks or for serving with salads. It is obtainable at most Greek and Italian grocery
stores, but is far too little known in the average household. Americans of Greek descent are passionately addicted to it, and so am I.
I had a good friend, Louis Throumoulos, who owned a small but
excellently stocked market in the comparatively small town of Biddeford, Maine. Until the war made it impossible for him to do so,
he customarily kept on hand about $10,000 worth of Greek cheese—
an indication of its popularity with persons who know about it.—
K.R.*

MACARONIS, RICE AND STUFFINGS

MAXIMS FROM MAINE KITCHENS

A small piece of butter dropped into the pan in which rice or spaghetti is cooking will prevent water from boiling over the sides.

❧

When boiling rice, the addition of a little lemon juice makes the rice whiter and keeps the grains well separated.

❧

Earthenware casseroles should be soaked 24 hours in cold water before being put on a range or over a gas flame.

❧

Copper ornaments are best cleaned with turpentine.

MACARONIS, RICE AND STUFFINGS

DISSERTATION ON SPAGHETTI, FETTUCINI, GNOCCHI, SPAGHETTI SAUCES, GRATED CHEESE AND ITALIAN COOKERY

By Kenneth Roberts

FOR TEN WINTERS, in order to make an almost non-existent income go as far as possible during the writing of books so lengthy I was sure nobody would ever buy them, I lived in a small town on the Tuscan seacoast, halfway between Rome and Leghorn and abreast of the southern tip of the island of Elba. From my Italian neighbors I learned something that everyone ought to know but doesn't—that practically everything is edible, and that any American ought to be able to get along on a fraction of the food he now consumes.

As a beauty spot Porto Santo Stefano was almost without a peer; as a place to work it was beyond compare; but it was blessed with few gastronomical delicacies of the sort that Americans regard as essential to their health and happiness.

Butter and cream weren't easy to get. Meat was always eaten the day it was killed, and consequently had to be sliced to paper thinness and stewed for hours with tomato sauce, garlic and olive oil to eradicate its leathery quality.

There was a plethora of fresh fish—many of them fish that are wasted in America: skate, dogfish, squid and octopus, for example. All these fish make excellent eating. Fillets from a 20-inch dogfish taste like a cross between sole and halibut. Long after I had abandoned my Italian workshop, my friend Rod Littlefield sent me packages of dogfish fillets from the Willard-Daggett fishing fleet in Portland. Guests who were fortunate enough to be on hand at such times were enraptured by their delicacy. To avoid misunderstandings we always told the guests that the fish was turbot.

America has no universally used staple that compares with the many forms of dried dough known to Italians as pasta—spaghetti, vermicelli, fettucini, or the romantically named capellini d'angeli, or angel hairs; with ravioli or gnocchi; with the various regional forms of thick soup known to Italians as minestrone. Any one of these things is a meal by itself and a satisfying one, and all of them somehow contrive to emerge successfully from the hands of even an incompetent cook.

Our cook was Maria Nobile, a pinheaded young woman unable to read or write, and with a mentality that left much to be desired. In spite of these (and a few other) drawbacks, Maria Nobile never failed in her preparation of fettucini, gnocchi and ravioli.

Why it is that all those dishes baffle so many American households I cannot say; nor can I say why an Italian, in his homeland, is able to eat four times as much spaghetti as an American. I have no idea why Americans cannot think of spaghetti without meat balls. In all the years I lived in Italy, I never heard of meat balls being served with spaghetti or any other form of pasta. Italians take their spaghetti straight on the theory that you shouldn't try to gild the lily.

Italians don't allow pasta to cook until it becomes glutinous, as so often happens in America. The Italian stops it from boiling while it still retains a slight tooth-resistant quality. Also the Italians deluge their pasta with semi-lubricant sauces based on what Italians call *guanciale di maiale,* or *grasso di prosciutto. Guanciale di maiale,* which the Italians also call *lardo,* or fat, means "bacon of pig." *Grasso di prosciutto* means "fat of ham." *Lardo di maiale* means pig fat. The Italian cook refers to all these things as "bacon." She slices her "bacon" into thin slices, puts it on her chopping board, hacks and mashes it with a chopping knife until it becomes a sort of paste; and this paste is the base of the sauces used on spaghetti, fettucini and all similar dishes.

My own experience has been that salt pork sliced thin is the equal of any Italian "bacon."

To make sure of the method used by the pinheaded and illiterate Maria Nobile in cooking her pasta, I went repeatedly to our Porto Santo Stefano kitchen and watched her operate. That kitchen was something to distress an American housekeeper beyond words. It was 14 feet square, its ceiling 12 feet high, and the floor made of

red tiles that had been badly laid a century before. The stove was
a raised platform of bricks. In the top of the platform were two
trenches, 8 inches wide and 8 inches deep. These trenches were the
fireboxes. When two handfuls of charcoal were put at the back ends
of the trenches and a grating placed over them, the stove was ready
for any culinary problem known to Italy.

The only storage place was a two-shelved, screened box that
hung on the wall like a bookcase. The only cupboard was a cur-
tained recess in one corner. On the three shelves of the recess were
blue enamel pots used in the morning to carry hot water to the
signori, and at noon and night to prepare dishes that left in the
pots a blended perfume of garlic and cabbage.

During the earlier part of the day all bits of refuse, such as lemon
peels, sardine heads, chicken feathers and eggshells, were thrown
on the floor, where they were kicked around until the noonday
policing.

It wasn't easy to obtain from Maria Nobile a logical description
of her methods, because she didn't know the names of many things,
and naturally couldn't spell the names of those she did know.

When Maria Nobile cooked pasta for six people, she put six quarts
of water in a kettle, and when the water was boiling, she dropped
in a handful of coarse cooking salt. If the salt had been finer, she
said, she'd have used a mere tablespoonful. Why? *Ma che!* Why
not!

The amount of pasta she used varied with the known pasta-eating
habits of those for whom she cooked. If, for example, there were
to be six people at the table, and two were true pasta gluttons—if,
that is to say, they piled their plates high, picked up large forkfuls
and drew them into their mouths with sonorous sucking sounds—
she used a pound and a half.

Her cooking time for fettucini and spaghetti was 13 minutes: no
more, no less. Fettucini are often known in America as noodles.
Egg noodles, which cook more quickly than ordinary fettucini,
should never be cooked more than eight minutes.

American cookbooks are inclined to recommend that spaghetti
be cooked twenty minutes and more. A leading American cookbook
even wants it cooked thirty-five minutes. Such overcooking makes
spaghetti too soft and slippery to handle effectively; and overcooked

pasta of any sort gives the eater a feeling of extraordinary distention —not just the stuffed feeling that goes with over-large meals, but the sensation of having swallowed a bag of Aroostook potatoes swathed in pink netting.

American cookbooks also insist that spaghetti or fettucini be washed in cold water after it has been cooked. Maria Nobile unhesitatingly condemned spaghetti-washing as being *pazza,* or cuckoo. Italians don't wash spaghetti. They cook it, drain it and serve it. Washing is not for what has been cooked! *Ma che!* Washing is for garments. To wash spaghetti after cooking is an *imbecillità*—a piece of pure insanity.

Having cooked the pasta thirteen minutes, Maria Nobile drained it in a colander, placed it on a heated platter, dappled it with butter, sprinkled over it four tablespoonfuls of grated Parmesan cheese, and stirred and tumbled the mass with a fork and a spoon until the butter and cheese were evenly distributed through the mound. Then she rushed it to the table with a tureen of tomato sauce and a dish of grated Parmesan cheese.

The double application of butter-and-cheese and sauce-and-cheese—first by the cook and then by the eater—is by no means universal in Italy, but it's the way good cooks handle pasta.

Alfredo, in Rome, made an international reputation for himself as a restaurateur because of the thoroughness with which he personally and with ludicrous violence worked butter and cheese into his platters of fettucini just before serving them. His fettucini was no better than anybody's fettucini; but the mere fact that he thoroughly buttered and cheesed his product before turning it over to his customers for a final saucing and cheesing added to its toothsomeness.

The sauces used by Italians on pasta vary as widely as recipes for ketchup in America. In some parts of Italy thick meat sauces are the rule: in other parts thin tomato sauces. Italian cookbooks seem chary of revealing anything about such matters, probably because all Italian cooks are supposed to understand from birth how to make them. American cookbooks never handle the subject satisfactorily.

All too frequently one comes across, both in Italy and in America, but more particularly in America, a recipe for a meat sauce that is almost incredibly rich. The trouble with these extremely rich sauces is that if enough is used to permeate the pasta, the eater develops a raging thirst and a feeling of having been inflated with helium.

In an American cookbook I came across one such sauce that had, among its ingredients, half a pound each of ground-up sausage meat, veal, beef, pork and mushrooms, a pound and a quarter of chopped onions, a quarter pound of butter, two cans of tomato purée, a cup of ketchup and a plentiful amount of green peppers, Worcestershire sauce, lemon juice, salt and pepper. The inventor of this sauce thought half a cup of water was enough to insure its fluidity, but he was wrong. A quart would have been better, but the sauce would still have been too rich.

I collected recipes for pasta sauces from Maria Nobile and in my travels through Italy. Those I give here are comparatively thin and easy to prepare. Tomato sauces are the most popular in Italy; and in our own small household, during our stay in Porto Santo Stefano, we kept a 5-gallon tin of tomato paste in the kitchen, ready for constant use. The same sort of tomato paste is obtainable in America, especially from shops which specialize in Italian foods.

A satisfactory sauce can be made by adding 1 tablespoon of butter, 1 tablespoon of grated onion and 1 cup of boiling soup stock to 2 cans of tomato purée—though the operation of sauce-making should be a little more elaborate for the best results. And every Italian cook knows that the longer the sauce simmers, the better it tastes.

EVERYDAY SAUCE

Put in a saucepan 1 tablespoon of butter or 2 tablespoons of olive oil; ½ onion cut fine; a single stalk of celery; 1 finely chopped carrot. Add a paste made of a 2-inch cube of salt pork, a mashed-up clove of garlic and a bunch of parsley.

Put over a moderate fire, stirring frequently and adding an occasional tablespoon of water so the herbs will cook and become golden without burning.

When this is ready, add 2 heaping tablespoons of tomato paste and 2 cups of water, stir well and season with salt and pepper. Cook 20 minutes, or until the sauce thickens. If fresh tomatoes are used instead of paste, use 3 pounds. This sauce can be made larger and richer by adding a can of mock turtle soup, 2 more cups of water and 1 more tablespoon of tomato paste.

WHOLE TOMATO SAUCE

Mix 1 quart of fresh or canned tomatoes, ½ sliced onion, a handful of herbs (parsley and celery), a tablespoon of olive oil (or a corresponding amount of butter), and salt to taste.

Put on the fire and when well cooked, rub through a sieve. Add twice as much oil or butter as originally used, cook a little more, and serve.

SIMPLE TOMATO SAUCE

Put a piece of butter in a casserole, add 2 cups of boiling water and ½ cup of tomato paste, a bunch of parsley, a single stalk of celery, a carrot, pepper and salt. Simmer slowly for 1½ hours, adding water as the original water evaporates. Before serving rub through a sieve.

MEATLESS MEAT SAUCE

Make a paste of a 4-inch cube of salt pork, 2 sliced onions, and salt and pepper to taste. Put on the stove in a saucepan. When the onions turn golden brown, add a 1¼ pound piece of lean pork or beef. Cook for 15 minutes; then add ½ glass of wine. When boiling again, add enough tomato purée or diluted tomato paste to cover the meat.

Continue cooking over a slow fire until the meat is done. The meat is removed from the sauce, thinly sliced, and served as a part of the sauce.

MEAT SAUCE

Make a paste of a 2-inch cube of salt pork, 1 onion, 1 carrot, 1 stalk of celery, ½ clove garlic. Put in a saucepan with 1 tablespoon of butter. Salt and pepper to taste. Add ¼ pound of hamburger. Add any sort of meat scraps or chicken livers cut in small pieces. Sauté well, stirring to prevent burning. When well cooked, add a small can of tomato paste diluted with a can of consommé. Cook until it thickens somewhat; then put in double boiler so it won't boil away. The longer it simmers, the better it is. Before serving, add ½ cup red or white wine.

Most Americans, when eating spaghetti or fettucini, are unable to use sauce and grated cheese with proper Italian abandon. An Italian, when he squares off before a plate of fettucini or spaghetti, covers the mound completely with tomato sauce, works it in with a sensuous movement of his fork, and adds a little more sauce for good luck. He then reaches for the grated cheese container and gives the whole mound a comprehensive dusting. This he twiddles with his fork until the cheese is worked into the mass; then, if the cheese container is still within reach, he absent-mindedly adds a little more. He then plunges his fork into the heap, as a farmer stabs a pitchfork into a mound of hay, and hoists the forkful to his mouth with a twisting motion. As the Italians say, *non c'è male*—not bad!

The regulation cheese used by Italians for grating and sprinkling on pasta is the wheel-shaped Parmesan or Parmigiano. Excellent replicas of Italian cheeses are being made in Wisconsin and Vermont. An American-made Romano is obtainable at all Italian-American food stores. It keeps as well as Parmesan, and when freshly grated is as satisfactory on pasta or rice. The ready-grated cheese available in envelopes and cartons is a miserable substitute for freshly grated Romano or Parmesan.

GNOCCHI

Another Italian dish that was as simple to make as it was easy to eat was the country-style gnocchi that Maria Nobile sent to the table once a week as our sole luncheon dish. Her gnocchi was made from the yellow corn meal known to Italians as *Gran Turco*. This is not corn flour, but corn meal—the same sort of corn meal from which johnnycake is made.

Maria mixed 1 cup of corn meal in 1½ cups of cold water. Then she put 2 cups of cold water in a saucepan, set it on the fire and brought it to a boil. When it was boiling, she poured into it the corn meal and cold water, added ½ cup of any sort of grated cheese, 2 heaping tablespoons of butter, 1 teaspoon of salt and a pinch of paprika. When it boiled she stirred it 5 minutes with a wooden spoon. Then she removed it from the fire and poured it evenly on a board, a scoured tabletop or any other flat surface. Five minutes later she cut it into oblong cakes 2 inches long, 1 inch wide and ½ inch thick. These cakes she arranged in a baking dish in three layers, sprinkling grated cheese and dots of butter over the two bottom layers. She explained to me, wagging a warning finger, that the little rectangles must be stiff or they'd run together, and that putting cheese on the top layer would result in a *sbaglio*—a pain in the neck. If sprinkled over the top layer, the cheese usually burns.

The baking dish was placed in the oven until the exposed surfaces of the squares showed signs of browning. It was then whisked out and rushed to the table, where it was handled like spaghetti or fettucini: each individual helping was covered generously with tomato sauce, then dusted with grated Parmesan cheese.

ITALIAN RICE

Maria Nobile was past mistress of the art of making leftovers go a long way, and what she could do with just one turkey leg was astounding.

First she made rice in the Italian manner—which is something worth knowing. She put 2 meat cubes into 1 quart of boiling, salted water; then added 1 cup of rice. At the end of 20 minutes the rice had absorbed the liquid, but was still glutinous. She added a dash of saffron powder—as much as could be picked up on the end of a penknife blade. This gave the rice a yellowish tinge and eliminated the flat taste peculiar to boiled rice. She also added 1 clove of garlic chopped fine and 1 tomato cut in small cubes.

She then minced the meat of a turkey leg on her chopping board and mixed it with 1 cup of mashed potatoes and ½ cup of turkey gravy, salting and peppering the mixture to taste.

She put a layer of this mixture into the bottom of small oval baking dishes, covered the layer with a layer of cooked rice, and on top of the rice broke a raw egg. The baking dishes were put into the oven until the eggs were cooked; then served with the conventional side dish of grated cheese.

She also made what she called *Gnocchi alla Tacchino,* or Turkey Gnocchi. First she broke up the turkey bones, covered them with cold water, and boiled them an hour, after which she strained off the liquid and picked off all the meat scraps. These she chopped fine with 1 cup of celery, added ½ cup of turkey fat, 1 quart of dried bread crumbs, a sprig of sage, a finely chopped clove of garlic, 1 cup of giblet gravy, 1 teaspoon of celery salt and pinches of salt and pepper. All these ingredients she chopped and mashed and re-chopped and remashed; then added to the broth from the turkey bones and set it on the stove to simmer.

When it was simmering well, she poured into it 1½ cups of corn meal, let it cook till the mixture thickened; then poured it into bread pans, filling the pans to the top.

After it had cooled, it could be sliced, and in a cold room would keep 3 weeks. When served, it was sliced and browned in a frying pan with a little olive oil or butter; then served like gnocchi—with tomato sauce and grated Parmesan cheese.

BASIC MINESTRONE

So far as I was able to learn, every Italian cook had the knack of making a filling minestrone for 6 or 8 people out of a little piece of meat that most Americans would consider an inadequate ration for a school child. When Maria Nobile made minestrone, she soaked 1 cup of white beans overnight. The next day she boiled them with a 2-inch cube of salt pork in 2 quarts of water for 2 hours. Then she added a pinch of rosemary, a finely chopped clove of garlic and 2 cups of diced potatoes and cooked them another half hour. She then added 2 cups of broken macaroni. When this had boiled 10 minutes, she put in any scraps of meat, chicken or chicken gizzards that she was able to find, ½ cup of grated cheese, 1 tablespoon of olive oil and pinches of salt and pepper. After a final 5 minutes of boiling, she sent it to the table, where each consumer added grated cheese to taste.

As a matter of fact, an Italian minestrone is any or all vegetables obtainable, cooked with rice, beans or macaroni, or with all three, and blended with a little salt pork. An Italian can live, and live well, on minestrone every noon for years on end—and so can I.

BOILED MACARONI

1 cup macaroni broken in 1-inch pieces	2 quarts boiling water 2 teaspoons salt

Boil macaroni in salted water 15 minutes or until soft. Drain in strainer.

MACARONI MOUSSE

1 cup cooked elbow macaroni 1 teaspoon salt
1½ cups scalded milk ⅛ teaspoon pepper
1 cup soft bread crumbs 1 tablespoon chopped onion
¼ cup melted butter 1 tablespoon chopped
¼ cup chopped pimento   parsley
1 cup grated American cheese 3 eggs, beaten

Pour milk over bread crumbs, add remaining ingredients and macaroni. Pour into a buttered baking dish, set in a pan of hot water and
bake in a moderate oven, 350 degrees, 50 minutes, or until firm.
Turn out on a platter and serve with Tomato Sauce, p. 213, or
Mushroom Sauce, p. 210. Serves 6.

MACARONI HADDIE CASSEROLE

Cover bottom of buttered baking dish with boiled macaroni. Spread
over this a layer of finnan haddie which has been simmered in hot
water 25 minutes and flaked. Add strips of pimento, another layer
of macaroni, grated mild cheese, a layer of fish and pimento. Fill
level of dish with Medium Cream Sauce, p. 215. Dot with butter
and bake in a moderate oven, 350 degrees, 20 minutes. Serve with
Tomato Sauce, p. 213.

BOILED NOODLES

Cook noodles 13 minutes in boiling salted water. If the noodles are
egg noodles, cook only 8 minutes. Drain, season with salt, pepper
and butter, and serve with Tomato Sauce, p. 241, and grated cheese.
(See p. 238.)

NOODLE RING

¾ cup noodles 2 tablespoons grated cheese
3 eggs ¼ teaspoon onion juice
½ cup light cream Salt and pepper

Cook and drain noodles. Add remaining ingredients, pour into buttered ring mold, set in pan of hot water and bake in a slow oven,
300 degrees, 1 hour. Fill center of ring with a creamed dish, such as
mushrooms or chicken. Serve on a platter with buttered spinach
around the outside of the ring.

NOODLES WITH HAM

Cover bottom of a buttered baking dish with boiled noodles, then add a layer of cold chopped ham, then a layer of noodles. Continue, leaving the top layer noodles. Beat 2 eggs with 2 cups milk and pour over all. Dot with butter and bake in a moderate oven, 350 degrees, until the top begins to brown. Serve with Tomato Sauce, p. 213.

SPAGHETTI CASSEROLE

Sauté leftover veal, lamb or pork in butter until brown. Season with salt and pepper, and chop fine. Put a layer of boiled spaghetti in a casserole, pressing it up around the sides; then fill the center with the meat, and cover with a layer of spaghetti. Top with buttered bread crumbs and grated cheese. Bake in a moderately hot oven, 375 degrees, 25 minutes. Serve with Tomato Sauce, p. 213.

RICE CAKES

Mix together 2 cups of cold cooked rice and a slightly beaten egg. Season with salt and pepper. Melt 1 tablespoon butter in a hot frying pan and drop rice mixture into the pan by spoonfuls. Sauté on both sides until brown. Serve as a side dish with Tomato Sauce, p. 213, or for breakfast, also with tomato sauce, and with crisp bacon on the side.

JAMBALAYA

Jambalaya, favored above all other dishes throughout Louisiana, is an ancient creole concoction based on the old Spanish custom of converting a handful of rice and food scraps into a dish so savory that it never palls.

For this recipe I am indebted to the Brezeales of New Orleans and Natchitoches, Louisiana.

An iron kettle is specified because rice cooks better in it than in shinier, more modern and less solid containers.

In a covered iron kettle heat 1 tablespoon lard, and in it brown 1 chopped onion and ½ clove of garlic. Into this stir 1 teaspoon flour; then add 2 large tomatoes (or ½ can). To this add any desired amount of chopped shrimp, chopped chicken, chopped ham or any chopped leftovers, or all of them mixed together.

Pour in 1½ cups boiling water, cover the pot and let it simmer 15 minutes.

Add 1 cup of well-washed uncooked rice, cover the pot, and let the rice boil without stirring until done—about 25 minutes. Season with 1 teaspoon celery salt, ¼ teaspoon pepper and a dash of red pepper.

If oysters are used, as is frequently the case in Louisiana, add them when the rice is done and cook only until their edges begin to curl.

MALABAR RICE

2 tablespoons butter	2 cups strained canned
1 tablespoon minced onion	tomatoes
1 cup rice	1 teaspoon salt
4 cups beef stock	⅛ teaspoon pepper

Sauté onion in butter until light brown; add rice, washed and drained. When rice is slightly browned add beef stock, strained tomatoes and seasonings. Simmer 30 minutes, or until rice is tender. Before serving add 2 tablespoons melted butter. Serve with grated cheese. Serves 6.

RICE OMELET

4 eggs, separated	1 tablespoon butter
⅛ cup hot water	⅛ teaspoon pepper
½ teaspoon salt	1 cup cooked rice

Beat yolks until thick and lemon-colored; add salt, pepper, hot water and butter. Add cooked rice to the stiffly beaten egg whites. Fold and cut into the yolk mixture with a knife. Cook in omelet pan; fold and turn on hot platter. Serve with Tomato Sauce, p. 213, or Cheese Sauce, p. 207. Serves 4.

BAKED RICE

Cook 1 cup rice in 1 quart of rapidly boiling salted water. Drain, flavor with a pinch of powdered saffron, mix with 1 cup light cream and season with salt and pepper. Pour into buttered baking dish and cover with thick layer of grated American cheese. Bake in a moderate oven, 350 degrees, until cheese is melted. Serves 6.

RICE PILAFF

1 cup rice   1 minced onion
1 cup stock   2 teaspoons minced parsley
1 cup strained tomatoes   Salt and pepper
                2 tablespoons butter

Boil rice in salted water 10 minutes; then drain off water and add
stock, tomatoes, onion, parsley and seasonings. Cook in double boiler
1 hour, or till rice absorbs all the liquor. Add butter. It should be
about the consistency of turnip or squash. Serve with Tomato Sauce,
p. 213, and grated cheese. Serves 6.

RICE CROQUETTES

1 cup cooked rice   ½ teaspoon salt
½ cup milk   1 egg
                1 tablespoon butter

Cook milk, rice and salt together. When it boils up, add the egg,
well beaten. Stir 1 minute, then remove from fire and spread on
platter to cool. Shape into small croquettes, dip into egg and crumbs,
and fry in deep fat, 390 degrees. Drain on brown paper. Serve with
Tomato Sauce, p. 213. Serves 4.

RICE AND OKRA CASSEROLE

1 cup cooked rice   1 minced onion
½ pound okra   1 tablespoon curry powder
⅓ cup butter   4 cups stewed tomatoes

Sauté onion in butter. Cut okra in small pieces, crosswise, and combine with all other ingredients. Season to taste. Put in a buttered
casserole and bake in a slow oven, 300 degrees, 2 hours.

BOILED WILD RICE

1 cup wild rice   3 cups boiling water
1 teaspoon celery salt   2 teaspoons butter

Wash rice thoroughly in cold water. Add salt to boiling water, then
add rice and let boil hard for 25 minutes, or until water is well
absorbed; then let steam until it is dry and fluffy. Add butter.

RISOTTO

2½ cups canned tomatoes	¼ teaspoon cloves (or not)
1 minced clove garlic	Dash cayenne (or not)
2 teaspoons celery salt	1 cup bouillon
1 chopped onion	2 tablespoons butter
1 teaspoon ginger (or not)	1 cup sliced mushrooms
½ teaspoon cinnamon (or not)	(or not)
	1½ tablespoons flour

1 cup cooked, chopped chicken livers (or anything else chopped)

Put tomatoes, garlic, celery salt, onion and seasonings in a saucepan and simmer 30 minutes; then add bouillon. Sauté mushrooms in butter for 5 minutes, add flour, blend, and add to tomato mixture. Add chicken livers and simmer 15 minutes. Serve on Italian Rice or spaghetti with grated Parmesan, Romano or any other hard cheese.

RICE AND CHICKEN CASSEROLE

2 cups boiled rice	2 tablespoons butter
2 cups milk	2 eggs, beaten

1½ cups diced cooked chicken

Mix together rice, milk, eggs and seasoning. Put a layer into a buttered casserole, then a layer of chicken, then the rice. Salt and pepper to taste. Bake in a moderate oven, 350 degrees, until browned. Serve with Tomato Sauce, p. 213. Serves 6.

BAKED HOMINY GRITS

¾ cup hominy grits	2 cups milk
1 cup boiling water	2 teaspoons sugar
½ teaspoon salt	¼ cup butter

2 eggs, well beaten

Pour grits into boiling salted water, stirring constantly. Boil 2 minutes. Add 1 cup of milk and cook in double boiler 30 minutes. Remove from fire, add remaining cup of milk, sugar, butter and well-beaten eggs. Return to double boiler and heat, stirring until mixture is smooth. Turn into buttered baking dish and bake in a moderate oven, 350 degrees, 45 minutes. Serves 6.

DRY STUFFING

4 cups bread crumbs	¼ teaspoon pepper
½ cup butter	1 teaspoon sage
1 teaspoon salt	1 teaspoon chopped parsley
	1 teaspoon minced onion

Cut crusts from bread 1 day old and crumble soft part with fingers. Melt butter in a frying pan, add crumbs and toss with a fork until well browned. Add seasonings and mix well.

MOIST STUFFING

4 cups diced bread crumbs	1 teaspoon poultry seasoning
1 teaspoon salt	1 teaspoon minced onion
¼ teaspoon pepper	¼ cup unmelted butter
	2 eggs, well beaten

Cut crusts from bread 1 day old, slice and dice. Add the seasonings and the butter, cut into small pieces. Add the beaten eggs, tossing the mixture with a fork. Stuff the bird at once, or put stuffing in the refrigerator until ready to use.

APPLE STUFFING

1 minced onion	2 tablespoons chopped
6 tablespoons butter	parsley
1 cup chopped celery	1 tablespoon celery salt
3 cups fine dry bread crumbs	½ teaspoon ground pepper-
4 cups diced apples	corns
	¼ cup seeded raisins

Sauté onion until brown in the butter, and then add remaining ingredients.

CUCUMBER STUFFING

2 eggs, beaten	1 minced onion
2 cups soft bread crumbs	3 tablespoons melted butter
1 cup chopped cucumber	1 tablespoon celery salt
	1 teaspoon black pepper

Mix all ingredients together and use to stuff a fish.

CELERY STUFFING

1 cup chopped celery	1 teaspoon celery salt
1 tablespoon minced onion	½ teaspoon pepper
1 tablespoon minced parsley	⅛ teaspoon sage
2½ cups bread crumbs	⅛ teaspoon celery seed

Chicken stock or water

Sauté celery, onion and parsley in butter. Add remaining ingredients and enough liquid to make the stuffing slightly moist.

CHESTNUT STUFFING

1 pound chestnuts	1 egg
2 cups chopped celery	6 cups bread crumbs
½ cup minced onion	1 cup hot stock or water
½ cup butter	2 teaspoons celery salt

¾ teaspoon pepper

Boil chestnuts 30 minutes; remove shells and skins while hot, and press through potato ricer. Sauté celery and onion in butter several minutes; add egg, bread crumbs, chestnuts, stock and seasonings. This recipe will fill a 10-pound turkey.

CORN BREAD STUFFING (1)

2 cups corn meal	2 tablespoons butter
½ teaspoon soda	1 finely chopped celery
2 cups buttermilk	heart
2 tablespoons melted butter	1 chopped onion
1 egg	1 cup hot light cream or
1 teaspoon celery salt	chicken stock
2 cups nut meats	3 eggs

The day before stuffing the turkey make a corn bread by combining corn meal, soda, buttermilk, melted butter, egg and salt. Beat thoroughly and bake until brown. The next day crumble the corn bread and add remaining ingredients. If stuffing is too dry, add more cream or stock. The stuffing that remains after the turkey has been stuffed may be baked in muffin tins and placed around turkey when served.

CORN BREAD STUFFING (2)

4 cups corn bread crumbs
4 cups dry bread crumbs
1 cup chopped celery
1 pint raw oysters
1 cup melted butter

1 minced onion
1 tablespoon poultry
   seasoning
2 teaspoons salt
1 teaspoon pepper

1 pint chicken stock

Mix ingredients and moisten with stock.

MUSHROOM STUFFING

⅓ cup chopped mushrooms
2 tablespoons butter
½ cup fine bread crumbs

2 tablespoons minced parsley
1 teaspoon grated onion
1 teaspoon celery salt

¼ teaspoon pepper

Sauté mushrooms in butter 5 minutes, stirring constantly. Add remaining ingredients and mix well.

WILD RICE STUFFING

2 cups wild rice
2 quarts boiling water
2 teaspoons celery salt
¾ pound sausage meat

1 teaspoon pepper
1 teaspoon poultry seasoning
2 tablespoons minced celery
   leaves

1 tablespoon minced parsley

Wash rice thoroughly in cold water; then cook rice in boiling salted water until tender and drain. Cook sausage meat in a frying pan until slightly browned, stirring with a fork. Pour over drained rice, add seasonings and mix thoroughly. This will stuff a 10-pound turkey.

SAUSAGE STUFFING

½ pound sausage meat
2 cups bread crumbs
1 minced onion

1 tablespoon celery salt
½ teaspoon black pepper
1 tablespoon minced parsley

Mix ingredients in order given.

OYSTER STUFFING (1)

¾ cup butter
2 tablespoons minced onion
2 tablespoons chopped parsley
2 cups chopped celery

6 cups soft bread crumbs
1 pint chopped oysters
1 tablespoon celery salt
1 teaspoon black pepper

Sauté onion, parsley and celery in melted butter. Add bread crumbs and heat well. Add chopped oysters and seasonings.

OYSTER STUFFING (2)

1 pint oysters
4 cups cracker crumbs
1 tablespoon celery salt

1 teaspoon pepper
¼ cup melted butter
1 tablespoon chopped celery

Wash oysters and remove tough muscles. Mix ingredients lightly with a fork.

POTATO STUFFING

2 cups hot mashed potatoes
1 stalk diced celery
1 minced onion
1 egg, beaten
1 tablespoon celery salt

¼ cup light cream
1 cup sausage meat
1 teaspoon dry English
     mustard
½ cup stale bread crumbs

Mix ingredients together.

FRUITS

MAXIMS FROM MAINE KITCHENS

A pinch of soda added to stewing rhubarb or other very acid fruit makes it more wholesome and saves sugar.

❦

Sliced apples or pears may be prevented from discoloring by dropping the slices into water to which a little lemon juice has been added.

❦

Remove spots from zinc table tops by rubbing with vinegar.

❦

New brooms dipped in hot suds for a few minutes and thoroughly dried will be tougher and more pliable than untreated brooms.

FRUITS

BAKED APPLES

Core medium-sized McIntosh Reds and place in baking dish. Fill cavity of each apple with 2 tablespoons brown sugar, dash of cinnamon and ½ teaspoon butter. Cover bottom of dish with boiling water and bake in hot oven, 400 degrees, until soft, basting often with syrup in dish. Serve with cream.

GLAZED BAKED APPLES

8 apples	1 cup boiling water	1 cup sugar

Wash apples, remove cores and skins from top of each apple, place close together in saucepan, peeled side up. Add the water and cook slowly, testing occasionally with a toothpick to see if they are soft. When done, place in a baking dish, sprinkle with sugar and cook in a hot oven, 400 degrees, basting with water in which they were originally cooked until the tops are brown. Serve cold with heavy cream.

CINNAMON APPLES

8 apples	½ pound small red cin-
1½ cups water	namon candies
1½ cups sugar	

Boil together the water, sugar and candies. Pare and core apples and simmer them in the syrup, basting often with syrup in pan. Cook until apples are tender. Serve cold with cream.

APPLESAUCE

Wash, core and quarter McIntosh Reds, add a very little water and cook until tender. Add a pinch of salt and sugar to taste, and cook 3 minutes. Strain.

STEWED DRIED APRICOTS

Wash dried apricots. Cover with cold water. Soak overnight; then cook slowly in same water until soft. Add sugar to taste.

AVOCADOS OR ALLIGATOR PEARS

Cut chilled avocados in half, remove stone, but do not peel. Sprinkle with lime or lemon juice and fill center with mayonnaise, French dressing or chopped garlic, celery salt and lemon juice. Or peel and slice avocados and marinate in over-salted French dressing.

BAKED BANANAS

6 bananas	3 tablespoons lemon juice
2 tablespoons melted butter	1/3 cup sugar

Remove skins from bananas, cut in halves lengthwise, and place in shallow pan. Mix the melted butter, sugar and lemon juice and pour over bananas. Bake in a slow oven, 300 degrees, 30 minutes.

FRIED BANANAS

Cut peeled bananas in halves crosswise and then lengthwise. Sprinkle with lemon juice, and dredge with flour seasoned with salt and pepper. Sauté in butter or bacon fat till a pale brown, and sprinkle with brown sugar.

STEWED BLUEBERRIES

Wash and pick over berries. Cook until soft in a syrup of sugar, water and small amount of lemon juice. Use just enough to prevent burning.

BROILED GRAPEFRUIT

Cut grapefruit in halves crosswise. Sprinkle each half with 1 tablespoon brown sugar or honey. Place on broiler under a moderate flame and broil until hot and slightly browned. Remove and add 1 tablespoon rum or sherry to each half. Serve at once.

BAKED PEACHES

Peel large peaches, cut in halves, and remove stones. Fill each cavity with 1 teaspoon sugar, ¼ teaspoon butter, a few drops of lemon juice and a dash of cinnamon. Bake in a moderate oven, 350 degrees, 20 minutes. Serve with cream.

FRIED PEACHES

Select solid peaches, halve them, remove stones, dust with celery salt and roll in brown sugar. Fry in bacon drippings and serve with crisp bacon for breakfast.

BAKED PEARS

Pare, halve and core pears. Put in a baking dish and fill hollows with brown sugar and butter. Cover bottom of dish with water, cover and bake in a moderate oven, 350 degrees, 25 minutes. Serve with cream.

STEWED PRUNES

Wash prunes thoroughly and soak in water overnight. Cook until soft in the same water. When nearly done, sweeten with sugar. Flavor with lemon juice or orange rind.

BAKED QUINCES

Wash, core and .parboil until almost tender; then place in baking dish, fill cavities with sugar and a dot of butter, pour water around them, and cook until soft in a slow oven, 300 degrees. Serve warm with cream.

RHUBARB SAUCE

Wash rhubarb and cut in 1-inch pieces. Cover with 1 cup sugar and ½ cup water to 1 pint of rhubarb. Let stand for 1 hour. Cook until rhubarb is tender. Serve cold.

JELLIES AND PRESERVES

MAXIMS FROM MAINE KITCHENS

A pinch of powdered alum makes jellies "jell" more easily.

❧

Lemons warmed in hot water will yield more juice.

❧

When making jellies, the use of underripe fruits and berries will result in better consistency and flavor.

JELLIES AND PRESERVES

APPLE JELLY

CUT APPLES in small pieces, cover with water, and cook till tender. Strain the juice through cheesecloth bag, allowing it to drain all night. Measure juice, and to each cup take ¾ cup sugar. Cook juice 10 minutes, then add sugar and stir constantly until sugar dissolves. Boil rapidly until mixture jells. Skim, fill glasses, seal and label.

APPLE BUTTER

Boil new cider down to one half. Pare and quarter sweet apples enough to fill up the cider. Boil slowly until the consistency of marmalade, stirring frequently. A small amount of lemon juice or cinnamon may be added if apples lack flavor 20 minutes before removing from fire. Fill glasses, seal and label.

BEACH PLUM CONSERVE

Beach plums (*Prunus maritimus*) grow on straggling bushes among sand dunes on the New England coast. They have a peculiarly delicious flavor when stewed with sugar or made into jelly or conserve. The latter confection is like the Mirabelle conserve so popular in France.

Maine cooks pick the plums when they are red, cover them with water and bring the water to a boil. The first water is thrown out, fresh water added, and the plums cooked until soft. The stones are removed; then as much sugar is added as there is liquid. Marbles are placed in the bottom of the kettle to prevent the conserve from sticking to bottom and burning. When the conserve jells when poured from spoon, remove from stove, pour into glasses, seal and label.

BLACKBERRY JAM

2 pounds blackberries   1½ pounds sugar

Wash and pick over the berries. In a large preserving kettle put a layer of berries, then a layer of sugar and continue until the ingredients are used. Let berries and sugar stand 1 hour before cooking. Cook until thick, stirring frequently. Pour into glasses, seal, and label.

CHERRY CONSERVE

4 pounds red cherries   ½ cup blanched almonds
4 pounds sugar   2 lemons, sliced thin
½ cup English walnuts   Grated rind of 1 lemon

Cook cherries and sugar over a slow fire for 1½ hours, stirring frequently. Add the remaining ingredients and cook ½ hour longer. Pour into glass jars, seal and label.

CRAB APPLE JELLY

Cut apples in halves and use an equal amount of apple juice and sugar. Follow Apple Jelly recipe, p. 260.

CURRANT JELLY

Wash, drain and pick over fruit, leaving it on the stems. Put into preserving kettle with a little water and mash with a potato masher. When the fruit is scalded, put in a jelly bag and allow the juice to drip through. Measure the juice and boil 5 minutes. Add the same amount of heated sugar as juice, stir, and boil 5 minutes longer. Skim, fill glasses, cool, seal and label.

GRAPEFRUIT MARMALADE

1 grapefruit   1 lemon
1 orange   Sugar   Water

Wipe fruit, remove seeds and core and put through a food chopper; then measure and add 3 times the amount of water. Let stand overnight. Next morning boil 10 minutes and leave until the next day. Add 1 pint of sugar to each pint of fruit, cook 3 hours, stirring occasionally. Pour into glasses, seal and label.

GRAPE JELLY

Pick over, wash, and remove stems from Concord grapes. Put in preserving kettle, heat to boiling point, mash, and boil 30 minutes. Pour into a jelly bag and permit juice to drip. Measure juice and boil 5 minutes. Add equal amount of sugar, stir and boil 5 minutes longer. Skim, fill glasses, cool and seal.

GRAPE MARMALADE

Pick over, wash, and remove stems from Concord grapes. Separate the pulp from skins, putting the pulp into a preserving kettle and skins into a dish. Heat pulp to boiling point, and cook slowly until seeds separate from pulp; then rub through a fine sieve. Return to kettle with skins and an equal amount of sugar, and cook slowly ½ hour, stirring occasionally. Put in jelly glasses, seal and label.

ORANGE MARMALADE

3 large oranges, or 6 small ones	1 large lemon
4 pounds sugar	9 cups cold water

Wash fruit and slice very thin. Cover with cold water and let stand overnight. Next morning bring to boiling point and add sugar. Remove from fire and let stand 24 hours. Put on fire and cook till like a jelly. Pour into jars and seal.

ORANGE, LEMON AND GRAPEFRUIT MARMALADE

6 oranges	1 grapefruit	2 lemons

Wash fruit, slice, remove seeds and put through meat chopper To a pint of fruit add a pint of water and let stand overnight. Boil 1 hour and let stand until the next morning. Measure mixture, bring to a boil, and to 1 pint mixture add 1¼ pounds sugar. Boil 1 hour, stirring occasionally. Pour into jars and seal.

QUINCES

Pare, quarter and core the fruit. Boil in clear water until tender. Make a syrup of ¾ pound of sugar to 1 pound of fruit, and a little water. When the syrup is boiling put in the fruit and cook slowly. Seal in glass jars.

PEACH AND PRUNE CONSERVE

6 cups sliced peaches	1 orange
2 cups sliced cooked prunes	1 lemon
4 cups sugar	½ cup English walnuts

Put peaches and prunes in kettle, sprinkle with sugar, and add grated rind and juice of orange and lemon. Mix together; then put over heat and simmer until thick. Add walnuts, and pour into glasses, seal and label.

PEAR AND GINGER PRESERVE

6 pounds juicy pears, sliced thin and chopped	1 pound preserved ginger, cut fine
6 pounds sugar	3 lemons (juice and chopped rind)

Boil ingredients together 10 minutes without stirring; stir, cool, and put in mason jars.

PLUM CONSERVE

4 quarts plums	1 pound raisins
5 pounds sugar	4 oranges
1 cup walnut meats	

Wash and pit the plums. Add sugar, raisins, grated rind of 2 oranges and pulp of 4 oranges. Add a little water and cook until set like jelly, about 1 hour and 20 minutes. Add nut meats. Pour into jars, seal and label.

PUMPKIN CHIPS

5 pounds pumpkin	5 pounds sugar
5 lemons	

Pare and slice pumpkin into thin slices. Sprinkle the pumpkin with half the sugar, the juice of the lemons and the grated rinds. Cover and let stand overnight. In the morning add the rest of the sugar, bring slowly to a boil, and then simmer until the chips are transparent. Take out pumpkin and spread on dishes to cool; cook down syrup, stirring frequently. Put pumpkin into jars, pour over boiling syrup, seal and label.

RHUBARB COMPOTE

1½ pounds unpeeled rhubarb   1 cup sugar
½ inch stick cinnamon

Cut rhubarb in 4-inch pieces. Put in a casserole, sprinkle with sugar and add stick cinnamon broken into small pieces. Cover and bake in a moderate oven, 350 degrees, 40 minutes. Stir once during cooking. Garnish with slices of orange.

RHUBARB CONSERVE

4 pounds rhubarb   ⅓ cup preserved orange
3 pounds white sugar   Grated rind and juice of
2 pounds brown sugar   2 lemons
½ cup preserved ginger   1 pound seedless raisins

Wash, peel and cut rhubarb in 1-inch pieces. Mix all the ingredients together and let stand ½ hour. Simmer for 2 hours, pour into jars, seal and label.

SUNBURNED STRAWBERRY JAM

Wash and hull freshly picked strawberries. Add equal amount of sugar, bring to a boil and cook 10 minutes. Spread mixture on large platters and cover with window glass. Place platters out of doors in the sun. Stir mixture carefully and thoroughly three or four times a day. It usually takes 4 or 5 days for the moisture to evaporate in the sun. This method keeps the berries whole and retains the brilliant red of the fruit. Raspberries may be preserved in the same manner.

TOMATO MARMALADE

5 pounds tomatoes   2 teaspoons grated ginger
2 lemons   root
4 pounds sugar

Peel and slice tomatoes, cut lemons in thin slices, add ginger root, put in kettle and cook 1 hour. Add sugar and cook until thick. Cool, pour into glasses, seal and label.

BREADS, BISCUITS AND DOUGHNUTS

MAXIMS FROM MAINE KITCHENS

Use measuring cups in the flour bucket and sugar bucket.

❧

If bits of egg yolks get into whites in separating, dip white cotton cloth in hot water, wring dry, and then touch yolk with it. The yellow will immediately be absorbed.

❧

Table silver blackened from eggs can be cleaned by rubbing with salt before washing.

❧

If biscuits are baked in pans about 1 inch deep, they will brown evenly on all sides.

BREADS, BISCUITS AND DOUGHNUTS

A LETTER FROM ELERY J. LYNDES TO MR. ROBERTS

"MY GRANDMOTHER, who lived all of her seventy-some years in central Vermont, and with whom most of my early years were spent, was a specialist at plain doughnuts. Unsweetened and unspiced—not the raised kind, but mixed up with sour milk, and a little saleratus. Left in the unscreened pantry window to cool, they would blow away in a good breeze, but eaten with maple syrup or perhaps good sharp country cheese, they were something to remember.

"Then she made fried pies: Doughnut dough rolled out about an inch thick and the size of a saucer, and cooked in the shallow iron doughnut kettle like doughnuts. While still warm, they were split and buttered and filled with a generous layer of home-cured dried apple, the kind you peeled, quartered and strung on a string and then hung up to dry and for the flies to walk on, over the kitchen stove on autumn evenings. This sweetened with maple sugar and generously sprinkled with grated nutmeg was a meal in itself and 'stuck to your ribs.' She also made chocolate custards, as did your grandmother, and also a cracker pudding, which contained an unbelievable quantity of raisins (the kind with the seeds still in 'em) and baked in a big earthen nappy, browned with years of use and good cooking.

"And boiled cider applesauce. Ever have it? If you haven't, you still have an experience due you. Pound Sweets, cored and quartered and cooked in tart new cider, then sweetened with maple sugar. It was placed in a 50-pound butter tub and put in the back shed to freeze. Wasn't fit to eat until it had frozen. It was dug out with a chisel in the winter, thawed on the stove and turned out a deep rich red like old wine and with fully as much bouquet.

"Too, I have her recipe for home-cured ham. The oak barrel was smoked with corncobs, rather than smoking the hams themselves, and then a pickle of brown sugar, saleratus and a little salt, was poured over them and they were left for two months, weighted down with a flat stone, before being ready to eat. The famed Virginia, peanut fed hams and Le jambon Bretagne which I have had in Paris, were like slices of wallboard, compared with them. That, with her home-made sausage, from which the fat had been kept for the lard kettle, and her home-cured dried beef and corned beef, were just about the best sort of 'vittles' a hungry youth ever set his teeth into.

"I see no particular reason why the 'Dirty Spoon Lunch' in Podunk Corners should list its fried Maine potatoes as 'pommes de terre frittes au Main,' or that good old Yankee apple pie should appear on the menus as 'tarts Normandie au mode.' We've got something to shout about in our own right."

WHITE BREAD

2 yeast cakes	2 tablespoons butter
1 quart lukewarm water	3 quarts sifted flour
2 tablespoons sugar	1 tablespoon salt

Dissolve yeast and sugar in lukewarm water, add butter, and half the flour. Beat until smooth, then add salt and balance of the flour. Knead until smooth and elastic. Place in greased bowl, cover and set aside in a moderately warm place, free from draft, until light (1½ hours). Knead, shape into 2 loaves; place in greased bread pans, filling them ½ full. Cover and let rise until double in bulk (1 hour). Bake in a hot oven, 450 degrees, 10 minutes, then reduce heat to moderate, 350 degrees, and bake 30 to 40 minutes longer.

BANANA BREAD

3 bananas	1 teaspoon soda
1 cup sugar	½ teaspoon salt
¼ cup melted butter	2 eggs, beaten
	1½ cups flour

Put bananas through potato ricer and then add other ingredients. Turn into a greased bread tin and bake in a moderate oven, 350 degrees, about 1 hour.

QUICK WHITE BREAD

3 cups sifted flour
3 teaspoons sugar
2 teaspoons salt
1½ yeast cakes

2 tablespoons lukewarm
water
1 cup lukewarm milk
3 tablespoons melted butter

Mix and sift dry ingredients. Dissolve yeast cakes in lukewarm water, then add to the milk. Gradually stir the liquid into the dry ingredients. Stir in butter and blend until dough is smooth. Knead on a floured board, cover dough with a cloth and let stand in a warm place 15 minutes. Knead dough for 10 minutes, shape into a loaf and place in a greased bread pan. Brush with melted butter, cover and let rise in a warm place for 1 hour. Bake in a moderately hot oven, 375 degrees, 40 minutes.

OATMEAL BREAD

2 cups boiling water
1 cup rolled oats
½ cup molasses
1 tablespoon melted butter

½ tablespoon salt
½ yeast cake dissolved in
½ cup lukewarm water
5 cups flour

Pour boiling water on rolled oats and let stand 1 hour; then add remaining ingredients. Let rise all day, beat thoroughly and put in 2 greased bread tins. Let rise and bake in a hot oven, 425 degrees, for 10 minutes. Reduce heat to moderate, 350 degrees, and bake 35 minutes more.

QUICK ROLLED OATS BREAD

1 quart boiling water
2 cups rolled oats
¾ cup molasses

3 tablespoons butter
1 teaspoon salt
1 yeast cake

Flour

Pour water over rolled oats, molasses, butter and salt. Let stand 1 hour. Add yeast cake and enough flour to handle. Knead well. Put into 2 buttered bread pans, let rise to twice its size and bake in a hot oven, 400 degrees, until light brown, then reduce heat to moderate, 350 degrees, and bake until done—about 1 hour in all.

SHREDDED WHEAT BREAD

5 shredded wheat	2 cups scalded milk
2 tablespoons lard	1 yeast cake dissolved in
½ cup molasses	½ cup lukewarm water
3 teaspoons salt	4 cups bread flour

Crumble shredded wheat and add lard, molasses, salt and milk. When the mixture is lukewarm add dissolved yeast cake. Gradually add flour and stir well with a wooden spoon. When thoroughly mixed turn dough out on board and knead with hands for 5 minutes. Put back in bowl and let rise to twice its size or more. Knead again for 5 minutes and divide in half. Then divide each half and knead in 4 round balls. Put 2 of these in 2 greased tins and let rise again. Bake in a moderate oven, 350 degrees, 45 minutes. When done brush tops of loaves with butter.

CINNAMON BREAD

1 cup flour	¾ teaspoon cinnamon
3 tablespoons sugar	1 egg, beaten
3 teaspoons baking powder	½ cup milk
½ teaspoon salt	3 tablespoons melted butter

Mix and sift dry ingredients; add beaten egg to milk and then add to the dry mixture. Stir in melted butter. Turn into a greased cake pan, sprinkle with 1 teaspoon sugar and ½ teaspoon cinnamon and bake in a quick oven, 425 degrees, 15 minutes.

GRAHAM BREAD

1 cup white flour	1 cup brown sugar
4 teaspoons baking powder	2 cups graham flour
1 teaspoon salt	½ cup raisins
2 tablespoons butter	¾ teaspoon soda
1¼ cups sour milk	

Sift white flour, baking powder and salt together twice. Cut in butter. Add sugar, unsifted graham flour and raisins. Dissolve soda in milk, then add to dry ingredients. Place in a greased bread tin and bake in a moderate oven, 350 degrees, about 1 hour.

DAYTIME BREAD

To 1 pint milk add 1 tablespoon butter, 1 tablespoon sugar and 1 teaspoon salt. Heat to the boiling point and then let cool until luke-warm. Add ½ cup warm water, ½ yeast cake, 4 cups flour. Knead. Place in a greased bread pan and let rise in a warm place 1 hour. Bake in a moderately hot oven, 375 degrees, about 45 minutes.

NUT BREAD

Mix and sift together 2 cups flour, ½ cup sugar, 4 teaspoons baking powder and 1 teaspoon salt. Work in 3 tablespoons butter and 2 tablespoons lard; then add 1 egg and 1 egg yolk well beaten, 1 cup milk and 1 cup chopped walnuts. Beat thoroughly and pour into buttered bread tin. Let stand 20 minutes, then bake in a moderate oven, 350 degrees, 45 minutes.

SOUR MILK NUT BREAD

2 cups sour milk	1 cup bread flour
1 teaspoon soda	⅛ teaspoon salt
1 cup brown sugar	2 teaspoons baking powder
2 cups entire wheat flour	1 cup chopped walnuts

Dissolve soda in sour milk, then add sugar. Mix and sift flours, baking powder and salt and add to milk mixture. Stir in nuts. Pour into buttered bread pan and bake in a moderate oven, 350 degrees, about 1¼ hours.

DATE AND NUT BREAD

1 cup chopped dates	1 cup sugar
1 teaspoon soda	2½ cups flour
3 tablespoons butter	1 teaspoon baking powder
1 cup boiling water	1 teaspoon salt
3 eggs	1 teaspoon vanilla

¾ cup chopped nuts

Mix dates, soda, butter and boiling water; allow to cool. Beat eggs, add sugar; then combine with date mixture. Sift flour, baking powder and salt together and stir into mixture. Add vanilla and nuts. Place the dough in a greased loaf pan. Bake in a moderate oven, 350 degrees, about 1 hour.

DARK NUT BREAD

2 cups pastry flour	1 egg
1 cup rye meal	½ cup molasses
1 teaspoon salt	¼ teaspoon soda
3 teaspoons baking powder	1 cup sweet milk
1 cup chopped nuts	

Mix pastry flour, rye meal, salt and baking powder. Stir soda into molasses, add milk, egg and nuts. Add liquid mixture to dry ingredients, pour into buttered bread pan and let stand 15 minutes. Bake in a moderate oven, 350 degrees, 45 minutes.

PEANUT BREAD

1 cup salted peanuts	1 teaspoon salt
4 cups flour	1 cup sugar
4 teaspoons baking powder	1 egg, well beaten
1½ cups milk	

Grind peanuts in meat grinder. Sift together the dry ingredients and add beaten egg, milk and peanuts. Beat well. Pour into buttered bread pan. Let stand 20 minutes. Bake in a moderate oven, 350 degrees, 40 minutes. Slice when 1 day old.

HONEY BREAD

1 cup graham flour	1 cup milk
1 cup white flour	½ cup strained honey
4 teaspoons baking powder	1 egg, beaten
1 teaspoon salt	½ cup chopped walnuts

Mix and sift dry ingredients. Add milk, honey, egg and nuts. Beat thoroughly. Bake in a greased loaf pan in a moderate oven, 350 degrees, about 1 hour.

BROWN BREAD BREWIS

2 cups dried brown bread	½ cup heavy cream
1½ cups milk	2 tablespoons butter
¼ teaspoon salt	

Scald milk, cream and butter together. Add crumbled brown bread and salt and simmer until the liquid is absorbed. Serve with cream.

BROWN BREAD (1)

1 cup yellow corn meal	1 teaspoon salt
1 cup graham meal	1 tablespoon sugar
½ cup maize	¾ cup molasses
½ cup rye flour	2 cups sour milk
2 teaspoons soda	¾ cup seeded raisins

Mix dry ingredients together. Combine molasses, milk and raisins and add to dry ingredients. Fill a buttered mold ⅔ full. Steam 3½ hours. If made in small molds, steam 1½ to 2 hours.

BROWN BREAD (2)

3 cups graham flour	2 teaspoons soda
1 cup white flour	1 cup molasses
1 teaspoon salt	2½ cups sour milk

Sift dry ingredients together, then add milk and molasses. Mix well. Fill a buttered mold ⅔ full. Steam 3 hours.

SALLY LUNN

½ cup melted butter	1 teaspoon soda
2 tablespoons sugar	2 well-beaten eggs
2 teaspoons cream of tartar	3 cups flour
1 cup milk	½ teaspoon salt

Mix ingredients in the order given. Pour into a shallow buttered pan and bake in a hot oven, 400 degrees, about 20 minutes. Cut the bread in squares and serve hot.

SPOON BREAD

2 cups milk	1 teaspoon baking powder
1 cup water	2 tablespoons melted
1 cup white corn meal	butter
1 teaspoon salt	3 eggs, well beaten

Scald milk and water and pour over mixed and sifted corn meal, salt and baking powder. Cook in double boiler, stirring constantly, until it thickens. Remove from fire and add melted butter. Cool slightly. Then add eggs. Pour into buttered baking dish and bake in a moderate oven, 350 degrees, 45 minutes. Serve from dish in which baked.

GINGERBREAD

2½ cups pastry flour	½ teaspoon salt
1 teaspoon soda	½ cup sugar
1 teaspoon ginger	½ cup molasses
¼ teaspoon cloves	1 tablespoon melted butter

1 cup sour milk

Mix and sift dry ingredients. Combine molasses, butter and milk; gradually add to dry ingredients, mixing well. Turn into a buttered shallow pan and bake in a moderate oven, 350 degrees, 45 minutes.

SOFT GINGERBREAD

1 cup molasses	1 teaspoon soda, dissolved
1 egg, beaten	in
½ cup melted butter	1 cup hot water
1 tablespoon ginger	2 cups sifted flour

Mix in order given. Beat well. Turn into a shallow buttered pan and bake in a moderate oven, 350 degrees, about 40 minutes.

SOUR CREAM GINGERBREAD

¼ cup butter	¼ teaspoon salt
½ cup sugar	1 teaspoon ginger
2 eggs, well beaten	2 teaspoons cinnamon
1¾ cups flour	½ cup sour cream
1 teaspoon soda	½ cup molasses

Cream butter, add sugar gradually; then add eggs. Mix and sift dry ingredients and add alternately with combined sour cream and molasses to creamed mixture. Pour into a shallow buttered pan or muffin tins and bake in a moderate oven, 350 degrees.

BAKED APPLE GINGERBREAD

Peel, core and cut 6 apples in eighths. Cook in syrup made of ½ cup sugar and ¼ cup water until half done. Drain off syrup and place apples in baking dish, pour over them a gingerbread batter and bake in a moderate oven, 350 degrees. Serve with whipped cream.

BLUEBERRY GINGERBREAD

To a gingerbread batter add 1 cup blueberries dusted with a little flour.

COFFEE CAKE

2 cups flour	½ teaspoon salt
⅓ cup sugar	3 tablespoons butter
3 teaspoons baking powder	1 egg, beaten
½ cup milk	

Mix and sift dry ingredients. Work in butter. Add egg and milk. Spread in shallow buttered pan. Sprinkle with sugar and cinnamon mixed together. Bake in a moderately hot oven, 375 degrees, about 20 minutes.

JOHNNYCAKE

1 cup corn meal	¼ teaspoon salt
½ cup sugar	1 cup milk
½ teaspoon soda	1 egg, well beaten
1 teaspoon cream of tartar	1 tablespoon melted butter
1 tablespoon molasses	

Mix and sift dry ingredients. Add remaining ingredients. Pour into a buttered shallow pan and bake in a hot oven, 425 degrees, 30 minutes.

SPIDER CAKE

¼ cup sugar	1 cup sour milk
⅔ cup Indian meal	1 teaspoon soda
2 eggs, beaten	1½ tablespoons butter
½ cup flour	1 cup sweet milk

Add the sugar and Indian meal to the beaten eggs; then add the flour alternately with the sour milk to which the soda has been added. Melt butter in a hot frying pan and turn in mixture. Pour the sweet milk slowly over the top of the mixture. Bake in a moderate oven, 350 degrees, until brown.

MOLASSES SUGAR CAKE

1 cup molasses	4 cups flour
1 cup boiling water	1 cup butter
1 teaspoon soda	1 cup sugar

Plain Pastry, p. 294

Mix the molasses, water and soda together. Combine the flour, butter and sugar, and work together. Line 2 pie plates with pastry; fill alternately with a layer of crumbs and a layer of liquid. Bake in a moderately hot oven, 375 degrees, 45 minutes.

CORN CAKE

1 cup corn meal	2 teaspoons baking powder
1/4 cup sugar	1 egg, beaten
1/2 teaspoon salt	1 cup milk
1 cup flour	1 tablespoon melted butter

Mix and sift dry ingredients; then add remaining ingredients. Bake in a shallow buttered pan or muffin pans in a hot oven, 425 degrees, about 20 minutes.

CROUTONS

Cut stale bread into 1/2-inch squares. Sauté in butter, turning constantly until evenly browned. Drain on brown paper and serve with soup.

HOT CROSS BUNS

1 cup scalded milk	1/4 cup lukewarm water
3 tablespoons melted butter	3 cups flour
1/2 cup sugar	3/4 teaspoon cinnamon
1/2 teaspoon salt	1 egg, well beaten
1 yeast cake dissolved in	1/2 cup raisins

Add butter, sugar and salt to milk. When lukewarm, add dissolved yeast cake, flour, cinnamon and egg. Add the raisins and mix thoroughly. Cover and let rise until double in bulk. Shape into large biscuits and place on a greased baking pan and let rise. Brush the top of each biscuit with beaten egg. Make a cross on each biscuit with a sharp knife. Bake in a moderately hot oven, 375 degrees, 20 minutes. Fill the cross with a plain frosting.

CINNAMON BUNS

Boil 6 medium potatoes, mash, and add 2 cups of sugar, 2 cups of milk, 1 yeast cake and enough flour to make a light batter. Let rise a few hours until light. Now add 1 cup melted butter, 4 eggs, and enough flour so that after it is kneaded it will form a light ball and not lose its shape. Let rise until light. Roll dough 1/4 inch thick, spread with soft butter; sprinkle with cinnamon and sugar. Roll and cut in 1 1/2-inch squares. Place in buttered pan 1/2 inch apart. Loosen rings a little when pieces are placed in the pan. Then sprinkle a little sugar on the top of each bun. Bake in a hot oven, 400 degrees. This makes about 3 dozen.

POTATO ROLLS

1 yeast cake	1/2 cup mashed potato
1/2 cup sugar	1 cup potato water
1 teaspoon salt	4 1/2 cups sifted flour
1/2 cup lukewarm water	1/4 cup melted butter

Crumble yeast cake and add sugar, salt and water. Stir in mashed potato, potato water and enough flour to make a soft sponge. Add melted butter, then remainder of flour, and knead until smooth. Put in greased mixing bowl and let rise for 2 hours. Knead. Let rise 45 minutes. Shape into round balls and put in greased muffin pans. Let rise 30 minutes. Bake in a hot oven, 425 degrees, about 25 minutes.

PARKER HOUSE ROLLS

1 yeast cake dissolved in	1 tablespoon sugar
1/3 cup lukewarm water	2 tablespoons butter
1/2 cup milk	1 teaspoon salt
2 1/2 cups sifted flour	

Warm milk, add sugar, dissolved yeast cake and butter. Sift flour and salt into mixture. Beat well, cover and let rise until double in bulk. Roll dough 1/4 inch thick, cut with biscuit cutter, and crease through the middle with dull edge of knife. Brush with melted butter, fold, press lightly and place on buttered pan. Cover, let rise, and bake in a hot oven, 425 degrees, about 20 minutes. Brush tops with butter just before removing from oven.

REFRIGERATOR ROLLS (1)

2 cups boiling water	2 yeast cakes dissolved in
½ cup sugar	½ cup lukewarm water
1 teaspoon salt	2 eggs, well beaten
¾ cup butter	Flour enough to make a
	soft dough

Add sugar and salt to boiling water, then add butter. Cool and add dissolved yeast cakes, eggs and flour. Let rise, then place in a covered bowl in the refrigerator until desired. Drop a little dough in buttered muffin pans, let rise 1 hour and bake in a hot oven, 425 degrees, about 15 minutes.

REFRIGERATOR ROLLS (2)

3 tablespoons butter	1 yeast cake dissolved in
1 cup sugar	¼ cup lukewarm milk
2 teaspoons salt	2 teaspoons baking powder
3¾ cups scalded milk	1 teaspoon soda
Flour (6–8 cups)	

Add butter, sugar and salt to scalded milk. When lukewarm, add dissolved yeast cake and mixed and sifted dry ingredients. Mix well, and place in a covered bowl in refrigerator 24 hours. Shape and let rise 2 hours before baking. Bake in a hot oven, 425 degrees. This mixture will keep for several days in refrigerator, and portions can be baked each day.

CLOVER–LEAF ROLLS

2 cups scalded milk	2 teaspoons salt
3 tablespoons butter	1 yeast cake dissolved in
3 tablespoons sugar	¼ cup lukewarm water
6 cups sifted flour (about)	

Add butter, sugar and salt to milk. When milk is lukewarm, add dissolved yeast cake and 3 cups sifted flour. Beat thoroughly, cover and place in refrigerator overnight. The next morning add enough flour to knead (about 2½ cups). Let rise until double in bulk. Knead and roll into small balls. Brush edges with melted butter and place 3 balls in each section of buttered muffin tins. Brush over with milk and bake in a hot oven, 425 degrees, 20 minutes.

SQUASH ROLLS

1 cup cooked strained squash	1 cup scalded milk
2 tablespoons melted butter	5 cups flour (about)
1 scant cup sugar	1 yeast cake dissolved in
1 teaspoon salt	¼ cup lukewarm water

Add butter, sugar and salt to squash. Pour in boiling milk; then add flour. When mixture is cool, add dissolved yeast cake. Let rise, shape like Parker House Rolls, p. 276, let rise again. Bake in a hot oven, 425 degrees, 15 minutes.

BAKING POWDER BISCUITS

2 cups flour	½ teaspoon salt
4 teaspoons baking powder	2 tablespoons butter
⅔ cup milk	

Mix and sift dry ingredients. Cut in butter with two knives or a pastry blender, or work it in with finger tips. Gradually add milk, stirring with a knife. Turn out on lightly floured board and shape into smooth ball. Roll lightly and pat ½ inch thick. Cut with biscuit cutter. Place on buttered baking sheet and bake in a hot oven, 425 degrees, 12 to 15 minutes.

CHEESE BISCUITS

Add ¾ cup grated cheese to dry ingredients in Baking Powder Biscuits.

DATE BISCUITS

Increase butter in Baking Powder Biscuits to ¼ cup and add ½ cup chopped dates.

ORANGE TEA BISCUITS

Prepare Baking Powder Biscuits. Roll lightly and pat ¾ inch thick. Cut with biscuit cutter. Break lumps of sugar in halves. Dip quickly in orange juice and press a half into each biscuit. Grate orange rind over each biscuit. Place on buttered baking sheet and bake in a hot oven, 425 degrees, 12 to 15 minutes.

ROLLED BISCUITS

Roll Baking Powder Biscuit dough ⅓ inch thick and spread with a
mixture of 1 teaspoon soft butter, ½ teaspoon cinnamon and 2
tablespoons sugar. Roll up and cut in slices ½ inch thick. Place close
together in a buttered pan and bake in a hot oven, 425 degrees, 12
to 15 minutes.

WHOLE WHEAT BISCUITS

1 cup whole wheat flour	¾ teaspoon salt
1 cup white flour	2 tablespoons sugar
4 teaspoons baking powder	3 tablespoons butter
¾ cup milk (about)	

Put whole wheat flour into a bowl. Sift together the remaining dry
ingredients and mix with whole wheat flour. Cut in butter until well
mixed. Add milk sufficient to make a soft dough. Dates or raisins
may be added if desired. Turn onto floured board and pat ¾ inch
thick. Cut with biscuit cutter and place on buttered baking sheet.
Bake in a very hot oven, 450 degrees, about 15 minutes.

SCONES

2 cups flour	½ cup butter
2 teaspoons baking powder	2 eggs, well beaten
¼ teaspoon salt	1 cup heavy cream

Mix and sift dry ingredients. Work in butter with finger tips. Add
the beaten eggs and cream. Toss on floured board and pat into
squares or diamonds ¾ inch thick. Bake in a hot oven, 450 degrees,
15 minutes.

SODA BISCUITS

2 cups flour	½ teaspoon salt
½ teaspoon soda	3 tablespoons butter
1 cup thick sour milk	

Mix as for Baking Powder Biscuits.

KENNEBEC TOAST

Make Baking Powder Biscuit dough, roll thin, cut in squares and bake. When done, split the squares, spread with softened butter and hot applesauce. Pile on a hot platter and serve at once.

MILK TOAST

2 tablespoons flour	½ teaspoon salt
3 tablespoons cold water	2 tablespoons butter
1 pint scalded milk	6 slices bread, ½ inch thick

Add water to flour gradually to make a smooth paste; add to milk, stirring constantly until thickened. Cover and cook 20 minutes; then add salt and butter. Toast bread until light brown. Put on serving dish and cover with sauce.

BLUEBERRY MUFFINS

2 cups sifted flour	2 cups blueberries
3 teaspoons baking powder	1 egg, well beaten
¼ cup sugar	1 cup milk
½ teaspoon salt	3 tablespoons melted butter or chicken fat

Mix and sift dry ingredients and add blueberries. Add milk to egg; then stir lightly into dry ingredients. Drop by spoonfuls in buttered muffin pans, and bake in a hot oven, 400 degrees, about 20 minutes.

BAHAMA FISH–TENDERS
(Corn meal fish cakes)

3 cups corn meal	1 teaspoon baking powder
1 cup flour	1 minced onion
1 teaspoon salt	1 egg
Milk	

While frying fish in deep fat, mix the dry ingredients together in a bowl, stir in onion, egg and sufficient milk to make a thick batter. Remove fish from deep fat, dip a tablespoon in the fat, and with it spoon the batter into the fat. Dipping the spoon into the fat prevents the batter from sticking. Fry the batter cakes to a deep brown and serve with the fish.

BRAN MUFFINS

1 cup flour	½ teaspoon salt
2 cups bran	½ cup molasses
1 teaspoon soda	1 egg, beaten
1 teaspoon baking powder	1 cup milk
½ cup raisins	

Mix dry ingredients together and then stir in molasses, egg, milk and raisins. Bake in buttered muffin pans in a hot oven, 400 degrees, about 25 minutes.

BREAKFAST MUFFINS

1 tablespoon sugar	2 cups flour
½ teaspoon salt	1 cup milk
1 teaspoon soda	1 egg, beaten
2 teaspoons cream of tartar	1 tablespoon melted butter

Mix and sift dry ingredients, and add combined milk, egg and butter. Drop by spoonfuls in buttered muffin pans and bake in a hot oven, 400 degrees.

CORN MEAL GEMS

½ teaspoon soda	1 cup corn meal
½ cup sour cream	1 cup flour
½ cup sour milk	1 teaspoon baking powder
1 tablespoon sugar	½ teaspoon salt
1 egg, beaten	

Add soda to sour cream and milk. Mix and sift dry ingredients; then add liquids and egg. Drop by spoonfuls in buttered muffin pans, and bake in a hot oven, 425 degrees, about 25 minutes.

HUSH PUPPIES

2 cups corn meal	¼ cup melted bacon fat
1½ cups milk	1 minced onion

Mix ingredients together and shape into oblong cakes ¾ inch thick. Place on a buttered baking sheet and bake in a moderate oven, 350 degrees, until cooked through.

MOLASSES CORN MUFFINS

1½ cups flour   1 teaspoon salt
¾ cup corn meal   ¼ cup molasses
¾ teaspoon soda   1 cup sour milk
1 teaspoon baking powder   1 egg
              2 tablespoons melted butter

Mix and sift dry ingredients. Add molasses, milk, beaten egg and
butter. Pour into buttered muffin tins. Bake in a hot oven, 400
degrees, about 20 minutes.

DATE MUFFINS

¼ cup sugar   ½ cup chopped dates
½ teaspoon salt   1 egg, beaten
4 teaspoons baking powder   1 cup milk
2 cups sifted flour   ¼ cup melted butter

Mix and sift dry ingredients, and add dates. Combine beaten egg,
milk and butter and add to dry ingredients. Drop by spoonfuls into
buttered muffin pans. Bake in a hot oven, 400 degrees, about 20
minutes.

GRAHAM MUFFINS

1½ cups graham flour   1½ cups sour milk
½ cup white flour   2 tablespoons molasses
1 teaspoon soda   1½ tablespoons melted
1 teaspoon salt   butter
              1 egg, beaten

Combine the dry ingredients. Stir the milk, molasses and butter into
the beaten egg, then add to the dry ingredients. Turn into hot
buttered muffin pans and bake in a moderately hot oven, 375
degrees, 25 minutes. Chopped dates may be added if desired.

HAM MUFFINS

¼ cup butter   5 teaspoons baking powder
¼ cup sugar   ½ teaspoon salt
1 egg, well beaten   1 cup milk
2 cups flour   ½ cup chopped cooked ham

Cream butter and sugar, and add egg. Mix and sift dry ingredients and add to creamed mixture alternately with milk. Stir in ham. Drop by spoonfuls in buttered muffin pans. Bake in a hot oven, 400 degrees, about 25 minutes.

RICE MUFFINS

2 eggs, separated	¼ cup melted butter
1 cup boiled rice	2½ cups flour
1 cup milk	2 teaspoons baking powder
½ teaspoon salt	

Beat egg yolks and add rice, milk and butter. Mix and sift dry ingredients and combine with liquids. Fold in stiffly beaten egg whites. Pour into buttered muffin tins and bake in a hot oven, 400 degrees, about 30 minutes.

RYE GEMS

Mix and sift twice 1 cup rye meal, ¼ cup sugar, ½ teaspoon salt, 2 teaspoons baking powder, 1 cup white flour. Add this to 1 egg mixed with 1 cup of milk. Bake in buttered gem pans in a hot oven, 400 degrees, about 20 minutes.

SURE SHOT MUFFINS

2 cups flour	1½ tablespoons sugar
¾ teaspoon salt	3 tablespoons butter
4 teaspoons baking powder	1 cup cold water

Mix dry ingredients in a big bowl; then knead and rub in the butter. Add the water to make the dough wet but not runny. Drop into ungreased muffin tins and cook in a hot oven, 450 degrees, 15 minutes.

WHOLE WHEAT MUFFINS

2 cups whole wheat flour	¼ cup molasses
1 teaspoon soda	1 egg, beaten
1 teaspoon salt	1 cup milk
2 teaspoons cream of tartar	1 tablespoon melted butter

Mix ingredients in order given. Drop by spoonfuls in buttered muffin pans and bake in a hot oven, 400 degrees, 20 minutes.

SQUASH MUFFINS

1 cup cooked strained	½ teaspoon salt
squash	3 teaspoons baking powder
2 eggs, well beaten	2 cups flour
2 tablespoons sugar	1 cup milk

2 tablespoons melted butter

Combine squash and eggs. Mix and sift dry ingredients and add alternately with milk to squash. Stir in butter. Bake in buttered muffin tins in a hot oven, 400 degrees, about 25 minutes.

POPOVERS (1)

1 cup flour	1 cup milk
½ teaspoon salt	1 egg

Mix the salt and flour. Beat the egg and mix with the milk; add to the dry ingredients. Pour into hot buttered gem pans or buttered custard cups. Bake in a hot oven, 450 degrees, 20 minutes, then reduce heat to moderate, 350 degrees, and bake 10 to 15 minutes longer. Remove from pans at once.

POPOVERS (2)

1 cup flour	1 cup milk
¼ teaspoon salt	1 egg, separated

Mix salt with flour; add part of the milk slowly until a smooth paste is formed. Add remainder of milk with beaten egg yolk, and lastly add the stiffly beaten egg white. Pour into hot buttered muffin pans, or buttered custard cups. Bake as for Popovers (1).

RICE POPOVERS

1 cup cold boiled rice	½ teaspoon salt
1 cup flour	1 tablespoon sugar
1 teaspoon baking powder	1 egg, separated

1 cup milk

Mash rice until smooth. Mix and sift dry ingredients together twice. Beat white of egg stiff, add beaten yolk and stir into rice. Add milk and dry ingredients alternately. Pour into hot buttered gem pans and bake as for Popovers (1).

GRIDDLECAKES

2 cups flour	1 ¾ cups sour milk
½ teaspoon salt	2 eggs, separated
1 teaspoon soda	2 tablespoons melted butter

Mix and sift dry ingredients. Combine well-beaten yolks and milk, and stir into dry ingredients. Add butter and beat to a smooth batter. Fold in stiffly beaten egg whites. Drop by spoonfuls on a hot greased griddle and brown on both sides. Serve with butter and maple syrup.

BLUEBERRY GRIDDLECAKES

2 cups flour	1 ½ cups sour milk or
2 teaspoons baking powder	buttermilk
½ teaspoon baking soda	1 egg
½ teaspoon salt	3 tablespoons melted butter
3 tablespoons sugar	1 cup blueberries

Mix and sift dry ingredients. Beat egg and milk together and gradually add to first mixture. Mix thoroughly. Add butter and blueberries. Drop by spoonfuls on hot greased griddle and brown on both sides.

BREAD GRIDDLECAKES

2 cups bread crumbs	1 teaspoon soda
2 cups sour milk	1 cup flour
1 egg, well beaten	1 tablespoon melted butter

Soak bread crumbs in milk till soft, then add egg. Mix and sift soda and flour and add to bread. Stir in butter. If too thin, add more flour. Cook on a hot griddle.

POTATO GRIDDLECAKES

6 potatoes	3 tablespoons milk
3 eggs, well beaten	3 tablespoons flour
2 teaspoons salt	

Peel potatoes and grate them coarsely. Add remaining ingredients and mix well. Drop by spoonfuls on a hot greased griddle. When brown on one side, turn with spatula and brown other side.

APPLE FLAPJACKS

1 tablespoon butter	1 teaspoon baking powder
1 tablespoon sugar	1 cup finely chopped
2 eggs, beaten	apples
1½ cups flour	1 teaspoon cinnamon

Milk

Cream butter and sugar, add eggs and sifted dry ingredients. Stir in chopped apples and gradually add enough milk to make a medium batter. Bake on a hot griddle. The best apple for this purpose is the McIntosh Red. Apple flapjacks are usually served in Maine with a syrup made by boiling sugar and water together.

RUSSIAN PANCAKES
(Blinis)

½ yeast cake	3 eggs, separated
2 cups warm milk	6 tablespoons soft butter
3 cups sifted bread flour	Scant teaspoon salt
1 tablespoon sugar	Black or red caviare

Dissolve yeast cake in warm milk, then stir in sugar and 1½ cups of the flour. Cover and put to rise in a warm place for 1½ hours. Beat egg yolks and stir in remaining 1½ cups flour, butter and salt. Beat this mixture into the dough and set to rise for another 1½ hours. Fold in stiffly beaten egg whites and let stand 15 minutes. Melt a little butter in a small frying pan, and pour in a little batter, keeping each cake very thin. Spread unbaked side with soft butter while cooking. Then spread with black or red caviare and roll into cylinder.

RICE GRIDDLECAKES

2 cups cold boiled rice	2 cups flour
1½ cups milk	1 teaspoon sugar
1 egg, well beaten	½ teaspoon salt

2 teaspoons baking powder

Press rice through strainer and add milk and egg. Mix and sift dry ingredients and add to rice mixture. Stir to a smooth batter and cook on hot griddle.

BUCKWHEAT CAKES

½ cup bread crumbs
½ teaspoon salt
2½ cups scalded milk
½ yeast cake

2 cups buckwheat flour
2 tablespoons molasses
¼ teaspoon soda
¼ cup lukewarm water

Add bread crumbs and salt to scalded milk. Cool. When lukewarm, add yeast cake, stirring till dissolved. Add buckwheat flour, stir until smooth and set in warm place overnight. In the morning add molasses, soda mixed with water, and beat smooth. Bake on a hot griddle. Serve with butter and maple syrup.

CORN MEAL GRIDDLECAKES

1 cup corn meal
1 cup flour
4 teaspoons baking powder

1 teaspoon salt
2 eggs, well beaten
2½ cups milk

¼ cup melted butter

Mix and sift dry ingredients. Combine well-beaten eggs and milk, and stir into dry ingredients. Add butter and beat to a smooth batter. Drop by spoonfuls on a hot greased griddle and brown on both sides. Serve with maple syrup.

RICE WAFFLES

2 eggs, separated
1 cup cooked rice
2 tablespoons melted butter

2 cups flour
3 teaspoons baking powder
1 teaspoon salt

Beat yolks of eggs, then add rice, butter, mixed and sifted dry ingredients; and then stiffly beaten egg whites. Add a little milk if necessary. Cook on hot waffle iron.

SOUR MILK WAFFLES

2 cups flour
1 teaspoon salt
1 teaspoon soda

1 tablespoon sugar
1½ cups sour milk
2 eggs, separated

2 tablespoons melted butter

Mix and sift dry ingredients. Add milk to beaten egg yolks; then add to dry ingredients. Stir in butter and lastly add stiffly beaten egg whites. Cook on hot waffle iron.

WAFFLES

2 egg yolks, well beaten	2 tablespoons sugar
2 cups milk	3 teaspoons baking powder
1 cup melted butter	1 teaspoon salt
2½ cups flour	2 egg whites, stiffly beaten

Beat together yolks and 1 cup of milk, then add other cup of milk and beat some more. Add melted butter. Mix and sift dry ingredients together; add liquids and beat until smooth; add egg whites stiffly beaten. Cook on hot waffle iron.

BANANA FRITTERS

6 bananas	¼ teaspoon salt
½ cup flour	1 tablespoon sugar
¾ teaspoon baking powder	1 egg yolk
⅓ cup milk	

Slice bananas lengthwise. Sift dry ingredients together. Beat egg yolk slightly, add milk, combine with dry ingredients and beat till smooth. Into this batter dip the banana slices; then fry in deep hot fat, 370 degrees, until light brown. Serve with powdered sugar and cream, or Lemon Sauce, p. 343.

CORN BREAD FRITTERS

1 cup corn meal	¾ teaspoon salt
1 cup flour	1 egg, beaten
2 teaspoons baking powder	Milk

Mix the corn meal, flour, baking powder and salt. Stir in beaten egg and enough milk to make a stiff batter. Drop by spoonfuls into deep hot fat, 370 degrees, and fry until brown. Drain on brown paper. Serve hot with maple syrup.

BREAKFAST FRITTERS

1 cup sour milk	1 egg, well beaten
1 tablespoon sugar	1 teaspoon soda
½ teaspoon salt	Flour to make a light batter

Mix ingredients in order given, and fry in deep hot fat, 370 degrees. Drain on brown paper.

APPLE FRITTERS

1 cup flour	¼ teaspoon salt
1½ teaspoons baking powder	⅓ cup milk
3 tablespoons powdered sugar	1 egg, well beaten
2 medium-sized sour apples	

Mix and sift dry ingredients. Add milk to egg and then stir into dry ingredients gradually. Mix well. Pare, core and slice apples into eighths. Stir into batter. Drop batter by spoonfuls into deep hot fat, 370 degrees, and fry until brown. Drain on brown paper. Serve with Lemon Sauce, p. 343.

PEACH FRITTERS

⅓ cup butter	3 teaspoons baking powder
½ cup sugar	½ teaspoon salt
2 eggs, well beaten	1 cup milk
2 cups flour	1 teaspoon lemon juice
1½ cups chopped peaches	

Cream butter and sugar; add eggs and beat well. Mix and sift dry ingredients and add to creamed mixture alternately with milk. Fold in peaches and lemon juice. Drop by spoonfuls into deep hot fat, 370 degrees, and fry until brown. Drain on brown paper. Serve sprinkled with powdered sugar.

CRULLERS

2 eggs, beaten	5 tablespoons melted butter
1 cup sugar	2 teaspoons baking powder
½ teaspoon salt	Flour enough to roll
1 cup milk	

Add sugar, salt and melted butter to beaten eggs. Mix and sift dry ingredients and add alternately with milk to egg mixture. Roll ½ inch thick, cut in strips 8 inches long and 1 inch wide and twist. Fry in deep hot fat, 370 degrees. Drain on brown paper.

FRIED CAKES

2 eggs	½ cup sweet milk
2 cups brown sugar	1 teaspoon soda
1 tablespoon melted butter	2 teaspoons baking powder
1 cup sour milk	½ teaspoon salt

Flour to handle

Beat eggs and sugar together, add melted butter. Put soda in the sour milk and then add with the sweet milk to the eggs and sugar. Add the dry ingredients. Shape into balls and fry in hot deep fat, 370 degrees, until light brown and cooked through. Drain on brown paper.

DOUGHNUTS

2 eggs, beaten	1 teaspoon soda
1 cup sugar	1 teaspoon salt
1 tablespoon melted butter	½ teaspoon nutmeg
3 cups pastry flour	1 cup sour milk

Gradually add sugar to eggs. Mix and sift dry ingredients and add to egg mixture alternately with milk. Turn on a floured board, roll ¼ inch thick and cut with floured doughnut cutter. Fry in hot deep fat, 370 degrees, until lightly browned. Turn doughnuts when they rise to top. Drain on brown paper.

RAISED DOUGHNUTS

1 pint milk	2 eggs, well beaten
½ cup butter	1 cup sugar
1 yeast cake dissolved in	1 tablespoon salt
¼ cup lukewarm water	⅓ teaspoon soda

Flour

Scald milk and butter together. Then cool, and when lukewarm add dissolved yeast cake and enough flour to make a stiff batter. Let rise overnight. Add eggs, sugar and salt. Beat well, then add soda and flour to knead. Let rise again. Turn out on floured board and roll ¾ inch thick. Cut with doughnut cutter and let rise until they have doubled in bulk. Fry in deep hot fat, 370 degrees. Drain on brown paper.

DROPPED DOUGHNUTS

2 eggs, well beaten
1 cup sugar
2 heaping teaspoons baking
    powder

½ teaspoon nutmeg
1 teaspoon salt
3 cups flour
1 cup milk

2 teaspoons grated lemon rind

Add sugar to eggs. Mix and sift dry ingredients and add alternately with milk to egg mixture. Add lemon rind. Drop from teaspoon into deep hot fat, 370 degrees. When brown on one side, turn and brown on other side. Drain on brown paper.

CHOCOLATE DOUGHNUTS

¼ cup butter
1¼ cups sugar
2 eggs, well beaten
1½ squares melted
    chocolate

½ teaspoon vanilla
4 cups flour
½ teaspoon salt
1 teaspoon cinnamon
1 cup sour milk

1 teaspoon soda

Cream butter and gradually add sugar; then eggs, chocolate and vanilla. Sift flour, salt and cinnamon together. Add to mixture alternately with sour milk in which soda has been dissolved. Roll, cut and fry in deep hot fat, 370 degrees. Drain on brown paper.

MOLASSES DOUGHNUTS

1 egg
½ cup sugar
1 cup molasses
½ cup sour milk
2 tablespoons melted butter

1 teaspoon salt
1 teaspoon cinnamon
1 teaspoon nutmeg
¾ teaspoon soda
5 teaspoons baking powder

5 cups sifted flour

Beat egg; gradually add sugar, molasses, milk and butter. Add mixed and sifted dry ingredients, stirring until well mixed. Turn out on floured board and roll ¼ inch thick. Cut with floured doughnut cutter and fry in hot deep fat, 370 degrees, until a golden brown. Drain on brown paper and sugar.

SOUR CREAM DOUGHNUTS

3 eggs, beaten	2 teaspoons soda
2 cups sugar	1 teaspoon salt
1½ cups sour milk	½ teaspoon cinnamon
½ cup sour cream	¼ teaspoon ginger

Flour

Mix ingredients in order given, using enough flour to mix as soft as can be handled. Roll, cut and fry, as in recipe for Doughnuts.

BUTTERMILK DOUGHNUTS

1 cup sugar	1 teaspoon salt
2 eggs, slightly beaten	1 teaspoon baking powder
1 teaspoon soda	½ teaspoon nutmeg
1 cup buttermilk	1 teaspoon ginger
2 tablespoons sour cream	Flour to handle

Gradually add sugar to eggs. Add soda to milk. Mix and sift dry ingredients and add alternately to egg mixture with liquids. Roll, cut and fry in deep hot fat, 370 degrees. Drain on brown paper.

PASTRIES AND PIES

MAXIMS FROM MAINE KITCHENS

To eliminate the taste of lard from pie crust, use a pinch of ginger when mixing.

❦

Vinegar or lemon juice added to milk will turn it sour in a few minutes.

❦

If cheese is cut in strips and put in a glass jar, it will keep fresh.

❦

Throw salt on burning fat to remove all odor and smoke.

❦

The easiest method of greasing a waffle iron is from an oilcan filled with salad oil.

❦

To prevent juices from running out of fresh fruit pies, add a little cornstarch or tapioca to the sugar.

PASTRIES AND PIES

PLAIN PASTRY

2 cups pastry flour
½ teaspoon salt

½ cup lard
1 cup butter

Cold water

Mix flour and salt. Work in lard and butter with finger tips, or two knives, until particles are size of a large pea. Add enough water to make particles hold together. Chill.

HOT WATER PASTRY

¼ cup boiling water
½ cup butter

1½ cups flour
⅓ teaspoon baking powder

1⅛ teaspoons salt

Pour boiling water over butter and beat with a fork until it becomes a smooth liquid. Sift flour, baking powder and salt into the liquid. Stir together, chill and roll out. Mixture keeps well in refrigerator.

APPLE CHEESE PIE

¾ cup milk
¼ cup heavy cream
1 teaspoon vanilla
2 eggs, beaten
⅓ cup sugar

½ teaspoon cinnamon
¼ teaspoon cloves
¼ teaspoon salt
2 tablespoons flour
½ cup cottage cheese

2 cups thinly sliced apples

Add milk, cream and vanilla to beaten eggs; then stir into mixed and sifted dry ingredients. Stir in cottage cheese, add apples and pour into unbaked pie shell. Bake in a hot oven, 450 degrees, 10 minutes; then reduce heat to moderately slow, 325 degrees, and bake 25 minutes longer.

APPLE PIE

Line a pie plate with pastry. Pare, core and slice tart, juicy apples.
Dip them in water and place on the bottom crust, packing closely
together. Add ¾ cup sugar, 1 teaspoon cinnamon and dots of butter.
Wet edges of the bottom crust, put on upper crust, pressing the two
together. Bake in a hot oven, 450 degrees, 10 minutes, then reduce
heat to moderate, 350 degrees, and bake 40 minutes, or until done.

APPLE CREAM PIE

¾ cup sugar	1 egg, well beaten
2 tablespoons flour	1 teaspoon lemon juice
1 cup sour cream	¼ teaspoon salt
2 cups finely chopped apples	

Combine sugar and flour and add cream, egg, lemon juice and salt.
Beat until smooth and add apples. Pour into unbaked pie shell
and bake in a hot oven, 450 degrees, 15 minutes; then reduce heat
to moderate, 350 degrees, and bake 30 minutes longer. Remove from
oven and over the top of pie pour ⅓ cup sugar mixed with 1 teaspoon cinnamon, ⅓ cup flour and ¼ cup melted butter. Bake another 20 minutes.

BANANA CREAM PIE

1 baked pie shell	½ cup cold milk
¼ cup flour	1½ cups scalded milk
6 tablespoons sugar	2 eggs, slightly beaten
Dash of salt	1 teaspoon rum or vanilla
Dash of nutmeg	3 ripe bananas
Whipped cream	

Combine dry ingredients, add cold milk and mix well. Add scalded
milk and cook in top of double boiler until thickened, stirring constantly. Pour small amount of mixture over beaten eggs, stir, and
return to double boiler. Cook for 5 minutes. Chill, then add flavoring. Slice 1½ bananas into the pie shell, cover with cream filling,
then top with remaining sliced bananas. Spread whipped cream
over the top and serve.

DEEP DISH APPLE PIE

Green apples
½ cup sugar
¼ teaspoon grated nutmeg
⅛ teaspoon salt

1 teaspoon lemon juice
1 teaspoon grated lemon
    rind
1 tablespoon butter

Line a baking dish with pastry. Cut up enough apples to fill it,
heaping a little in the center. Mix remaining ingredients, except
butter, and sprinkle over apples. Dot with butter. Cover with pastry
and bake in a moderate oven, 350 degrees, 45 minutes. Serve with
cream. This may be made with no under crust.

BANANA GRAHAM PIE

1¼ cups finely crushed
    graham crackers
⅓ cup butter
1 tablespoon sugar

2 ripe bananas
1 cup sugar
⅛ teaspoon salt
2 egg whites

¼ teaspoon vanilla

Mix crackers, softened butter and tablespoon of sugar and press
in an even layer against the bottom and sides of a buttered pie
plate. Mash bananas and add 1 cup sugar and salt. Stir stiffly beaten
egg whites into banana mixture. Add vanilla and pour into crumb-
lined pie plate. Bake in a moderate oven, 350 degrees, 15 minutes;
then lower temperature to 300 degrees and bake 15 minutes longer.
Chill and serve topped with whipped cream.

BANBURY TARTS (1)

1 cup chopped raisins
¾ cup sugar
1 egg, beaten

1½ tablespoons cracker
    crumbs
Juice and grated rind 1
    lemon

Mix ingredients in order given. Roll pastry ⅛ inch thick and cut
in 3-inch squares. Place 1 tablespoon of the mixture on each square
of pastry and fold to form a triangle. Moisten edges of pastry with
cold water and press together with the prongs of a fork. Bake in
a hot oven, 450 degrees, 15 minutes.

BANBURY TARTS (2)

1 cup seedless raisins	1 egg
1 cup pitted dates	1 cup sugar
Juice and grated rind 1 lemon	1 tablespoon melted butter

Put raisins and dates through meat chopper. Add remaining ingredients. Continue as for Banbury Tarts (1).

BANANA MERINGUE PIE

Line a deep pie plate with pastry and spread 3 tablespoons orange marmalade on bottom of plate. Peel and thinly slice 8 ripe bananas and mix well with ¼ cup sugar and ½ teaspoon vanilla. Pour over marmalade and bake in a moderate oven, 350 degrees, 30 minutes. Remove and top with meringue made of 3 stiffly beaten egg whites, 2 tablespoons sugar and 1 teaspoon rum. Return to oven 10 minutes. Serve either hot or cold.

BLACK BOTTOM PIE

1 baked pie shell	¼ cup sugar
1 tablespoon gelatin	¼ teaspoon cream of
¼ cup cold water	tartar
4 eggs, separated	Dash of salt
2 cups scalded milk	2 tablespoons rum
½ cup sugar	1 cup whipped cream
3 teaspoons cornstarch	2 tablespoons confectioner's
1½ squares melted chocolate	sugar
1 teaspoon vanilla	½ square shaved chocolate

Soak gelatin in cold water. Beat egg yolks until light, then add scalded milk and combined sugar and cornstarch. Cook in double boiler 20 minutes, or until custard coats a spoon heavily. Remove 1 cup of custard and add to it the melted chocolate. Beat with egg beater until cool, add vanilla and pour into baked pie shell. Chill. Stir the soaked gelatin into the remaining hot custard; then permit it to cool, but not stiffen. Beat egg whites, ¼ cup sugar, cream of tartar and salt until stiff, then fold into custard with rum. Pour over the chocolate custard, and chill until set. Spread with whipped cream to which confectioner's sugar has been added. Sprinkle shaved chocolate over top.

BLACK WALNUT PIE

1 cup sugar	¼ teaspoon salt
6 tablespoons flour	1 tablespoon butter
2 egg yolks	1 teaspoon vanilla
2 cups milk	1 cup black walnuts

Mix sugar and flour, gradually stir in beaten egg yolks and milk. Cook in double boiler until thick. Add salt, butter and vanilla. Cool. Add walnuts and pour into a baked pastry shell. Cover with whipped cream.

BLUEBERRY PIE

3 cups blueberries	2 tablespoons flour
¾ cup sugar	Pinch of salt

Wash, drain and pick over berries. Line a pie plate with pastry, and add berries which have been dredged lightly with flour. Sprinkle sugar and salt over the berries and put on top crust. Bake in a hot oven, 450 degrees, 10 minutes, then reduce heat to moderate, 350 degrees, and bake 35 minutes.

CHESS PIE

1½ cups butter	3 egg yolks
2 cups sifted sugar	2 tablespoons brandy
1 cup chopped walnuts	

Cream butter and sugar, then add remaining ingredients. Pour into unbaked pie shell and bake in a hot oven, 450 degrees, 10 minutes; then reduce heat to moderate, 350 degrees, and bake until a silver knife comes out clean.

CHERRY PIE

Line a pie plate with pastry and sprinkle 1 tablespoon flour over the bottom. Half fill the plate with ripe, stoned cherries, sprinkle with 1 cup of sugar and 1 teaspoon flour, and dot with butter. Cover with an upper crust and bake in a hot oven, 450 degrees, 10 minutes; then reduce heat to moderate, 350 degrees, and bake 40 minutes, or until done.

BUTTERSCOTCH PIE (1)

1 baked pie shell
½ cup brown sugar
⅓ cup flour
¼ teaspoon salt
2 cups scalded milk
3 egg yolks, well beaten
3 tablespoons butter

In a double boiler mix sugar, flour and salt, and gradually stir in scalded milk. Cook until thick and smooth, stirring occasionally. Slowly stir mixture over beaten egg yolks. Return to double boiler and cook 3 minutes. Add butter. Pour into baked pie shell. Make meringue with the 3 egg whites, spread on top of pie and bake in a slow oven, 300 degrees, 15 minutes, or until meringue is light brown. Serve cold.

BUTTERSCOTCH PIE (2)

1½ cups butter
2 cups light brown sugar
3 eggs, separated
1 cup chopped pecans
2 tablespoons brandy

Cream butter and sugar; then add beaten yolks, pecans and brandy. Pour into unbaked pie shell. Cover with a meringue made with the 3 egg whites. Bake in a hot oven, 450 degrees, 10 minutes; then reduce heat to moderate, 350 degrees, and bake until knife comes out clean.

COCONUT CUSTARD PIE

1 egg white, unbeaten
5 eggs, slightly beaten
¾ cup powdered sugar
½ teaspoon salt
1 tablespoon vanilla
2 cups milk, scalded
½ cup heavy cream, scalded
1¾ cups grated coconut

Brush bottom of unbaked pie shell with unbeaten white of egg. Chill. Add sugar, salt, vanilla, scalded milk and cream to slightly beaten eggs. Put coconut in pie shell and strain custard over it. Bake in a hot oven, 450 degrees, 10 minutes, reduce heat to moderate, 350 degrees, and bake 20 minutes longer.

CUSTARD PIE

½ cup sugar   1 teaspoon vanilla
3 cups scalded milk   Pinch of salt
                3 eggs, well beaten

Add sugar, scalded milk, vanilla and salt to eggs. Strain into an
unbaked pie shell, sprinkle with nutmeg and bake in a hot oven,
450 degrees, 10 minutes; then reduce heat to slow, 300 degrees, and
bake until firm when tested with a silver knife.

RASPBERRY CUSTARD PIE

Raspberry jam   3 tablespoons sugar
4 eggs, beaten   ⅛ teaspoon salt
2 cups scalded milk   Whipped cream

Cover the bottom of an unbaked pie shell with raspberry jam 1 inch
thick. Combine eggs, milk, sugar and salt and pour over jam. Bake in
a hot oven, 450 degrees, 10 minutes; then reduce heat to moderate,
350 degrees, and bake until firm when tested with silver knife. Chill
and top with whipped cream.

DATE PIE

1 baked pie shell   ¼ teaspoon cinnamon
1 pint milk   ⅛ teaspoon salt
1¼ cups chopped dates   2 eggs

Cook milk and dates together in double boiler 20 minutes. Add
cinnamon and salt and slightly beaten eggs. Cook slowly until thick.
Fill baked pie shell and top with whipped cream.

PORTSMOUTH DATE PIE

2 eggs   ½ teaspoon salt
1½ cups sugar   1 cup sour cream
                1 cup chopped dates

Combine ingredients and pour into an unbaked pie shell. Bake in
a hot oven, 450 degrees, 10 minutes, then in a slow oven, 300 degrees, 15 minutes.

CRANBERRY PIE

1 cup sugar	1 cup chopped raisins
1 tablespoon flour	⅛ teaspoon salt
½ cup boiling water	½ teaspoon vanilla
1 cup chopped cranberries	

Mix sugar and flour, add water, then raisins. Beat smooth and stir in remaining ingredients. Put into an unbaked pie shell and cover with a lattice top. Bake in a hot oven, 450 degrees, 10 minutes; then reduce heat to moderate, 350 degrees, and bake 40 minutes longer.

CREAM PIE

1 tablespoon butter	½ teaspoon cinnamon
2 tablespoons flour	¼ teaspoon nutmeg
¾ cup sugar	⅛ teaspoon salt
1½ cups heavy cream	

Cream butter and flour, then stir in mixed dry ingredients. Gradually stir in cream, and when well blended pour into an unbaked pie shell, cover with a top crust, and bake in a hot oven, 450 degrees, 10 minutes; then reduce heat to moderately slow, 325 degrees, and bake about 25 minutes.

GRAHAM CRACKER CREAM PIE

20 graham crackers, rolled fine	1 tablespoon cinnamon
½ cup melted butter	3 egg yolks
½ cup sugar	2 cups milk
1 teaspoon flour	2 tablespoons cornstarch
	½ cup sugar
1 teaspoon vanilla	

Lightly mix crackers, butter, sugar, flour and cinnamon. Reserve ¼ of the crumbs and line a pie plate with the remainder. Chill the shell. Make a cream filling of the egg yolks, milk, cornstarch, sugar and vanilla. Cook until thick; then pour into crumb-lined plate. Cover with meringue, sprinkle rest of crumbs on top and bake in a slow oven, 300 degrees, until brown.

LEMON MERINGUE PIE (1)

2 tablespoons butter
⅔ cup sugar
4 eggs, separated

1 tablespoon cold water
Juice of 1 lemon
Grated rind ½ lemon

Cream butter and sugar, add yolks beaten lightly, water, lemon juice and rind. Pour into an unbaked pie shell and bake in a slow oven, 300 degrees, until set and a light brown. Cool. Add 2 tablespoons powdered sugar to the stiffly beaten egg whites, pile on top of pie and bake in a slow oven, 250 degrees, until brown.

LEMON MERINGUE PIE (2)

1 baked pie shell
¼ cup cornstarch
1 cup sugar
1 cup boiling water

Pinch of salt
Juice of 2 lemons
Grated rind of 1 lemon
1 tablespoon butter

3 eggs, separated

Combine the cornstarch and sugar in a double boiler and add the boiling water, salt, lemon juice and grated rind. Cook until thick and clear; then add the butter and well-beaten egg yolks. Remove top of double boiler from water and cook over fire for a minute. Beat the egg whites stiff and lift the beater into the lemon filling, and beat once. This will give the filling a cloudy look, and is the final touch to make it perfection. Cool and pour into pie shell. To the stiffly beaten egg whites add 6 tablespoons sugar. Dot meringue carelessly on pie and bake in a slow oven, 250 degrees, until browned.

LEMON MERINGUE PIE (3)

1½ cups sugar
½ cup cornstarch
2 cups boiling water

2 egg yolks
2 tablespoons butter
Juice and rind of 1 lemon

Mix sugar and cornstarch in a double boiler, and gradually stir in boiling water. Cook 20 minutes, then add beaten egg yolks and butter. Cook until a paste, then add lemon juice and grated rind. Cool, pour into a baked pastry shell and cover with meringue.

FRIED PIES

2 cups flour	½ cup butter
1 teaspoon salt	⅓ cup cold water

Stewed fruit

Sift flour and salt together; cut in butter and add water. Roll out on a floured board ⅛ inch thick. Cut in rectangular pieces 4 by 2 inches. Place 1 tablespoon sweetened, mashed stewed fruit (peaches, prunes or thick applesauce) on half of each piece, moisten edges with cold water, fold over and press edges together with a fork. Fry in hot, deep fat, 370 degrees, until lightly browned.

MAPLE SYRUP PIE

1 baked pie shell	1 cup maple syrup
1½ tablespoons butter	½ cup water
2 tablespoons flour	½ cup chopped walnut
2 egg yolks	meats

Cream butter and flour; then add egg yolks, maple syrup and water. Cook in a double boiler until thick. Add nut meats. Pour into a baked pie crust and cover with meringue or whipped cream.

MINCEMEAT

2¼ pounds venison, cut up	1 teaspoon mace
6 pounds russet apples and juice from grinding	6 heaping teaspoons salt
1 pound ground currants	1 cup vinegar
1 pound ground raisins	2 pounds white sugar
½ cup molasses	½ cup lemon peel
½ cup ground citron	½ cup orange peel
1 tablespoon each of cinnamon, allspice and cloves	½ pound ground beef suet
	Few shakes white pepper
	½ cup lemon juice

Cook venison in boiling water to cover until tender, and cool in the broth. Put venison through a food chopper and return to broth with remaining ingredients. Simmer slowly 1½ hours, stirring frequently. Pour into clean hot jars. Add 2 teaspoons brandy on top of pint jars, and 1 tablespoon to quarts. Seal.

GRANDMA'S MINCEMEAT

In my grandmother's house, mincemeat was made in bulk and kept in a stone crock in the chilly storeroom where unused garments, blankets, comforters and bed linen were stored. The fragrance from that mincemeat percolated through the locked door, since it was redolent of rum and richness; and whenever the door was carelessly left unlocked, I helped myself to a cupful and for the remainder of the day was more offensively active than usual.—K.R.

3 quarts lightly cooked and finely chopped venison, p. 99, from which all gristle has been removed

1 quart fat from outside of the best beef, chopped fine

6 quarts apples, peeled, cored and chopped fine (russet apples if possible)

1 pint boiled cider[1]

2 pounds brown sugar

1 pound white sugar

1 pint black molasses

5 pounds finely chopped seeded raisins

1 pint finely chopped candied orange peel

1 pound finely chopped citron

½ cup lemon juice

¼ cup salt

1 quart brandy

¼ cup ground cloves

¼ cup powdered cinnamon

1 whole nutmeg grated

Simmer together for 2 hours everything except brandy, cloves, cinnamon and nutmeg. At the end of 2 hours, remove from stove and add remaining ingredients. The result may be kept in a crock (stirred frequently) in a cold room, put up in mason jars or frozen in small containers.

STRAWBERRY PIE (1)

Arrange 2 cups strawberries in baked pie shell. Mash another 2 cups of berries and add to it ⅔ cup sugar and 2 tablespoons cornstarch. Cook until thick in double boiler; then pour over berries in pie shell. Chill. Top with whipped cream.

---

[1] Boil 2 quarts fresh cider, uncovered, until reduced to 2 cups. Stir frequently as it thickens to avoid burning.

STRAWBERRY PIE (2)

1 baked pie shell	1 cup boiling water
2 tablespoons sugar	3 tablespoons cornstarch
1 tablespoon water	dissolved in
1 quart fresh strawberries	¼ cup cold water
1½ cups sugar	Whipped cream

Boil the 2 tablespoons sugar and 1 tablespoon water 3 minutes, and brush over hot baked pie shell. Return shell to oven 2 minutes; then cool. Hull, wash and drain berries, and set aside 12 nice ones. Put 3 cups of berries in the pie shell. Mash the remaining cup of berries, add the sugar and boiling water and simmer 5 minutes; then rub through a sieve. Add dissolved cornstarch and cook 5 minutes, until clear. Remove from fire and beat hard 2 minutes, then pour over berries in shell. Chill. Cover with whipped cream sweetened with sugar and vanilla. Place the 12 berries which were set aside on top of whipped cream.

MOLASSES PIE

½ cup sugar	1 cup molasses
3 tablespoons cornstarch	½ teaspoon cinnamon
1¼ cups water	¼ teaspoon nutmeg

Cook sugar, cornstarch, water and molasses in double boiler until thick. Cool and add spices. Pour into an unbaked pie shell, cover with a top crust, and bake in a hot oven, 425 degrees, 30 minutes.

PEACH PIE

1 cup graham cracker crumbs	2 eggs, slightly beaten
⅓ cup melted butter	Dash of salt
3 tablespoons confectioner's	1 cup sour cream
sugar	⅓ cup sugar
2 cups sliced peaches	

Mix crumbs, melted butter and confectioner's sugar and press on the sides and bottom of a pie plate. Add salt, sour cream and sugar to eggs, and mix well. Stir in peaches. Pour into pie shell and bake in a moderately slow oven, 325 degrees, 1 hour, or until custard is set.

PECAN TARTS

¼ cup butter	¾ cup molasses
½ cup sugar	Juice of 1 lemon
3 eggs, unbeaten	1 cup chopped pecans

Line muffin tins with thinly rolled pastry. Cream butter and sugar, then add eggs, molasses and lemon juice. Beat with egg beater until well mixed. Add pecans. Pour into tart shells. Bake in a hot oven, 400 degrees, 10 minutes; then reduce to moderate, 350 degrees, and bake 20 minutes longer, or until firm. Serve with whipped cream.

RASPBERRY PIE

1 baked pie shell	1 teaspoon grated lemon
1 quart raspberries	rind
¾ cup sugar	Dash salt
½ cup boiling water	1 tablespoon gelatin
1 tablespoon lemon juice	¼ cup cold water
1 teaspoon vanilla	

Crush berries and stir in sugar and boiling water. Let stand 30 minutes, then drain. Bring the juice to a boil and add lemon juice, rind, salt, and gelatin which has been soaked 5 minutes in the cold water. Cool, and when slightly thick, stir in vanilla. Put the berries in the pastry shell and pour the gelatin mixture over them. Chill.

CREAM PRUNE PIE

2 eggs, separated	1 cup prune pulp
½ cup sugar	1 cup heavy cream
1 teaspoon vanilla	

Beat yolks of eggs and sugar; add prune pulp, cream and vanilla. Pour into a slightly baked pie shell and bake in a slow oven, 325 degrees, until set. When cool, cover with meringue made of stiffly beaten egg whites and 2 tablespoons sugar. Bake in a slow oven until meringue is delicately browned.

PUMPKIN PIE

2 cups canned pumpkin
2 cups rich milk
¾ cup sugar

2 eggs
¼ teaspoon ginger
½ teaspoon salt

1 teaspoon cinnamon

Mix pumpkin with milk, sugar, beaten eggs, ginger, salt and cinnamon; beat 2 minutes. Pour into unbaked pie shell and bake in hot oven, 450 degrees, for 10 minutes, then reduce heat to moderate, 350 degrees, and bake 45 minutes.

PUMPKIN CHIFFON PIE

1 baked pie shell
1 tablespoon gelatin
¼ cup cold water
1 cup brown sugar
3 eggs, separated
½ cup milk

1½ cups canned pumpkin
2 teaspoons cinnamon
½ teaspoon ginger
½ teaspoon salt
2 tablespoons granulated
    sugar

Soften gelatin in water. Combine brown sugar, egg yolks, milk, pumpkin, spices and salt. Cook in double boiler until thick. Add softened gelatin and cool. Fold in egg whites beaten with granulated sugar. Pour into baked pie shell and chill.

SOUR CREAM RAISIN PIE

2 eggs, beaten
¾ cup sugar
½ teaspoon cinnamon
½ teaspoon nutmeg

¼ teaspoon cloves
½ teaspoon salt
1 tablespoon vinegar
1 cup sour cream

1 cup chopped raisins

Mix ingredients together and pour into unbaked pie shell. Bake in a hot oven, 450 degrees, 10 minutes; then reduce heat to moderate, 350 degrees, and bake 30 minutes longer. Cool.

RHUBARB PIE

1 cup chopped rhubarb	1 egg, beaten
1 cup sugar	1 teaspoon lemon juice
2 tablespoons flour	1/8 teaspoon salt

Mix in order given. Pour into unbaked pie shell and cover with a top crust or a lattice top. Bake in a hot oven, 450 degrees, 10 minutes; then reduce to moderate, 350 degrees, and bake about 40 minutes.

SQUASH PIE

1 cup canned squash	1 cup light cream
1 cup brown sugar	1 teaspoon cinnamon
2 eggs, beaten	1/4 teaspoon ginger
1/4 teaspoon nutmeg	

Mix squash with sugar, eggs, cream and seasonings; beat well. Pour into a pastry-lined plate and bake in a hot oven, 400 degrees, until of a custard consistency, about 30 minutes.

DESSERTS AND DESSERT SAUCES

MAXIMS FROM MAINE KITCHENS

A pinch of salt and a few grains of grated nutmeg improve the taste of any pudding.

☙

When boiled custard curdles, set in a dish of cold water and beat with egg beater till smooth.

☙

When making French toast, use water rather than milk with the egg; the toast will be more tender.

DESSERTS AND DESSERT SAUCES

BERNICE WING TO MR. ROBERTS CONCERNING CREAMED CODFISH, STRAWBERRY SHORTCAKE, PANCAKES, DRIED BEEF, FISH CHOWDER, BOILED CIDER PIE AND OTHER DAINTIES

"YOU SPOKE of pouring thick cream on top of chocolate custards. Cream was used by my grandmother as we would use milk. Creamed codfish was just that, creamed with real cream, as well as potatoes cooked on the back of the stove in cream and butter.

"But to get back to the shortcake. At least two layers, and sometimes three, of hot biscuit dough, unsweetened, made from sour cream or buttermilk, was piled on a large old blue platter. The platter was probably over 100 years old, but that didn't make the taste bitter. While hot, the layers were heavily buttered, and over each layer, before piling up, crushed fresh strawberries, sweetened, were poured thickly. Then wedges of this were cut, and from a pitcher always on the table, heavy yellow cream could be poured on it. Never, never, whipped cream. In raspberry and blackberry season we had a cake made of those berries in the same way, and they required thick cream too.

"On my great-great grandmother's pancake griddle, cakes made from buttermilk, ten at a time, were heaped in a covered dish. The first ten or so were eaten with sausage; the last ten with either shaved maple sugar or syrup or just plain thick cream and sugar, the latter the best of all. Don't you have sweet-smelling buckwheat fields up in Maine, either? Didn't you ever see the big pitcher 'set' with buckwheat batter, foaming and running over, and used morning after morning, until the first signs of a rash breaking out on the family, when it was dropped for a while? And the sausage was something to talk about. I agree with you that it wasn't our youthful appetites that made these foods perfect. They were perfect. My aunts made the same sausage this butchering time, and sent me some, and there is none like it anywhere. For the sausage, they always grind their own pepper, raise their own sage, and look over and wash each leaf of sage separately, so that no worm can creep in. The meat is seasoned just right, packed in large cloth bags. When it is fried, very little grease comes out, since they use only the best lean meat. No beef is ever used. City sausage doesn't deserve the stolen name. Then the thick slices are browned slowly, so that the centers are done.

"Their head-cheese, too, is seasoned right, and packed in bags. Only lean meat from the head is cooked and pressed for that. Our dried beef wasn't smoked. The hooks used to hang in the ceiling of the living room where my ancestors hung this beef to dry. Then we used frozen beef, sliced off paper-thin, and fried in butter. Your beans sound fine, just like grandmother used to make. For chowder we mostly used fresh water fish from the lake: bass, pickerel, perch, bull-heads, etc. They were always dipped in a mixture of meal and flour, salted, and fried in butter (never in salt pork) until they would break in two with crispness, the inside white meat falling from the backbone. Your tripe sounds familiar. My grandfather loved that. He ate vinegar on it. How about your chicken dinners? Nothing could compare to ours. The biscuit alone would melt in your mouth, so flaky and light, made with butter and sour cream. The chicken was taken out when done, and fried brown in butter.

"I didn't hear you mention boiled cider pie. Sweet cider boiled down, sweetened and thickened, and put in an open crust, with latticed crust on top. And a real cream pie, too. Not a custard, although they made that, with four or five eggs. But a cream pie is something. What we would call a sweetened white sauce was cooked, to which was added plenty of thick yellow cream, until the mixture would be just right to cut when cold. This was put in a raw crust, and baked until bubbly brown. Their ice cream was also made of pure cream (not whipped, Heaven forbid), with no milk at all, and with plenty of eggs. Good? Don't you eat in your part of Maine?

"This was their usual breakfast, after the family had been up from four o'clock in the summer: Baked potatoes, or hash, meat, or sausage with pancakes, apple sauce or fruit, plenty of pancakes

with syrup, or Johnny cake. Coffee with cream. Homemade doughnuts, made with sour cream. Such Johnny cake, too, brown and
with a cream taste. We, too, had our three jars, one with hermits,
one with doughnuts, and in place of your sugar cookies, one filled
with sour cream cookies, which my aunt makes today, and which
are soft and luscious, like none ever tasted now. Sometimes they
were full of butternut or hickory nut meats. Then there were the
hickory nut meats, too. Don't they grow in your part of Maine?
To sit down in the evening and pick out a dish of hickory nuts
was the usual occupation in the fall. I never see them any more.

"Their mince meat was the real thing, too. No tomatoes or imi-
tations. Such pies! My aunts and grandmother were overcome with
neatness, too. I have seen my grandmother throw away her heaped
up plate, at the table, because someone got too near it, and she
was afraid a hair had dropped into it. When she visited away from
home, she always carried her own butter, for fear that that of her
hosts was dirty."

SOFT CUSTARD

2 cups milk	¼ cup sugar
3 eggs, separated	¼ teaspoon salt
½ teaspoon vanilla	

Scald milk in double boiler. Gradually add beaten egg yolks, stirring constantly. Cook until mixture coats a spoon. Add sugar and
salt and remove from stove. Cool; then add vanilla and beaten
egg whites. Chill. Serves 4.

MACAROON CUSTARDS

1½ cups thin cream	⅛ teaspoon salt
1½ cups milk	8 crumbled almond maca-
1 tablespoon grated lemon rind	roons
¼ cup sugar	4 slightly beaten eggs
	Nutmeg

Scald cream, milk, lemon rind, sugar and salt in top of double boiler.
Strain and add macaroons, stirring until blended. Remove from stove
and add eggs. Turn into buttered molds and sprinkle with nutmeg.
Bake in moderate oven, 350 degrees, until firm. Serves 6.

GRANDMA NASON'S CHOCOLATE CUSTARDS

3 scant tablespoons corn-
    starch
3 cups milk

5 heaping tablespoons sugar
2 tablespoons water
2 squares chocolate

Dissolve cornstarch in ½ cup of the milk. Heat remaining 2½ cups of milk in double boiler. Put sugar, water and chocolate in a saucepan and dissolve over boiling water; then place on fire, boil 2 minutes and then add to the hot milk. When this has the appearance of chocolate milk, add the cornstarch mixture. Stir until slightly thickened, pour into goblets, cool and place in refrigerator. Serve with cream.

CHOCOLATE CUSTARDS

2 eggs
2 egg yolks
1 cup cold milk
1 cup heavy cream
2 squares chocolate

3 tablespoons sugar
½ teaspoon vanilla or sherry to
    taste
⅛ teaspoon salt
1 teaspoon sugar

Beat the 2 eggs and 1 egg yolk in top of double boiler with milk and cream. Stir in melted chocolate, 3 tablespoons sugar, flavoring and salt. Heat slowly, stirring constantly. When mixture thickens, stir in remaining egg yolk beaten with 1 teaspoon sugar. Continue to cook and stir until slightly thick. Pour into custard cups, chill, and serve with heavy cream. Serves 4.

BAVARIAN CREAM

2 tablespoons gelatin
⅓ cup cold water
1 cup boiling pineapple juice
1 tablespoon lemon juice

¼ cup orange juice
¼ cup sugar
1 cup sliced dates
½ cup diced pineapple

¼ cup chopped almonds

Soak gelatin in cold water for 5 minutes. Dissolve in boiling pineapple juice. Add fruit juices and sugar. Chill until slightly thick; then beat until frothy and add remaining ingredients. Turn into a mold and chill. Unmold and serve with heavy cream. Serves 4.

COFFEE BAVARIAN CREAM

2 tablespoons gelatin   1 cup strong coffee
⅓ cup cold water   1 cup sugar
               1 pint heavy cream, whipped

Dissolve gelatin in cold water; then pour in boiling coffee and add sugar. Strain into a bowl set in ice water. Beat till it begins to thicken; then add the cream. Turn into mold and chill. Serves 6.

MACAROON BAVARIAN CREAM

¾ cup sugar   2 tablespoons cold water
½ cup boiling water   1 teaspoon vanilla
2 egg whites   1 cup heavy cream
1 tablespoon gelatin   ½ cup crumbled macaroons

Boil sugar and water 5 minutes; then add the gelatin which has soaked in the cold water 15 minutes. Pour over the stiffly beaten egg whites, beating constantly until cold. Fold in stiffly beaten cream, vanilla and macaroon crumbs. Turn into a mold and chill. Serves 4.

STRAWBERRY BAVARIAN CREAM

2 tablespoons gelatin   ½ cup sugar
1 cup water   2 cups hulled strawberries
               2 cups heavy cream, whipped

Soak gelatin in ½ cup water for 10 minutes. Mix the remaining ½ cup of water and sugar in a saucepan, add the berries and bring to a boil. Add the gelatin and cool. Fold in the whipped cream, turn into a mold and chill. Serves 6.

ZABAGLIONE

Beat the yolks of 6 eggs with 3 tablespoons powdered sugar until thick and lemon-colored. Put in top of a double boiler and beat with a wire whisk. Gradually add ⅓ cup sherry or brandy, and continue beating until mixture is custardy. Put into sherbet glasses and serve immediately. Serves 4.

TAPIOCA CREAM

2 tablespoons quick-cooking tapioca	2 eggs, separated
1 pint milk	½ cup sugar
	½ teaspoon vanilla

Put tapioca in top of double boiler and add enough hot water to cover. When water has been absorbed, add milk and cook till tapioca is soft. Beat egg yolks and add sugar. Pour hot milk and tapioca on eggs, and cook till custardy. Remove from fire and add stiffly beaten egg whites. Stir well, and when cool add vanilla and a dash of salt. Turn into serving dish and chill. Serves 4.

LEMON TAPIOCA

Soak ½ cup pearl tapioca in 3 cups cold water overnight. Add rind and juice of 1 lemon and cook in double boiler until tapioca is clear. Remove lemon rind and add juice of another lemon, 1 cup sugar and ⅛ teaspoon salt. Mix and bring to a boil. Turn into a mold and chill. Serve with sugar and cream. Serves 6.

PINEAPPLE TAPIOCA

5 tablespoons quick-cooking tapioca	⅛ teaspoon salt
¼ cup sugar	2 cups hot pineapple juice
	2 cups boiling water
1 cup chopped pineapple	

Cook tapioca, sugar, salt, pineapple juice and water in a double boiler 15 minutes. Remove from heat and add pineapple. Chill and serve with cream and sugar. Serves 6.

SPANISH CREAM

2 tablespoons gelatin	4 eggs, separated
1 quart milk	6 tablespoons sugar
1 teaspoon vanilla	

Scald milk with gelatin. Beat yolks of eggs and sugar; then add to milk. Cook until custardy. Remove from fire and add stiffly beaten egg whites. Beat in vanilla. Pour into a mold and chill. Serve with cream. Serves 6.

MAPLE CREAM

1 envelope gelatin	3 eggs, separated
2½ cups milk	¼ teaspoon salt
⅔ cup maple syrup	1 teaspoon vanilla

Dissolve gelatin in milk in top of double boiler. Place over hot water, add maple syrup and stir until well blended. Beat yolks and salt slightly and pour milk mixture over them. Return to double boiler and stir constantly until mixture thickens. Remove from fire, add vanilla and fold in stiffly beaten egg whites. Pour into molds or custard cups and chill. Serves 6.

SEA MOSS BLANCMANGE

½ cup Irish moss	Pinch of salt
3 cups milk	1 teaspoon vanilla

Soak moss 15 minutes in cold water; reject discolored pieces, then add remainder to milk and cook in double boiler 25 minutes. Strain. Add salt and vanilla. Turn into molds, chill and serve either with sliced bananas, sugar and cream, or with cream and sugar alone.

CHOCOLATE MOUSSE

1 cup chocolate bits	4 eggs, separated
¼ cup water	2 tablespoons rum or sherry

Melt chocolate bits in water. Remove from fire and stir in beaten egg yolks, flavoring and stiffly beaten egg whites. Pour into sherbet glasses and chill in refrigerator. Serves 6.

PEACH MOUSSE

1 cup peach pulp	2 cups heavy cream,
¾ cup sugar	whipped
	1 teaspoon vanilla

Mix peach pulp and sugar; then fold into the whipped cream and add vanilla. Mold and freeze. Serves 4.

VANILLA MOUSSE

½ cup water
½ cup sugar
Pinch of salt

2 eggs, separated
1 pint heavy cream,
    whipped

1 teaspoon vanilla

Boil sugar and water until syrup threads. Pour over beaten egg yolks and cook in double boiler until thick, stirring constantly. Remove from heat, fold in stiffly beaten egg whites and cool in refrigerator. Fold in cream, add vanilla and freeze. Serves 4–6.

FRUIT PUDDING

1 ½ tablespoons gelatin
2 tablespoons cold water
½ cup boiling water
¼ cup lemon juice

¼ cup orange juice
½ cup grape juice
1 cup sugar
Whites of 2 eggs

1 cup heavy cream, whipped

Soften gelatin in cold water; add boiling water, fruit juices and sugar and chill until slightly thickened. Fold in egg whites, stiffly beaten, and whipped cream. Turn into a mold and chill until firm. Serves 6.

JUDGE PETERS' PUDDING

2 tablespoons gelatin
1 cup cold water
1 cup boiling water
1 ½ cups sugar
2 oranges

Juice of 2 lemons
2 sliced bananas
8 chopped figs
¼ cup chopped walnuts
¼ cup chopped dates

Soak gelatin in cold water until soft; add boiling water and stir until gelatin is dissolved; add sugar, strain, and cool until thickened. Peel and cut oranges into small pieces and stir into the gelatin with the remaining ingredients. Pour into a mold and chill. Turn onto a platter and put around pudding 1 pint whipped cream to which has been added ½ cup sugar, ½ teaspoon vanilla and a pinch of salt. Serves 6.

RUM PUDDING

2 tablespoons gelatin
1 pint milk
1 cup sugar

10 egg yolks, well beaten
1 pint heavy cream
½ cup rum

Juice of 1 lemon

Soak gelatin in the milk 5 minutes, then heat until dissolved, stirring constantly. Add sugar. Stir cream into egg yolks, then beat with a wire whisk into gelatin mixture. Bring to boiling point and remove from fire. When cool, add rum. Pour into large or individual molds and chill. Squeeze lemon juice over it before serving.

SNOW PUDDING

2 tablespoons gelatin
¼ cup cold water
1 cup boiling water

¾ cup sugar
½ cup lemon juice
3 egg whites, stiffly beaten

Soak the gelatin in the cold water 5 minutes; then add boiling water and stir until dissolved. Stir in sugar and lemon juice, and when sugar is dissolved allow mixture to cool until slightly thickened. Then set the bowl in a pan of ice water and beat mixture until it is foamy. Fold in the egg whites and continue to beat until the mixture holds its shape. Pour into a mold and chill till firm. Unmold and scrve with Custard Sauce, p. 340, around the mold. Serves 6.

COFFEE JELLY

1 tablespoon gelatin
¼ cup cold water

6 tablespoons sugar
⅛ teaspoon salt

1¾ cups hot strong coffee

Soak gelatin 5 minutes in cold water. Add sugar, salt and hot coffee and stir until gelatin dissolves. Turn into molds and chill until firm. Serve with plain or whipped cream.

WINE OR CIDER JELLY

Soak 2 tablespoons gelatin in 1 cup cold water. Add 1 cup boiling water, 1 cup sugar and 1 cup wine (1 cup old cider and 1 teaspoon lemon extract for cider jelly may be substituted for wine). Pour into mold and chill. Serve with whipped cream.

APRICOT WHIP

1 cup stewed apricot pulp	3 egg whites, stiffly beaten
½ cup sugar	¾ teaspoon salt
1 teaspoon gelatin	1 cup heavy cream
1 teaspoon cold water	1 teaspoon vanilla

Heat pulp with sugar; then add gelatin, softened in cold water. Fold mixture into stiffly beaten egg whites to which salt has been added. Pour into pudding dish and chill. Whip cream, add vanilla and serve on pudding.

PINEAPPLE WHIP

3 eggs, separated	⅔ cup canned grated pineapple
Grated rind 1 lemon	
Juice of 1 lemon	1 tablespoon gelatin
½ cup sugar	3 tablespoons cold water
Few grains salt	1½ cups heavy cream

Beat yolks of eggs and add grated rind, lemon juice, salt and sugar. Cook in double boiler, stirring constantly, until thick. Remove from fire and add pineapple and the gelatin which has been soaked in the cold water 15 minutes. Chill until mixture begins to thicken; then add stiffly beaten egg whites and stiffly beaten cream. Turn into mold and chill. Serves 4.

PRUNE WHIP

1 pound stewed prunes, stoned	4 egg whites, stiffly beaten
	¼ teaspoon soda
1 cup sugar	¼ teaspoon salt

Cut prunes fine and add sugar. Mix egg whites with soda and salt, and add to prunes and sugar. Put in a baking dish, set in pan of hot water and bake in a slow oven, 300 degrees, 45 minutes. Serve cold with Custard Sauce, p. 340. Serves 6.

BOSTON CREAM PIE

Put Cream Layer Cake, p. 349, together with Cream Filling, p. 375, and sprinkle the top with powdered sugar.

WILD STRAWBERRY DESSERT

1 quart wild strawberries	3 tablespoons powdered
1 pint water	sugar
1 cup sugar	1 tablespoon butter

4 eggs, separated

Cook berries in water until tender, add sugar, butter and egg yolks beaten light. Mix well. Pour into serving dish. Add powdered sugar to stiffly beaten egg whites, heap on berries and chill. Serves 6.

CHOCOLATE SOUFFLÉ

1 ½ squares chocolate	4 ½ tablespoons confec-
3 tablespoons butter	tioners' sugar
3 tablespoons flour	3 egg yolks
½ teaspoon salt	1 teaspoon vanilla
¾ cup milk	3 egg whites

Melt chocolate over hot water. Melt butter, add flour and gradually add milk, stirring until mixture is smooth. Add powdered sugar and stir until it begins to boil. Remove from fire, add chocolate and egg yolks beaten until light. Cool, flavor with vanilla, then fold in egg whites stiffly beaten. Pour into baking dish, set in a pan of hot water, and bake in a moderately hot oven, 375 degrees, 20 minutes. Serve immediately with heavy cream. Serves 4.

LEMON SOUFFLÉ

4 eggs, separated	Rind and juice of 1 lemon

1 cup sugar

Beat egg yolks until thick and lemon-colored. Gradually add sugar and continue beating. Then add lemon juice and grated rind. Cut and fold in stiffly beaten egg whites. Turn into buttered baking dish, set in pan of hot water and bake in a moderately slow oven, 325 degrees, 35 to 40 minutes. Serve with Foamy Sauce, p. 341. Serves 4.

BOWDOIN SPECIAL

Put Cream Layer Cake, p. 349, together with Cream Filling, p. 375, and frost the top and sides with Fudge Frosting, p. 376.

COFFEE PARFAIT

½ cup strong coffee   2 cups heavy cream
½ cup sugar   1 teaspoon vanilla
2 eggs   Pinch of salt

Add ¼ cup of coffee to sugar and boil until mixture threads. Pour slowly over well beaten eggs, stirring constantly. Cook in double boiler 5 minutes, stirring constantly. Remove from fire and chill. Beat cream until stiff, add vanilla and remaining coffee. Fold cream into egg mixture, stirring as little as possible. Freeze in ice and salt, or in mechanical refrigerator. Serves 4.

MAPLE PARFAIT

1 cup maple syrup   3 egg whites
          1 pint heavy cream, whipped

Heat maple syrup to boiling point and pour slowly over stiffly beaten egg whites, beating constantly. Beat until mixture is cold. Fold whipped cream into egg mixture. Turn into mold and freeze in ice and salt 3 hours, or turn into trays in mechanical refrigerator and freeze 2 to 3 hours. Serves 4.

APPLE SNOW

6 apples   Sugar
          3 egg whites, beaten stiff

Peel and core apples and boil in a little water until soft enough to sieve. Sweeten, beat in egg whites, and serve with cream.

LEMON CREAM SHERBET

1 cup sugar   ½ cup lemon juice
1 cup water   1 cup heavy cream,
                               whipped

Mix sugar and water. Cook over low heat until sugar is dissolved. Cool. Add lemon juice and whipped cream, turn into refrigerator tray, and freeze, stirring at least twice during the freezing process. Serves 4.

LEMON SHERBET

8 lemons   6 cups milk   2 cups sugar

Squeeze and strain lemons; then add sugar. Add milk just before turning into freezer. Serves 6.

ORANGE SHERBET

½ cup sugar   1 cup evaporated milk,
1½ cups unstrained orange   chilled
     juice   2 tablespoons lemon juice

Dissolve sugar in orange juice and chill in refrigerator. Whip cold evaporated milk until stiff, fold in lemon juice and orange-sugar mixture. Pour into a cold freezing tray and freeze. Serves 4.

RASPBERRY SHERBET

2 tablespoons gelatin   2 cups sugar
3 cups cold water   1 cup strained raspberry
1 cup boiling water   juice
       3 tablespoons lemon juice

Soften gelatin in ½ cup cold water; dissolve in boiling water, and add sugar, fruit juices and remaining 2½ cups cold water. Strain and freeze. Serves 6.

LEMON ICE

1 quart water   2 cups sugar
       ¾ cup lemon juice

Boil water and sugar 5 minutes. Add lemon juice, cool, strain and freeze. Serves 6.

WASHINGTON PIE

Put the layers of Cream Layer Cake, p. 349, together with raspberry jam and sprinkle the top generously with powdered sugar.

VANILLA ICE CREAM

2 cups milk	⅛ teaspoon salt
1 cup sugar	4 egg yolks
1 tablespoon flour	1 tablespoon vanilla

2 cups heavy cream

Scald milk in double boiler and gradually add mixture of sugar, flour and salt. Cook 5 minutes, stirring constantly. Thin slightly beaten egg yolks with a little of the scalded milk mixture, and then add this to mixture in double boiler. Cook 2 minutes, stirring constantly. Chill, add vanilla and cream and freeze. Serves 6.

REFRIGERATOR ICE CREAM

½ pound marshmallows	2 cups heavy cream
3 cups milk	1 teaspoon vanilla

Pour milk over marshmallows and cook slowly till dissolved. Cool, put in refrigerator trays and freeze to a mush. Whip cream and vanilla and add to mixture. Freeze, stirring 2 or 3 times while freezing. Serves 6.

ICEBOX CAKE

3 squares melted chocolate	3 eggs, separated

Beat yolks into melted chocolate, and add stiffly beaten whites. Place between layers of sponge cake and put in icebox for several hours. Serve with whipped cream.

CHOCOLATE ROLL

6 egg yolks, beaten	1 teaspoon baking powder
½ cup confectioners' sugar	½ teaspoon salt
2 squares melted chocolate	6 egg whites, stiffly beaten
2 tablespoons pastry flour	1 teaspoon vanilla

Mix ingredients in order given. Spread thin on a buttered baking sheet and bake 20 minutes in a moderate oven, 350 degrees. Turn out on a damp cloth. When cool, spread with whipped cream flavored with vanilla and sugar. Roll like a jelly roll and cut in slices for serving.

CREAM CAKES

1 cup water	1 cup pastry flour
½ cup butter	4 eggs

Boil water and butter together. While on the stove add flour and beat well. Remove from heat, add eggs one at a time, beating 2 minutes after each is added. Drop mixture by spoonful on buttered sheet and bake in a moderately hot oven, 375 degrees, about 30 minutes. Cut cakes in half and fill with Cream Filling, p. 375.

STRAWBERRY SHORTCAKE

2 cups flour	2 tablespoons sugar
4 teaspoons baking powder	⅓ cup butter
½ teaspoon salt	⅔ cup milk

1 quart strawberries, crushed and sweetened

Mix and sift dry ingredients. Cut in butter. Add milk gradually and mix lightly to a soft dough. Turn onto a floured board, knead slightly, roll or pat dough ¼ inch thick and cut with biscuit cutter. Place half the rounds on a buttered cooky sheet, spread lightly with melted butter and place remaining halves on top. Bake 12 minutes in a hot oven, 450 degrees. Separate halves, spread with softened butter and part of strawberries. Place other half on top and cover with remaining berries. Serve with heavy cream.

CHOCOLATE REFRIGERATOR CAKE

2 dozen ladyfingers	4 eggs, separated
4 ounces chocolate	½ pint heavy cream,
1 cup confectioners' sugar	whipped
9 tablespoons water	1 teaspoon vanilla

Few drops almond extract

Line sides and bottom of a mold with ladyfingers, rounded side out. Melt chocolate and add sugar and water. Stir until smooth and then add beaten egg yolks. Cool. Fold in stiffly beaten egg whites and cream. Flavor. Pour into mold and arrange ladyfingers on top in the form of spokes. Place in refrigerator 24 hours. Serves 12.

ORANGE REFRIGERATOR CAKE

2 cups water	2 cups heavy cream,
1 cup sugar	whipped
2 tablespoons gelatin	½ pound marshmallows
2 tablespoons lemon juice	2 dozen ladyfingers
Pulp of 1 orange, shredded	1 cup chopped nuts

Boil water and sugar 20 minutes. Dissolve gelatin in cold water
to cover for 10 minutes; then add to boiling syrup. Add lemon
juice and strain. Add orange pulp and juice and put in refrigerator
1 hour to chill. Beat with wire whisk till light. Add whipped cream
and marshmallows and beat thoroughly. Separate ladyfingers, line
sides of baking dish with them and crumble some in the bottom.
Over the crumbs put a layer of chopped nuts, then a layer of the
mixture. Continue in this manner until ingredients are gone. Put
in refrigerator overnight.

DUTCH APPLE CAKE

¼ cup butter	3 heaping teaspoons baking
¾ cup sugar	powder
2 eggs	½ teaspoon salt
2 cups flour	¾ cup milk
1 teaspoon vanilla	

Cream butter and sugar together. Add beaten eggs and mix well.
Mix and sift flour, baking powder and salt, and add alternately
with milk to first mixture. Add vanilla and beat thoroughly. Pour
into well-greased, shallow pan, having batter ¾ inch deep. Arrange
thinly sliced apples close together in rows on top of batter. Sprinkle
generously with mixture of brown sugar and cinnamon and dot
with small bits of butter. Bake in moderate oven, 350 degrees, 45
minutes or until apples are tender.

SPONGE CAKE PUDDING

Break pieces of leftover sponge cake in individual custard cups or a
baking dish. Moisten with any sort of wine, sherry, rum or other
liquor. Pour over them either Soft Custard, p. 312, or Chocolate
Custards, p. 313. Bake in a 300-degree oven for 15 or 20 minutes.
Serve either hot or chilled with heavy cream.

APPLE DUMPLINGS

Make a rich baking powder biscuit dough, roll ¼ inch thick and cut in 4-inch squares. Peel and core apples and place one in the middle of each square of dough. Fill cavity with sugar and cinnamon and a small piece of butter. Fasten the four corners of the dough over the apple. Bake in a moderate oven, 350 degrees, 20 minutes.

APPLE PUDDING (1)

Green apples	1 cup sugar
3 tablespoons lemon juice	¾ cup flour
¼ cup water	¼ teaspoon salt
1 teaspoon cinnamon	6 tablespoons butter

Pare, core and slice enough apples to fill a baking dish. Add lemon juice and water. Mix cinnamon with half the sugar and sprinkle over apples. Combine remaining sugar with flour and salt and work in butter with finger tips until crumbly. Sprinkle over apples and pat smooth with back of spoon. Bake 40 minutes in a 375-degree oven. Serve with cream or Hard Sauce, p. 341. Serves 6.

APPLE PUDDING (2)

8 apples	¼ teaspoon salt
¾ cup brown sugar	½ cup molasses
½ teaspoon cinnamon	3 tablespoons warm water
¼ teaspoon nutmeg	¼ cup butter
Baking Powder Biscuit crust	

Peel, core and slice apples and put them in bottom of a buttered baking dish. Add sugar, spices, salt, molasses, water and dot with butter. Cover and bake in a hot oven, 400 degrees, for 45 minutes. Make half the Baking Powder Biscuit recipe, p. 278, roll dough lightly and pat ¾ inch thick. Remove pudding from oven and put on crust. Bake in a 450-degree oven for 15 minutes. Serve with Hard Sauce, p. 341, or cream. Serves 6.

APPLE CRUMB PUDDING

Fill buttered baking dish with applesauce. Melt 3 tablespoons butter in frying pan and add ½ cup brown sugar and a dozen graham crackers rolled into crumbs. Mix well and spread over sauce. Bake in hot oven, 400 degrees, 10 minutes. Serve hot or cold with Hard Sauce, p. 341.

BROWN BETTY

2 cups chopped apples	1 teaspoon cinnamon
1 cup bread crumbs	Grated rind and juice of
¼ cup butter	½ lemon
½ cup brown sugar	¼ cup hot water

Butter a pudding dish and put a layer of apples in the bottom. Sprinkle with sugar and cinnamon, dots of butter, some rind and lemon juice and bread crumbs. Continue layers until dish is filled, topped with bread crumbs. Cover with water and bake, covered, in a moderate oven, 350 degrees, 40 minutes. Uncover and brown crumbs. Serve with cream. Serves 4.

BANANA BETTY

2 cups bread crumbs	1 teaspoon cinnamon
¼ cup melted butter	¾ cup brown sugar
3 tablespoons lemon juice	6 bananas
1½ cups milk	

Moisten bread crumbs in melted butter and lemon juice and combine with sugar and cinnamon. Slice 3 bananas in the bottom of a baking dish; sprinkle with half the bread crumb mixture. Repeat with bananas and crumbs. Pour milk over all and bake in a moderate oven, 350 degrees, 30 minutes. Serve with whipped cream. Serves 6.

VIRGINIA PUDDING

Beat together ½ cup butter, ½ cup sugar, 1 teaspoon soda; then add ½ cup molasses, beaten yolks of 4 eggs, beaten whites of 4 eggs, 2 cups sifted flour. Pour into a buttered baking dish and bake in a moderately slow oven, 325 degrees, 1 hour. Serve with a wine sauce. Serves 6–8.

BLUEBERRY COBBLER

1 quart blueberries	3 teaspoons baking powder
1 cup sugar	¼ teaspoon salt
¼ cup melted butter	Pinch of nutmeg
Juice of ½ lemon	3 tablespoons lard
1 cup cake flour	1 egg
	¼ cup milk

Put blueberries, sugar, butter and lemon juice in a baking pan. Mix and sift dry ingredients and cut in lard. Beat egg and milk together, then stir into dry ingredients. Cover the blueberries with this mixture. Bake in a moderate oven, 350 degrees, 40 minutes. Cut in squares and serve with liberal amount of Pudding Sauce (3), p. 342.

BLUEBERRY CRUMBLE

3 cups blueberries	¼ teaspoon cinnamon
¾ cup sugar	¾ cup flour
Juice of 1 lemon	½ teaspoon salt
	⅓ cup butter

Put blueberries in buttered baking dish and add half the sugar, lemon juice and cinnamon. Mix remaining half of sugar, flour, salt and butter into a crumble, then sprinkle over blueberries. Bake in a moderate oven, 350 degrees, about 40 minutes. Serve with heavy cream or vanilla ice cream. Serves 6.

BLUEBERRY PUDDING

¼ cup butter	2 cups blueberries
¾ cup sugar	¼ cup water
4 cups bread cubes	1 tablespoon lemon juice

Cream butter and sugar; then add remaining ingredients. Mix well. Put in a buttered baking dish and bake in a moderately hot oven, 375 degrees, 35 minutes. Serve hot with Hard Sauce, p. 341, heavy cream or vanilla ice cream. Serves 6.

DATE–NUT CRUMBLE

2 eggs, beaten	1 teaspoon baking powder
¾ cup white or brown sugar	1 cup chopped nuts
2 tablespoons flour	1 cup chopped dates

Mix ingredients in order given. Spread in shallow, buttered pan, sprinkle with cinnamon and bake in moderate oven, 350 degrees, 30 to 40 minutes. Cool. Crumble and serve with whipped cream. Serves 4.

FRIED MUSH

Pack thick, cooked cereal in a buttered bread tin. Cover and chill. Slice ¼ inch thick and sauté in bacon fat or butter until browned on both sides. Serve hot with butter and maple syrup.

BREAD PUDDING

1 cup bread crumbs	¼ teaspoon nutmeg
¼ cup butter	¼ teaspoon salt
¼ cup sugar	2 eggs, slightly beaten
½ teaspoon cinnamon	2 cups scalded milk
½ cup chopped raisins	

Arrange bread crumbs in buttered baking dish. Dot with butter. Combine dry ingredients and add to eggs with scalded milk and raisins. Pour over bread crumbs. Set in pan of hot water and bake in a moderate oven, 350 degrees, 40 minutes, or until firm. Serve with Hard Sauce, p. 341. Serves 4.

CHOCOLATE BREAD PUDDING

Soak 2 cups stale bread crumbs in 2 cups hot milk for 30 minutes. In a double boiler melt 2 squares of chocolate, add ½ cup sugar and stir this into the bread crumbs, with 2 more cups of hot milk, ½ cup sugar, 2 eggs slightly beaten, a pinch of salt and 1 teaspoon vanilla. Bake in a buttered baking dish in a moderate oven, 350 degrees, 1 hour. Serve with Hard Sauce, p. 341, or Pudding Sauce (3), p. 342. Serves 6.

CARAMEL BREAD PUDDING (1)

½ cup sugar
2 cups scalded milk
1 cup bread crumbs

1 egg
¼ teaspoon salt
½ teaspoon vanilla

Caramelize sugar by melting it over moderate heat in heavy, shallow pan, stirring constantly. Then add it to scalded milk. When the sugar has dissolved, add bread crumbs, beaten egg, salt and vanilla. Turn into buttered baking dish and bake in moderate oven, 350 degrees, about 1 hour. Serve with whipped cream. Serves 4.

CARAMEL BREAD PUDDING (2)

3 cups buttered bread cubes
2⅓ cups milk
1 cup brown sugar

2 eggs
½ teaspoon cinnamon
¼ teaspoon nutmeg

1 teaspoon vanilla

Sprinkle sugar in bottom of buttered baking dish and add bread cubes. Beat eggs, gradually add milk, spices and vanilla, and pour over bread cubes. Bake in a moderate oven, 350 degrees, about 1 hour. Serve with Hard Sauce, p. 341, or cream. Serves 6.

RICE PUDDING (1)

1 quart milk
3 tablespoons rice

½ cup sugar
2 tablespoons butter

½ grated nutmeg

Mix ingredients, pour into a buttered baking dish and bake in a moderately slow oven, 325 degrees, 3 hours. Whenever it browns, stir it. When slightly cool cover with marshmallows, and return to oven until marshmallows brown. Serve warm with cream. Serves 6.

RICE PUDDING (2)

½ cup rice
½ teaspoon cinnamon

⅛ teaspoon salt
½ cup molasses

1 quart milk

Wash rice and put in a buttered baking dish. Add remaining ingredients and bake in a moderately slow oven, 325 degrees, 3 hours. Stir occasionally. Serves 6.

DEVIL'S FLOAT

1 cup flour	2 tablespoons melted butter
1½ tablespoons cocoa	½ cup chopped nuts (if
¾ cup sugar	desired)
½ teaspoon salt	½ cup milk
2 teaspoons baking powder	1 teaspoon vanilla

Mix and sift dry ingredients, add butter, nuts, milk and vanilla. Pour into a buttered square pan. Make a sauce by mixing together ½ cup granulated sugar, ½ cup brown sugar, 5 tablespoons cocoa and 1 cup hot water. Pour this sauce over the batter. Bake in a hot oven, 400 degrees, 30 minutes. Do not open oven door while baking. Cut in squares and serve hot with whipped cream or ice cream.

FIVE-MINUTE DESSERT

2 eggs, beaten	2 tablespoons flour
3 tablespoons sugar	1 teaspoon baking powder

Dash of salt

Beat sugar into eggs. Mix and sift flour, baking powder and salt and add to eggs. Put into buttered muffin tins and bake in a moderate oven, 350 degrees, 5 minutes. Serve with whipped cream. Melted chocolate may be added if desired, in which case increase the sugar to ¼ cup.

INDIAN PUDDING[1]

Boil 1 pint of milk, stir in ¼ cup corn meal, cook 10 minutes and then add: ½ cup molasses, ½ cup sugar, ½ teaspoon salt, ½ teaspoon cinnamon, 1 egg, well beaten, 2 tablespoons butter, ½ cup raisins. Mix all together, add 1 pint cold milk and bake in a slow oven, 250 degrees, for 2 hours. When it has baked ½ hour, stir and add 1 cup of cold milk. Serves 8.

---

[1]A Letter to Mr. Roberts from F. E. Thompson on Indian Pudding:

"Our baked Indian pudding was made with sour cream skimmed from the pan (not by separator), sweetened with the old New Orleans black molasses and spiced with nutmeg. My Grandmother in Union, Maine, back in 1875, used to feed me on it and I would gain a pound a day on it when I was a boy."

INDIAN COCONUT PUDDING

⅓ cup yellow corn meal   ½ teaspoon cinnamon
⅓ cup cold water   ½ teaspoon nutmeg
1 quart milk   ½ cup molasses
½ teaspoon salt   1 egg
½ cup shredded coconut

Combine corn meal and water. Scald milk; add moistened corn meal and cook 20 minutes in double boiler, stirring constantly. Add salt, cinnamon, nutmeg and molasses. Pour into baking dish and bake in slow oven, 250 degrees, ½ hour. Stir beaten egg into pudding slowly; sprinkle with coconut and bake 1 hour longer. Serve with cream. Serves 8.

WHITE CORN MEAL PUDDING

Heat 2½ cups of milk, add ½ cup white corn meal, stir well and then remove from fire. Add ⅓ cup molasses, ¼ cup brown sugar, ½ teaspoon salt, 1 tablespoon butter, 1 teaspoon cinnamon and ½ teaspoon ginger. Cool. Add 2½ cups milk and 1 beaten egg. Pour into buttered baking dish and set in pan of hot water. Bake in a slow oven, 250 degrees, 3 hours. Serve with cream. Serves 8.

PEACH COBBLER

1½ cups flour   4 cups sliced peaches
¾ teaspoon baking powder   ¾ cup brown sugar
¼ teaspoon salt   1 teaspoon cinnamon
2 tablespoons sugar   Grated rind and juice of
¼ cup butter   1 lemon
1 egg yolk, beaten   2 tablespoons butter
½ cup milk   ¼ cup water

Mix and sift flour, baking powder, salt and sugar. Cut in butter; then stir in combined egg yolk and milk. Roll ¼ inch thick on floured board. Place peaches in buttered baking dish and sprinkle with brown sugar, cinnamon, lemon juice and rind. Dot with butter and add water. Cover with dough. Cut several gashes in top. Bake in a hot oven, 400 degrees, 15 minutes; then reduce heat to moderate, 350 degrees, and bake 20 minutes longer. Serve with cream or Hard Sauce, p. 341. Serves 6.

GRAHAM CRACKER PUDDING

3 eggs, separated	1 cup graham cracker
¾ cup sugar	crumbs
½ teaspoon baking powder	1 teaspoon vanilla

Beat egg yolks till thick and lemon-colored. Add sugar and baking powder mixed together; add crumbs, vanilla and stiffly beaten egg whites. Put in a buttered baking dish and bake in a moderate oven, 350 degrees, 35 minutes. Serve with whipped cream. Serves 4.

LEMON CRUMB PUDDING

2 cups scalded milk	1 egg, well beaten
2 cups dry bread crumbs	Grated rind of 1 lemon
¼ teaspoon salt	3 tablespoons lemon juice
¼ cup sugar	1 tablespoon melted butter

Pour scalded milk over fine bread crumbs and add remaining ingredients. Pour into a buttered baking dish and bake in a moderate oven, 350 degrees, 45 minutes. Serve hot with Lemon Sauce, p. 343. Serves 4.

RASPBERRY SLUMP

1 quart raspberries	1½ teaspoons baking
1½ cups sugar	powder
1 cup flour	¼ cup sugar
½ teaspoon salt	2 tablespoons melted butter
½ cup milk	

Wash berries and put in buttered baking dish; sprinkle with sugar. Make a smooth batter of remaining ingredients and pour it over berries. Bake in a moderately hot oven, 375 degrees, 45 minutes. Serves 6.

JELLY ROLL

4 egg whites	1 tablespoon lemon juice
1 cup sifted sugar	⅞ cup sifted cake flour
4 egg yolks	1¼ teaspoons baking
3 tablespoons cold water	powder
¼ teaspoon salt	

Beat egg whites until stiff, but not dry. Gradually add 4 tablespoons sifted sugar and continue beating. Beat egg yolks, water and lemon juice till lemon-colored and thick. Beat in remaining sugar. Fold egg whites into the yolk mixture and gradually cut in mixed and sifted dry ingredients. Do not beat after adding dry ingredients. Line the bottom of a 17 by 11 dripping pan with paper. Butter paper and sides of pan. Spread cake mixture evenly, and bake in a moderate oven, 350 degrees, 12 minutes. Turn out on paper sprinkled with powdered sugar. Remove bottom paper. Cut off thin strips from sides and ends of cake. Spread with jelly that has been beaten a little so as to spread easily. Wrap in waxed paper till cool. Work quickly or cake will crack.

DATE AND NUT TORTE

2 eggs	⅓ cup flour
1 cup sugar	1 teaspoon baking powder
1 cup chopped pecans	Dash of salt
1 cup chopped dates	1 tablespoon sherry

Whipped cream

Beat eggs and gradually add sugar; then add pecans, dates, flour, baking powder and salt. Pour into a shallow buttered pan and bake in moderate oven, 350 degrees, ½ hour. When cold, sprinkle with sherry and cover with whipped cream.

STEAMED FIG PUDDING

⅓ cup flour	1 egg
½ teaspoon baking powder	½ pound chopped figs
¼ teaspoon mace	1 teaspoon grated orange
⅛ teaspoon salt	rind
1 cup ground suet	½ cup bread crumbs
⅓ cup sugar	¼ cup milk

2 tablespoons brandy

Mix and sift flour, baking powder, mace and salt. Cream suet and sugar together; then stir in unbeaten egg, figs and orange peel. Mix well. Add sifted dry ingredients and crumbs alternately with milk and brandy. Beat well. Pour into buttered mold, cover tightly and steam 1 hour. Serve with Foamy Sauce (1), p. 341, or Orange Sauce, p. 343.

SNOWBALL PUDDING

½ cup butter	¼ teaspoon salt
1 cup sugar	1 cup milk
2 cups flour	1 teaspoon vanilla
2 teaspoons baking powder	Whites of 3 eggs

Cream butter and add sugar gradually. Alternately add the mixed and sifted dry ingredients with the milk. Stir in the vanilla and the stiffly beaten egg whites. Fill buttered custard cups ⅔ full and steam 40 minutes. Serve with Hard Sauce, p. 341, or Strawberry Sauce, p. 344. Serves 6.

SUET PUDDING

1 cup ground suet	3 cups flour
1 cup molasses	3 teaspoons baking powder
1 cup seeded raisins	½ teaspoon salt
½ cup currants	1 cup milk
	1 egg, beaten

Combine suet, molasses, raisins and currants. Mix and sift dry ingredients; add to suet mixture alternately with milk; add the beaten egg. Turn into a buttered mold, cover and steam 3 hours. Serve with Hard Sauce, p. 341. Serves 6–8.

RASPBERRY PUDDING

2 cups pastry flour	½ teaspoon salt
1 teaspoon soda	4 tablespoons butter
2 teaspoons cream of tartar	⅔ cup milk
	1 can raspberries

Sift dry ingredients together three times, work in butter with a fork and gradually add milk. Roll on floured board. Divide dough into 2 parts. Roll first half thin and line a greased mold. Divide second half of dough into 2 parts and roll thin. Drain raspberries and save juice for sauce. Spread half of raspberries over dough in mold, add ¼ cup sugar, dash of nutmeg and dots of butter. Cover with a piece of rolled dough. Repeat raspberries, sugar, nutmeg and butter. Cover with second piece of dough, cut slits in top to allow escape

of steam. Cover mold tightly with greased top and steam 1½ hours.
Serve with Hot Raspberry Sauce, p. 344.

DARK STEAMED PUDDING

1 egg, beaten	1 teaspoon soda
½ cup molasses	¼ teaspoon cloves
½ cup milk	¼ teaspoon nutmeg
¼ cup melted butter	½ teaspoon cinnamon
1½ cups sifted graham flour	1 cup chopped raisins

Add molasses, milk and butter to beaten egg, then stir in mixed and
sifted dry ingredients. Add raisins. Turn into a buttered mold and
steam 4 hours. Serve with Foamy Sauce, p. 341, or Hard Sauce,
p. 341. Serves 6.

STEAMED DATE PUDDING

1 pound dates	¼ teaspoon nutmeg
4 tablespoons brown sugar	½ teaspoon salt
¾ cup flour	1 egg
½ cup finely chopped suet	1 teaspoon baking powder

Scald dates in enough boiling water to cover; let dry; remove
stones; chop fine. Put flour, salt, sugar, suet, nutmeg and baking
powder in a bowl and moisten with egg and as little milk as possible. Turn into a buttered baking dish, cover tightly and steam 4
hours. Serves 4.

STEAMED CHOCOLATE PUDDING

3 tablespoons butter	3 teaspoons baking powder
⅔ cup sugar	¼ teaspoon salt
1 egg, well beaten	2½ squares unsweetened
1 cup milk	chocolate
2 cups flour	

Cream butter; gradually add sugar and egg. Mix and sift flour,
baking powder and salt and add alternately with milk to creamed
mixture. Then add chocolate which has been melted in double
boiler. Turn into buttered mold and steam 1½ hours. Serve hot
with cream or Hard Sauce, p. 341. Serves 6.

PLUM PUDDING

1 pound stale bread crumbs
2 cups flour
1 pound minced beef suet
6 eggs, well beaten
1 cup milk
1 pound seeded raisins
1 pound washed and dried
  currants

¼ cup chopped candied
  orange peel
½ cup chopped candied
  lemon peel
2 tablespoons cinnamon
½ tablespoon ginger
1 grated nutmeg
Dash of salt

½ cup brandy or rum

Mix the bread crumbs, flour and suet together. Combine the beaten eggs and milk, and stir into the dry ingredients with a wooden spoon. Then add the remaining ingredients, mixing well. The pudding can be either baked or steamed. If baked, turn into a buttered baking dish and bake in a moderate oven, 350 degrees, 1½ hours. If steamed, turn into a buttered mold, close cover tightly, and steam 6 hours. Serve with Hard Sauce, p. 341, or Pudding Sauce (2), p. 342. Serves 8.

STEAMED BLUEBERRY PUDDING (1)

2 cups flour
4 teaspoons baking powder
1 teaspoon salt
1 tablespoon butter

¾ cup milk
4 cups blueberries
2 cups sugar
2 teaspoons lemon juice

Mix and sift flour, baking powder and salt; work in butter with finger tips. Gradually add the milk and mix well. Mix berries, sugar and lemon juice and add to the batter. Pour into a buttered mold, cover tightly and steam 45 minutes. Serve with cream. Serves 6–8.

STEAMED BLUEBERRY PUDDING (2)

Spread thick slices of white bread with butter and fill a buttered baking dish. Pour stewed blueberries sweetened with sugar over the bread; add 1 tablespoon lemon juice and steam 30 minutes. Serve with Blueberry Sauce, p. 338.

BLUEBERRY SAUCE

¾ cup sugar   ½ cup crushed blueberries
¼ cup cornstarch   ½ cup whole blueberries
Dash of nutmeg   ¼ cup butter
1½ cups boiling water   ¼ cup rum

Mix sugar, cornstarch and nutmeg in a saucepan and gradually stir in boiling water. Bring to a boil, stirring constantly, and when mixture thickens add blueberries and butter. Just before serving add rum. Serve on ice cream, or Cottage Cake, p. 353, or Steamed Blueberry Pudding (2), p. 337.

BLUEBERRY PUDDING SAUCE

¼ cup butter   1 teaspoon vanilla
1 cup sugar   ½ nutmeg grated
              1 tablespoon sherry

Cream butter and sugar and add flavorings. Just before serving add 1 egg and beat whole over hot water for 5 minutes.

BRANDY SAUCE

½ cup melted butter   ¼ cup brandy
1 cup powdered sugar   1 egg white, stiffly beaten

Add sugar to melted butter and bring to a boil, stirring constantly. Remove from fire and stir in brandy; then fold in stiffly beaten egg white. Serve on steamed puddings.

CHOCOLATE SAUCE (1)

1 square chocolate   1 tablespoon flour
1 cup milk   1 tablespoon butter
⅓ cup sugar   1 teaspoon vanilla

Heat chocolate and milk in double boiler and blend with egg beater. Mix sugar and flour, add gradually to chocolate mixture and cook till thickened, stirring constantly. After cooking another 5 minutes add butter and vanilla. Serve on ice cream.

CHOCOLATE SAUCE (2)

1 cup powdered sugar | ½ cup milk
½ cup cocoa | ½ cup water
¼ teaspoon salt | ½ teaspoon vanilla

Sift sugar, cocoa and salt together; then add milk and water and blend to a smooth paste. Cook mixture in top of double boiler over hot water for 25 minutes, stirring frequently. Add vanilla. Serve on ice cream, meringues, Cottage Cake, p. 353.

SEMI–SWEET CHOCOLATE SAUCE

1 package semi-sweet | ¼ cup sugar
chocolate | ½ teaspoon cornstarch
2 tablespoons butter | Pinch of salt
1 cup light corn syrup | ¼ cup water
½ teaspoon vanilla

Melt chocolate and butter in top of double boiler. Add syrup; then sugar mixed with cornstarch and salt. Bring to a boil. Add water and vanilla, stir, and cook about 5 minutes longer. Serve hot.

SUGARLESS CHOCOLATE SAUCE

1 cup chocolate milkshake | 1 can evaporated milk
powder | 1 tablespoon butter
½ teaspoon cornstarch | 2 grains saccharine, dis-
1 tablespoon flour | solved
¼ teaspoon salt | 1 teaspoon vanilla

Mix ingredients together and cook 25 minutes in top of double boiler, stirring occasionally.

THIN CHOCOLATE SAUCE

1 cup sugar | 1½ squares grated chocolate
½ cup water | ½ teaspoon vanilla
1 tablespoon butter

Combine the sugar, water and chocolate and boil 5 minutes. Cool slightly and add vanilla and butter.

BUTTERSCOTCH SAUCE

1 cup brown sugar 　　　　 ¼ cup butter
½ cup maple syrup 　　　　 ½ cup thin cream

Boil sugar, syrup and butter in double boiler 2 minutes. Do not stir. Take from stove and stir in cream. Keep hot over water. Serve on ice cream, meringues, or Cottage Cake, p. 353.

CARAMEL SAUCE

Heat 1 cup sugar in a heavy pan over moderate heat, stirring till melted and light brown. Add 1 cup boiling water, stir and simmer 10 minutes. Serve cold. Juice of ½ orange may be added if desired. Serve on plain custards.

COFFEE SAUCE

3 eggs 　　　　 ⅛ teaspoon salt
¼ cup sugar 　　　　 1 cup strong coffee

Beat eggs slightly, add sugar and salt. Gradually pour on coffee. Cook in double boiler until thickened, stirring occasionally.

COTTAGE PUDDING SAUCE

¼ pound butter 　　　　 1 tablespoon vanilla
1 cup sugar 　　　　 2 eggs, well beaten
1 nutmeg 　　　　 Rum or brandy

Cream butter and sugar; then add grated nutmeg and vanilla. Place over hot water, add beaten eggs and flavor with rum or brandy.

CUSTARD SAUCE

2 egg yolks, stirred 　　　　 Pinch of salt
2 tablespoons sugar 　　　　 1 cup scalded milk
⅔ teaspoon vanilla

Stir egg yolks, sugar and salt into the milk. Cook over hot water, stirring constantly, until mixture will coat a silver spoon. Remove immediately from hot water, add vanilla and chill. Serve on Snow Pudding, p. 318, or Prune Whip, p. 319.

FOAMY SAUCE (1)

¼ cup milk	2 eggs, separated
1 cup sugar	2 tablespoons rum

Heat milk in double boiler, add sugar and stir a few minutes. Add beaten egg yolks, stirring until mixture thickens. Remove from fire, cool, then beat in stiffly beaten egg whites and rum. Serve on puddings.

FOAMY SAUCE (2)

2 eggs, separated	1 cup heavy cream,
2 cups powdered sugar	whipped
1 teaspoon vanilla	

Add the sugar to the stiffly beaten egg whites; stir in unbeaten egg yolks; add the whipped cream; then the vanilla. Serve on puddings.

HARD SAUCE (1)

½ cup butter	1 teaspoon lemon juice
3 teaspoons hot light cream	¼ teaspoon salt
2 cups sifted confectioners' sugar	

Mix ingredients with a fork and beat until creamy. Chill.

HARD SAUCE (2)

Cream together ½ cup butter and 1 cup powdered sugar. Add rind and juice of ½ lemon, 1 teaspoon vanilla, nutmeg, yolk of 1 egg well beaten, and white of 1 egg beaten stiff. The sauce needs to be well beaten to be smooth.

HARD SAUCE (3)

⅓ cup butter	1 egg yolk
1 cup sugar	3 tablespoons brandy
Chopped Maraschino cherries	

Cream the butter and sugar, then add beaten egg yolk. Beat until light, then add brandy and cherries.

STRAWBERRY HARD SAUCE

⅓ cup butter   1 egg white, stiffly beaten
1 cup sifted confectioners'   ½ cup mashed strawberries
   sugar

Cream butter and then add sugar and stiffly beaten egg white.
Gradually beat in strawberries. Mix well and chill thoroughly.
Serve on hot bread pudding.

MOLASSES SAUCE

1 cup molasses   1½ tablespoons butter
          1½ tablespoons lemon juice

Boil molasses and butter 5 minutes. Remove from fire and slowly
stir in lemon juice.

PUDDING SAUCE (1)

1 cup white sugar   2 tablespoons brandy
1 cup light brown sugar   1 cup sherry
1 egg   ½ nutmeg

Mix all ingredients together in a double boiler. Stir constantly and
bring to a boil.

PUDDING SAUCE (2)

¼ cup milk   2 eggs, separated
1 cup sugar   Vanilla, brandy or rum

Heat milk in double boiler and stir in sugar and beaten egg yolks.
Continue to stir and cook until mixture thickens. Remove from fire
and cool; then add stiffly beaten egg whites and flavoring. Beat
thoroughly.

PUDDING SAUCE (3)

3 eggs, separated   1 pint heavy cream
½ cup sugar   2 teaspoons vanilla

Beat yolks of eggs with ¼ cup sugar. Beat whites of eggs until stiff
and add the other ¼ cup sugar. Beat cream until stiff and then add
yolks, whites and vanilla. Serve on Chocolate Bread Pudding, p. 329.

LEMON SAUCE

½ cup sugar   1 cup boiling water
3 teaspoons cornstarch   1½ tablespoons lemon juice
            1 tablespoon butter

Mix sugar and cornstarch, stir in boiling water; add butter, lemon juice and grated rind of ½ lemon. Boil 5 minutes, stirring constantly. Serve on fruit fritters or puddings.

MARSHMALLOW SAUCE

¾ cup sugar   ½ pound marshmallows
¼ cup milk   2 tablespoons water

Boil sugar and milk to thread stage; then cool and beat until thick and white. Set in boiling water and stir until thin enough to pour. Cut marshmallows in pieces and melt with water in double boiler. Add syrup to marshmallows and beat together. Serve warm on puddings, chocolate soufflé or ice cream.

ORANGE SAUCE (1)

¼ cup butter   3 egg whites
½ cup sugar   Juice of 2 oranges
½ cup boiling water   Juice of ½ lemon

Cream butter and sugar and put in a double boiler. Add boiling water; then beat in stiffly beaten egg whites and fruit juices. Beat until light and foamy.

ORANGE SAUCE (2)

¾ cup sugar   1 tablespoon grated orange
3 tablespoons flour   rind
¼ cup orange juice   1 egg
            1 cup heavy cream, whipped

Mix together sugar, flour, orange juice, grated rind and egg in double boiler. Cook 10 minutes, or until thick, stirring constantly. Cool, then fold in whipped cream.

RASPBERRY SAUCE

1½ cups raspberry juice	2 tablespoons flour
½ cup water	Pinch of salt
1 cup sugar	2 tablespoons butter

Bring raspberry juice and water to boiling point; then add sugar, flour and salt. Boil gently for 5 minutes. Remove from heat and add butter. Serve hot.

STRAWBERRY SAUCE

½ cup butter	1 egg white
1 cup sugar	1 cup strawberries

Cream the butter and add sugar gradually; then the stiffly beaten white of egg and the strawberries put through a strainer.

CAKES, COOKIES AND FROSTINGS

MAXIMS FROM MAINE KITCHENS

To improve the flavor of fresh cookies, put an apple or orange in the container with them. Cake and bread will keep fresh for a long time if a cut apple is put in the cake or bread tin.

✿

To prevent cake icing from sticking to knife, dip knife in hot water.

✿

To remove stains from copper or brass, dip ½ lemon into salt and rub on the metal.

✿

To prevent nuts and fruit from sinking to the bottom of cakes, heat them in oven and mix with a little flour.

CAKES, COOKIES AND FROSTINGS

"MY MEMORIES of my grandmother's kitchen are fond ones. One who stood persistently beside the stove on baking days could usually obtain permission to lick the large iron spoons with which the chocolate, orange and vanilla frostings had been applied to the cakes.

"There was also an excellent chance that the cook's attention would be so caught by an occurrence in the outer world that a deft bystander could thrust a prehensile forefinger into the frosting pan and extract a delectable morsel without detection.

"Opposite the stove was the pantry, with a barrel of flour and a barrel of sugar beneath the bread-shelf. An excellent confection could be obtained from the sugar barrel by dropping a spoonful of water into it, and carefully removing the resulting blob of moist sugar with a fork.

"Yes, I knew the kitchen well; and from occasionally sleeping above it, I became an expert on its intricate and absorbing sounds: the rhythmic thumping of the hash-chopper, muffled by the mound of potatoes and corned beef through which it was driven by Katie's tireless arms, and the occasional muted rasp when the scattered mound was reassembled for further chopping; the delicate gritting of an iron spoon against a saucepan at the culmination of a successful frosting-making; the faint bubbling which accompanied the manufacture of doughnuts; the soft clanking that announced the removal of the lid of the mincemeat jar. Many of these sounds, of course, left me unmoved, but others brought me hurriedly down the winding back stairs—so hurriedly that I usually fell the last half-dozen steps, having learned that the compassion aroused by such a fall would unfailingly bring me a doughnut, a frosting spoon to lick, or at the worst a slice of new bread, well buttered and sprinkled with sugar."

—KENNETH ROBERTS, *Trending into Maine*

ANGEL FOOD CAKE

1 cup egg whites	1¼ cups sifted sugar
3 tablespoons cold water	1 cup cake flour
1 teaspoon cream of tartar	¼ teaspoon salt
	1 teaspoon vanilla

Beat egg whites and water until foamy. Add cream of tartar and beat until stiff, but moist. Add ½ cup sugar, 1 tablespoon at a time, and continue beating. Sift remaining sugar, salt and flour together four or five times. Fold into egg mixture, 2 tablespoons at a time, using a whisk. Add vanilla. Pour into a large unbuttered angel food tin and bake in a slow oven, 300 degrees, 50 minutes.

GOLDEN ANGEL SPONGE CAKE

5 eggs, separated	1 teaspoon orange extract
¾ teaspoon cream of tartar	¼ teaspoon almond extract
½ cup cold water	1½ cups cake flour
1½ cups sugar	1 teaspoon baking powder
	½ teaspoon salt

Beat egg whites and cream of tartar until high, but not dry. Add water to egg yolks and beat vigorously until light and high, then add sugar and flavoring. Add mixed and sifted flour, baking powder and salt, and beat for 2 minutes. Fold in the egg whites. Pour into a large unbuttered pan and bake in a slow oven, 300 degrees, 1 hour. Remove cake from oven and turn upside down on a cake rack for 1 hour before removing from pan.

OLD–FASHIONED SPONGE CAKE

5 eggs	Juice and rind of 1 lemon
1½ cups powdered sugar	1 cup flour
	1 teaspoon salt

Separate eggs, beat yolks with sugar for 10 minutes; then add lemon juice and rind. Beat egg whites stiff, fold into mixture and slowly sift in flour and salt, stirring gently. Pour into an unbuttered tube pan and bake in a moderately slow oven, 325 degrees, about 1 hour.

SPONGE CAKE

1 ½ cups sugar
½ cup water
6 eggs, separated

1 cup sifted flour
1 teaspoon vanilla
1 tablespoon orange juice

Grated rind of 1 orange

Boil sugar and water until it threads, then pour over beaten egg whites, beating while pouring. Continue beating until cool, then beat in egg yolks. Fold in flour and flavorings. Pour into an unbuttered tube pan, sprinkle with powdered sugar and bake in a moderately slow oven, 325 degrees, about 1 hour. Invert when done and let remain in pan till cold.

ORANGE SPONGE CAKE

4 eggs, separated
2 cups sugar
½ cup melted butter
2 cups flour

2 teaspoons baking powder
½ teaspoon salt
1 tablespoon grated orange rind

½ cup orange juice

Beat yolks until light and gradually add sugar; then add butter. Mix and sift flour, baking powder and salt and add to creamed mixture. Add orange rind and juice and lastly the stiffly beaten egg whites. Pour into unbuttered tube pan and bake in a moderately slow oven, 325 degrees, about 1 hour.

DAFFODIL CAKE

1 cup egg whites
3 tablespoons cold water
¼ teaspoon salt
1 teaspoon cream of tartar

1 ¼ cups sugar
1 teaspoon vanilla
1 ⅛ cups sifted cake flour
6 egg yolks

Whip egg whites, water and salt until foamy. Add cream of tartar. Beat until stiff, but moist. Sift sugar and fold in gradually. Add vanilla. Divide mixture in half. Resift flour 3 times. Beat egg yolks until thick and fold into one half with ¾ cup of flour. Fold ½ cup flour into other half. Pour batter in unbuttered angel-cake tin, alternating the yellow and white mixture. Bake in a slow oven, 300 degrees, 50 to 60 minutes. Invert on cake rack until cool, about 1 hour.

WHITE LAYER CAKE (1)

½ cup butter
1½ cups sugar
½ cup milk
½ cup water

3 cups cake flour
¼ teaspoon salt
3 teaspoons baking powder
1 teaspoon vanilla

3 egg whites

Mix flour, baking powder and salt and sift together three times. Cream butter and sugar until light. Add flour mixture alternately with milk and water. Add vanilla. Fold in stiffly beaten egg whites. Pour into 3 buttered layer-cake pans and bake in a moderately hot oven, 375 degrees, about 25 minutes. Put together and cover with any desired filling or frosting.

WHITE LAYER CAKE (2)

¾ cup butter
2 cups sugar
4 eggs, beaten
3 cups flour

3 teaspoons baking powder
½ teaspoon salt
1 cup milk
1 teaspoon vanilla

2 teaspoons lemon juice

Cream butter and sugar; add well-beaten eggs. Mix and sift flour, baking powder and salt, and add alternately with milk to first mixture. Add flavorings. Pour into 3 buttered layer-cake pans and bake in a moderately hot oven, 375 degrees, about 25 minutes. Put together and cover with any desired filling or frosting.

CREAM LAYER CAKE

1 cup sugar
1 cup heavy cream
2 eggs, beaten

1 teaspoon vanilla
2 cups flour
1 teaspoon cream of tartar

1 teaspoon soda

Combine the sugar and cream and beat in eggs and vanilla. Stir in mixed and sifted dry ingredients. Pour into 2 buttered layer-cake tins and bake in a moderate oven, 350 degrees, 30 minutes. Put layers together and cover with any desired filling or frosting.

PEANUT BUTTER LAYER CAKE

¼ cup peanut butter
2 tablespoons butter
2 squares melted chocolate
1¾ cups sifted cake flour

1 cup sugar
¾ teaspoon soda
½ teaspoon salt
1 cup milk

1 teaspoon vanilla

Cream butters until well blended, then add melted chocolate. Mix dry ingredients and sift together three times; then add alternately with the milk to the chocolate mixture. Add vanilla and beat hard 1 minute. Pour into 2 buttered layer-cake pans and bake in a moderate oven, 350 degrees, 25 minutes. Put together and cover with Seven-Minute Frosting, p. 378.

LADY BALTIMORE CAKE

1 cup butter
2 cups sugar
3½ cups sifted pastry flour
2 teaspoons baking powder

Pinch of salt
1 cup milk
1 teaspoon vanilla
6 egg whites, stiffly beaten

Cream butter and sifted sugar. Mix dry ingredients together and add alternately with the milk to the creamed mixture. Then add the vanilla and fold in the stiffly beaten egg whites. Bake in 3 buttered layer-cake tins in a moderately hot oven, 375 degrees, about 25 minutes. Frost and spread between layers with Lady Baltimore Frosting, p. 377.

ORANGE LAYER CAKE

3 eggs, separated
¼ teaspoon cream of tartar
1 cup sugar
1 tablespoon grated orange rind

½ cup orange juice
1¼ cups flour
1½ teaspoons baking powder
¼ teaspoon salt

Beat egg whites and cream of tartar until stiff, then add egg yolks one at a time. Gradually beat in sugar, grated rind and orange juice. Fold in mixed and sifted flour, baking powder and salt. Pour into 2 buttered layer-cake pans and bake in a moderate oven, 350 degrees, about 20 minutes. Put layers together with Orange Filling, p. 375, and cover with Orange Frosting, p. 378.

DEVIL'S FOOD CAKE

½ cup butter   2 squares chocolate
1¼ cups brown sugar   1¼ cups cake flour
2 eggs, well beaten   1 teaspoon baking soda
1 teaspoon vanilla   ½ teaspoon baking powder
½ cup boiling water   ½ teaspoon salt
                ½ cup sour milk

Cream butter and gradually add sugar; then beat in eggs and vanilla.
Pour the boiling water over the chocolate, stir over fire until smooth
and thick, cool, and add to egg mixture. Mix and sift dry ingredients and add alternately with milk to chocolate mixture. Pour into
2 buttered layer-cake pans and bake in a moderately hot oven, 375
degrees, about 25 minutes. Cover with Uncooked Chocolate Frosting (1), p. 377, or Boiled Frosting (2), p. 376.

EGGLESS CHOCOLATE CAKE

1 cup sugar   3 tablespoons hot water
½ cup cocoa   1½ cups flour
1 cup sour milk   5 tablespoons melted butter
1 teaspoon soda dissolved in   1 teaspoon vanilla

Mix sugar and cocoa, and add remaining ingredients. Pour in buttered cake pan and bake in a moderate oven, 350 degrees, 35 minutes. Frost with Mocha Frosting (2), p. 378.

CHOCOLATE LAYER CAKE (1)

1¼ cups brown sugar   2 cups sifted cake flour
½ cup butter   1 teaspoon soda
3 squares melted chocolate   1 teaspoon salt
3 eggs   1 cup milk
                1 teaspoon vanilla

Cream butter and sugar; then add melted chocolate and beat thoroughly. Drop eggs into the creamed mixture one at a time and beat.
Add mixed and sifted dry ingredients alternately with milk. Add
vanilla. Pour into buttered layer-cake pans and bake in moderate
oven, 350 degrees, 30 minutes. Put layers together and cover with
any desired frosting.

CHOCOLATE LAYER CAKE (2)

2 squares chocolate

½ cup milk

2 eggs, separated

1 cup sugar

Pinch of salt

1½ cups flour

1 teaspoon baking powder

1 teaspoon vanilla

Melt chocolate in milk; cool. Beat egg yolks until light and add mixed and sifted sugar, salt, flour and baking powder. Add the chocolate mixture, stiffly beaten egg whites and vanilla. Pour into 2 buttered layer-cake pans and bake in a moderate oven, 350 degrees, 30 minutes. Put layers together and cover with any desired frosting.

CHOCOLATE CAKE

½ cup butter

1 cup sugar

1 egg yolk

1 teaspoon soda dissolved in

1 cup sour milk

2 cups sifted pastry flour

2 teaspoons baking powder

¼ teaspoon salt

1 teaspoon vanilla

2 squares melted chocolate

Cream butter and sugar, add egg. Mix and sift flour, baking powder and salt, and add to creamed mixture alternately with milk. Add vanilla and chocolate. Pour into buttered cake tin and bake in a moderate oven, 350 degrees, about 30 minutes.

CHOCOLATE CINNAMON CAKE

½ cup butter

1½ cups sugar

2 squares chocolate

½ cup hot water

2 eggs, beaten

1 teaspoon baking powder

1 teaspoon cinnamon

2 cups flour

½ teaspoon soda

½ cup sour milk

1 teaspoon vanilla

Cream butter and sugar. Add the chocolate to the hot water and cook until thickened. Add to the creamed mixture with the beaten eggs. Dissolve the soda in the sour milk and add to the creamed mixture alternately with the mixed and sifted baking powder, cinnamon and flour. Stir in the vanilla. Pour into a buttered loaf pan and bake in a moderately hot oven, 375 degrees, about 30 minutes.

FUDGE CAKE

¼ cup butter
1 cup sugar
2 eggs, beaten
1¼ cups flour

1 teaspoon baking powder
½ cup milk
2 squares chocolate
½ cup chopped walnuts

Cream together butter and sugar, and add eggs. Sift the flour and baking powder, and add alternately with milk to the creamed mixture. Melt the chocolate over hot water and then add to mixture with the walnuts. Pour into a buttered loaf pan and bake in a moderate oven, 350 degrees, 45 to 50 minutes. Cover with either Fudge Frosting, p. 376, Mocha Frosting, p. 378, or Uncooked Chocolate Frosting, p. 377.

STICKY–BOTTOM CAKE

3 tablespoons melted butter
½ cup brown sugar
Chopped dates
½ cup nut meats
¼ cup butter
½ cup sugar

1 egg, separated
1 cup flour
1 teaspoon baking powder
½ teaspoon salt
½ cup milk
1 teaspoon vanilla

Put melted butter in an 8-inch cake pan, sprinkle with brown sugar, a layer of dates and a layer of nut meats. Cream ¼ cup butter, add sugar and beaten egg yolk. Mix and sift dry ingredients and add to creamed mixture alternately with milk. Add vanilla and stiffly beaten white of egg. Pour into cake pan and bake in a moderate oven, 350 degrees, about 30 minutes. Turn onto serving dish, sticky-bottom side up. Serve with whipped cream.

COTTAGE CAKE

¼ cup butter
½ cup sugar
1 egg, well beaten
1½ cups flour

2 teaspoons baking powder
¼ teaspoon salt
½ cup milk
1 teaspoon vanilla

Cream butter and sugar, and add egg. Mix and sift dry ingredients and add alternately with milk to creamed mixture. Add vanilla. Pour into a buttered shallow cake pan and bake in a moderate oven, 350 degrees, about 25 minutes.

GRAHAM CRACKER CAKE

½ cup butter
1 cup sugar
3 eggs
½ cup flour

1½ teaspoons baking
powder
1½ cups rolled graham
cracker crumbs

¾ cup milk

Cream butter and add sugar gradually. Add the eggs and beat thoroughly. Mix together flour, baking powder and graham cracker crumbs, which have been rolled fine. Add dry and liquid ingredients alternately to the creamed mixture. Pour into buttered and floured layer-cake pans. Bake in a moderate oven, 350 degrees, about 25 minutes. Put whipped cream between the layers and on top of cake.

APPLESAUCE CAKE

½ cup butter
1 cup sugar
1 egg
1 teaspoon vanilla
1 cup chopped dates
1 cup chopped nuts

2 cups chopped raisins
1½ cups applesauce
2 cups flour
1 teaspoon cinnamon
½ teaspoon cloves
2 teaspoons baking soda

¼ teaspoon salt

Cream butter and sugar. Add well-beaten egg and vanilla. Then add dates, nuts, raisins, applesauce and mixed and sifted dry ingredients. Turn into buttered loaf pan and bake in a moderate oven, 350 degrees, 1 hour.

ONE–EGG CAKE

¼ cup butter
1 cup sugar
1 egg
2 cups sifted flour

2 teaspoons baking powder
¼ teaspoon salt
¾ cup milk
½ teaspoon vanilla

Cream butter and sugar; then add egg. Mix dry ingredients, sift twice and add alternately with milk to creamed mixture. Add vanilla. Pour into a buttered loaf or layer-cake pan and bake in a moderate oven, 350 degrees, about 30 minutes.

EGGLESS CAKE

½ cup butter
1 cup sugar
2 cups sifted flour
½ teaspoon soda

½ teaspoon cloves
½ teaspoon cinnamon
⅛ teaspoon salt
½ cup sour milk

1 cup chopped raisins

Cream butter and sugar; then add mixed and sifted dry ingredients alternately with the milk. Beat in the raisins. Pour into a buttered cake pan and bake in a moderate oven, 350 degrees, about 45 minutes.

FRUIT CAKE

1 cup butter
1 cup sugar
3 eggs
½ cup molasses
2½ cups flour
1 teaspoon soda

1 teaspoon cinnamon
½ teaspoon cloves
¼ teaspoon mace
⅛ teaspoon salt
½ cup sour milk
2 cups raisins

½ cup currants

Cream the butter, gradually add the sugar; then the beaten eggs and molasses. Add the mixed and sifted dry ingredients alternately with milk. Stir in the fruit. Turn into 2 buttered and floured loaf pans and bake in a slow oven, 300 degrees, about 1½ hours.

RAISIN CAKE

1 cup butter
2 cups sugar
4 eggs
1 cup milk

2½ cups flour
1 teaspoon soda
2 teaspoons cream of tartar
¼ teaspoon nutmeg

1 cup raisins

Cream butter until soft; gradually add sugar, creaming until fluffy, and beat in eggs. Mix and sift the dry ingredients and add them to the butter mixture alternately with the milk. Add the raisins, turn into a buttered cake pan and bake in a moderate oven, 350 degrees, 45 minutes.

SPICE CAKE

5 tablespoons butter
1⅓ cups brown sugar
2 eggs
½ cup cold water

1¾ cups pastry flour
3 teaspoons baking powder
½ teaspoon nutmeg
¼ teaspoon cloves

1 cup chopped raisins

Cream the butter and sugar until smooth and beat in 1 egg at a time. Add the mixed and sifted dry ingredients alternately with the water, then beat in the raisins. Pour into a buttered loaf or tube pan and bake in a moderate oven, 350 degrees, about 50 minutes.

DATE SPICE CAKE

½ cup butter
1⅓ cups brown sugar
2 eggs, well beaten
1¾ cups flour
3 teaspoons baking powder

½ teaspoon cinnamon
½ teaspoon cloves
½ teaspoon salt
½ cup milk
1 cup chopped dates

Cream butter and sugar; then stir in eggs. Mix and sift dry ingredients and add alternately with milk to creamed mixture. Beat well and add dates. Pour into a buttered loaf pan and bake in a moderate oven, 350 degrees, about 40 minutes.

FARMER'S CAKE

2 cups dried apples
2 cups molasses
1 cup butter
1 cup sugar

2 eggs
1 teaspoon each cloves,
    cassia and ginger
1 teaspoon soda

3½ cups flour

Soak the apples overnight in cold water; then chop fine. Add them to the molasses and simmer slowly 1 hour. Cream the butter and sugar, add beaten eggs and mixed and sifted dry ingredients. Add the apple-molasses mixture. Pour into a buttered and floured loaf pan and bake in a moderate oven, 350 degrees, about 1 hour.

BLUEBERRY CAKE (1)

½ cup butter
1 cup sugar
2 eggs, well beaten
1½ cups flour

1 teaspoon baking powder
1½ cups blueberries
⅓ cup milk
1 teaspoon vanilla

Cream together butter and sugar; then add eggs. Sift flour, baking powder and pinch of salt and stir in blueberries. Add dry ingredients alternately with milk to creamed mixture. Add vanilla. Pour into shallow buttered pan and bake in moderate oven, 350 degrees, 35 minutes. Serve hot, cut in squares.

BLUEBERRY CAKE (2)

2 cups flour
1 teaspoon soda
½ teaspoon each nutmeg,
   cinnamon and cloves

1 egg
1 cup sugar
½ teaspoon salt
1 cup sour cream

1 cup fresh blueberries

Mix and sift flour, soda and spices. Beat egg and gradually add sugar and salt. Add dry ingredients alternately with sour cream. Add blueberries, slightly floured. Pour into a buttered layer-cake or loaf pan and bake in a moderately hot oven, 375 degrees, 20 to 30 minutes.

DARK CAKE

2 cups sugar
2 cups chopped seeded raisins
3 tablespoons butter
3 teaspoons cinnamon
1 teaspoon nutmeg

½ teaspoon cloves
2 cups cold water
3 cups flour
1 teaspoon soda
⅛ teaspoon salt

Combine sugar, raisins, butter and spices in water and boil 5 minutes. When cool, add mixed and sifted flour, soda and salt. Pour into 2 small buttered and floured loaf tins and bake in a moderate oven, 350 degrees.

HICKORY NUT CAKE

¾ cup butter	1 teaspoon baking powder
1½ cups sugar	2 cups chopped hickory
¾ cup milk	nuts
2½ cups flour	5 egg whites

Cream butter and sugar and add liquid alternately with mixed and sifted flour and baking powder. Add stiffly beaten egg whites and nuts. Pour into a buttered cake pan and bake in a moderate oven, 350 degrees. Frost with Boiled Frosting, p. 376, and sprinkle with chopped hickory nuts.

DATE AND NUT CAKE

1½ cups chopped dates	4 tablespoons flour
1½ cups English walnuts	1½ teaspoons baking
1½ cups sugar	powder

3 eggs

Mix the sugar with chopped dates and nuts; break in eggs and stir well; add the sifted flour and baking powder. Pour into a shallow buttered pan and bake in a moderate oven, 350 degrees, 30 minutes.

WAR CAKE

2 cups brown sugar	¼ teaspoon cloves
½ cup hot water	1 teaspoon cinnamon
½ cup raisins	Pinch of salt
2 tablespoons butter	1 teaspoon soda

3 cups flour

Boil sugar, water, raisins, butter, spices and salt 5 minutes. Cool; then add soda and flour. Pour into a buttered cake pan and bake in a moderate oven, 350 degrees.

POUND CAKE (1)

1 pound butter	10 eggs, separated
1 pound sugar	1 wineglass brandy

1 pound flour

Cream butter and sugar together; then add egg yolks beaten until thick and lemon-colored, and brandy. Add the stiffly beaten egg whites alternately with the flour. Beat well, turn into a deep buttered cake pan and bake in a slow oven, 300 degrees, 1¼ hours.

POUND CAKE (2)

1 cup butter	½ teaspoon baking powder
1⅔ cups sugar	¼ teaspoon salt
5 eggs	½ teaspoon nutmeg
2 cups flour	1 teaspoon lemon juice

Cream butter and sugar until light; add eggs, one at a time, and beat thoroughly. Mix and sift dry ingredients and gradually add to egg mixture with the lemon juice. Turn into a buttered loaf pan and bake in a moderate oven, 350 degrees, 1 hour.

IMPERIAL CAKE

1 cup butter	1 cup chopped walnuts
1 cup sugar	1 cup chopped raisins
5 eggs	¼ cup chopped citron
¼ cup brandy	2 cups flour
½ teaspoon mace	

Cream butter and sugar; beat in eggs one by one; add brandy, chopped fruit and then flour and mace. Beat well together, pour into a buttered loaf pan and bake in a moderate oven, 350 degrees, 1 hour.

HONEY CAKE

½ cup butter	1 teaspoon baking soda
¾ cup honey	½ teaspoon cinnamon
2 eggs	½ teaspoon ginger
2 cups flour	⅛ teaspoon salt
⅔ cup sour cream	

Cream the butter and honey together and add the beaten eggs. Mix and sift dry ingredients and add alternately to the creamed mixture with sour cream. Pour into a buttered cake pan and bake in a moderate oven, 350 degrees, 40 minutes.

WALNUT MOCHA CAKE

½ cup butter	2½ teaspoons baking
1 cup sugar	powder
½ cup strong coffee	3 egg whites, stiffly beaten
1½ cups pastry flour	¾ cup walnut meats

1½ teaspoons vanilla

Cream butter and sugar; then add remaining ingredients in order given. Pour into a buttered shallow cake pan and bake in a moderate oven, 350 degrees, about 45 minutes. Frost with Boiled Frosting, p. 376, or Mocha Frosting, p. 378.

TEA CAKES (1)

2 cups cake flour	¼ cup butter
½ teaspoon salt	¾ cup milk
3 teaspoons baking powder	1 egg, beaten

Sift dry ingredients together and cut in butter. Add milk to beaten egg. Add enough of liquid mixture to dry ingredients to make a soft dough, reserving the rest to brush over top. Roll dough ¼ inch thick on floured board. Cut 12 pieces with small round cutter and 12 with a doughnut cutter the same size. Brush plain pieces with remaining egg-and-milk mixture. Place doughnut-shaped circles on top, sprinkle with powdered sugar and place on buttered cooky sheet. Bake in a hot oven, 400 degrees, about 12 minutes. Remove from cooky sheet and put jelly in center.

TEA CAKES (2)

2½ cups pastry flour	½ teaspoon salt
½ teaspoon soda	1 cup milk
1 teaspoon cream of tartar	1 tablespoon melted butter
½ cup sugar	1 egg, beaten

Mix dry ingredients and sift twice. Add milk and butter to egg, then add sifted dry ingredients. Add 1 cup of berries in berry season. Pour into buttered muffin pans and bake in a moderately hot oven, 375 degrees.

HUCKLEBERRY TEA CAKES

½ cup butter
1½ cups sugar
2 eggs
3 cups flour

3 teaspoons baking powder
¼ teaspoon salt
1 cup milk
1 cup huckleberries

1 teaspoon vanilla

Cream butter and sugar and add well-beaten eggs. Mix and sift flour, baking powder and salt and add to mixture alternately with milk. Add huckleberries which have been slightly floured. Pour into buttered muffin pans and bake in a moderate oven, 350 degrees, about 25 minutes. Sprinkle with powdered sugar while still warm.

SPICE CUPCAKES

½ cup butter
2½ cups sugar
2 teaspoons soda dissolved in
2 cups sour cream
3½ cups sifted flour
2 teaspoons cinnamon

1 teaspoon cloves
1 teaspoon salt
1 cup seeded raisins
1 cup seedless raisins
1 cup walnut meats
4 eggs, well beaten

Cream butter and sugar; add cream alternately with sifted dry ingredients. Soak raisins in a little cold water and then put through meat chopper. Add raisins, nut meats and eggs to mixture. Pour into small buttered muffin tins and bake in a moderate oven, 350 degrees, 15 to 20 minutes.

MOLASSES DROP CAKES

½ cup butter
½ cup brown sugar
1 cup molasses
1 teaspoon soda

1 cup sour milk
⅛ teaspoon ginger
1 teaspoon cloves
1 teaspoon cinnamon

3 cups flour

Cream butter and sugar; then add molasses and soda dissolved in milk. Add the flour mixed with spices. Drop by spoonfuls on buttered cooky sheet, sprinkle with sugar and cinnamon and bake in a moderate oven, 350 degrees, 10 to 15 minutes.

SOUR MILK CAKES

½ cup butter
1 cup sugar
2 eggs

½ teaspoon soda
½ cup sour milk
1¼ cups flour

1 teaspoon vanilla

Cream butter and sugar; then add eggs. Add soda to sour milk and add alternately with the flour to the creamed mixture; add vanilla. Pour into buttered muffin tins, saving out 2 tablespoons of the dough. To this add 1 square of melted chocolate; then drop a little in the center of each cake. Bake in a moderate oven, 350 degrees, about 30 minutes. Frost with Boiled Frosting, p. 376.

SPONGE DROPS

2 eggs, separated
1 cup sugar
1 cup flour

1 rounded teaspoon baking
powder
½ teaspoon salt

⅓ cup boiling water

Beat yolks of eggs light and gradually add sugar. Mix and sift dry ingredients and add alternately with water. Lastly add stiffly beaten egg whites. Pour into unbuttered muffin tins and bake in a moderate oven, 350 degrees, 20 to 30 minutes.

LADYFINGERS

⅔ cup powdered sugar
½ cup sifted flour

⅛ teaspoon salt
3 eggs, separated

½ teaspoon vanilla

Mix flour, ⅓ cup of the sugar and salt and sift together 3 times. Gradually beat remaining sugar into stiffly beaten egg whites. Fold in vanilla and egg yolks beaten until thick and lemon-colored. Gradually fold in the flour-sugar mixture. Bake in ladyfinger pans, or shape in oblongs, 4 by 1 inches, on unbuttered paper-lined cooky sheets. Dust with additional powdered sugar and bake in a moderate oven, 350 degrees, 10 to 12 minutes. Dough may be dropped from teaspoon to make rounds, or it may be baked in small buttered muffin pans.

SODA CAKES

¼ cup butter	1 teaspoon cinnamon
1 cup brown sugar	½ teaspoon cloves
1 egg	¼ teaspoon nutmeg
1 teaspoon vanilla	½ teaspoon soda
1 cup milk	2 teaspoons baking powder
2 cups flour	½ teaspoon salt

Cream together butter, sugar and egg. Add vanilla. Mix and sift dry ingredients and add to creamed mixture alternately with milk. Mix well, pour into buttered muffin tins and bake in a moderate oven, 350 degrees, 15 to 20 minutes. Frost with Chocolate Frosting, p. 377.

BROWN SUGAR DROP COOKIES

½ cup butter	½ teaspoon soda
1 cup brown sugar	3 tablespoons milk
Pinch of salt	1 teaspoon vanilla
1 egg	2 cups flour
½ cup chocolate bits	

Cream butter, sugar and salt, then beat in egg. Dissolve soda in milk, then add to creamed mixture with vanilla, flour and chocolate bits. Mix well. Drop from teaspoon on a buttered cooky sheet. Bake in a moderately hot oven, 375 degrees, about 10 minutes.

BROWN SUGAR ICEBOX COOKIES

2 eggs, well beaten	3½ cups sifted flour
2 cups brown sugar	1 teaspoon soda
1 cup melted butter	1 teaspoon vanilla
¼ teaspoon salt	

Mix in order given. Shape into a roll, wrap in wax paper and put in icebox overnight. Slice with a knife and place on buttered cooky sheet. Bake in moderate oven, 350 degrees. One half cup walnut meats may be added if desired.

BUTTERSCOTCH COOKIES

1 cup butter	2½ cups flour
1¾ cups brown sugar	¼ teaspoon soda
1 teaspoon vanilla	1 teaspoon baking powder
2 eggs	½ teaspoon salt

1 cup chopped pecans

Cream butter and gradually add sugar; then beat in vanilla and eggs. Mix and sift dry ingredients and add to creamed mixture with nuts. Drop from a teaspoon on a buttered cooky sheet and bake in a moderately hot oven, 375 degrees, for 10 minutes.

BUTTERSCOTCH SQUARES

¼ cup butter	1 teaspoon vanilla
1 cup brown sugar	⅔ cup flour
1 egg	½ teaspoon salt
½ cup chopped nuts	1 teaspoon baking powder

Melt butter, then add brown sugar, unbeaten egg, nuts and vanilla. Mix and sift the dry ingredients and add to first mixture. Bake in a shallow buttered pan in a moderate oven, 350 degrees, for 30 minutes.

CHOCOLATE GRAHAM CRACKER BROWNIES

2 cups crushed graham crackers	1 cup condensed milk
	1 package chocolate bits

Mix ingredients together, place in buttered pan and bake in a moderate oven, 350 degrees, until chocolate bits are melted. When cool, cut into squares.

BROWNIES (1)

2 eggs	½ cup butter
1 cup sugar	½ cup flour
2 squares chocolate	1 cup chopped walnut meats

Beat eggs and add sugar. Melt chocolate and butter together and add to egg mixture. Stir in flour and nuts. Spread evenly in shallow buttered pan and bake in a slow oven, 300 degrees, 40 minutes. Cut in squares when cool.

BROWNIES (2)

⅓ cup butter	¾ cup flour
1 cup sugar	1 teaspoon baking powder
2 eggs	¼ teaspoon salt
2 squares melted chocolate	1 cup chopped nuts
	½ teaspoon vanilla

Cream butter and sugar, beat in eggs and melted chocolate. Add flour sifted with baking powder and salt; stir in nuts. Add vanilla. Turn into shallow buttered pan and bake in a moderate oven, 350 degrees, 25 minutes. Cut in squares before removing from pan.

CHOCOLATE COOKIES

1 cup butter	3 squares melted chocolate
2 cups sugar	1½ cups bread flour
3 eggs	1 cup chopped walnuts
	1 teaspoon vanilla

Cream butter and sugar and stir in remaining ingredients. Drop from a spoon on a buttered cooky sheet. Bake in a moderate oven, 350 degrees, 12 to 15 minutes.

CHOCOLATE COCONUT MACAROONS

1 cup sugar	2 squares melted chocolate
¼ teaspoon salt	1½ cups grated and
3 egg whites, beaten stiff	chopped coconut
	½ teaspoon vanilla

Combine sugar and salt. Fold gradually into beaten egg whites. Add vanilla, chocolate and coconut. Drop from spoon on buttered cooky sheet. Bake in a slow oven, 300 degrees, 20 minutes.

MERINGUES, OR KISSES (1)

3 egg whites	3 teaspoons baking powder
1¼ cups granulated sugar	1 teaspoon vanilla

Beat egg whites stiff and fold in sugar, baking powder and vanilla. Drop by spoonfuls on a cooky sheet lined with brown paper and bake in a very slow oven, 250 degrees, about 1 hour.

MERINGUES, OR KISSES (2)

4 egg whites   ½ teaspoon vanilla
1½ cups powdered sugar

Beat whites till stiff, gradually add ⅔ cup sugar and beat until mixture holds its shape. Add vanilla and remainder of sugar and beat. Shape with spoon on a baking sheet or wet board covered with paper. Bake 40 minutes in a very slow oven, 250 degrees. Scoop out center, fill with ice cream or whipped cream flavored with vanilla and sugar. Serve with chocolate or butterscotch sauce.

COCONUT DROP COOKIES

1 cup butter   1 teaspoon soda
2 cups brown sugar   ¾ cup shredded coconut
3 eggs, well beaten   ¼ cup chopped raisins
3 cups flour   1 teaspoon lemon extract

Cream butter and sugar; then add eggs. Mix and sift dry ingredients and add to first mixture. Add coconut, raisins and lemon extract. Drop from a spoon on buttered cooky sheet. Bake in a moderate oven, 350 degrees, about 10 minutes.

COFFEE SUGAR COOKIES

1 cup brown sugar   1 teaspoon cream of tartar
½ cup butter   ½ teaspoon soda
¼ cup strong cold coffee   ⅛ teaspoon salt
1 egg   Flour to make soft dough

Cream butter and sugar, and add remaining ingredients. Roll thin, sprinkle with granulated sugar and gently roll in. Place on buttered cooky sheet and bake in a moderately hot oven, 375 degrees, about 8 minutes.

FILLED COOKIES

½ cup butter   ½ cup milk
1 cup sugar   2½ cups flour
1 egg, beaten   4 teaspoons baking powder
                1 teaspoon vanilla

Cream butter and sugar and add egg. Mix and sift flour and baking powder and add to creamed mixture alternately with milk. Add vanilla. Roll thin and cut with cooky cutter. Place half the cookies on a buttered sheet and put a teaspoon of Raisin Filling, p. 375, on each. Place the other half of cookies on top, press edges together and prick with fork. Bake in a moderately hot oven, 375 degrees, about 12 minutes.

DATE SQUARES

2 cups chopped dates	1½ cups sifted flour
½ cup water	1 cup brown sugar
½ cup sugar	¾ cup butter
Juice of 1 lemon	½ teaspoon soda
1½ cups rolled oats	⅛ teaspoon salt
(oatmeal)	

Cook dates and water until dates are tender, about 5 minutes. Add sugar and lemon juice; cool. Combine rolled oats, flour, brown sugar, butter, soda and salt and mix until it resembles crumbs. Place ⅔ of mixture in a buttered square pan. Cover with the date mixture and sprinkle remaining crumbs over the top, pressing lightly. Bake in a moderate oven, 350 degrees, 25 to 30 minutes. Cool and cut in squares.

DATE BARS

¾ cup butter	3 cups flour
1½ cups sugar	1 teaspoon baking powder
1 cup sour milk	1 teaspoon salt
½ teaspoon soda	1 cup chopped dates
1 cup chopped nut meats	

Cream butter and sugar, and stir in milk which has been mixed with soda. Then add mixed and sifted flour, baking powder and salt, dates and nuts. Pour into a shallow pan lined with waxed paper. Bake in a moderate oven, 350 degrees, 20 minutes. Cut into bars and roll in powdered sugar while warm.

GINGERSNAPS

½ cup butter	1 teaspoon cinnamon
½ cup molasses	½ teaspoon salt
1 cup brown sugar	1 scant dessertspoon soda
2 teaspoons ginger	1 egg
3½ cups pastry flour	

Heat butter, molasses, sugar, spices, salt and soda to boiling point. Remove from heat and add egg and flour. Chill. Roll very thin, cut in strips and place on buttered cooky sheet. Bake in a hot oven, 400 degrees.

HERMITS

⅓ cup butter	2 tablespoons light cream
⅔ cup sugar	¼ teaspoon cloves
⅓ cup chopped raisins	¼ teaspoon nutmeg
1 egg	2 teaspoons baking powder
1¼ cups flour	

Cream butter and sugar. Add raisins, beaten egg and cream. Mix and sift dry ingredients and add to mixture. Drop from teaspoon on buttered cooky sheets and bake in a moderate oven, 350 degrees, about 15 minutes.

ICE CREAM WAFERS

½ cup butter	¾ cup flour
½ cup sugar	¼ teaspoon salt
1 egg	½ teaspoon vanilla

Cream butter and sugar thoroughly, then add well-beaten egg and flour sifted with salt. Beat vigorously and add vanilla. Drop by teaspoonfuls on buttered cooky sheet, well apart. Place a nut on each cooky. Bake in a moderate oven, 350 degrees, 10 minutes.

ICEBOX COOKIES

1½ cups butter	1 teaspoon soda
1 cup white sugar	2 tablespoons hot water
1 cup brown sugar	4 cups flour
2 eggs	1 cup chopped raisins
½ cup chopped nuts	

Cream butter and gradually add the sugars, then the eggs. Dissolve the soda in the hot water and add to the butter mixture. Stir in the flour, raisins and nuts. Form into a roll and chill in the refrigerator. Cut in thin slices, place on buttered cooky sheet and bake in a hot oven, 400 degrees, about 10 minutes.

MOLASSES ICEBOX COOKIES

1 cup sugar	1 teaspoon cinnamon
2 eggs, well beaten	½ teaspoon cloves
1 cup melted butter	½ teaspoon nutmeg
½ cup molasses	1 teaspoon soda
4½ cups flour	1 teaspoon salt

Add beaten eggs, butter and molasses to sugar. Mix and sift dry ingredients and add to first mixture. Shape into a roll, wrap with wax paper and chill. Slice thin and place on buttered cooky sheet. Bake in a hot oven, 400 degrees, about 8 minutes.

ROLLED MOLASSES COOKIES

1 cup butter	⅛ teaspoon nutmeg
1 cup sugar	⅛ teaspoon salt
1 cup molasses	2 teaspoons soda
½ teaspoon cinnamon	Flour to roll, about 3½
¼ teaspoon allspice	cups
1 cup thick sour cream	

Cream butter; gradually beat in sugar, then molasses. Mix and sift dry ingredients and add to creamed mixture alternately with sour cream. Roll ⅓ inch thick, cut, and place on buttered cooky sheet. Bake in a moderate oven, 350 degrees, about 10 minutes.

OATMEAL MACAROONS

1 egg, beaten	¼ teaspoon salt
½ cup sugar	½ teaspoon baking powder
¼ cup melted butter	1 cup rolled oats (oatmeal)
2 tablespoons flour	½ teaspoon vanilla

Mix in order given. Drop from spoon on buttered cooky sheet. Bake in a moderate oven, 350 degrees, 10 minutes.

OATMEAL HERMITS

3 cups flour	2 cups brown sugar
1 teaspoon cinnamon	2 eggs
1 teaspoon cloves	1 teaspoon soda
1 cup rolled oats (oatmeal)	1/4 cup hot water
1/4 cup chopped raisins	1/4 cup light cream
1 cup butter	1 teaspoon vanilla

Mix and sift flour and spices and stir in oatmeal and raisins. Cream butter, gradually beat in sugar, then eggs. Dissolve soda in hot water and add it alternately with flour-oatmeal mixture to the creamed mixture. Stir in cream and vanilla. Drop from a teaspoon on buttered cooky sheet and bake in a moderately hot oven, 375 degrees, 15 minutes.

OATMEAL COOKIES (1)

1/2 cup butter	Pinch of salt
2/3 cup sugar	1/2 teaspoon soda
1 egg	1 cup rolled oats (oatmeal)
3/4 cup flour	2 tablespoons milk
1 teaspoon cinnamon	1 tablespoon molasses
1/2 teaspoon vanilla	

Cream butter, gradually beat in sugar, then egg. Mix and sift flour, cinnamon, salt and soda; stir in rolled oats. Add dry ingredients to creamed mixture alternately with milk to which the molasses has been added. Stir in vanilla. Drop from teaspoon on buttered cooky sheet and bake in a moderate oven, 350 degrees, about 15 minutes.

OATMEAL COOKIES (2)

2 eggs, beaten	1 cup flour
1 cup sugar	2 teaspoons baking powder
1 cup melted butter	1/2 teaspoon salt
2 cups rolled oats (oatmeal)	1 teaspoon vanilla

Add sugar, melted butter and rolled oats to beaten eggs. Mix and sift flour, baking powder and salt and add to first mixture with vanilla. Drop by teaspoonfuls on buttered cooky sheet. Spread very thin with knife dipped in hot water. Bake in a moderate oven, 350 degrees, until a golden brown.

OLD–FASHIONED SUGAR COOKIES

½ cup butter	2 teaspoons baking powder
1 cup sugar	½ cup milk
1 egg	1 teaspoon vanilla
3 cups flour	1 egg white

Cream butter and sugar; add egg and beat well. Mix and sift dry ingredients and add to first mixture alternately with milk and vanilla. Turn onto a floured board, roll ⅛ inch thick and cut with cooky cutter. Place on buttered cooky sheet. Brush each cooky with unbeaten egg white and sprinkle with sugar. Bake in a moderately hot oven, 375 degrees, 10 minutes.

ORANGE COOKIES

¼ cup butter	3 cups flour
¾ cup sugar	2 teaspoons baking powder
¼ cup orange juice	½ teaspoon salt
1 egg, well beaten	½ teaspoon vanilla

Cream butter and sugar; then add orange juice and grated rind of 1 orange. Add egg and mixed and sifted flour, baking powder and salt. Stir in vanilla. Place on floured board, roll thin, cut and place on buttered cooky sheet. Bake in a moderately hot oven, 375 degrees, about 8 minutes.

ROCKS

1 cup butter	½ teaspoon salt
1½ cups brown sugar	1½ cups chopped raisins
3 eggs, well beaten	1 cup chopped walnut meats
3 cups flour	1 teaspoon soda, dis-
1 teaspoon cinnamon	solved in
1 tablespoon hot water	

Cream butter, gradually add sugar; then eggs. Mix and sift flour, cinnamon and salt and add raisins and nuts to dry ingredients. Beat the dry ingredients into creamed mixture and lastly add dissolved soda. Drop by spoonfuls onto buttered cooky sheets and bake in a hot oven, 400 degrees, about 8 minutes.

DROP SUGAR COOKIES

½ cup butter	2½ cups flour
1 cup sugar	⅔ cup milk
1 small teaspoon soda	1 egg
2 teaspoons cream of tartar	1 teaspoon vanilla

Cream butter and sugar. Mix and sift dry ingredients and add alternately with milk to creamed mixture. Add beaten egg and vanilla. Drop from a spoon on a buttered cooky sheet. Sprinkle each cooky with sugar and put a raisin in the center. Bake in a moderately hot oven, 375 degrees, until a light brown.

SOUR CREAM COOKIES

1 cup butter	3 eggs, well beaten
2 cups brown sugar	4 cups flour
1 cup sour cream	½ teaspoon cinnamon
3 teaspoons soda	½ teaspoon nutmeg
1 teaspoon vanilla	

Cream butter and sugar; then add sour cream in which soda has been dissolved. Add the eggs. Mix and sift flour, cinnamon and nutmeg and add to creamed mixture. Stir in vanilla. Drop by spoonfuls on buttered cooky sheet. Bake in a moderate oven, 350 degrees, about 12 minutes.

SAND TARTS (1)

½ cup butter	½ teaspoon salt
1 cup sugar	1 teaspoon vanilla
1 egg, well beaten	1 egg white, unbeaten
1¾ cups pastry flour	1 teaspoon sugar
1 teaspoon baking powder	¼ teaspoon cinnamon
Split blanched almonds	

Cream butter and sugar and add egg, mixed and sifted dry ingredients and vanilla. Chill in refrigerator several hours. Turn onto a floured board, roll ⅛ inch thick and cut with a cooky cutter. Place on buttered cooky sheet. Brush each cooky with unbeaten egg white and sprinkle with mixed sugar and cinnamon. Decorate with almonds. Bake in a moderate oven, 350 degrees, 10 to 15 minutes.

SAND TARTS (2)

4 tablespoons powdered sugar
½ pound butter

2 cups flour
1 teaspoon vanilla

Cream butter and sugar together and add flour, then vanilla. Roll and cut into small squares. Place on buttered cooky sheet. Bake in moderate oven, 350 degrees, until a light brown. Sprinkle with powdered sugar while hot.

SCOTCH SHORTBREAD (1)

½ cup powdered sugar   1 cup butter
4 cups flour

Mix sugar and butter, but do not cream. Rub this mixture into the flour with your hands until it resembles putty. Pat dough on a floured board to ¼-inch thickness. Cut in desired shapes and place on cooky sheets. Bake in a slow oven, 300 degrees, till light brown.

SCOTCH SHORTBREAD (2)

1 cup butter
½ cup confectioners' sugar

2 cups sifted bread flour
¼ teaspoon baking powder
¼ teaspoon salt

Cream butter and gradually add sugar. Cream well, then add mixed and sifted dry ingredients. Turn onto a floured board and roll dough ⅓ inch thick. Cut with cooky cutter and place on a buttered cooky sheet. If desired, sprinkle with a mixture of sugar and cinnamon. Bake in a moderate oven, 350 degrees, 20 to 25 minutes.

PEANUT COOKIES

2 tablespoons butter
½ cup sugar
1 egg, well beaten
½ teaspoon soda

2 tablespoons milk
1 cup flour
1 teaspoon cream of tartar
1 cup chopped peanuts

Cream butter and sugar and add egg. Dissolve soda in milk; then add to creamed mixture. Add flour, cream of tartar and peanuts. Drop by spoonfuls on buttered cooky sheet. Bake in a moderate oven, 350 degrees, about 12 minutes.

VANILLA WAFERS

1 cup flour	1/2 cup butter
1 1/8 teaspoons baking	1 egg yolk
powder	1/2 cup sugar
1/8 teaspoon salt	3 tablespoons cold water

Sift flour, baking powder and salt 4 times; then cut in the butter until well mixed. Beat egg yolk and sugar until creamy; then add to dry ingredients. Add the water by the spoonful. Beat. Drop from spoon on a buttered baking sheet. Spread smoothly and bake in a hot oven, 400 degrees.

BUTTERSCOTCH FILLING

3/4 cup brown sugar	2 eggs, slightly beaten
1/3 cup flour	2 cups scalded milk
1/4 teaspoon salt	2 tablespoons butter
	1 teaspoon vanilla

Mix dry ingredients and add to eggs. Stir in enough scalded milk to make a thin paste, then add to scalded milk. Add butter. Cook in double boiler 15 minutes, stirring constantly until mixture thickens. Cool and add vanilla.

COCONUT RAISIN FILLING

2/3 cup sugar	1 egg white
1/4 cup hot water	1/2 cup chopped raisins
	3 tablespoons coconut

Heat sugar and water, stirring constantly until sugar dissolves and mixture boils. Remove from heat, stir until cool; then add stiffly beaten egg white, raisins and coconut. Flavor with vanilla.

LEMON FILLING

1 egg, beaten	Juice and grated rind of
1 cup sugar	1 lemon
1 grated apple	1 tablespoon butter

Cook egg, sugar, grated apple, lemon rind and juice in double boiler until thick, stirring constantly. Add butter and cool.

CREAM FILLING

1 pint milk	⅔ cup sugar
1 tablespoon cornstarch	1 tablespoon butter
1 egg	1 teaspoon vanilla

Dissolve cornstarch in ¼ cup of milk. Scald the rest of the milk in a double boiler. Beat egg and sugar together and stir into milk. Add cornstarch and stir until thickened. Add butter. Cool and flavor.

BANANA CREAM FILLING

Prepare Cream Filling and add either 1 cup mashed bananas or 1 cup thinly sliced bananas before spreading.

CHOCOLATE CREAM FILLING

Prepare Cream Filling, but scald 2 squares chocolate with the milk.

ORANGE FILLING

2 tablespoons butter	½ cup orange juice
¼ cup sugar	1 tablespoon grated orange
2 eggs, well beaten	rind
½ tablespoon lemon juice	

Mix in order given. Cook 10 minutes in double boiler, stirring constantly. Cool.

RAISIN FILLING

½ cup water	1 teaspoon flour
½ cup sugar	1 cup chopped raisins

Mix the above ingredients and cook until thick.

STRAWBERRY OR RASPBERRY FILLING

1 cup heavy cream, whipped	¼ cup sugar
2 egg whites, stiffly beaten	1 cup crushed berries

Combine whipped cream and egg whites. Add sugar to berries, then fold into the first mixture.

BOILED FROSTING (1)

1 cup sugar
⅓ cup cold water

⅓ teaspoon vinegar
1 egg white, stiffly beaten

1 teaspoon vanilla

Boil sugar, water and vinegar till the syrup spins a long thread when dropped from the spoon. Pour syrup slowly over egg white, beating constantly. Add vanilla and beat until it thickens.

BOILED FROSTING (2)

1½ cups sugar
½ cup water
1 teaspoon cream of tartar

2 egg whites
Dash of salt
1 teaspoon vanilla

Cook sugar, water and cream of tartar in a saucepan until sugar is dissolved; then cover and boil 3 minutes. Remove cover and boil, without stirring, until mixture forms a soft ball when dropped into cold water. Pour syrup gradually over stiffly beaten egg whites, beating constantly. Add salt and vanilla and continue to beat until frosting is of the right consistency to spread.

BUTTER FROSTING

2 tablespoons butter
1 cup sifted confectioners'
　　sugar

1 tablespoon light cream
½ teaspoon vanilla

Cream butter, gradually add part of sugar and mix thoroughly. Add remaining sugar and cream, beating well. Add vanilla.

FUDGE FROSTING

3 squares chocolate
2 cups brown sugar

½ cup sour cream
1 tablespoon butter

1 teaspoon vanilla

Melt chocolate over hot water, add sugar and mix well. Gradually stir in cream. Add butter and boil until mixture forms a soft ball when tried in cold water. Add vanilla, cool and then beat until right consistency to spread. Chopped nut meats may be added if desired.

UNCOOKED CHOCOLATE FROSTING (1)

¼ cup melted butter   ¼ cup light cream
2 squares melted chocolate   2 cups confectioners' sugar
1 teaspoon vanilla

Mix butter and chocolate; add cream, sugar and vanilla.

UNCOOKED CHOCOLATE FROSTING (2)

1 cup confectioners' sugar   2 squares melted chocolate
1 egg   2 tablespoons milk

Combine ingredients in a bowl and set bowl in a larger bowl of ice
or snow. Beat ingredients until stiff, then stop. If overbeaten, the
frosting will become runny again.

UNCOOKED CHOCOLATE FROSTING (3)

3 egg yolks, beaten   Powdered sugar to thicken
1 square melted chocolate   ½ teaspoon vanilla

Mix in order given.

LADY BALTIMORE FROSTING

3 cups sugar   3 egg whites, stiffly beaten
1 cup boiling water   ½ cup walnut meats
6 chopped figs

Cook sugar and water, stirring until sugar is dissolved, to 238
degrees, or until syrup spins a long thread. Remove from fire and
slowly pour over stiffly beaten egg whites, stirring constantly. Reserve half the frosting for top and sides of cake, and add nuts and
figs to the remaining half for filling between the layers.

LEMON FROSTING

1 egg yolk   1 tablespoon grated orange rind
1½ tablespoons lemon juice   Confectioners' sugar

Mix together egg yolk, lemon juice and orange rind. Gradually stir
in sugar until of right consistency to spread.

MOCHA FROSTING (1)

1 tablespoon butter
Cold strong coffee

1 cup confectioners' sugar
8 teaspoons cocoa

Melt butter in cup and add enough coffee to make ¼ cup. Mix cocoa and sugar and slowly stir in liquid.

MOCHA FROSTING (2)

¾ cup confectioners' sugar
¼ cup melted butter

2 tablespoons hot coffee
2 tablespoons marshmallow
    fluff

Stir butter, coffee and marshmallow fluff into the sugar and mix well.

ORANGE FROSTING

½ teaspoon gelatin
½ teaspoon flour
½ cup sugar

2 eggs, beaten
½ cup orange juice
Grated rind of 1 orange

1 cup heavy cream, whipped

Mix gelatin, flour and sugar and then add eggs, juice and grated rind. Cook in double boiler until thick. Cool and add whipped cream.

SEVEN–MINUTE FROSTING

2 egg whites, unbeaten
1½ cups sugar
⅛ teaspoon cream of tartar

Pinch of salt
5 tablespoons cold water
1 teaspoon vanilla

Combine all the ingredients except vanilla in top of double boiler. Beat with egg beater 7 to 9 minutes, or until frosting will stand up in peaks. Remove from boiling water, add vanilla and beat until thick enough to spread. If desired, add ½ cup grated coconut or chopped nut meats.

PEPPERMINT FROSTING

Prepare Seven-Minute Frosting, but replace vanilla with 2 drops oil of peppermint or 1 crushed stick of peppermint candy.

CANDIES

MAXIMS FROM MAINE KITCHENS

Meats of pecans may be easily removed if nuts are first placed in a pan and boiling water poured over them. Leave them in the water 20 minutes.

❦

Almonds and other nuts may be blanched by removing shells, covering with boiling water, and letting stand until dark skin rubs off easily. Then put in cold water, rub off skins and dry between towels.

❦

Aluminum articles are best cleaned by standing 24 hours in a strongish solution of oxalic acid.

❦

To make a small piece of candle burn all night, put fine salt on the candle till it covers the wick as high as the black part.

CANDIES

CARAMELS

1 ½ cups heavy cream   ½ cup corn syrup
1 cup sugar   1 teaspoon vanilla

Put sugar, syrup and ½ cup cream in pan and cook until it forms a soft ball when tried in cold water. Stir constantly. Add ½ cup cream and boil until mixture will again form a soft ball in cold water. Add remainder of cream and cook until mixture makes a firm ball when tried in cold water. Add vanilla and pour into buttered pan. Cool, cut in squares and wrap in wax paper.

CHOCOLATE CARAMELS

To the preceding recipe add 3 squares of chocolate with the last ½ cup of cream.

FONDANT

4 cups sugar   Pinch of salt
1 cup hot water   Pinch of cream of tartar
                1 teaspoon vanilla

Mix sugar, water, salt and cream of tartar. Place on heat, but don't stir. Boil till mixture will spin a thread, or 238 degrees. Remove from heat and keep fingering to see when it is cool. Then add vanilla and beat till creamy. Make into little balls and put a walnut meat on each side. Delicious used to stuff dates.

FUDGE

1 cup sugar	2 tablespoons butter
½ cup milk	1 square melted chocolate

½ teaspoon vanilla

Boil sugar, milk and butter until it forms a soft ball when tested in cold water, or to 234 degrees. Remove from heat and add chocolate, vanilla and walnut meats. Beat. Pour into a buttered pan, cool and cut in squares.

PEANUT BUTTER FUDGE

3¾ cups confectioners' sugar	1 cup canned marshmallow
⅔ cup evaporated milk	fluff
1 teaspoon vanilla	½ cup peanut butter

Cook sugar and milk, stirring constantly, until it forms a soft ball when tested in cold water, or to 234 degrees. Remove from heat and add other ingredients. Beat until nearly stiff, then pour into a buttered pan, cool and cut in squares.

GLACÉ NUTS

1 cup sugar	⅓ cup water

⅛ teaspoon cream of tartar

Mix ingredients in saucepan and boil without stirring until syrup begins to discolor. Remove from saucepan and put in double boiler over boiling water. Dip in nuts separately, and then place on waxed paper.

MINT PASTE

1½ packages minute gelatin	1 cup sugar
¼ cup boiling water	¼ cup water
½ package pink coloring	1 tablespoon lemon juice

5 drops oil of peppermint

Add gelatin to hot water with coloring. Boil sugar and water 1 minute, add gelatin mixture and boil 5 minutes. Add remaining ingredients, put in a pan and cool. Cut in squares and roll in powdered sugar.

MOLASSES POPCORN BALLS

1 cup molasses	1 tablespoon vinegar
½ cup honey	3 tablespoons butter
¼ cup corn syrup	3 quarts salted popped corn

Cook molasses, honey, syrup, vinegar and butter until mixture forms a hard ball when tried in cold water. Stir occasionally. Remove from heat, pour over corn and allow to cool a little. Butter fingers lightly and mold corn into balls. Cool on a buttered dish.

MOLASSES TAFFY

2 cups molasses	⅛ teaspoon soda
1 cup sugar	¼ cup butter
¾ cup water	½ teaspoon vanilla

Cook molasses, sugar and water slowly, stirring constantly, until it is brittle when tried in cold water, 256 degrees. Remove from fire and add soda, butter and vanilla. Pour into buttered pan. When cool enough to handle, pull until light-colored. Cut in small pieces with scissors.

NOUGAT

1 cup blanched almonds, chopped fine	2 cups powdered sugar

Melt sugar in a heavy pan, stirring constantly. Add nuts and spread very thin on a buttered cooky sheet.

PANOCHA
(Penuchy)

1 pound light brown sugar	3 tablespoons butter
½ cup rich milk	1 teaspoon vanilla
½ cup walnut meats	

Mix sugar, milk and butter and boil till it will form a soft ball when tested in cold water. Remove from heat and beat in vanilla and nut meats. Beat until mixture thickens and is of a creamy consistency. Pour into a buttered pan, cool and cut in squares.

PRALINES

2 cups brown sugar 1 tablespoon lemon juice
⅔ cup water ½ cup chopped nuts
1 teaspoon vanilla

Melt sugar in water and lemon juice. When sugar is dissolved, boil until a soft ball is formed in cold water, 234 degrees. Remove from fire and let stand until lukewarm. Add nuts and vanilla. Beat till creamy. Drop from tip of spoon on waxed paper.

SEA FOAM CANDY

3 cups brown sugar ¼ teaspoon salt
¾ cup water 2 egg whites, stiffly beaten
1 teaspoon vanilla

Put sugar, water and salt in saucepan, place on fire and stir until sugar is dissolved. Continue cooking until syrup reaches 255 degrees. Remove from fire and gradually pour it over the stiffly beaten egg whites, beating while pouring. Continue beating until candy cools and will hold its shape when dropped from a spoon. Add vanilla and drop on waxed paper. Nuts may be added if desired.

WHITE TAFFY

2 cups sugar ½ cup white vinegar
½ cup water 1 teaspoon butter
1 tablespoon vanilla

Put sugar, water, vinegar and butter in a saucepan and stir over slow heat until sugar is dissolved. Then cook, without stirring, until mixture forms a hard ball when tried in cold water. Add vanilla. Pour on oiled slab or platter. When cool enough to handle pull with finger tips, then clip into chewable pieces with buttered scissors.

CYCLONE CANDY

1 cup sugar	2 tablespoons butter
1 cup molasses	1 teaspoon vanilla
3 tablespoons vinegar	1¼ teaspoons baking soda

Cook sugar, molasses, vinegar and butter in a heavy saucepan until it forms a hard ball when tried in cold water. Then add vanilla and soda, and stir well. Pour into a shallow, lightly buttered pan and do not touch or move until cool.

ROSE CANDY

Pick rose petals early in the morning while still dewy. Put a 1-inch layer of petals in a stone crock. Cover the layer with a generous amount of brown sugar. Add alternate layers of rose petals and sugar, pressing them down tightly until crock is full, with a layer of sugar on top. Cover crock and let it stand for 3 months, at the end of which time the petals and sugar will have candied and will be ready to scoop out and eat.

DIET

DIET

By Kenneth Roberts

A NOVELIST, in consulting references on any given subject, is usually forced to discard the majority as inaccurate, biased, unreliable or untruthful, and to retain a few dependable ones as his chief sources of information. This is because too many writers of reference books are careless about their facts, and willing to conceal evidence in order to make a good case for their unsound theories.

Books on diet ought to be different; for most of them are written by medical experts who have studied for years to find out exactly what happens to seven cents' worth of liver when it meets a Welch's bacillus in the upper colon of a sedentary worker aged forty-five.

Diet books ought indeed to be different; yet when I first looked into some of them, I found myself entertaining grave doubts.

From each book, for example, I learned that all diets, except the one advocated by the author of that particular book, are either based on the erroneous ideas of a faddist, or are downright dangerous. I learned that I had eaten incorrect foods all my life and must do something about it in a hurry. What that something should be, however, was a problem.

From a cursory survey of the most advanced diet books I gathered that nearly every disease in the world is not only the result of eating improper foods, but also the result of eating proper foods in improper combinations.

I further discovered that although a person may consider himself in perfect health, and may feel comfortable and happy, he is—unless he is eating foods that the diet books say he ought to eat—as effectively poisoned as though nurtured for years on poison-ivy salads with bichloride-of-mercury dressing.

I also learned that almost every sort of illness—according to the most advanced school of diet thought—can be prevented or cured by proper diet; and that the only way in which any person can save himself from a fatal sickness is by ceasing to eat nearly everything to which he has hitherto been addicted and devoting the rest of his life to devouring foods he wouldn't ordinarily eat except on a bet.

I learned, with considerable distress, that the person who permits himself to eat starches, meats and sweets must be in a constant state of internal ferment. Not only is intestinal fermentation inevitable, but those who suffer from it are nervous, timid, afraid, irritable and suspicious; they are quick-tempered, disagreeable and easily offended; under the influence of intestinal ferment a splendid mind often loses its faculty of reasoning and thinking.

I discovered, with steadily growing apprehension, that if a person is so ignorant as to permit fermentable foods to pass his lips, he is doomed, because no amount of exercise, medicines or outdoor life can counteract the harmful effects of fermented foods. They give him acidosis; and what acidosis does to him, in a quiet way, almost passes belief.

Acidosis is too large a subject for me to handle, in these few notes, except in the sketchiest manner. Not even the authors of the diet books are able to handle it satisfactorily. However, all of us are suffering from acidosis; and so far as I can tell, everybody has suffered from acidosis since the beginning of the world—unless he has been so happy as to stumble on the proper diet.

Among the unfortunates who must have been afflicted with it are Chaucer, Martin Luther, Julius Cæsar, Christopher Columbus, William Shakspere, Michael Angelo, George Washington, Napoleon Bonaparte, and all other great leaders, thinkers, fighters and philosophers, as well as everybody who is or has ever been afraid of thunderstorms.

For many years I have been partial to large sirloin steaks, preferably those about three inches thick, which have been broiled six to eight minutes on each side.

Such a sirloin steak, accompanied by a mealy Aroostook potato, a plateful of buttered toast and a lettuce salad thoroughly moistened with a garlic-perfumed dressing composed of two parts oil and one part lemon juice, has always struck me as one of civilization's noblest products, especially when followed by a flaky fragment of apple pie tasting of cinnamon.

I have also viewed with favor a commodious platter of corned beef hash, or a savory mess of pea beans impregnated with pork, molasses, mustard and onion in the proper proportion; then baked all day Saturday in a well-ripened bean pot.

My baked-bean record, to the best of my knowledge and belief, compares favorably with that of any New Englander. From my earliest years I have had what might almost be called an affinity for baked beans, especially when lubricated with homemade tomato ketchup from which all sweetening has been religiously excluded.

When confronted with a successful baking of beans, I have frequently attacked them enthusiastically on Saturday night, gladly repeated on Sunday morning, then toyed with two or three platefuls, cold, on Sunday evening, and made a final clean-up of the bean situation at my Monday morning breakfast.

Blueberry pie, too, appeals to me strongly—especially the honest variety that makes the inside of the mouth look like a miniature stage setting of the Cave of the Winds at midnight. Blueberry pie, I have felt, is hard to beat as a climax to a tasty meal, provided the upper and under crusts are not flexible and inclined to adhere to the roof of the mouth, and if the consistency of the pie's interior is in that delicate state of transition when it is too loose to be called solid, but not sufficiently loose to be called runny.

There are, in short, a number of New England dishes that have given me pleasure for many years; and without knowing anything about it, I have taken it for granted that they were as nourishing as they were enjoyable. My ideas were probably based on the knowledge that people from Maine have lived on similar dishes since time immemorial, and have apparently thrived on them. That is to say, it has not been unusual for them to keep their health and strength until they were eighty-five or ninety years of age, and then meet untimely ends through being lost at sea or falling off a roof.

However, they were great bean and hash eaters, and many of them—especially the seafaring people from my section—frequently lived for weeks on end on one of the most trying dietary combinations known to dietitians: salt pork, ship's bread, and coffee tasting like a blend of boiled stockings and lobster bait.

Therefore I take it for granted, in view of what I have acquired from diet books, that they really weren't healthy at all, in spite of their long lives. Unquestionably they were victims of intestinal ferment, these seafaring State-of-Mainers that I had always regarded as models of sturdiness. They were not, apparently, the bold mariners I had thought them, willing to crack on sail in strange waters; but must have been in a constant state of nervousness and timidity, and frequently lacking in reasoning faculties.

A casual glance into the pages of the most popular diet books was enough to make this point clear. From one I learned my errors in regard to sirloin steak dinners, as outlined above. Beefsteak is a protein. A potato is a starch. The combination is dreadful. Buttered toast is largely starch, and therefore makes the terribleness more pronounced. Lemon juice is an acid: to eat an acid with a protein is almost suicidal. As for the apple pie, it contains starch in its crust and sugar in its stuffing; and to drop those ingredients on top of steak and potatoes is little different from touching a match to a celluloid collar.

I was aroused to the horrors of baked beans and tomato ketchup. Baked beans are as full of starch, if not fuller, than a dress shirt. Tomato ketchup is made of acid fruit. When these are placed together in the human stomach, a fermentation takes place. Fermentation results in acidosis.

Corned beef hash is no better, unless some of the best diet books are grievously at fault. Corned beef hash is made, if made properly, by chopping corned beef and boiled potatoes together. Corned beef, unfortunately, is a protein, and potatoes are a starch. When simultaneously digested, the diet books say, the resulting fermentation is somewhat similar, in its effect on the stomach, to a lighted pinwheel.

I would have been glad, of course, to be free of the curse of acidosis; but the deeper I delved in the diet books, especially those of the anti-acidosis school, the more it seemed to me that each one evinced a singular amount of irritation at the ideas of other dietitians.

As I understand it, you cannot feel irritation if you are free of acidosis. If that is correct, then the anti-acidosis experts are themselves troubled with acidosis. At all events, there was something about the situation that led me to think it might be wise to settle on a composite diet from a number of books rather than trust blindly to one book whose author might have been mistaken in his calculations.

Fasting, according to several of the most modern diet books, is a sure cure for acidosis, smallpox, acute appendicitis, pernicious anemia, rheumatism, colds in the head; for nearly every ailment, in short, that you can imagine.

Unfortunately there is a difference of opinion on the matter. I say "unfortunately" because the most earnest supporters of the fasting theory say that a thirty-day fast is easy of accomplishment: that the person participating in the fast has no desire for food after the first two or three days: that during the remainder of the fasting period there is, generally speaking, no depression; no hunger; no mental or physical fatigue; nothing but increased strength, mental clarity and elation.

One of the diet books, written by Dr. Hay, impressed me deeply. It was being written, the author stated, during a thirty-day fast; and at the end of the thirty-day period, the author intended to subsist entirely on grapes for another thirty days.

After reading Dr. Hay's impressive diet book, which spoke so highly of the beneficial effects of a thirty-day fast, I thought for a time of cleaning up the entire acidosis situation by fasting for thirty days.

Shortly thereafter I read another authoritative book which stated casually that fasting isn't a bad thing if proper care is observed in preparing for and recovering from the fast. If precautions are not taken, the book added, the nervous system may receive a shock from which it will never recover.

This gave me, as the saying goes, pause; for I had contrived to struggle along fairly well even though I did—according to the diet books—have acidosis. It occurred to me at once that acidosis might be preferable to an incurable shock to the nervous system; so I hurriedly ran through all my diet books to see what the rest of them thought about fasting.

A large number of them seemed to have no thoughts on the subject. That is to say, they made no mention of it, which I assume they would have if they had regarded it with either favor or disfavor. One of them seemed to think that a ten-day fast might be beneficial; and another advocated fasting one day out of each month, but no more. Another declared flatly that fasting should under no circumstances be indulged in, inasmuch as it poisons the system.

Because of this divergence of opinion, I decided to do nothing definite about fasting until the diet experts could reach an agreement.

Having disposed of fasting to my own satisfaction, I found myself enmeshed in the subject of breakfast. Some of our leading dietitians believe that a person who wishes to be truly healthy should eat no breakfast at all; but when they have delivered themselves of this opinion, they immediately print a large number of breakfast menus. I must confess to being confused at this singular contradiction; and from time to time I wonder whether the dietitians may not be slightly confused themselves. Probably they are not. Probably their reasons for condemning breakfasts in one breath and recommending them in the next are excellent; but this is only conjecture on my part.

What to eat for breakfast is obviously one of the many baffling problems with which dietitians wrestle. According to some dietitians, there is nothing so nourishing and healthy as an egg. According to others, an egg is too rich for the human frame; and they stubbornly refuse to mention eggs in their diet books.

According to some, a griddlecake is one of the most pernicious foods yet evolved by civilized peoples; but on the other hand one of the most earnest advocates of thirty-day fasts and a breakfastless diet favors a breakfast made up of whole wheat pancakes, maple syrup, butter and black coffee.

Another thinks that the best of all possible breakfasts is a plate of vegetable soup.

Still another, who has specialized on the sort of foods to feed people so they may live to be excessively old and overpoweringly healthy, thinks a normal middle-aged person should have, for breakfast, melon, baked sweet potato, an extra-ripe banana with cream, and milk or cocoa. The same expert urges, as a preventive of obesity, a breakfast of melon, peaches or berries, broiled fish, and a baked potato or a bran muffin.

Some say that coffee and tea are highly injurious. Some say they are only injurious if taken with sugar or cream. Some say they aren't injurious at all, no matter how taken.

Some say cereals are bad, and others say cereals are splendid. Some say you must not eat toast made from white bread; but others strongly recommend toast made from white bread.

Whole wheat bread or toast, many insist, is the only sort of bread that should be eaten, and it can be eaten with anything at any time. Others say that whole wheat bread or toast is a starch, and therefore must not—absolutely must *not*—be eaten at the same meal with meat, eggs, fish or cheese, which are proteins, or with any food containing sugar, or with any acid fruit.

Nearly all dietitians hold out for a light breakfast, but one dietitian whose reputation is world-wide states clearly and emphatically that a frugal breakfast is bad.

In my first fright at the acidosis threat which was held over my head by so many diet books, I abandoned the breakfast on which I had subsisted for many years—two eggs, two slices of dry toast, a cup of coffee and a reasonable helping of any marmalade except quince. The eggs contained protein, the toast contained starch and the marmalade contained sugar; and any such mixture, as I have before intimated, does shocking things to your insides—unless a number of dietitians of high standing are sadly in error.

I shifted first to tomato juice and whole wheat toast. I seemed to be getting along on it all right, when somebody carelessly called my attention to the fact that whole wheat toast was a starch, whereas tomato juice ranks as acid fruit—a dangerous combination according to doctors who ought to know what they're talking about.

I then turned to coddled eggs, bran embellished with milk and honey, and a spot of coffee—a breakfast strongly recommended by a diet expert whose books are regarded with veneration by large numbers of diet enthusiasts. There was something wrong with this breakfast, though I couldn't at the moment put my finger on the trouble. It gave me the unaccustomed feeling of having swallowed a polo ball; and at the risk of inflaming my acidosis, I was obliged to go back to my old original breakfast in order to be comfortable again.

For a time I thought the polo-ball feeling was due to the fact that my breakfast contained an improper number of calories; but a study of the calory theory convinced me that it must have been caused by something else.

The calory theory of diet is, I assume, familiar to all. Roughly speaking, the theory contends that every edible thing contains so many calories or heat units—three figs, 100 calories; one potato, 100 calories; one banana, 75 calories; one half cup beans, 100 calories; seven half walnuts, 100 calories; one egg, 75 calories; one cup skimmed milk, 90 calories; medium serving of meat, 300 calories, and so on.

The normal moderately strenuous person requires about 2400 calories a day, whereas a coal heaver should have between 4000 and 5000 calories, and a heavy sitter only about 1800 calories. If, therefore, the moderately strenuous person wishes to gain weight, he adds a few hundred calories to his diet. If he wishes to lose weight, he cuts his daily ration to about 1200 calories.

That is the theory; but some of the modern diet books say the calory theory is all wrong: wrong and dangerous.

They say the calory theory encourages people to eat starches and proteins at the same time—which causes acidosis.

They say it permits the eating of starches, sugar and acid fruits together—which also causes acidosis.

They point out it is little short of madness to think a coal heaver needs over 4000 calories a day. They say if this were so, and the coal heaver were fed milk, his daily requirements would be ten quarts, which is enough to make even a rubber-skinned man explode with a loud majority report. They also say if foods are not properly combined, a man can starve to death on 4000 calories a day and gain weight on 1200 calories a day; and they may, of course, be right.

I would like to have it borne in mind that I am merely quoting from the books. I have nothing whatever against the calory theory. I am always happy to hear from readers: but I trust, in this particular case, that those who believe in the calory theory will not write long, indignant letters to show me where I am wrong. The persons to whom they should write their letters are the acidosis theorists. In fact, I may as well state here and now that if I receive vituperative letters from acidosis theorists, I shall forward them to a calory expert without comment; and if a calory theorist undertakes to drag me over the coals in a letter, I shall merely pass the letter to an acidosis expert.

I think I would probably be glad to answer all letters in person if the business of dieting were not so involved. It is so involved that persons who go into it in a serious way have little time for anything else. The most recent diet books, in extolling the advantages of an anti-acidosis diet, say that brain-workers find their brains much clearer and their inventiveness greatly improved if they give up all their old habits of eating and consume only such foods as are properly combined and prepared—consume starchy foods only with starchy foods and vegetables; proteins only with other proteins and vegetables.

Authors, they say, would do infinitely more work, and better work, if they would follow this system. I have no doubt that this is true; but in my own case, I am obliged to spend so much time hunting through diet books to find out what I ought to eat, and when to eat it, and what to eat with it, and in tinkering with my vegetable steamer, and in worrying about my acidosis, that I have almost been obliged to stop writing entirely.

Possibly William Shakspere, if he could have been persuaded to cut out all liquors and restrict his foods largely to steamed vegetables and salads, might have written better plays; and then, again, he might have spent so much time steaming his spinach and thinking about his health, to say nothing of arguing with cooks who didn't care to have Shakspere or anybody else tell them how to cook vegetables, that he would have had no time at all in which to write anything.

One might think that such a small and apparently harmless thing as a drink of water would present no problem to experienced dietitians; but one who thought in that manner would be displaying lamentable ignorance.

A few diet experts think the time to drink water is when the prospective drinker thinks he would like a drink of water: when, in short, he feels thirsty. Other dietitians say this is all wrong: one should never drink when he feels thirsty, but only one half hour before meals. Others say nobody can be healthy unless he drinks at least six quarts of water a day; but this belief is derided by equally prominent dietitians, who declare firmly that large amounts of water put an intolerable burden on the heart and other organs and result in serious diseases and death. The ideal state of affairs, they say, is to drink as little water as possible. Some say no water should be drunk during meals, while others are equally positive in saying there is no better time for water-drinking.

At first blush, as the saying goes, the student of diets thinks there is one form of sustenance that has the unqualified approval of all dietitians: to wit, salads. Each and every one of them says "Eat lots of salad"—though none of them is able to dispose of salads in so few words. In that respect the diet books are somewhat similar to those that tell people how to play golf. A book on golf usually needs three chapters to tell a would-be golfer how to place his left hand on the club; and the diet books usually devote three chapters to telling their disciples to eat lots of salad. When, however, one dietitian says "salad," he means his own brand of salad: not salads advocated by other dietitians.

One of my favorite diet authors, for example, says "salads, with plenty of fine first-press olive oil and a little malt vinegar, should form a part of the midday or evening meal."

From other diet authors one learns that vinegar is all right on a salad, whereas olive oil is all wrong. "There is less danger," declares one diet authority, "from the teaspoon of alcohol in a stein of beer than from the teaspoon of oil in salad dressing."

The most modern diet books are inclined to take the opposite viewpoint. Vinegar, they think, is one of the great curses of modern life, whereas olive oil is essential to health. Vinegar on salads or on anything else, they say, must be shunned as though it contained cholera bacilli. Lemon juice must be used in place of vinegar, they declare: the man who refuses it is beyond all human help.

Others say salads should never be eaten if they contain either oil or vinegar, but should be garnished with a dressing of lemon juice and salt. Still others say salt is bad on a salad—very bad. It causes hardening of the arteries and destroys the delicate flavor of the salad.

There are also those who protest vigorously against lemon juice, which is an acid fruit; for if a salad garnished with lemon juice enters the stomach in company with a piece of toast or a fragment of meat, eggs, fish or cheese—with a starch or a protein, that is to say—fermentation ensues at once, and the salad eater is about as badly off as though he had inadvertently consumed a toadstool.

Potatoes are either beneficial or ruinous for one who wishes to live healthfully. Some say one thing and some another.

Rice is either splendid as a food or dreadful. Several books state clearly that nations given to a rice diet have enormous endurance, and that people who live on rice can fight and toil tirelessly, whereas meat eaters fade like wilted flowers over the same tasks.

These statements baffled me. Years ago, when the United States was allied with Japan, and every Japanese officer and soldier was heartily disliked and distrusted by every American, I found myself in uniform and in Siberia, sourly observing the antics of our brothers-in-arms, at that time affectionately known to all as "those little yellow monkeys." Two of our regiments, the 27th and 31st Infantry, enervated by a tour of duty in the tropical Philippines, set out on a five-hundred-mile march with two Japanese regiments fresh from the rigorous climate of the Hokkaido, the northern island of Japan. The Japanese ate rice; the Americans ate meat. The Americans out-marched the Japanese, and had to wait around, every little while, for the Japanese to catch up. Still, the dietitians, being doctors, ought to know what they are talking about when they arbitrarily announce that rice eaters have more endurance than meat eaters.

Don't eat nuts, some say. Others say nuts must be eaten.

Stick to vegetables, say others, and you'll be free of all ills. On the other hand there are many experts who issue heartfelt warnings against the indiscriminate use of vegetables. A distinguished German dietitian darkly reminds his readers that Cameroon Negroes subsist entirely on vegetables but seldom live to be more than forty years old. Others say that if you renounce meat in favor of vegetables, you will be pure as the driven snow, and will probably live a hundred years unless unexpectedly struck on the head with a club.

A great international diet specialist says firmly that a vegetable diet is unhealthful, dangerous and irrational. In Germany, he says, he has observed patrons of vegetarian restaurants eating green vegetable soup; then carrots or spinach with potatoes, followed by applesauce and a helping of nuts and fruits. In his opinion, all of them looked pretty sick; and he considers the diet a breeder of anemia and tuberculosis.

It mustn't be thought, from the foregoing paragraphs, that I have never been able to form any definite opinions of my own.

In 1943 and 1944 I was afflicted with steadily increasing pains in my hands and arms, which finally became so severe that I could hardly lift a book or close my fingers around a pen. Various celebrated specialists examined me, tapped me, X-rayed me and tested me in every possible way, and made various stabs at the causes and nature of my ailment. One said arthritis, another said neuritis, another said polyneuritis, another said gout. They prescribed massive daily injections of thiamin chloride, Vitamin C, cholesterol and other things: they fed me innumerable pills containing vitamins of every known and unknown sort—and the pain in my arms and hands grew worse and worse and worse. Eventually Dr. Donald Munroe, at that time a member of the staff of Boston's Peter Bent Brigham Hospital, came around to see me, listened carefully to my story, and then addressed several other medical notables who had gathered around my bed of pain, doubtless in the hope of snickering quietly at Munroe's bafflement.

But Munroe wasn't baffled. "Listen," he said to them, "where do you get all this stuff about neuritis and gout and polyneuritis and arthritis? He hasn't got any of 'em. He's as healthy as any of you— yes, healthier! All he's got is a twisted nerve at the base of his neck, as a result of leaning on his left elbow for thirty years and writing novels!" To me he added, "Keep off your left elbow and sleep flat on your back without pillows, and your pain'll start leaving you in a week. In six weeks you won't have any."

He was right.

The point of that story is this: because of the intense pain in my hands and arms I had to stop taking daily exercises over a period of two years. I couldn't play tennis—couldn't even grip the steering wheel of an automobile. As a result I gained weight with startling rapidity. The weight-gaining came to a climax early in 1945, when I was incarcerated in Boston's Baptist Hospital with a neck infection, and stuffed with rich and unaccustomed foods by my attentive nurses. I left that hospital at the end of January, 1945, weighing a dreadful 195 pounds. My chest measure was 41 inches, midrib measure 41, waist 39, hips 42.

On March first I started exercising again, and discovered Ida Jean Kain's *Prescription for Slimming,* published by David McKay Company, Philadelphia, 1940. That book was the only wholly sensible diet book I ever read, because a person who follows its precepts is scarcely conscious of dieting. So I followed the directions in Ida Jean Kain's book.

Roughly speaking, all I did was this:

In ten minutes each morning I took eight or ten stretching exercises.

I trimmed the fat from all meat I ate . . .

. . . used a salad dressing made of two parts of·mineral oil and two scant parts of lemon juice, flavored with garlic and vegetable salt

. . . used only vegetable salt—Vegesal—or celery salt when salt was needed

. . . used saccharine in coffee and tea in place of sugar

. . . used no butter and ate Ry-Krisps in place of bread or toast

. . . ate grapefruit sweetened with saccharine for all desserts

. . . drank no water half an hour before meals, during meals, or for an hour after meals

. . . but otherwise did as I pleased.

On March eighth I weighed 188; on April first, 183; on May twelfth, 176; on June ninth, 171; on July twenty-first, 163; on August twenty-fifth, 160. I had taken off 35 pounds, and my chest measure had faded from 41 to 38 inches; midrib from 41 to 36, waist from 39 to 33, hips from 42 to 37.

So the diet books don't confuse me any more. I *know* now.

INDEX

(Index by John Askling)